MULTIPLE PERSPECTIVES ON THE EFFECTS OF EVALUATION ON PERFORMANCE

Toward an Integration

MULTIPLE PERSPECTIVES ON THE EFFECTS OF EVALUATION ON PERFORMANCE

Toward an Integration

edited by

Stephen G. Harkins
Northeastern University

KLUWER ACADEMIC PUBLISHERS
Boston / Dordrecht / London

Distributors for North, Central and South America:
Kluwer Academic Publishers
101 Philip Drive
Assinippi Park
Norwell, Massachusetts 02061 USA
Telephone (781) 871-6600
Fax (781) 681-9045
E-Mail <kluwer@wkap.com>

Distributors for all other countries:
Kluwer Academic Publishers Group
Distribution Centre
Post Office Box 322
3300 AH Dordrecht, THE NETHERLANDS
Telephone 31 78 6392 392
Fax 31 78 6546 474
E-Mail <services@wkap.nl>

Electronic Services <http://www.wkap.nl>

Library of Congress Cataloging-in-Publication Data

Multiple perspectives on the effects of evaluation of performance: toward an integration / edited by Stephen G. Harkins.
p. cm.
Papers presented at a symposium at the Midwestern Psychological Association meeting in May 1998.
Includes bibliographical references and indexes.
ISBN 0-7923-7526-2 (alk. paper)
1. Employees—Rating of—Congresses. 2. Intrinsic motivation—Congresses. 3. Goal setting in personnel management—Congresses. 4. Personnel management—Psychological aspects—Congresses. I. Harkins, Stephen G., 1948-
HF5549.5.R3 M835 2001
658.3'125—dc21 2001038561

Printed on acid-free paper. Printed in the United States of America

For Ivy and Max

TABLE OF CONTENTS

Contributors ix

Preface xi

1. **Social Loafing and Expectancy-Value Theory**

   James A. Shepperd 1

2. **Goal Setting Research in Industrial/Organizational Psychology**

   Mark E. Tubbs 25

3. **The Social Psychology of Creativity: Effects of Evaluation on Intrinsic Motivation and Creativity of Performance**

   Beth A. Hennessey 47

4. **Evaluation and Intrinsic Motivation: The Double-Edged Sword**

   John M. Tauer and Judith M. Harackiewicz 77

5. **The Role of Task Complexity, and Sources and Criteria of Evaluation in Motivating Task Performance**

   Stephen G. Harkins 99

6. **Performance Among Individuals and Groups: The Implications of Parallel Research Traditions for Social Loafing**

   James A. Shepperd 133

7. **External Performance Evaluations and Task Motivation: Some Suggestions**

   Mark E. Tubbs 155

8. **Attending to the Details**

Beth A. Hennessey 173

9. **Just Do It: Remaining Task Focused When Performance Outcomes Loom Large**

Amanda M. Durik, John M. Tauer, and
Judith M. Harackiewicz 189

10. **The Three-Variable Model: From Occam's Razor to the Black Box**

Stephen G. Harkins 207

Author Index 261

Subject Index 271

CONTRIBUTORS

Amanda M. Durik, Department of Psychology, 1202 West Johnson Street, University of Wisconsin, Madison, WI 53706, U.S.A.

Judith M. Harackiewicz, Department of Psychology, 1202 West Johnson Street, University of Wisconsin, WI 53706, U.S.A.

Stephen G. Harkins, Department of Psychology, 125 NI, Northeastern University, Boston, MA 02115, U.S.A.

Beth A. Hennessey, Department of Psychology, Wellesley College, Wellesley, MA 02481, U.S.A.

James. A. Shepperd, Department of Psychology, P.O. Box 112250, University of Florida, Gainesville, FL 32611-2250, U.S.A.

John M. Tauer, Department of Psychology University of St. Thomas, ALB LL56, 2115 Summit Avenue, St. Paul, MN 55105, U.S.A.

Mark E. Tubbs, Department of Psychology, 325 Stadler Hall, University of Missouri-St. Louis, 8001 Natural Bridge Road, St. Louis, MO 63121, U.S.A.

PREFACE

In psychology, research areas often develop in relative isolation. Researchers in different areas are either not aware of, or seem to fail to see the relevance of, findings from other areas, even though, it would seem that the findings are directly relevant to their own. One striking example of this is to be found in research that focuses on the effects of evaluation on performance. There are at least five research traditions in which it can be argued that the potential for evaluation affects task performance: social loafing; goal setting; intrinsic motivation/creativity; achievement goals; and social facilitation.

Social loafing refers to the finding that people put out less effort when working together than when working alone (Latané, Williams, & Harkins, 1979). Harkins (1987) has suggested that this reduction in effort stems from the fact that, in this research, when participants "work together," their outputs are pooled, and the participants can receive neither credit nor blame for their performances. Consistent with this analysis, in a meta-analysis of social loafing effects, Karau and Williams (1993) report that: "In fact, social loafing was eliminated when evaluation potential was not varied across coactive (*individual outputs identifiable*) and collective (*individual outputs pooled*) conditions" (p. 696; italicized text added). Thus, the potential for external evaluation eliminates the social loafing effect.

In summarizing a second research tradition that encompasses nearly 400 studies which have used 40,000 participants in eight countries, 88 different tasks, and time spans ranging from one minute to three years, Locke and Latham (1990a) report that participants urged to strive to attain a specific, difficult level of performance do better than participants asked to do their best. They argue that the *goal setting effect* is produced by the opportunity to compare one's performance to the specific, difficult criterion represented by the goal. Thus, it is the opportunity for self-evaluation that is supposed to be responsible for the goal setting effect.

In a third research tradition, Deci and Ryan (1985) have argued that when individuals are intrinsically motivated, they attempt to stretch their abilities and derive enjoyment from the challenge associated with the task itself. In contrast, when individuals are extrinsically motivated, they are focused on factors such as reward, deadlines, surveillance, and evaluation. In much of this research, the dependent variable has been subsequent interest in the task. However, Amabile and her colleagues (e.g., Amabile, 1979; Amabile, Hennessey & Grossman, 1986) have shown that extrinsic motivation not only undermines subsequent interest in the tasks, but also disrupts performance on these tasks. So, for example, Amabile (1979) has shown that the extrinsic motivation produced by the potential for external evaluation leads to less creativity than the intrinsic motivation resulting from task performance with no evaluation.

A fourth research tradition distinguishes between two types of goals that people can adopt in settings that involve achievement motivation. "*Performance goals* highlight normatively based standards and promote the demonstration of ability relative to others, whereas *mastery goals* are self-referential, focusing on the development of skill and competence relative to the task and one's own past performance" (p. 2, Harackiewicz, Barron & Elliot, 1998). The achievement goals tradition would suggest that evaluation that involves the comparison of one's performance to the performance of others (performance goals) leads to poorer performance than the comparison of one's performance to one's previous performance (mastery goals).

The fifth relevant tradition is described by the generic term "social facilitation." In this literature, it has been found that the presence of coactors leads to enhanced performance on simple tasks, and debilitated performance on complex tasks. However, there is little agreement on what it is about the presence of these others that produces these effect (Geen, 1989). However, all of the theories that attempt to explain the phenomenon focus on the effects of one or both of the same two features of the facilitation paradigm: the mere presence of others, and/or the potential for evaluation that these others represent. Although, these factors have been pitted against each other as rival explanations for facilitation effects, Markus (1981) pointed out that both factors could contribute to facilitation effects. In a pair of experiments that used different tasks, Harkins (1987) found that each did, and in an additive fashion. Thus, the basic notion here is that the potential for evaluation represented by presence of a coactor leads to improved performance on simple tasks, and to debilitated performance on complex tasks (see Jackson & Williams, 1985; Sanna, 1992).

These five research traditions have developed in parallel. In two of them, achievement goals and intrinsic motivation/creativity, the potential for evaluation appears to debilitate performance. In two of them, goal setting and social loafing, the potential for evaluation appears to facilitate performance. Finally, in the social facilitation literature, largely ignored in recent years, both facilitation and debilitation have been found. In the belief that each of the areas, as well as psychology as a whole, would benefit from an integration of these different traditions, I invited researchers known for their work in each of these traditions to participate in a symposium at the Midwestern Psychological Association meeting in May, 1998.

The present volume represents a continuation of the effort to effect an integration of these various traditions. The participants in the symposium each wrote initial chapters in which they provided overviews of research in their particular area and/or described their own work which is representative of work in their particular tradition. In Chapter 1 Shepperd uses expectancy-value theory to organize the social loafing literature. Tubbs, in Chapter 2, provides an overview of research in the goal setting domain. In Chapter 3, Hennessey describes work in the intrinsic motivation/creativity area. In Chapter 4 Tauer and Harackiewicz describe their work in the achievement goal tradition. Finally, in Chapter 5, I present the fifth tradition, social facilitation, but I do so in the context of a first attempt to suggest a simple integration of these various traditions.

After reading these first chapters, the contributors were asked to write second chapters in which they commented on the relevance of these other traditions to their own. In my own second chapter, I argue that the three-variable model that I proposed remains viable as a first approximation of an integration of the various traditions. Of course, I would not necessarily expect the other contributors to agree. But even if an overall integration of these traditions is not in the offing, at the very least I would hope that the current volume serves to encourage researchers in the various traditions to look at their own work from new perspectives, allowing them to make progress in their own research that otherwise would not have been possible.

Chapter 1

SOCIAL LOAFING AND EXPECTANCY-VALUE THEORY

James A. Shepperd
University of Florida

Most people who have worked in group settings have likely had the experience that the input of group members are not equal, and that they are working harder or are contributing more to the group effort than are other group members. To the extent that group members share equally in the rewards generated by the group, unequal contributions can create considerable frustration and annoyance. In response, people leave or restructure such groups, or they adjust their contributions in an attempt to make inputs more equitable. On the other hand, some more insightful people may occasionally realize, perhaps with some chagrin, that they at times have been on the other end of the stick, contributing less to the group (but enjoying no less of the benefits) than their fellow group members. Although the inequity in contributions among group members and the negative feelings that result are undoubtedly commonplace and would seem to lead people to avoid working in groups, the fact remains that many human endeavors cannot be accomplished individually, requiring instead that people combine their efforts towards a common goal. Building a bridge, producing a play or movie, playing a team sport such as football or baseball, and completing a group project such as writing a group paper, all require that individuals pool their efforts to produce the desired outcome.

This chapter examines social loafing and related behaviors. The specific question I address is why do some people who work on a common task or pool their efforts toward a common goal loaf or free-ride on the contributions of others. And, just as important, what can be done about it? In the last twenty-five years researchers have demonstrated social loafing in a variety of tasks. For example, investigators have noted that individuals pull a tug-of-war rope less hard when they believe they are pulling the rope as part of a group, than when they believe they are pulling the rope alone (Ingham, Levinger, Graves, & Peckham, 1974). Reduced effort among individuals working collectively has also been shown on other physical tasks such as clapping and cheering (Harkins, Latané, & Williams, 1980; Jackson & Harkins, 1985; Latané, Williams, & Harkins 1979), swimming in a relay race (Williams, Nida, Baca, & Latané, 1989), and pumping air (Kerr & Bruun, 1981; Kerr, 1983), and on cognitive tasks such as evaluating a poem, editorial, or job (Petty, Harkins, Williams, & Latané, 1977; Weldon & Gargano, 1988), visual vigilance (Harkins & Petty, 1982; Harkins & Szymanski, 1988, 1989) solving mazes (Jackson & Williams, 1985), making paper moons (Zaccaro, 1984), and generating uses for objects (Harkins & Petty, 1982). In addition, researchers have documented a variety of causes of social loafing, and have proposed several cures (see Karau & Williams, 1993; Shepperd, 1993 for reviews). More importantly, there is growing recognition that low motivation and effort in collective settings is best conceptualized within an expectancy-value theoretical framework (Karau & Williams, 1993; Kerr, 1983, 1986; Shepperd, 1993, 1995; Stroebe & Frey, 1982; Williams & Karau, 1991).

This chapter reviews recent research examining components of an expectancy-value model as they pertain to effort and motivation in collective settings. In a prior articles (Shepperd, 1993, 1995), I proposed that social loafing arises from three conditions: (a) people perceive their contributions as unneeded, (b) people perceive their contributions as unrewarded, and (c) the costs of contributing are excessive, exceeding any benefit or reward that might be linked to contributing. In this chapter I present a revised model in which I combine the second (rewards) and third (costs) conditions under the general topic of value, and separated the first category into expectancy (effort expectations) and instrumentality (performance expectations).

I begin with a general overview of expectancy-value theory as it pertains to effort on individual and group tasks. This overview is followed by a review of research and findings on social loafing and a description of how these findings can be conceptualized within an expectancy-value framework. Although expectancy-value frameworks typically have three components (expectancy, instrumentality and value), most of this chapter focuses on the components of expectancy and outcome value because these are the components that have received most attention from researchers. The modest attention given to instrumentality should not be interpreted as evidence that instrumentality is relatively unimportant, but as a statement of gaps in our knowledge and directions for future research.

EXPECTANCY-VALUE THEORY

Expectancy-value theories typically consist of three components: expectancy, instrumentality, and value (Karau & Williams, 1993; Mitchell, 1974, 1982; Porter & Lawler, 1968; Vroom, 1964). The *expectancy* component refers to the perception that performance is contingent on effort; i.e., that greater effort will result in better performance. For example, a student may believe that if she works hard, she can write a good term paper (high effort expectancy). Alternatively, she may believe that writing a good paper is beyond her ability or that the amount of effort she devotes to writing a paper and the quality of the paper that emerges are unrelated (low effort expectancy).

The *instrumentality* component refers to the perception that the consequence of the performance outcome is contingent on performance; i.e., that performance will determine the outcome. In a sense, it also reflects a type of expectation, but an expectation about performance rather than an expectation about effort. In the term paper example, the student may believe that a good paper will receive a good grade, and that a poor paper will receive a bad grade (high instrumentality). On the other hand, the student may view the teacher as capricious and thus perceive no relationship between the quality of the paper and the grade received (low instrumentality).

The *value* component refers to how much value or importance the person attaches to achieving the outcome of the performance minus any costs involved. In the term paper example, the student's course grade may depend largely on the grade received on the term paper, thus making the term paper grade important (high value). Alternatively, the term paper grade may have a negligible impact on the student's course grade (low value). Importantly, value does not depend solely on how important or rewarding the person regards the outcome. It also depends on the costs (psychological and material) associated with achieving the outcome (Shepperd, 1993). Thus, outcome value represents the difference between the reward for achieving the outcome and the cost of achieving the outcome. For many events, there are multiple values. There may be value attached to completing a task, such as completing the term paper, independent of any external rewards received for performance.

Figure 1 presents the three components of expectancy-value theory. The first component, Expectancy (E), represents the probability that effort will lead to performance and ranges from 0 (effort and performance are unrelated) to 1 (the greater the effort, the better the performance). The second component, instrumentality (I), represents the probability that performance will result in the outcome and also ranges from 0 (performance and outcome are unrelated) to 1 (the better the performance the more likely the outcome will be attained). The third component, value (V), represents the difference between the reward for achieving the outcome and the cost (psychological, physical, and material) of achieving the outcome. In short, Value = Reward - Cost. The value component ranges from -1 (the outcome is not rewarding and very costly) to +1 (the outcome is highly rewarding or important and the costs are negligible).

The product of expectation, instrumentality and outcome value is effort motivation (EM). Effort motivation represents how much effort a person is willing to exert on a task or toward a goal. As effort motivation

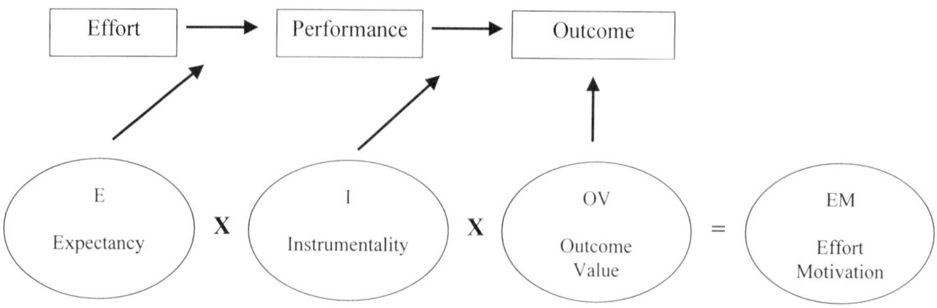

Figure 1. Expectancy -Value Theory

approaches 1, effort should be high. As such, it is a measure of intended effort and should be highly related to actual task effort. As effort motivation approaches 0 or becomes negative, effort should be low. Effort motivation in collective settings should be high when people (a) perceive a contingency between effort and performance (high E), (b) perceive a contingency between performance and the outcome (high I), and (c) value the outcome (the benefits associated with contributing or the outcome significantly exceed the costs of contributing; high V).

The multiplicative nature of the model reveals that effort motivation will be low if any of the three components of the model are low. Thus, motivation will be low and people will loaf if expectancy is low even though instrumentality and value are quite high. Our student, for example, may place a high value on a course, and perceive that the course grade is closely linked to performance on the paper, but nevertheless will exert low effort if she perceives that she personally is incapable of writing a good paper.

The multiplicative model expressed in Figure 1 is not entirely unique. Organizational psychologists have also expressed multiplicative models for understanding job effort (see Porter & Lawler, 1968; Mitchell, 1974, 1982; Vroom, 1964). However, organizational psychologists have not applied multiplicative models to understanding and predicting contributing in collective settings. In addition, the present model is distinct in the way it defines mathematically instrumentality and value. Elsewhere instrumentality has been defined as a correlation ranging from -1 to +1 rather than a probability (Vroom, 1964; see Evans, 1991, for criticisms of the correlation approach). In addition, other models have neglected to consider the costs of contributing and thus have conceived value as ranging from 0 to 1.

Importantly, effort motivation is a product of the *perceived* expectancy, instrumentality, and outcome value (Karau & Williams, 1993). The perceptions may only loosely correspond to actual contingencies and value. Moreover, as noted earlier a given situation may have multiple values and costs each with its own set of expectations and utilities. As a result, the model can lead to actions that are rational to the actor yet appear irrational to observers. For example, a woman may spend an inordinate amount of time working on a task that she realizes she has no hope of successfully completing (the project's effort expectancy is low) or for which any external reward is negligible (outcome value appears low). However, she may devote effort to the task out of a sense of obligation or duty, because performing the task is intrinsically enjoyable, or because important others will notice and supply nontangible rewards (respect, praise, etc.) for high effort. These outcomes, although valued by the person, may go unnoticed by observers, leading to the conclusion that the person's behavior is irrational.

In summary, effort motivation in groups will be low and people will loaf if they perceive little or no contingency between their effort and the performance, if they perceive little or no contingency between performance and the outcome, or if outcome value is low (i.e., the costs associated with contributing or achieving the outcome exceed the benefits of contributing). Of course, as the term paper example illustrates, these three conditions can occur among persons working individually. However, in group settings where efforts are pooled, these three conditions are particularly likely to occur. In groups, individual efforts are often redundant or relatively inconsequential, resulting in low expectancy. In addition, in groups, instrumentality may be low because of the often tenuous relationship between individual performance and attaining the group outcome. A group may be rewarded for a good group performance even though one's personal performance was poor. Likewise, a good individual performance may go unrewarded because the collective performance of the group was poor. Finally, the group outcome may not be equally valuable to all members of the group. Thus, members of a group may vary in the efforts or resources they contribute because of differences in the value placed on the achieving the group outcome. Other things being equal, members who value the outcome will contribute more than will members who value the outcome less.

RESEARCH ON EFFORT EXPECTANCY

The Dispensability of Individual Contributions

As noted earlier, effort expectancy refers to the contingency between individual efforts and performance. People will work hard if they believe high efforts will lead to a good performance. In individual settings, the contingency is between individual effort and individual performance. In collective settings, the contingency is between individual effort and the performance of the collective or group. Researchers have traditionally examined this contingency by manipulating the extent to which individual efforts or contributions are necessary to achieve a good group performance. People working in collective settings often perceive their personal contributions as unnecessary or inconsequential in achieving a good group performance. When individuals perceive their contributions as dispensable, they may opt to free-ride on the efforts of others, thereby enjoying the fruits of a good collective performance (if it is achieved) while bearing little of the costs associated with contributing.

Researchers have manipulated the dispensability of individual contributions in several ways. The first involves persuading individuals that, due to the difficult, challenging nature of the task, their contributions are unlikely to be duplicated by fellow workers. For example, participants in one study received instructions to generate as many uses as they could for either an easy object with many possible uses (a knife) or a difficult object with relatively few possible uses (a detached door knob) while working alone (identifiable condition) or as part of a nine-person collective (anonymous condition). Presumably, participants working on the difficult task would perceive their contributions as needed and thus would work harder even when efforts were anonymous. The results revealed that participants generated more ideas for the easy object than for the difficult object. More importantly, although the number of uses generated for the easy object varied as a function of the identifiability of contributions, the number of uses generated for the difficult object did not. Thus, regardless of whether contributions could identified, participants working on a difficult task exerted high effort (Harkins & Petty, 1982, Experiment 1).

Researchers have also manipulated the dispensability of individual contributions by increasing the uniqueness (or apparent uniqueness) of contributions. Similar to task difficulty, when people perceive their contributions as unique or as nonredundant with the contributions of others, they are likely to view their efforts as needed. This, in turn, should lead them to expend greater effort to insure the group's success. Harkins and Petty (1982, Experiment 3) demonstrated the effect of making contributions unique by having participants perform a signal detection task on a television screen divided into four quadrants. Some participants believed that they watched the same quadrant as three other participants (redundant contribution condition), whereas other participants believed that they watched a quadrant different from other participants (unique contribution condition). In addition, participants believed that their inputs were identifiable or were anonymous. Participants made the most errors on the task (i.e., exerted the least effort) when inputs were both anonymous and redundant. When individual efforts were either identifiable or unique, participants made few errors.

Finally, researchers have manipulated the dispensability of individual contributions by leading people to infer that achieving a good collective performance is dependent on their personal efforts (Kerr, 1983; Kerr & Bruun, 1983; Williams & Karau, 1991). For example, in a study by Kerr and Bruun (1983), participants working in pairs believed that they were more or less able than their partner at an air-blowing task. In addition, participants believed that the pair's performance would be equal to the performance of the least able member of the pair (a conjunctive task), or would equal the performance of the most able member of the pair (a disjunctive task). Kerr and Bruun found that high ability participants exerted greater effort on the disjunctive task than on the conjunctive task, whereas low ability participants exerted greater effort on the conjunctive task than on the disjunctive task. In short, when participants saw their contributions as crucial (indispensable) for a good collective performance, they worked harder. When they saw their contributions as dispensable, they loafed.

Kerr and Bruun's findings suggest that individuals are likely to infer that a good collective performance is dependent on their contributions (and, consequently, are likely to contribute more) if the task is structured in a way that makes individual contributions seem uniquely essential. Other research suggests that people will also draw this inference if they perceive that coworkers are unable or unwilling to make adequate contributions (Williams & Karau, 1991). In three experiments participants anticipating a poor performance from a coworker compensated by exerting high effort (Williams & Karau, 1991). In the first experiment, participants who were dispositionally inclined to believe that a coworker would free-ride on their efforts (i.e., low trusters) worked harder in an effort to compensate for the poor performance that they anticipated from their coworker. In the second experiment, participants who heard a coworker announce that he would exert low effort on a forthcoming meaningful task (one that had implications for intelligence) compensated by working harder. Finally in the third experiment, participants working with a partner whom they believed was incapable of making adequate contributions exerted higher effort to ensure a good collective performance, but only when they valued the collective performance. When participants did not value the collective performance, they withheld effort. Taken together, these findings suggest that, when individuals perceive that the performance of the collective is dependent on their personal contributions, they will exert greater effort.

Each of the studies described thus far manipulated the contingency between individual and group performance by varying the dispensability of individual contributions. In the first study (Harkins & Petty, 1982, Experiment 1), dispensability was manipulated by varying the difficulty of the task. In the second study (Harkins & Petty, 1982, Experiment 2) dispensability was manipulated by varying the uniqueness of contributions. And in the final studies (Kerr & Bruun, 1983; Williams & Karau, 1991), dispensability was manipulated by varying the extent to which achieving a good group performance was dependent on personal performance. In each case, the crucial comparison was between a condition in which a good performance could be achieved only if the participant worked hard and a condition in which a good performance could be achieved regardless of whether the participant worked hard or loafed.

The Likelihood of a Good Group Performance

Occasionally, however, people find themselves working on group tasks in which the likelihood of a good performance is remote. That is, due to lack of ability, training, time, sufficient group members, or some other factor, the group is unlikely to perform well even if the group members uniformly exert high effort. Such a situation often appears in sports settings where mismatched teams are competing and the less capable team has no prayer of winning no matter how hard the individual team members try. In such settings, high effort seems an exercise in futility. Of course, people facing insurmountable odds may work hard not to achieve a "good" group performance, but to avoid humiliation. Thus, the members of a weak football team facing a game against a nationally ranked opponent may be motivated to practice and play hard, not out of an illusion that they can somehow upset their opponent, but out of a desire to avoid humiliation. However, in the absence of these external incentives for working hard, will group members work hard when the chances of a good group performance are grim?

In a sense, this question addresses a twist of the dispensability concern documented in the studies just described. These studies compared contributing in a condition in which personal efforts were indispensable to achieving a good group performance with a condition in which personal efforts were dispensable in that a good group performance was likely regardless of whether individual group members worked hard. The present idea, by contrast, compares contributing in a condition in which personal efforts are indispensable to achieving a good group performance with a condition in which the chance of a good group performance is remote regardless of the level of personal contributions. In this latter condition, personal contributions can also be thought of as dispensable in that they are inconsequential in influencing the outcome of the group. That is, in the bigger scheme of things, the group will perform inadequately regardless of whether individual group members work hard.

Kevin Taylor and I addressed whether group members will work hard when the chance of a good group performance is remote by manipulating the probability that the group could achieve a good group performance (Shepperd & Taylor, 1999, Study 1). Participants working in groups generated uses for an object and believed that their individual contributions could or could not be identified and evaluated. In addition, participants were offered a reward for a good group performance. That is, participants believed that groups that performed well on the task (i.e., in the top 10% of all groups) would receive a prize -- certificates for free pizza or movies. Based on bogus feedback on performance from a series of practice trials, participants came to believe that their group was likely or unlikely to perform well enough to receive the prize. In the high expectancy condition participants learned from the practice trials that their group consistently performed around the top 10%. Thus, if group members worked hard on the final trial, they stood a good chance of winning the reward. In the low expectancy condition, participants learned from the practice trials that their groups performed mediocre at best. Thus, their group was unlikely to perform well enough in the experimental trial to win the reward.

Table 1 presents the number of uses participants generated by condition during the final, experimental trial. The design included two additional cells in which no reward was offered for performance and in which individual efforts could or could not be identified. These cells permitted comparison of the results with findings from past research. Consistent with prior research, participants worked hard when the experimenter could evaluate their individual efforts regardless of whether they were offered a reward for a good group performance and regardless of whether their group's ostensible likelihood of achieving the reward. More interesting are the responses of participants in the no evaluation cells. Participants in the high expectancy condition who stood a good chance of winning the reward for a good group performance worked hard, generating a high number of uses for the object, even though their individual contributions ostensibly could not be evaluated. In contrast, participants

Table 1. Number of uses generated as a function of effort expectancy (expectancy) and evaluation.

	Control	Low Instrumentality	High Instrumentality
Evaluation	28.4	37.9	28.4
No Evaluation	20.0	21.1	28.4

in the low expectancy condition who faced a remote chance of winning the reward for a good group performance, loafed.

Within the evaluation condition, the number of uses generated by low expectancy participants is strikingly high. Their high effort was apparently not due to a feeling of personal responsibility for their group's poor practice trial performance and a desire to demonstrate to the experimenter that they could do better. Responses to manipulation checks revealed that low expectancy participants were just as likely as high expectancy participants to believe that they personally could achieve the prize if the brainstorming task were an individual one rather than a group one. The implication is that participants viewed the poor group performance as caused by other group members. The greater effort also does not seem to result from a belief by low expectancy/evaluation participants that the experimenter would erroneously attribute a poor group performance on the final task to them. After all, participants in the evaluation conditions knew that the experimenter could monitor who was and who was not loafing.

The most likely explanation is that participants worked hard initially to compensate for their underperforming coparticipants during the practice trials. The initial high effort trapped these low expectancy participants, whose personal efforts were identifiable to the experimenter, into working hard on the final trial. After all, anything less would be perceived as inconsistent (and as loafing) in the eyes of the experimenter.

Summary

In summary, people working in collective settings will work hard provided they perceive a contingency between their efforts and performance. In collective settings, the contingency is between individual efforts and the group's performance. When people perceive their efforts as dispensable either because they are redundant with the efforts of others, because the task is easy and thus a good performance can be achieved from the contributions others, or because they infer that the group performance is decided by how others perform and not how they perform, they loaf. By contrast, when people perceive their efforts as indispensable to a good group performance they work hard. In addition, people loaf if they view the likelihood of good group performance as remote regardless of how hard they work.

RESEARCH ON PERFORMANCE EXPECTANCY (INSTRUMENTALITY)

Instrumentality refers to the contingency between performance and the outcome. In individual settings, the contingency is between individual performance and the outcome. In collective settings, the contingency is either between individual performance and the group outcome or between the group performance and the group outcome. Specifically, it refers to the likelihood that a good individual or group performance will be rewarded. Other things being equally, people in collective settings will work hard if they believe that their performance will be rewarded.

Remarkably, few studies have examined the effect of the contingency between group performance and outcome on effort in collective settings. Within organizational psychology, some studies have manipulated the effect of group performance on group outcome. However, these studies have most often examined self-reported rather than actual effort (e.g., Mitchell, 1982). In the few studies that have examined actual effort, instrumentality was naturally occurring and thus uncontrolled, or individual efforts were easily identifiable and thus open to evaluation by the experimenter (e.g., Ilgen, Nebeker, & Pritchard, 1981; Peters, 1977; Pritchard & De Leo, 1973).

In the social loafing literature, Kevin Taylor and I examined the contingency between group performance and group outcome by varying the probability that a good group performance on a task would be rewarded (Shepperd & Taylor, 1999, Experiment 2). Participants generating uses for an object as part of a group believed that the uses they individually generated could or could not be identified and evaluated by the experimenter. In addition, participants were offered a reward for good group performance. In the *high instrumentality* condition participants learned that, of the 10 groups participating in the experiment, members of the seven groups that generated the most uses for the object would be rewarded with a certificate for pizza. Thus, these participants had a 70% chance of receiving the reward. In the *low instrumentality* condition participants learned that, of the 40 groups participating in the experiment, only the group generating the most uses would be eligible for the reward, and that from this top group, only one name would be selected randomly to actually receive the reward. Thus, these participants had only a 1 in 200 chance of receiving the reward.

Table 2 presents the number of uses that participants generated in each condition. The design included two additional cells in which no reward was offered for performance but in which individual efforts could or could not be identified to permit a comparison of the results with findings from past research. Consistent with prior research, participants generated more uses when the experimenter could evaluate individual efforts. Evaluation led to high effort irrespective of whether participants anticipated a reward for a good group performance (i.e., the control condition), and irrespective of their expectations regarding the probability that a good group performance would be rewarded (i.e., the high and low instrumentality conditions). In the absence of external evaluation, however, participants worked hard only when instrumentality was high. That is, in the no evaluation condition, participants generated a high number of uses only when a reward was offered for a group collective performance, and only then when the probability of achieving the reward was high. When no reward was offered (control condition), or when the probability was low that a good group performance would be rewarded (low instrumentality condition), participants loafed.

Table 2. Number of uses generated as a function of performance expectancy (instrumentality) and evaluation.

	Control	Low Instrumentality	High Instrumentality
Evaluation	20.9	24.2	24.4
No Evaluation	16.1	16.3	23.6

In sum, research on outcome expectancy and contributing in groups is notably sparse. Nevertheless, the results suggest that people are sensitive to the contingency between performance and outcomes. Other things being equal, people will contribute when they perceive contingency between performance and the outcome. That is, group members will work hard if they believe that there is a high probability that a good group performance will be rewarded. If they believe that the probability of reward for a good group performance is low, they will loaf.

RESEARCH ON OUTCOME VALUE

A number of studies have examined the link between outcome value and contributing in collective settings. The consistent finding is that people contribute more when there is some value or incentive associated with contributing, and the value exceeds any costs associated with contributing. The incentives for contributing can be internal or external and can be linked to individual performance or group performance.

Incentives for Individual Performance

External Incentives

Typically when people think of incentives, they think of tangible rewards such as bonuses, raises and gifts. These tangible rewards can have a powerful impact on behavior, countering the reduction in effort typically found among people pooling their efforts in collective settings. Indeed, numerous researchers have documented the fact that people will exert greater effort when they believe their efforts will be rewarded than when they believe their efforts will go unrewarded (Locke, 1975; Mitchell, 1974; Vroom, 1964).

Researchers examining social loafing, however, have more often examined intangible, social rewards for contributing rather than tangible rewards. The promise of social rewards, such as liking, approval, and status, for individual contributions (or social sanctions for failing to contribute) can also elicit greater contributing. Moreover, the social rewards need not be explicitly promised to be effective. Rather the mere potential for gaining social rewards (or avoiding social sanctions) can serve as a motivation for greater effort. Researchers have typically manipulated the potential of social rewards and sanctions by varying the extent to which individual contributions can be evaluated. Other things being equal, the opportunity for (or risk of) evaluation can motivate individuals to exert greater effort.

The most straightforward method of manipulating evaluation in social loafing studies is to vary the extent to which individual efforts are identifiable. In the typical study, participants work either alone such that individual efforts are identifiable, or collectively such that individual efforts are anonymous. The recurring finding is that people work hard when efforts are identifiable, and loaf when they are not. For example, in a study by Williams et al. (1981, Experiment 1), participants wearing blindfolds and headsets and placed in a soundproof room participated in an experiment that ostensibly examined the effects of sensory feedback on sound production. Participants believed that they were shouting alone in some trials and in combination with one or five other participants in other trials. All participants actually shouted alone; however, the blindfolds and headphones concealed this fact. Participants shouted less in the combined conditions where efforts presumably were unidentifiable, than in the alone condition where efforts clearly were identifiable.

Importantly, it was the inability to identify individual contributions and not the mere fact that participants worked in a group that led to loafing in the collective condition. In a second part of the experiment, participants again believed that they shouted alone on some trials and in combination with one or five other participants on other trials. In addition, participants wore individual microphones and were instructed that how loud they shouted could be identified across all trials. Participants shouted equally loudly in all conditions. In sum, regardless of whether people are working alone or as part of a group, they exert greater effort when they believe their contributions are identifiable.

When people pool their efforts and individual contributions cannot be identified, the social rewards for contributing or social sanctions for failing to contribute cannot be administered. According to Latané et al. (1979), when people pool their efforts, they can "hide in the crowd," a strategy unavailable to individual performers. With efforts pooled and thus less noticeable, people experience less pressure to work hard, either because they cannot be held accountable for a poor performance, or because they cannot enjoy the "proper benefits" deserved for an outstanding performance (Kerr & Bruun, 1981; Williams, Harkins, & Latané, 1981). By contrast, when people perform alone or when their inputs are identifiable, they can be associated more easily with their efforts: they can be evaluated negatively should they perform poorly or fail, and positively should they perform well or succeed.

Importantly, making personal contributions identifiable reduces social loafing only to the extent that the contributions can be evaluated. In the absence of other motivational factors, if personal contributions cannot be evaluated, then people will likely loaf regardless of whether contributions are or are not identifiable. This point is illustrated in a study that separated the ability to identify personal contributions and the ability to evaluate them (Harkins & Jackson, 1985). Participants performing a brainstorming task believed either that the uses they generated for an object would be individually identifiable, or would be pooled with the uses generated by other participants, thereby making individual contributions anonymous. In addition, half of the participants believed that all participants were generating uses for the same object, making it possible to evaluate personal contributions relative to the contributions of other participants, or that each participant was generating uses for a different object, making impossible any evaluation of personal performance. In truth, all participants generated uses for the same object. Participants making identifiable contributions exerted greater effort on the task than did participants making unidentifiable contributions, but only when they believed that their efforts could be evaluated. When participants believed that their identifiable contributions could not be evaluated, they exerted no more effort than did participants making unidentifiable contributions.

In sum, one way to increase the value of contributing is to offer external incentives (either economic or social) for individual efforts or contributions. Although the incentive can be explicit as in the promise of a reward or the threat of sanction, the research on the effect of evaluation suggests that merely alerting people that their individual contributions can be evaluated serves as a sufficient incentive to contribute.

Internal Incentives

Internal rewards tap a person's capacity for self-reward and, like economic and social rewards, can lead to greater effort and contributing in collective settings. One internal, individual incentive comes from the value that people personally place on performing well on the task. To some extent this value is necessarily subjective and can depend on the nature of the task itself. However, people can attach value to their performance on even mundane tasks (e.g., generating uses for an object, visual vigilance) provided they personally can evaluate their performance. When people can personally evaluate their performance (either against an objective standard, a social standard, or their own previous performances), they exert greater effort (Harkins & Szymanski, 1988; Szymanski & Harkins, 1987). Apparently, people are not only concerned that others evaluate them favorably, they are also concerned with evaluating themselves favorably. When people can evaluate their personal efforts or performance, they often work hard or contribute more in order to produce a favorable self-evaluation. For instance, participants in a study by Szymanski and Harkins (1987) believed that the experimenter would or would not be able to evaluate their performance on a forthcoming brainstorming task. In addition, some participants believed that they could evaluate their own performance on the task, whereas others did not. Not surprisingly, participants were worked hard when they believed that the experimenter could evaluate performances. However, the opportunity for self-evaluation also elicited greater effort even in the absence of external evaluation.

A second internal, individual incentive for performing well in collective settings is present when people find the task intrinsically interesting, either because the task is enjoyable or meaningful, or because the outcome of the task is personally relevant. Two studies demonstrate that people exert higher effort on a collective task when they find the task intrinsically interesting than when they do not. The first study examined dispositional differences intrinsic interest by using the need for cognition scale (Cacioppo & Petty, 1982). People scoring high in the need for cognition are dispositionally prone to find effortful, cognitive tasks intrinsically interesting, whereas people scoring low in need for cognition are not so prone. As might be expected, participants high in the need for cognition exerted higher effort on a cognitive task and lower effort on physical tasks than did participants low in the need for cognition (Petty, Cacioppo, & Kasmer, 1985).

The second study manipulated intrinsic interest by varying the personal relevance or importance of the experimental task to participants. Specifically, students generated thoughts about senior comprehensive exams that were proposed for their school (high personal relevance), for another school (low personal relevance), or for their school 6 years from now (well after their own graduation -- low personal relevance). In addition, the students believed that they were working individually or in pairs. Participants generated more thoughts when working individually than when they worked in pairs. However, within the pair condition participants generated more thoughts when personal relevance was high than when personal relevance was low (Brickner, Harkins, & Ostrom, 1986).

In sum, similar to external incentives, internal incentives for individual performance enhance contributing in collective settings by increasing the value associated with contributing. Internal incentives are present when people personally value the collective performance or when people find the task itself intrinsically interesting. However, with internal incentives the motivation to contribute arises from personal benefits associated with performing the task or achieving the outcome and not from external benefits received for contributing.

Incentives for a Good Collective Performance

Providing incentives for individual contributions necessitates that individual contributions can be identified and evaluated. In many groups, however, contributions are pooled and individual efforts cannot easily be identified or evaluated. For example, in a tug-of-war match it is impossible, outside of the elaborately furnished experimental laboratory, to monitor the magnitude of effort expended by individual participants. As an alternative, some researchers have examined incentives for the collective performance rather than for individual performances, a strategy that is similar to the business practices of profit or gainsharing (Doyle, 1983). The typical finding is that people work harder in the presence of an incentive for a good group performance than when no such incentive is available. Similar to incentives for a good individual performance, the incentives for a good group performance can be internal or external.

External Incentives

Two studies have demonstrated that an external incentive for a good collective performance can decrease social loafing. In the first study the incentive was extra experimental credit (Zaccaro, 1984). In the second study, the incentive was avoidance of a tedious memorization task (Shepperd & Wright, 1989). Both studies demonstrated that, when individual efforts could not be evaluated, participants nevertheless worked hard when an incentive was offered for a good group performance. For example, in a study by Shepperd and Wright (1989), participants generated uses for an object either alone or as part of group in which individual contributions would be anonymous. In addition, some participants learned that participants (groups) performing above criterion could leave the experiment and that participants (groups) performing below criterion would have to remain and perform a tedious memorization task. Participants generated fewer uses in the group condition than in the individual condition, but only when no incentive was offered for a good group performance. When an incentive was offered for a good group performance, participants working in groups performed as well as participants working individually.

Internal Incentives

Internal incentives for achieving a good collective performance exist when group members identify with, or feel a sense of pride in or duty toward their group. These group qualities facilitate group cohesiveness and can elicit high effort because the group members personally value the success of the group and are motivated to work hard to insure success. These group qualities likely develop slowly, and are rarely found among aggregates of strangers who meet once or only briefly for a psychology experiment. Perhaps as a consequence, only two studies have examined the effect of internal incentives for a good group performance.

The first study investigated the effect of group cohesiveness on typing speed among students at a secretarial school (Karau and Williams, 1997, Study 1). Participants believed that their typing speed would be evaluated individually or would be combined with the typing speed of others and evaluated collectively. In the collective condition, participants believed either that the other participants were three self-chosen friends or three participants chosen randomly. Participants in the randomly assigned (low cohesion) conditions typed more slowly than individual participants, whereas participants in the friend (high cohesion) conditions tended to type faster than individual participants. The second study examined the effect of group cohesiveness on a brainstorming task among friends (high cohesion) vs. strangers (low cohesion) working coactively or collectively (Karau and Williams, 1997, Study 2). All participants believed that their coparticipant was high in ability on the task. Participants in the low cohesion group loafed, working harder coactively than collectively. By contrast, participants in the high cohesion group worked just as hard collectively as they did coactively. Apparently, being part of a cohesive group provided an incentive for exerting high effort, countering low productivity arising as a result of contributions being anonymous (see also Harkins & Szymanski, 1989).

Addressing the Costs of Contributing

As noted earlier, outcome value refers to the value or importance a person attaches to achieving an outcome *minus any costs involved*. If the cost of achieving the outcome is excessive, exceeding the available benefits, then the person will loaf. The costs can be material such as a depletion of personal energy or resources, or lost opportunity associated with taking time and energy from more profitable ventures. In the classroom paper described earlier, if the time required to write a good paper necessitates that the student forfeit studying for an exam for another, more important class, the student will likely opt to study for the exam rather than write the paper. Researchers examining social loafing, however, have focused more often on psychological costs associated with contributing in group settings. Psychological costs refer to the inequity experienced when one believes that others are free-riding on one's personal contributions. The aversion to being a "sucker" of others' free-riding attempts can lead people to reduce or withhold contributions (Orbell & Dawes, 1981; Kerr, 1983).

In a clever demonstration of the sucker effect, Kerr (1983) had participants work on a physical task (pumping air) either (a) individually, (b) with a capable partner who worked hard in all conditions, (c) with a capable partner who appeared to free-ride on their efforts, or (d) individually, but in the presence of a capable coactor who nevertheless exerted low effort. This fourth condition was included to examine whether participants might exert low effort on the task merely because their partner modeled lazy behavior. Consistent with the free-rider effect, participants working with a capable, hardworking partner, exerted less effort than did control participants, thereby free-riding on their partner's high efforts. Consistent with the sucker-effect, participants working with a capable partner who attempted to free-ride on the participants' efforts exerted less effort than did participants working individually. Importantly, the low effort of participants working with free-riding partner appeared to result from an attempt to avoid the free-riding attempts of their partner and not to their partner modeling low effort. Participants working individually but in the presence of a capable yet poor performing coactor (a confederate who "modeled" low effort), exerted high effort, equaling the effort exerted by control subjects. These findings suggest that having a capable partner free-ride on one's own efforts can lead people to exert less effort presumably in an attempt to reestablish equity in contributions.

An examination of the literature suggests three ways to reduce the psychological costs associated with feeling that one is the sucker of the free-riding attempts of others. First, one can change the nature of the group task itself by partitioning it into individual tasks in which all members have their individual jobs (Edney, 1980; Lynn & Oldenquist, 1986; Samuelson & Messick, 1986). This partitioning represents a sort of privatization of the group task. By partitioning a group task into individual tasks, group members can no longer fall victim to the free-riding attempts of others. As a consequence, the cost arising from a perception of inequitable contributions is eliminated. With the collective good privatized, individuals enjoy the fruits (as well as suffer the consequences) of their personal contributions. In work settings, paying workers piecework for their efforts represents one means of privatizing of the collective good.

Some research suggests that people working in groups will opt for partitioning the group task if given the opportunity. Specifically, in a study by Yamagishi (1988), Japanese and American students working in triads performed several trials of a verbal recognition task in which free-riding on the part of coworkers was a threat. At the beginning of each trial, students could choose to remain in the triad and share equally the rewards of the trial with the other remaining participants, or exit from the triad and be rewarded solely for their individual performance. The results revealed that both American and Japanese students opted to exit from the triad. Moreover, students whose initial contributions to the triad were high were more likely to exit from the triad than were students whose contributions were low. These findings suggest that the people who were most likely to feel exploited by their fellow group members were most eager to remove themselves from the group.

It is noteworthy that the Japanese students were more likely to exit from the group than were the American students. Yamagishi (1988) argued that collective systems in Japan are sustained externally by mutual monitoring and sanctioning whereas in America collective systems are sustained internally by feelings of obligation or duty (see Benedict, 1946), and that a system that sanctions free-riding externally escalates free-riding when the sanctions are removed (Taylor, 1976). The conditions in the Yamagishi study provided no opportunity for students to monitor and possibly sanction coworker performance. As a consequence, the Japanese students chose more often to exit from the group to avoid being a victim of free-riding from coworkers.

Of course, in real world settings it often is impossible or unfeasible to partition a public resource into individual portions. In a tug-of-war game, for example, dividing the task into individual, private portions is rarely a realistic or desirable solution.

An alternative way that leaders can reduce the psychological costs of contributing is to inform group members that their fellow members are making (or will make) equitable contributions toward the group. The idea is that people are less likely to think that they are victims of others' free-riding attempts if they believe that coworkers are making equitable contributions. Indeed, people may even exert higher effort to insure that their own contributions are equitable. For example, participants in one study learned that their coparticipant in a sound production experiment shouted on a series of practice trials louder than expected on the basis of her lung capacity. These participants later shouted more loudly themselves even when their efforts were ostensibly unidentifiable (Jackson & Harkins, 1985). Apparently, the belief that one's own contributions may be inequitably low led participants to contribute more in an attempt to reestablish equity.

Importantly, it may be impossible to convince group members that coworkers are making equitable contributions. Unless everyone is contributing his or her share, group members may quickly realize from monitoring the effort of coworkers or the group product that efforts are not equitable and that that they are being played the sucker. A second drawback is that this solution inadvertently may elicit free-riding from the target of the feedback. That is, people may reason that the high efforts of the coparticipant make their personal efforts dispensable. In addition, it is possible that group members will perceive the contributions as dispensable and will loaf when they believe that others are exerting high efforts. This possibility was demonstrated in the study by Kerr (1983; see also Williams & Karau, 1991) described earlier. Specifically, participants working toward a preestablished criterion on a physical task with a capable, hardworking partner exerted less effort on the task than did control participants, thereby free-riding on their partner's high efforts.

A final way to reduce the psychological costs of contributing is to conclude that free-riders will be punished. Research suggests that some group members attempt this approach informally by threatening would be free-riders that behaving contrary to the group goal will be met with unpleasant consequences (Dawes, McTavish, & Shaklee, 1977). In addition, equity researchers have noted that people spontaneously convince themselves (and perhaps others) that free-riding will be punished in a variety of settings for a multitude of transgressions when they say or think, "what goes around, comes around" (Walster, Walster, & Berscheid, 1978). Finally, parents, teachers, and religious leaders sometimes use this strategy to control behavior when they inform those they wish to influence that "God is watching." The knowledge that others who free-ride will suffer negative consequences can diminish the aversive experience of being a sucker. Moreover, this perception can eliminate free-riding to the extent that people infer that their own free-riding attempts also will be punished.

We are quick to note that the cost of contributing must be viewed relative to the benefits of contributing. It is not necessary that all costs be eliminated, but that the costs not exceed the benefits. Thus, in situations where people withhold contributions to avoid being a sucker, an alternative remedy might be to increase the value or benefit associated with achieving the collective good, a strategy discussed earlier under incentives. Williams and Karau (1991) illustrate this approach in a study described earlier. Participants who anticipated that a coworker would free-ride on their contributions responded by exerting higher effort in an attempt to compensate for the coworker's poor performance. This compensatory effort occurred, however, only when the collective performance was valued. When the collective performance was not valued, participants did not exert higher effort. This research suggests that people will compensate for a free-riding coworker even though they find such compensation aversive, provided they place a high value on a good group performance.

Summary

In summary, other things being equal, people working in collective settings will work hard provided they value the outcome or the behavior leading to the outcome. The value can be linked to individual performance or group performance and can be internal (tapping the individual's capacity for self-reward) or external (rewards provided by external sources). Importantly, contributing in collective settings involves expending personal resources and people will work hard only in so far as the costs of contributing do not exceed the benefits. Perhaps the most insidious costs are psychological, and come from perceiving others as free-riding on one's personal efforts. People who perceive they are suckers to the free-riding attempts of others will often reduce their efforts in response unless they can (a) change the nature of the group task, making it an individual task rather than a group task, (b) convince themselves that fellow group members are contributing equitably, or (c) convince themselves that free-riders will be punished.

CONCLUSIONS

Social loafing is pervasive in collective settings where people combine their efforts toward a common goal. The reduction in contributing perhaps should not be surprising given that individual efforts in collective settings are often unidentifiable and redundant, making the links between personal effort, the group's performance, and the consequence of that performance weak. The present analysis suggests that social loafing and free-riding are not inevitable consequences of working in groups. People will work hard in group settings provided they (a) believe that performance is dependent on their efforts, (b) believe that the outcome is dependent on performance, and (c) value the outcome or the behavior leading to the outcome, and this value exceeds the costs associated with contributing.

REFERENCES

Benedict, R. (1946). *The chrysanthemum and the sword: Patterns of Japanese culture.* Boston: Houghton-Mifflin.

Brickner, M., Harkins, S., & Ostrom, T. (1986). Personal involvement: Thought-provoking implications for social loafing. *Journal of Personality and Social Psychology, 51*, 763-769.

Cacioppo, J. T., & Petty, R. E. (1983). The need for cognition. *Journal of Personality and Social Psychology, 42*, 116-131.

Dawes, R. M., McTavish, J., & Shaklee, H. (1977). Behavior, communication, and assumptions about other people's behavior in a commons dilemma situation. *Journal of Personality and Social Psychology*, 35, 1-11.

Doyle, R. J. (1983). *Gainsharing and productivity: A guide to planning, implementing and development.* New York: American Management Association Book Division.

Edney, J. J. (1980). The commons problem: Alternative perspectives. *American Psychologist, 35*, 131-150.

Evans, M. G. (1991). The problem of analyzing multiplicative composites: Interactions revisited. *American Psychologist, 46*, 6-15.

Harkins, S. G., & Petty, R. E. (1982). Effects of task difficulty and task uniqueness on social loafing. *Journal of Personality and Social Psychology, 43*, 1214-1229.

Harkins, S. G., & Szymanski, K. (1988). Social loafing and self-evaluation with an objective standard. *Journal of Experimental Social Psychology, 24*, 354-365.

Harkins, S. G., & Szymanski, K. (1989). Social loafing and group evaluation. *Journal of Personality and Social Psychology, 56*, 934-941.

Harkins, S. G., & Jackson, J. (1985). The role of evaluation in eliminating social loafing. *Personality and Social Psychology Bulletin, 11*, 457-465.

Harkins, S. G., Latané, B., & Williams, K. (1980). Social loafing: Allocating effort or taking it easy? *Journal of Experimental Social Psychology, 16*, 457-465.

Ilgen, D. R., Nebeker, D. M., & Pritchard, R. D. (1981). Expectancy theory measures: An empirical comparison in an experimental simulation. *Organizational Behavior and Human Performance, 28*, 189-223.

Ingham, A. G., Levinger, G., Graves, J., & Peckham, V. (1974). The Ringelmann effect: Studies of group size and group performance. *Journal of Experimental Social Psychology, 10*, 371-384.

Jackson, J. M., & Harkins, S. G. (1985). Equity in effort: An explanation of the social loafing effect. *Journal of Personality and Social Psychology, 49*, 1199-1206.

Jackson, J. M., & Williams, K. D. (1985). Social loafing on difficult tasks: Working collectively can improve performance. *Journal of Personality and Social Psychology, 49*, 937-942.

Karau, S. J., & Williams, K. D. (1993). Social loafing: A meta-analytic review and theoretical integration. *Journal of Personality and Social Psychology, 65*, 681-706.

Karau, S. J., & Williams, K. D. (1997). The effects of group cohesiveness on social loafing and social compensation. *Group Dynamics: Theory, Research, and Practice, 1*, 156-168.

Kerr, N. L. (1983). Motivation losses in small groups: A social dilemma analysis. *Journal of Personality and Social Psychology, 45*, 819-828.

Kerr, N. L. (1986). Motivational choices in task groups: A paradigm for social dilemma research. In H. A. M. Wilke, D. M. Messick, & C. G. Rutte (Eds.), *Experimental Social Dilemmas* (pp. 1-27). New York: Lang.

Kerr, N. L., & Bruun, S. E. (1981). Ringelmann revisited: Alternative explanations for the social loafing effect. *Personality and Social Psychology Bulletin, 7*, 224-231.

Kerr, N. L., & Bruun, S. E. (1983). Dispensability of member effort and group motivation losses: Free-rider effects. *Journal of Personality and Social Psychology, 44*, 78-94.

Latané, B., Williams, K., & Harkins, S. (1979). Many hands make light the work: The causes of consequences of social loafing. *Journal of Personality and Social*

Psychology, 37, 822-832.
Locke, E. A. (1975). Personnel attitudes and motivation. *Annual Review of Psychology, 26*, 457-480.
Lynn, M., & Oldenquist, A. (1986). Egoistic and nonegoistic motives in social dilemmas. *American Psychologist, 41*, 529-534.
Mitchell, T. R. (1974). Expectancy models of job satisfaction, occupational preference and effort: A theoretical, methodological, and empirical appraisal. *Psychological Bulletin, 81*, 1053-1077.
Mitchell, T. R. (1982). Expectancy-value models in organizational psychology. In N. T. Feather (Ed.), *Expectations and actions: Expectancy-value models in psychology* (pp. 293-312). Hillsdale, NJ: Erlbaum.
Orbell, J., & Dawes, R. (1981). Social dilemmas. In G. Stephenson & H. H. Davis (Eds.), *Progress in applied social psychology* (Vol. 1). New York: Wiley.
Peters, L. H. (1977). Cognitive models of motivation, expectancy theory and effort: An analysis and empirical test. *Organizational Behavior and Human Performance, 20*, 129-148.
Petty, R. E., Cacioppo, J. T., & Kasmer, J. A. (1985). *Individual differences in social loafing on cognitive tasks.* Paper presented at the Midwestern Psychological Association, Chicago, IL.
Petty, R. E., Harkins, S. G., Williams, K., & Latané, B. (1977). The effects of group size on cognitive effort and evaluation. *Personality and Social Psychology Bulletin, 3*, 579-582.
Porter, L. W., & Lawler, E. E., III. (1968). *Managerial attitudes and performance.* Homewood, IL: Dorsey Press.
Pritchard, R. D., & De Leo, P. J. (1973). Experimental test of the valence-instrumentality relationship in job performance. *Journal of Applied Psychology, 57*, 264-270.
Samuelson, C. D., Messick, D. M. (1986). Alternative structural solutions to resource dilemmas. *Organizational Behavior and Human Decision Processes, 37*, 139-155.
Shepperd, J. A. (1993). Productivity loss in groups: A motivation analysis. *Psychological Bulletin, 113*, 67-81.
Shepperd, J. A. (1995). Remedying Motivation and Productivity Loss in Collective Settings. *Current Directions in Psychological Science, 4*, 131-134.
Shepperd, J. A., & Taylor, K. M. (1999). Social loafing and expectancy-value theory. *Personality and Social Psychology Bulletin, 25*, 1147-1158.
Shepperd, J. A., & Wright, R. A. (1989). Individual contributions to a collective effort: An incentive analysis. *Personality and Social Psychology Bulletin, 15*, 141-149.
Stroebe, W., & Frey, B. S. (1982). Self-interest and collective action: The economics and psychology of public goods. *British Journal of Social Psychology, 21*, 121-137.
Szymanski, K., & Harkins, S. G. (1987). Social loafing and self-evaluation with a social standard. *Journal of Personality and Social Psychology, 53*, 891-897.
Taylor, M. (1976). *Anarchy and cooperation.* New York: Wiley.
Vroom, V. H. (1964). *Work and motivation.* New York: Wiley.
Walster, E., Walster, G. W., & Berscheid, E. (1978). *Equity: Theory and research.* Boston: Allyn Bacon.
Weldon, E., & Gargano, G. M. (1988). Cognitive loafing: The effects of accountability and shared responsibility on cognitive effort. *Personality and Social Psychology Bulletin, 14*, 159-171.
Williams, K. D., & Karau, S. J. (1991). Social loafing and social compensation: The effects of expectations of co-worker performance. *Journal of Personality and Social Psychology, 61*, 570-581.
Williams, K. D., Harkins, S. G., & Latané, B. (1981). Identifiability as a deterrent to social loafing: Two cheering experiments. *Journal of Personality and Social Psychology, 40*, 303-311.
Williams, K. D., Nida, S. A., Baca, L. D., & Latané, B. (1989). Social loafing and swimming: Effects of identifiability on individual and relay performance of intercollegiate swimmers. *Basic and Applied Social Psychology, 10*, 73-81.

Yamagishi, T. (1988). Exit from the group as an individualistic solution to the free rider problem in the United States and Japan. *Journal of Experimental Social Psychology*, *24*, 530-542.

Zaccaro, S. J. (1984). Social loafing: The role of task attractiveness. *Personality and Social Psychology Bulletin*, *10*, 99-106.

Chapter 2

GOAL SETTING RESEARCH IN INDUSTRIAL/ORGANIZATIONAL PSYCHOLOGY

Mark E. Tubbs
University of Missouri - St. Louis

In the Forward to Locke and Latham's (1990) "A Theory of Goal Setting and Task Performance," Albert Bandura wrote: "The regulation of motivation by goal setting is a remarkably robust phenomenon. Converging lines of evidence from laboratory and field studies involving heterogeneous task domains reveal goal effects to be highly reproducible and of substantial magnitude. Despite this unprecedented level of empirical support, goal theory has not been accorded the prominence it deserves in mainstream psychology. Perhaps it is because this line of theorizing and research has been featured mainly in publications in the organizational field" (p. xii).

It was in a similar spirit of integration that Steve Harkins organized the present volume and the earlier symposium on the effects of performance evaluation, as conceived and operationalized in several different research domains. The purpose of the present chapter is to briefly review the applied psychology literature on performance goal setting for readers not familiar with that research tradition nor, perhaps, with the field of industrial/organizational psychology itself. I will begin with a brief discussion of the field itself and the manner in which individual evaluations, including goals, are utilized in research and practice. Next I'll describe both the traditional paradigm on performance goal setting and the generally accepted conclusions of the voluminous empirical research conducted over the past 35 years. As Bandura observed, there is considerable and relatively consistent support for the influence of assigned performance goals on task performance. I will conclude with a discussion of recent efforts to describe and explain the processes underlying the empirical goal setting effect.

INDUSTRIAL/ORGANIZATIONAL PSYCHOLOGY

Branches and Subdisciplines

The field of industrial/organizational (I/O) psychology is concerned, broadly speaking, with both organizations per se and the behavior of people in organizations (Dunnette & Hough, 1991). The former orientation of the field represents an interest in the organization as the unit of analysis, and offers theories on the nature of organizations as well as research into their productivity and economic survival (Bedeian & Zammuto, 1991; Etzioni, 1964; Lawrence & Lorsch, 1967). That orientation is therefore not directly relevant to this volume's focus on the impact of evaluations on personal behavior and performance. Whether this macro-organizational emphasis should even be considered a component of the psychological discipline is perhaps a matter of opinion, but research and theory from that viewpoint are definitely present in psychology journals and at national conventions. On the other hand, its roots in classic management theory and its links to systems theory, sociology, and organizational development do set the macro orientation somewhat apart in terms of subject matter from traditional psychology (Greenberg & Baron, 1993; Lawrence, 1987).

In contrast to the macro approach, the more mainstream micro orientation in the field can in many ways be considered an extension of traditional individual-level psychological concerns into the arena of human work behavior. Elements of social, cognitive, personality, behavioral, and differential psychology are clearly present in the I/O perspective and form the basis for (or are at least consistent with) many of the theoretical orientations taken in the I/O literature (Landy & Trumbo, 1980; Muchinsky, 2000).

The industrial branch of the field is concerned rather directly with the actual "maintenance" of individuals in organizations. Recruitment, employment testing, test validation, job analysis and design, personnel selection, training, performance measurement and appraisal, supervision, compensation, as well as related legal concerns (e.g., fairness and discrimination), are specific topics of interest (Muchinsky, 2000). Research and theory in this area is naturally focused on solving practical problems and, as a consequence, is relatively atheoretical, although increasingly less so. The organizational branch of the field is somewhat more theoretical and mirrors social psychology with its concern for motivation, leadership, decision making, and work attitudes such as job satisfaction, job involvement, and organizational commitment (Katz & Kahn, 1978). The related fields of human resources management and organizational behavior parallel the industrial and organizational branches of the psychological discipline from the business management perspective. As such, they cover much of the same topical ground but with a more practical, managerial, bent (O'Reilly, 1990; Schmitt & Klimoski, 1991).

A Brief History of Industrial/Organizational Psychology

In his review of the early years of I/O psychology, Landy (1997) noted that the first I/O text was published in 1910 and that the *Journal of Applied Psychology* (still a primary outlet for I/O psychologists) was founded in 1917. Because the first general psychology journals and the American Psychological Association (APA) itself did not appear until the 1890s, Landy argues that "it would appear that I/O psychology existed at the beginning" (1997, p. 467). Indeed, three of the four founding figures of the field (Hugo Munsterberg, James McKeen Cattell, Walter VanDyke Bingham, and Walter Dill Scott) began their careers as psychologists by studying Structuralism with Wilhelm Wundt in Germany in the late nineteenth century. All later turned to more applied interests. Munsterberg, for example, studied the safety of trolley car operation. Cattell was an early advocate of the practicality of "mental" testing and founder of the Psychological Corporation, which pioneered the use of psychological tests in organizations. Scott and Bingham were, among many other accomplishments, instrumental in the development of procedures for selecting and training soldiers during World War I. Another central figure in the development of the field was Frederick Taylor. An engineer by training, Taylor was among the first to offer a systematic model for job design, as outlined in his classic, *The Principles of Scientific Management* (1911). Though widely criticized over the years as being exploitative of workers, scientific management's influence was far reaching.

Between the world wars applied research expanded in scope. Probably the most influential and ambitious effort in the history of the field were the Hawthorne studies, conducted at the Western Electric Company in Hawthorne, Illinois just outside Chicago (Roethlisberger & Dickson, 1939). In Blum and Naylor's (1968) words, the Hawthorne studies were "the most significant research program undertaken to show the enormous complexity of the problem of production in relation to efficiency" (p. 306). Not only was the famous "Hawthorne effect" observed (i.e., improved performance as a result of being studied rather than as a result of the intervention itself), but the existence of informal work groups and norms, the importance of employee attitudes and sympathetic supervision, and the complexity of organizational life in general became apparent for the first time. Consequently, avenues of inquiry previously untapped became fertile ground for the next generation of I/O psychologists. What came to be known as the Human Relations school (Argyris, 1964; Likert, 1967; McGregor, 1960) emphasized the person in the organization, in contrast to the mechanistic views of Scientific Management. Informal organizational structures and patterns of communication, norms, participative decision making, and job attitudes like satisfaction and commitment all became primary emphases (Greenberg & Baron, 1993; Muchinsky, 2000).

During World War II, I/O psychologists had a major role, developing the Army General Classification Test, devising selection and training programs for OSS agents, and human factors engineering of aircraft instruments, among other activities. The most important postwar influence on the field has been the 1964 Civil Rights Act which, with its emphasis on fairness in testing and selection, instigated widespread efforts to ascertain the validity of employment selection tests. More recently, the 1990 Americans with Disabilities Act and the revised 1991 Civil Rights Act have further cemented I/O psychology's link with the legal issues of discrimination and fairness.

Early on, the APA was reluctant to formally embrace the application of psychological theories and methods, once even rejecting a proposal for a division of industrial psychology (Napoli, 1981). In 1921 applied psychologists finally formed their own organization to address their concerns, the American Association of Consulting Psychologists, which later merged with the Clinical division of the APA to form the American Association for Applied Psychology. That organization rejoined the APA in 1945, spawning 5 of the APA's original 18 divisions, including Division 14, originally known as the Division of Industrial and Business Psychology and now as the Society for Industrial and Organizational Psychology (Benjamin, 1997). Currently, approximately 4% of all psychologists are I/O by training (Muchinsky, 2000).

ORGANIZATIONS AS EVALUATION SYSTEMS

The context for the study of I/O psychology, organizational life, represents what might be thought of as a more rigid version of life in human society, the latter instead being the focus of social psychology. In organizations, many of the same concerns relevant to everyday society are amplified due to the work-for-money nature of the individual-organization relationship. Appropriate behavior is rewarded, inappropriate behavior punished, and opportunities for training and advancement are available, much as in everyday life. However, the organization's control over individual behavior is more immediate and direct. Organizational theorists (Taylor, 1911; Weber, 1921; McGregor, 1960; Likert, 1967) have long speculated on the proper model for organization-person relationships -- from autocratic to participative -- but even in the latter case the organization's power over the individual is relatively direct as compared to that of society. For example, even in the most participative of decision making techniques, the employee still must participate.

The result is that I/O psychology, as a field, examines human behavior in what must be viewed as very strong situations relative to those typically studied in most social psychological research. That is, the very purpose of an organization is to organize and control human behavior (and other resources) in order to produce some "product" and, typically, a profit (Bedeian & Zammuto, 1991; Etzioni, 1964). Integral to this effort is the creation of clear and powerful motivation and reward contingencies to guide employees' behavior (Naylor et al., 1980; Mitchell, 1997). And, of course, the ultimate contingency is that employees might be fired if behavior is not appropriate. Not only are motivational contingencies strong, but employees who wish to retain their jobs will always be at least somewhat willing to comply with reasonable organizational demands. People enter into the described quid pro quo with the organization of their own free wills (more or less), and fully expect that they will be asked to perform certain tasks within certain time limits. So, even for the least talented and most intrinsically uninvolved employees there is some willingness to respond to motivational contingencies -- at least to the minimal extent that pay is received and the relationship continues. As a result of both (a) the formal authority granted to the organization by a person's contractual arrangements, and (b) the person's own desire to live up to agreed-upon commitments (at least to a point), procedures for evaluating and influencing behavior may have rather different effects in the workplace than in contexts where such powerful situational contingencies are absent.

Techniques for evaluation of individual behavior in organizations are many. Employees are often tested when hired, when trained, and, sometimes, when promoted. Everyday performance is appraised and fed back at periodic performance reviews. Incentives are offered for project completion, reaching a sales target, or other performance outcomes. And, of most direct interest here, performance goals are set. The pervasive and logical use of goals in organizations (e.g., Bedeian & Zammuto, 1991, referred to organizations as "goal setting social systems," p. 25) have made them a topic of interest in the I/O literature for decades.

THE I/O PSYCHOLOGY LITERATURE ON GOAL SETTING

Any discussion of goal setting must begin with a mention of Edwin Locke. Locke and his colleagues (most notably Gary Latham) have, from the mid 1960s to the present day, formed the core group of researchers involved in a widespread empirical effort to understand and explain the effects of assigned goals on work performance. There have been literally hundreds of studies conducted on the effects of goal setting. And it is no doubt accurate to say that every goal setting researcher has either worked with Locke directly or been strongly influenced by his published work. His views on goal setting have clearly dominated the field, and his research paradigm for examining the effects of goals has been the basis for countless masters theses and doctoral dissertations, along with the published articles.

Locke and his colleagues have written extensive reviews of the literature (Latham & Yukl, 1975; Locke, Feren, McCaleb, Shaw, & Denny, 1980; Locke, Shaw, Saari, & Latham, 1981; Locke & Latham, 1990), which were supplemented by several meta-analyses of the empirical findings (Chidester & Grigsby, 1984; Guzzo, Jette, & Katzell, 1985; Mento, Steel, & Karren, 1987; Tubbs, 1986; and Wood, Mento, & Locke, 1987). Rather than trying to reinvent the wheel, I will rely heavily on these earlier works, especially Locke and Latham's (1990) book, which must be considered the ultimate source on the topic. I will also briefly review the literature on goal setting published subsequent to Locke and Latham's (1990) volume and the meta-analyses.

Foundations of the Modern Goal Setting Tradition

As reviewed by Locke and Latham (1990), an academic focus on goals began with Germany's Wurzburg school. Ach (1935), for example, conducted research on the relation between task difficulty and performance. Concurrently in England, Mace (1935) published perhaps the first research on the effects of specific difficult goals versus "do your best" goals. A philosophical foundation for what was to emerge as a cognitive theory of deliberate behavior on work tasks was provided by Lewin's (1951) concept of intention, and Ryan's (1958, 1970) subsequent work on intentions was, in turn, a direct influence on Locke (Locke & Latham, 1990). In the world of industry, Taylor's Scientific Management can be viewed as a precursor to Management by Objectives, or MBO (Drucker, 1954; Greenwood, 1981; Rodgers & Hunter, 1991). MBO is a widely-used coordinated system of organization-wide goal setting, incentives, and feedback, and was thus a salient factor from the private sector motivating early academic research on the efficacy of performance goals.

Towards a Theory of Goal Setting

Initial research efforts were often atheoretical and focused primarily on the question of whether goals affected performance and under what conditions. So a shortcoming of much early research is that it did not satisfactorily address the issue of what occurred between goal assignment and performance. How and why were assigned goals evaluated, accepted, or rejected? Researchers began to ask subjects whether they accepted the goal they were assigned and how committed to the goal they were, in essence assessing subjects' motivation for the goal. Other studies took expectancy-valence theory, control theory, or even behaviorist views of the goal setting, motivation, and choice process. Soon, theoretical perspectives attempting to explain the phenomenon were presented (Campion & Lord, 1982; Hollenbeck & Klein, 1987; Kanfer & Ackerman, 1989; Klein, 1989; Locke & Latham, 1990; Naylor & Ilgen, 1984; Reidel, Nebeker, & Cooper, 1988; Tubbs & Ekeberg, 1991).

Though differing in foci, the common thread in the various approaches is that behavior is assumed to be purposeful, goal directed, and intentional; that goals are incorporated into one's motivational scheme because the person (at some level) chooses to do so. Some of the specifics of these models of goal setting will be considered later, after a review of the results of the empirical research on the basic question of whether goal setting is effective and when. For now, it should be noted that evaluations of theories in the organizational sciences have given goal setting theory high ratings. For example, Pinder (1984) concluded that goal theory was the most scientifically valid of the theories of work motivation. Similarly, Miner (1984) rated goal theory as one of the top 4 (out of 32) theories of organizational behavior (i.e., including nonmotivation theories).

The Goal Setting Research Paradigm

Ranging from simple laboratory experiments with brainstorming or clerical performance tasks to full-scale longitudinal field experiments, early goal setting studies compared the performance of groups assigned specific and difficult numerical performance goals with those assigned either easy goals or no specific goals. This reflected the two main goal setting hypotheses: (1) that specific, difficult, assigned goals lead to higher performance than more vague "do your best" goals, and (2) that difficult assigned goals lead to higher performance than easy assigned goals. The first of these, the goal specificity hypothesis, is the fundamental test of the goal setting procedure in that it compares goal setting to what might occur otherwise, that is, telling workers to do their best. In other words, it asks the question of whether specific assigned goals are an effective method for improving work performance. Besides the self-explanatory goal difficulty hypothesis, other notable research trends included investigating the necessity of accurate performance feedback (i.e., knowledge of results) for the effectiveness of goal setting and the relative effectiveness of assigned versus participatively-set goals.

THE EMPIRICAL RESULTS OF GOAL SETTING RESEARCH

Locke et al. (1981) reviewed the empirical literature from 1969 to 1980 and found strong support for the basic hypotheses. They reported that 51 of 53 studies found support for the goal specificity hypothesis, and 48 of 57 studies found support for the goal difficulty hypothesis. Evidence was consistent with the prediction that specific difficult goals do result in higher performance as long as subjects reported acceptance of, and/or commitment to, the goals. In terms of practical significance, Locke et al. (1980) reported that the median performance gain in experimental field studies of goal setting effects was 16%, which no doubt translated into a considerable cost savings for the companies involved.

That a goal setting effect existed was apparent. Consequently, several groups of investigators (Chidester & Grigsby, 1984; Guzzo et al., 1985; Mento et al., 1987; Tubbs, 1986; and Wood et al., 1987) sought to provide meta-analytic estimates of the magnitude of that effect. Their studies differed in various ways (e.g., Guzzo et al., 1985, only examined actual organizational interventions), but reached generally similar conclusions regarding the effectiveness of goal setting.

Goal Specificity and Goal Difficulty

The results of the meta-analyses of the goal specificity hypothesis are shown in Table 1. In all the empirical reviews, effect sizes were represented as d statistics, which reflect, in this case, the number of standard deviations by which task performance differed between groups given specific difficult goals versus those given "do your best" or no goals (Hunter, Schmidt, & Jackson, 1982). Mean ds in the meta-analyses ranged from .42 to .65. Even the most conservative estimate translates into an

Table 1. Meta-analyses of Main Goal Setting Hypotheses

	Goal Specificity		Goal Difficulty	
	k	mean d	k	mean d
Chidester & Grigsby (1984)	17	.51	12	.52
Guzzo, Jette, & Katzell (1985)	74	.65	-	-
Mento, Steel, & Karren (1987)	49	.42	70	.55
Tubbs (1986)	48	.50	56	.82
Wood, Mento, & Locke (1987)	53	.43	72	.58

k = number of results

average performance difference of 8.4% between conditions (Locke & Latham, 1990). As ds of .2, .5, and .8 are generally considered small, medium, and large, respectively (Cohen, 1988), the magnitude of goal setting's effect in the studies reviewed was moderate on average.

Table 1 also shows the results for the goal difficulty hypothesis, where mean ds computed in the meta-analyses ranged from .52 to .82. The most conservative estimate represents an average performance difference of 10.4% between easy-goal and difficult-goal conditions (Locke & Latham, 1990). The empirical effects can be considered to be of moderate to strong magnitude.

The overall conclusion is that goal setting has been effective. These results represent findings across roughly 90 different tasks, from 8 different countries, using many different performance criteria, and with subjects ranging from college students to loggers, marines, factory workers, scientists, and college professors (Locke & Latham, 1990). So, some evidence for the external validity and generalizability of the goal setting procedure does appear to exist. However, there was variability in the observed effects. Probably the three most important moderators of the goal setting effects were: (a) setting (laboratory vs. field), (b) performance feedback (present or absent), and (c) task complexity.

Moderating Effects of Setting

Mento et al. (1987) and Tubbs (1986) reported moderating effects for setting on both the goal specificity and goal difficulty findings, with results somewhat stronger in the laboratory. (See Table 2.) For the results compiled in Tubbs (1986), the lab versus field distinction accounted for 9% of the variance in the goal specificity effect sizes, and 14.4% of the variance in the goal difficulty effects. It does make sense that laboratory

Table 2. Moderating Effects of Setting

	Goal Specificity Results				Goal Difficulty Results			
	Mento et al. (1987)		Tubbs (1986)		Mento et al. (1987)		Tubbs (1986)	
Setting	k	mean d	k	mean d	k	mean d	k	mean d
Laboratory	26	.569	34	.575	47	.649	45	.897
Field	23	.350	14	.427	23	.492	11	.520

k = number of results

research would produce somewhat stronger effects in the case of goal setting. In the typical laboratory study, experimenter control over the situation is high -- tasks are usually fairly simple, distractions are absent, and time allotments are short -- thus simplifying the situation within which task performance occurs. And while no long-term financial relationship exists between experimenter and subject, the strong demand existing in the laboratory is well known (Orne, 1962) and has been argued to be similar to that existing between manager and worker (Locke, 1986). In the field, where real-life jobs are more complex, more difficult to change, and many other influences besides assigned goals are present, somewhat smaller effects are to be expected. However, it should be noted that substantial goal setting effects were still observed in the field.

Moderating Effects of Performance Feedback

Table 3 presents the breakdowns of the goal specificity and goal difficulty findings reported by Mento et al. (1987) and Tubbs (1986) by whether or not performance feedback was available to subjects when pursuing their assigned goals. A difference between the meta-analyses was

Table 3. Moderating Effects of Feedback

	Goal Specificity Results				Goal Difficulty Results			
	Mento et al. (1987)		Tubbs (1986)		Mento et al. (1987)		Tubbs (1986)	
Feedback	k	mean d	k	mean d	k	mean d	k	mean d
None	28	.408	11	.488	34	.573	5	.349
Informal	-	-	22	.462	-	-	28	.885
Explicit	14	.504	8	.570	31	.614	14	.763

k = number of results

that Tubbs (1986) attempted to separate those studies without explicit formal feedback into those where: (a) informal performance feedback was available to subjects, and (b) no feedback whatsoever was present. Overall, goal setting effects were somewhat smaller in studies where explicit feedback was absent, as goal theory predicts (Locke et al., 1981). In Tubbs' (1986) results, the feedback variable accounted for 12.2% of the variance in goal difficulty effects and 2% of the goal specificity effects.

Moderating Effects of Task Complexity

Perhaps the most important moderator of the effectiveness of goal setting is task complexity. Wood et al. (1987) provided the most extensive analysis of this variable by coding tasks with Wood's (1986) 10-point complexity measure. They found that the majority of tasks used in goal setting research were fairly simple, although a sizeable minority (34 out of the 125 they reviewed) were reasonably complex, and included: college coursework, employee supervision, middle management, technician work, and science/engineering work (Locke & Latham, 1990). These all represented rather complex real-life tasks quite different from the typical "widget-making" tasks found in many laboratory studies. According to Wood et al.'s (1987) analyses, effect sizes were somewhat larger on less complex tasks, although they remained moderate even on the most complex tasks examined. See Table 4.

Table 4. Moderating Effects of Task Complexity

	Goal Specificity Results				Goal Difficulty Results	
	Wood et al. (1987)		Tubbs (1985)		Wood et al. (1987)	
Task Complexity	k	mean d	k	mean d	k	mean d
Low	19	.473	18	.624	33	.694
Moderate	21	.434	40	.562	18	.499
High	13	.358	5	.236	21	.478

k = number of results

A moderating effect for task complexity on goal specificity effects was also observed by Tubbs (1985), although it was not reported in the published article (i.e., Tubbs, 1986). Using a less precise measure of complexity than did Wood et al. (1987), studies subjectively coded as involving extremely simple, fairly simple, and fairly complex tasks reported ds averaging between .624 and .504. In contrast, the 5 studies coded as involving extremely complex tasks reported effects averaging .236. Note that in Table 4 the studies originally coded as fairly simple and fairly complex were combined and considered moderate for purposes of comparison with Wood et al.'s (1987) findings.

Direct Tests of Feedback's Influence on Goal Setting

By actually manipulating the presence and absence of feedback within a study, a more direct test (i.e., relative to the across-study moderator analyses) of the importance of performance feedback for successful goal setting is obtained. Locke and Latham (1990) reported that 17 out of 18 studies which directly compared goals-plus-feedback with goals alone found significantly higher performance in the goal-plus-feedback condition. Tubbs (1986) found only 3 studies that tested that hypothesis and also had the necessary information to code an effect size. However, the mean d in those studies was .564, indicating a clear, albeit somewhat tentative (due to the small number of codable effects), facilitating effect of performance feedback on goal setting effects.

Employee Participation in Goal Setting

Another trend in the literature has been to investigate the impact of assigned versus participatively-set goals. Although the Human Relations school would predict that participatively-set goals are superior to assigned goals, the evidence is equivocal. Locke and Latham (1990) make a strong case that there is no evidence in terms of differing performance outcomes and goal commitment levels supporting the participative approach, and the meta-analyses bear this out to some extent, at least regarding performance outcomes. Mento et al. (1987) found a mean d of only .202 on performance (favoring participation) for the 6 studies they reviewed, all of which controlled goal level. That is, many tests of this hypothesis held goal level constant across goal conditions because differing goal levels between assigned and participative groups would confound any estimate of the effect of participation per se on performance differences. Tubbs (1986) reviewed 17 studies, 6 of which controlled goal level and 11 which did not. Performance differences between assigned and participative conditions were negligible in both types of studies (controlled d = .107, uncontrolled d = -.034).

Many psychologists would no doubt like to believe the jury is still out on this issue. Perhaps the proper criteria to distinguish the procedures have not been examined yet. And some might even argue that participation solely for the sake of participation is still desirable -- that is, even if there is no easily demonstrable benefit to the procedure. But such discussions quickly become ideological and that is not the purpose here. At least in terms of performance outcomes, there would seem to be no clear trend favoring either approach. Perhaps future research will provide a new perspective on this topic.

Goal Setting Failures

Although examining moderator variables in meta-analyses can give one a general idea of the factors influencing goal setting effects, Locke and Latham (1990) presented a detailed review of every goal setting study up to that time that failed to produce the hypothesized effect on task performance. Most of their assessments of the apparent reasons for failure fell into one of several categories. First, in some studies it appeared that goal acceptance and/or goal commitment was lacking. In other words, the subjects were, for whatever reasons, not very motivated to pursue the assigned goals and thus performed poorly. Second, in some failures the tasks were complex and novel, with no training or false training. Third, occasionally the variable used to assess the outcome of goal setting was not the same as the variable on which the goal was set; that is, there was a goal-outcome mismatch. Fourth, in some studies there was no performance feedback or false feedback given to subjects. Fifth, sometimes there was an insufficient range of goal levels examined to produce an effect.

Though based on post hoc categorizations, these interpretations are in general agreement with the moderator analyses from the meta-analyses. The apparent lack of acceptance or commitment in many failures was a major impetus for researchers to begin closer study of those concepts. Often defined as the initial adoption of a goal, acceptance eventually fell from favor and is now infrequently discussed. Perhaps this is because success on most tasks requires that people persist in their attempts to reach the goal, and it is that long-term willingness to pursue a goal that defines the concept of commitment (Hollenbeck & Klein, 1987; Locke & Latham, 1990).

Summary

The effectiveness of assigned goal setting must be qualified somewhat. For example, assigned goals are less effective when accurate performance feedback is absent. Clearly, any benefit from the presence of a specific performance standard will be diminished without the availability of feedback to monitor progress toward that goal. Goal setting is also somewhat less effective with complex tasks. Various explanations for that finding have been put forth, but basically the notion is that when adequate strategies for successfully performing a complex task are not available, an assigned outcome goal can distract one from focusing on learning and performing the task, and may thus actually be counterproductive. This situation is most likely to occur with inexperienced performers and tasks which are both novel and complex (Earley, Lee, & Hanson, 1990). In novel task situations, Andia, Kristoff-Brown, Brown and Locke (1996) suggested that gradually increasing goals may be superior to starting with a single difficult goal, so that expectations are not so high when the person is still learning the task.

Goal setting effects have generally been stronger in laboratory settings, but it should be noted that there may be considerable overlap between setting and task complexity variables. It is inevitable that the real jobs examined in field studies are usually going to rate higher in complexity than are the kind of tasks commonly used in laboratory research. Some evidence for that trend was reported in Tubbs (1985), where a coded lab-versus-field variable and the task complexity coding described earlier correlated .76 across all studies examined. There are obviously other features that distinguish laboratory from field studies, most prominently the relative lack of control over both experimental and contextual factors that exists in field research, but the nature of the task would be a key difference. However, this is not to lose sight of the fact that goal setting has been moderately effective even in field studies involving fairly complex tasks.

MODELS OF GOAL SETTING'S EFFECT ON PERFORMANCE

Much speculation is required to comment on the nature of the mechanism by which a formal assigned goal influences behavior and task performance. One can either avoid such speculation or cautiously embrace it, and in the I/O literature on goals and motivation the latter course is clearly followed. If our hope in this volume is to better understand why performance goals are effective in some research contexts and not in others, it likewise seems necessary to consider potential explanations for a goal's influence on performance.

Most models of motivation presented in the goal setting literature reflect the influence of theoretical perspectives from the psychological literature on behavioral intentions, expectancy-valence judgments, and cybernetic control systems (e.g., Bandura, 1977; Carver & Scheier, 1982; Fishbein & Ajzen, 1975; Vroom, 1964). In models of intentional behavior, a person's intention is the focal point. Intention is defined as a cognitive representation of one's plans for future behavior, including both intended end states (e.g., goals) and intended action plans or strategies (Tubbs & Ekeberg, 1991). Some theories of motivation have focused more on how intentions are chosen (Fishbein & Ajzen, 1975; Vroom, 1964), others on monitoring and maintenance of intentions (Carver & Scheier, 1982; Campion & Lord, 1982), still others on moderators on the intention-behavior link (Kanfer & Ackerman, 1989; Kuhl, 1985).

Given goal setting's beginnings as an applied motivational technology, it is not surprising that the earliest attempts to elaborate on the factors intervening between assigned goals and performance were very goal centered. That is, the main focus was to ascertain whether goal assignment was successful, much as in a manipulation check. This led to emphasis on assessing whether subjects accepted goals and were committed to them. Hollenbeck and Klein (1987) and Locke and Latham (1990) compiled lists of factors that should affect and enhance one's commitment to an assigned goal. Using an expectancy-valence theory framework, they grouped the factors into influences on the expectancy (i.e., likelihood) and valence (i.e., value or importance) of successful goal attainment. Influences on valence included incentives and rewards (including self-rewards), publicness of goal setting, personality, ego involvement in the task, and the presence of authority figures and coworkers,. Expectancy of success would be influenced by prior performance levels, task self-efficacy, attributions for past performance, performance constraints, and perceived ability.

Other approaches to understanding the goal setting phenomenon

(Campion & Lord, 1982; Kanfer & Ackerman, 1989; Klein, 1989; Locke & Latham, 1990; Reidel, Nebeker, & Cooper, 1988; Tubbs & Ekeberg, 1991) took a less goal centered view in that the assigned goal was viewed as but one -- albeit very salient -- environmental event which, combined with other information, was evaluated and perhaps incorporated into one's intentions. That is, rather than just assessing whether or not an assigned goal was accepted, the effect of the assigned goal on a person's overall motivational system was considered. Despite differing details, the basic notion of all such models is that people are somehow motivated to pursue certain courses of action more than others and choices are made. The nature of this evaluation and choice process and the degree of automaticity involved have, of course, been the source of much speculation, but those elaborations are unimportant here. What is relevant is that the cognitive orientation of the models is consistent with the assumption that some, at least partially conscious and deliberate, choice occurs. What is chosen is an intention, which in turn serves as a direct impetus to action.

Effects of an Assigned Goal

From an expectancy-valence theory perspective, the most immediate influence of an assigned goal should be on one's judgments of the valence and expectancy attached to the task itself and to the performance of levels above and below the assigned goal. This is the most direct effect of the evaluation contingencies communicated by goal assignment. Naylor and Ilgen (1984) provided a particularly explicit discussion of the nature of those contingencies. If the effect on the contingencies is powerful enough, a change (or choice) of intention will result. One's personal goal or intention is, of course, the target of the goal setting procedure (Locke, 1968).

Taking a somewhat different approach, Locke and Latham (1990) broke the effect of goals into four mechanisms. The first three, directing attention, mobilizing effort, and encouraging persistence, are motivational in nature and can be seen as related to the three facets of behavior: direction, intensity, and duration. Goals direct attention in that they help lead to intentions consistent with reaching desired outcomes. A goal thus creates a focus that facilitates successful performance -- in fact, it defines successful performance for a worker. The more specific the goal, the more clear that focus is, and the better guide for one's intention it provides. Goals also mobilize effort and other resources until the goal is achieved, and thus encourage persistent behavior. A fourth, more cognitive, mechanism comes into play in the case of complex tasks where available knowledge may not suffice to allow successful performance. Locke and Latham (1990) believed goals encourage the development of more appropriate task performance strategies in that context.

Whichever view one takes, the basic idea is still that goal assignment results in changes in one's intentions, both in terms of intended outcomes (like goal levels) and in terms of actual intended behaviors (like task strategies). These changes will take place to the extent that the goal is sufficiently motivating to the individual such that it defines or significantly alters the contingencies for good and poor performance. The choice process should result in intentions consistent with achievement of an assigned goal when incentives, norms, resources, the person's personality and perceived abilities, etcetera, are all conducive to such a result. And such an intention will lead to the desired performance when the person has the requisite skills, knowledge and abilities for successful maintenance and enactment.

RECENT GOAL SETTING RESEARCH

Some previous trends have continued to the present. For example, a number of studies have addressed the conception and measurement of goal commitment (DeShon & Landis, 1997; Hollenbeck, Klein, O'Leary, & Wright, 1989; Klein & Mulvey, 1995; Tubbs & Dahl, 1991; Tubbs, 1993, 1994; Wright, O'Leary-Kelly, Cortina, Klein, & Hollenbeck, 1994). Some others have continued the attempt to explain goal setting effects from an expectancy-valence theory perspective (Klein, 1991; Tubbs, Boehne, & Dahl, 1993). Still others have further examined the relation between goals and monetary incentives (Lee, Locke, & Phan, 1997; Wood, Atkins, & Bright, 1999; Wright, 1989, 1992).

Another series of recent studies have focused on goal orientation, an individual difference variable hypothesized to moderate the effectiveness of goal setting (Button, Mathieu, & Zajac, 1996; Phillips & Gully, 1997; VandeWalle, Brown, Cron, & Slocum, 1999). Basically, people with a learning goal orientation are thought to take goals as more of a positive challenge, whereas those with a performance goal orientation view goals as more of a threat. Results have provided some support for the notion that assigned goals are more effective for individuals who have a learning orientation. Another individual difference variable, conscientiousness, has also lately been linked to goal setting. Barrick, Mount, and Strauss (1993) reported that salespersons high in conscientiousness were more likely to spontaneously set their own specific performance goals.

Arguably the most important trend in the current literature has been the investigation of possible explanations for the relatively weak (and sometimes detrimental) effects of assigned goals on complex tasks. DeShon, Brown, and Greenis (1996) noted that three possible explanations have been offered. First, Earley (Earley, Connolly, & Ekegren, 1989; Earley, Connolly, & Lee, 1989) has suggested that the pressure to meet goals leads to dysfunctional strategy choices. Second, Kanfer and Ackerman's (1989) model hypothesizes that, because of the presence of a specific performance goal, attentional resources which would better be spent on skill acquisition are instead expended on self-regulation activities like performance monitoring, resulting in poor performance (Kanfer, Ackerman, Murtha, Dugdale, & Nelson, 1994). Third, DeShon and Alexander (1996) and Wood and Locke (1990) have suggested that goals on complex tasks may be improperly framed. Empirical findings do not clearly support any one explanation, indicating the need for more work in this area.

CONCLUSIONS

It is understandable that assigned goals have a positive influence on performance on work tasks. If reaching an assigned goal is instrumental in obtaining valued outcomes or avoiding unpleasant ones, then it is logical that a person should accept that goal and try to reach it. Not that people always behave logically, or in their best long-term interests, but it is reasonable to assume that most individuals in job contexts will choose to accept reasonable work assignments when given, and usually remain committed to them until completion. If they do not, they probably will not fare very well in the organization, and they know it. As mentioned earlier, organizations are strong systems, with the formal authority to reward and punish.

If the goals and their consequences are valent enough to alter one's perception of evaluations contingencies, more difficult assigned goal levels should result in different intentions (e.g., stronger effort, longer hours, more efficient strategies) geared to reach the tougher standard. If a time goal (a deadline) is assigned, an altered strategy to allow quicker completion may be formed. More specific goals should likewise result in intentions matched more closely to the assignment. When goal specificity is defined in terms of a specific number of "widgets," a more specific outcome is assigned, giving the person a clearer referent against which to measure progress and alter intentions if necessary. The feedback loop analogy is of course borrowed from control theory and also explains why goal setting effects are stronger when accurate feedback is provided. Without such knowledge of one's progress on the task, the processes of pacing oneself and knowing when to alter strategies or tactics are greatly complicated.

It also makes sense that assigned goals are somewhat less effective, at least initially, with complex and novel tasks. Whatever the exact explanation for this finding, it is no surprise that adding the pressure of an assigned goal into a situation where someone is trying to learn a new and difficult task can hurt performance. The real question is why we would want to assign a difficult goal to that person at all. Gradually increasing goals may be more appropriate (Andia et al., 1996). And in some jobs -- for example, where the work pace is externally determined (as in many service jobs) or in jobs with creative products -- specific quantitative output goals may not be a good fit anyway. Time goals or quality goals may be better suited to those contexts, if goals are indeed warranted.

Of course, a major factor in the typical success of goal setting in work contexts is the context itself. From Scientific Management onward, the aim of organizational theorists has been to create systems to meet organizational objectives, sustain levels of production, and compete with rivals, meaning that factors conducive to successful goal setting (e.g., training programs, reward systems, accurate feedback) abound in effective organizations. Constructing organizational systems where employee motivation is high for pursuing shared goals is the whole idea of modern organizational design (Bedeian & Zammuto, 1991; Greenberg & Baron, 1993; Ivancevich, Szilagyi, & Wallace, 1977). In well-run organizations offering equitable incentives and involving people in their work, there is reason to hope for such a mutually beneficial outcome.

REFERENCES

Ach, N. (1935). *Analyse des willens.* Berlin: Urban & Schwarzenberg.

Andia, G., Kristoff-Brown, A., Brown, K., & Locke, E. A. (1996). Relation of goals and microlevel work processes to performance on a multipath manual task. *Journal of Applied Psychology, 81*, 483-497.

Argyris, C. (1964). *Integrating the individual and the organization.* New York: Wiley.

Bandura, A. (1977). Self-efficacy: Toward a unifying theory of behavioral change. *Psychological Review, 84*, 191-215.

Barrick, M. R., Mount, M. K., & Strauss, J. P. (1993). Conscientiousness and performance of sales representatives: Test of the mediating effects of goal setting. *Journal of Applied Psychology, 78*, 715-722.

Bedeian, A. G., & Zammuto, R. F. (1991). *Organizations: Theory and design.* Chicago: Dryden.

Benjamin, L. T. (1997). Organized industrial psychology before division 14: The ACP and the AAAP (1930-1945). *Journal of Applied Psychology, 82*, 459-466.

Blum, M. L., & Naylor, J. C. (1968). *Industrial psychology: Its theoretical and social foundations.* New York: Harper & Row.

Button, S., Mathieu, J., & Zajac, D. (1996). Goal orientation in organizational behavior research: A conceptual and empirical foundation. *Organizational Behavior and Human Decision Processes, 67*, 26-48.

Campion, M. A., & Lord, R. G. (1982). A control systems conceptualization of the goal-setting and changing process. *Organizational Behavior and Human Performance, 30*, 265-287.

Carver, C. S., & Scheier, M. F. (1982). Control theory: A useful conceptual framework for personality-social, clinical, and health psychology. *Psychological Bulletin, 92*, 111-135.

Chidester, T. R., & Grigsby, W. C. (1984). A meta-analysis of the goal setting performance literature. *Academy of Management Proceedings*, 202-206.

Cohen, J. (1988). *Statistical power analysis for the behavioral sciences.* Hillsdale, NJ: Erlbaum.

DeShon, R. P., & Alexander, R. (1996). Goal setting effects on implicit and explicit learning of complex tasks. *Organizational Behavior and Human Decision Processes, 65*, 18-36.

DeShon, R. P., Brown, K. G., and Greenis, J. L. (1996). Does self-regulation require cognitive resources? Evaluation of resource allocation models of goal setting. *Journal of Applied Psychology, 81*, 595-608.

DeShon, R. P., & Landis, R. S. (1997). The dimensionality of the Hollenbeck, Williams, and Klein (1989) measure of commitment on complex tasks. *Organizational Behavior and Human Decisions Processes, 70*, 105-116.

Drucker, P. (1954). *The practice of management.* New York: Harper.

Dunnette, M. D., & Hough, L. M. (Eds.). (1991). *Handbook of industrial and organizational psychology*, (Vol. 2). Palo Alto, CA: Consulting Psychologists Press.

Earley, P. C., Connolly, T., and Ekegren, G. (1989). Goals, strategy development, and task performance: Some limits on the efficacy of goal setting. *Journal of Applied Psychology, 74*, 24-33.

Earley, P. C., Connolly, T., & Lee, C. (1989). Task strategy interventions in goal setting: The importance of search in strategy development. *Journal of Management, 15*, 589-602.

Earley, P. C., Lee, C., & Hanson, L. A. (1990). Joint moderating effects of job experience and task component complexity: Relations among goal setting, task strategies, and performance. *Journal of Organizational Behavior, 11*, 3-16.

Etzioni, A. (1964). *Modern organizations.* Englewood Cliffs, NJ: Prentice-Hall.

Fishbein, M., & Ajzen, I. (1975). *Belief, attitude, intention, and behavior: An introduction to theory and research.* Reading, MA: Addision-Wesley.

Greenberg, J., & Baron, R. A. (1993). *Behavior in organizations.* Boston: Allyn & Bacon.

Greenwood, R. G. (1981). Management by objectives: As developed by Peter Drucker, assisted by Harold Smiddy. *Academy of Management Review, 6,* 225-230.

Guzzo, R. A., Jette, R. D., & Katzell, R. A. (1985). The effects of psychologically based intervention programs on worker productivity: A meta-analysis. *Personnel Psychology, 38,* 275-291.

Hollenbeck, J. R., & Klein, H. J. (1987). Goal commitment and the goal-setting process: Problems, prospects, and proposals for future research. *Journal of Applied Psychology, 72,* 212-220.

Hollenbeck, J. R., Klein, H. J., O'Leary, A. M., & Wright, P. M. (1989). Investigation of the construct validity of a self-report measure of goal commitment. *Journal of Applied Psychology, 74,* 951-956.

Hunter, J. E., Schmidt, F. L., & Jackson, G. B. (1982). *Meta-analysis: Cumulating research findings across studies.* Beverly Hills, CA: Sage Publications.

Ivancevich, J. M., Szilagyi, A. D., & Wallace, M. J. (1977). *Organizational behavior and performance.* Santa Monica, CA: Goodyear.

Kanfer, R. (1996). Self-regulatory and other non-ability determinants of skill acquisition. In P. M. Gollwitzer & Bargh (Eds.), *The psychology of action: Linking cognition and motivation to behavior* (pp. 404-423). New York: Guilford.

Kanfer, R., & Ackerman, P. L. (1989). Motivational and cognitive abilities: An integrative/aptitude-treatment interaction approach to skill acquisition. *Journal of Applied Psychology, 74,* 657-690.

Kanfer, R., Ackerman, P. L., Murtha, T. C., Dugdale, B., & Nelson, L. (1994). Goal setting, conditions of practice and task performance: A resource allocation perspective. *Journal of Applied Psychology, 79,* 826-835.

Katz, D., & Kahn, R. (1978). *The social psychology of organizations.* New York: Wiley.

Klein, H. J. (1989). An integrated control theory model of work motivation. *Academy of Management Review, 14,* 150-172.

Klein, H. J., & Mulvey, P. W. (1995). Two investigations of the relationships among group goals, goal commitment, cohesion, and performance. *Organizational Behavior and Human Decision Processes, 61,* 44-53.

Kuhl, J. (1985). Volitional mediators of cognition-behavior consistency: Self-regulatory processes and action versus state orientation. In J. Kuhl & J. Beckmann (Eds.), *Action control: from cognition to behavior* (pp. 101-128). Berlin: Springer-Verlag.

Landy, F. L. (1997). Early influences on the development of industrial and organizational psychology. *Journal of Applied Psychology, 82,* 467-477.

Landy, F. L., & Trumbo, D. A. (1980). *Psychology of work behavior.* Pacific Grove, CA: Brooks/Cole.

Latham, G. P., & Yukl, G. A. (1975). A review of research on the application of goal setting in organizations. *Academy of Management Journal, 18,* 824-845.

Lawrence, P. R. (1987). Historical development of organizational behavior. In J.W. Lorsch (Ed.), *Handbook of organizational behavior* (pp. 1-9). Englewood Cliffs, NJ: Prentice-Hall.

Lawrence, P. R., & Lorsch, J. W. (1967). *Organizations and environment.* Homewood, IL: Irwin.

Lee, T. W., Locke, E. A., & Phan, S. H. (1997). Explaining the assigned goal-incentive interaction: The role of self-efficacy and personal goals. *Journal of Management, 23,* 541-559.

Lewin, K. (1951). *Field theory in social science.* New York: Harper.

Likert, R. (1967). *The human organization.* New York: McGraw-Hill.

Locke, E. A. (1968). Toward a theory of task motivation and incentives. *Organizational Behavior and Human Performance, 3,* 157-189.

Locke, E. A. (1986). *Generalizing from laboratory to field settings.* Lexington, MA: Lexington.
Locke, E. A., & Latham, G. P. (1990). *A theory of goal setting and task performance.* Englewood Cliffs, NJ: Prentice-Hall.
Locke, E. A., Feren, D. B., McCaleb, V. M., Shaw, K. N., & Denny, A. T. (1980). The relative effectiveness of four methods of motivating employee performance. In K. D. Duncan, M. M. Gruneberg, & D. Wallis (Eds.), *Changes in working life* (pp. 368-388). London: Wiley.
Locke, E. A., Shaw, N. R., Saari, L. M., & Latham, G. P. (1981). Goal setting and task performance: 1969-1980. *Psychological Bulletin, 90*, 125-152.
Mace, C. A. (1935). Incentives: Some experimental studies. *Industrial Health Research Board, Report number 72.*
McGregor, D. (1960). *The human side of enterprise.* New York: McGraw-Hill.
Mento, A. J., Steel, R. P., & Karren, R. J. (1987). A meta-analytic study of the effects of goal setting on task performance: 1966-1984. *Organizational Behavior and Human Decision Processes, 39*, 52-83.
Miner, J. B. (1984). The validity and usefulness of theories in an emerging organizational science. *Academy of Management Review, 9*, 296-306.
Mitchell, T. R. (1997). Matching motivational strategies with organizational contexts. In B. M. Staw & L. L. Cummings (Eds.), *Research in Organizational Behavior, 19*, 57-149.
Muchinsky, P. M. (2000). *Psychology applied to work.* Belmont, CA: Wadsworth.
Napoli, D. S. (1975). *The architects of adjustment: The practice and professionalism of American psychology.* Ann Arbor, MI: University Microfilms.
Naylor, J. C., & Ilgen, D. R. (1984). Goal setting: A theoretical analysis of a motivational technology. In B. M. Staw & L. L. Cummings (Eds.), *Research in organizational behavior, 6*, (pp. 95-140). Greenwich, CT: JAI.
Naylor, J. C., Pritchard, R. D., & Ilgen, D. R. (1980). *A theory of behavior in organizations.* New York: Academic Press.
O'Reilly, C. A., III. (1990). Organizational behavior: Where we've been and where we're going. *Annual Review of Psychology, 42*, 427-458.
Orne, M. T. (1962). On the social psychology of the psychological experiment with particular reference to demand characteristics. *American Psychologist, 17*, 776-783.
Phillips, J. M., & Gully, S. M. (1997). Role of goal orientation, ability, need for achievement, and locus of control in the self efficacy and goal setting process. *Journal of Applied Psychology, 82*, 792-802.
Pinder, C. C. (1984). *Work motivation.* Glenview, IL: Scott-Foresman.
Reidel, J. A., Nebeker, D. M., & Cooper, B. L. (1988). The influence of monetary incentives on goal choice, goal commitment, and task performance. *Organizational Behavior and Human Decision Processes, 42*, 155-180.
Rodgers, R., & Hunter, J. E. (1991). Impact of management by objectives on organizational productivity. *Journal of Applied Psychology, 76*, 322-336.
Roethlisberger, F. J., & Dickson, W. J. (1939). *Management and the worker.* Cambridge, MA: Harvard University Press.
Ryan, T. A. (1958). Drives, tasks, and the initiation of behavior. *American Journal of Psychology, 71*, 74-93.
Ryan, T. A. (1970). *Intentional behavior: An approach to human motivation.* New York: Ronald.
Schmitt, N. W., & Klimoski, R. J. (1991). *Research methods in human resources management.* Cincinnati, OH: South-Western.
Taylor, F. (1947). *Scientific Management.* New York: Harper & Row.
Tubbs, M. E. (1985). *A meta-analysis of the goal-setting/performance literature.* Unpublished doctoral dissertation, University of Houston.
Tubbs, M. E. (1986). Goal setting: A meta-analytic examination of the empirical evidence. *Journal of Applied Psychology, 71*, 474-483.

Tubbs, M. E. (1993). Commitment as a moderator of the goal-performance relation: A case for clearer construct definition. *Journal of Applied Psychology*, *78*, 86-97.

Tubbs, M. E. (1994). Commitment and the role of ability in motivation: A reply to Wright, O'Leary-Kelly, Cortina, Klein, and Hollenbeck. *Journal of Applied Psychology*, *79*, 804-811.

Tubbs, M. E., Boehne, D. M., & Dahl, J. G. (1993). Expectancy, valence, and motivational force functions in goal setting research: An empirical test. *Journal of Applied Psychology*, *78*, 361-373.

Tubbs, M. E., & Dahl, J. G. (1991). An empirical comparison of self-report and discrepancy measures of goal commitment. *Journal of Applied Psychology*, *76*, 708-716.

Tubbs, M. E., & Ekeberg, S. E. (1991). The role of intentions in work motivation: Implications for goal-setting theory and research. *Academy of Management Review*, *16*, 180-199.

VandeWalle, D., Brown, S. P., Cron, W. L., & Slocum, J. W. (1999). The influence of goal orientation and self-regulation tactics on sales performance: A conceptual field test. *Journal of Applied Psychology*, *84*, 249-259.

Vroom, V. (1964). *Work and motivation.* New York: Wiley.

Weber, M. (1921). *Theory of social and economic organization.* London: Oxford University Press.

Wood, R. E., Atkins, P. W. B., & Bright, J. E. H. (1999). Bonuses, goals and instrumentality effects. *Journal of Applied Psychology*, *84*, 703-720.

Wood, R. E., Mento, A. J., & Locke, E. A. (1987). Task complexity as a moderator of goal effects: A meta-analysis. *Journal of Applied Psychology*, *72*, 416-425.

Wood, R. E., & Locke, E. A. (1990). Goal setting and strategy effects on complex tasks. In B. Staw & L. Cummings (Eds.), *Research in Organizational Behavior*, *12*, (pp. 73-109). Greenwich, CT: JAI.

Wright, P. M. (1989). Test of the mediating role of goals in the incentive-performance relationship. *Journal of Applied Psychology*, *74*, 699-705.

Wright, P. M. (1992). An examination of the relationships among monetary incentives, goal level, goal commitment and performance. *Journal of Management*, *18*, 677-693.

Wright, P. M., O'Leary-Kelly, A. M., Cortina, J. M., Klein, H. J., & Hollenbeck, J. R. (1994). The meaning and measurement of goal commitment. *Journal of Applied Psychology*, *79*, 795-803.

Chapter 3

THE SOCIAL PSYCHOLOGY OF CREATIVITY: EFFECTS OF EVALUATION ON INTRINSIC MOTIVATION AND CREATIVITY OF PERFORMANCE

Beth A. Hennessey
Wellesley College

In this chapter, I will describe research and findings resulting from the study of the social psychology of creativity. Rather than attempting to specify the personality traits that distinguish creative persons or the steps of the creative process, social psychologists have focused their attention on the impact of situational factors on creative performance. Investigations carried out over the past two decades clearly demonstrate that there is a direct link between the motivational orientation brought by an individual to a task and the creativity of their performance on that task; and it is the environment, or at least certain aspects of the environment, that in large part determine that motivational orientation. Researchers working within this tradition have identified a number of environmental factors that kill intrinsic motivation and creativity. These include expected reward, competition, surveillance and time limits. But often the most deleterious extrinsic constraint of all has been found to be expected evaluation. Perhaps because situations of evaluation often combine aspects of each of the other "killers," the expectation of evaluation has been shown to severely undermine the intrinsic motivation and creativity of performance of persons across the entire age span, individuals from all walks of life, from preschoolers to professionals whose very livelihood depends upon the creativity of their work.

An examination of the diaries and letters of creative persons, both past and present, provides real-world evidence of the devastating effects of expected evaluation. The personal accounts of Sylvia Plath are particularly revealing. Plath, who felt especially debilitated by competitive evaluation, wrote: "Yes, I want the world's praise, money, and love, and I am furious with anyone . . . getting ahead of me" (Hughes & McCullough, 1982, p. 305).

"I want . . . to feel my work good and well-taken. Which ironically freezes me at my work, corrupts my nunnish labor of work-for-itself-as-its-own-reward" (p. 305).

THE INTRINSIC MOTIVATION PRINCIPLE OF CREATIVITY

A long tradition of carefully-conceived empirical research corroborates the view that extrinsic constraints, like evaluation, can have severely negative consequences. The first published studies to investigate the impact of environmental constraints on motivation and performance appeared over 25 years ago and were focused on the effects of expected reward (e.g., Deci, 1971, 1972; Garbarino, 1975; Greene & Lepper, 1974; Kernoodle-Loveland & Olley, 1979; Kruglanski, Friedman, & Zeevi, 1971; Lepper, Greene, & Nisbett, 1973; McGraw & McCullers, 1979; Pittman, Emery, & Boggiano, 1982; Shapira, 1976). While, over the years, experimental approaches have become increasingly complex, the basic message has remained the same. Hundreds of published investigations reveal that the promise of a reward made contingent on task engagement can often serve to undermine intrinsic task motivation and qualitative aspects of performance, including creativity.

Building on this body of evidence, researchers have gone on to uncover the deleterious impact of a variety of other environmental constraints, such as deadlines and surveillance. The data reveal that expected reward is not the only "killer" of motivation and creativity. In recent years, the investigative focus has also been expanded to include the impact of evaluation. For persons who initially display a high level of interest in a task, working under the expectation of an evaluation both decreases their motivation and undermines the creativity of their performance.

Intrigued by these research findings, a small group of investigators and theorists who had been trained primarily as social psychologists began to explore the mechanism behind these effects. Over the years, the research evidence has grown to reveal a direct link between the motivational orientation brought by an individual to a task and creativity of performance on that task. Whether 3 or 83, if individuals are to reach their creative potential, they must engage in an activity for the sheer pleasure and enjoyment of the task itself, rather than for some extrinsic goal (such as a positive evaluation). So certain are many researchers about the crucial role played by intrinsic interest in the creative process that they have come to subscribe to what Amabile terms the "Intrinsic Motivation Principle of Creativity" (Amabile, 1983, 1996): Intrinsic motivation is conducive to creativity and extrinsic motivation is almost always detrimental.

In order for an individual's creative potential to be realized, she must approach a task with intrinsic motivation -- she must engage in that task for the sheer enjoyment and pleasure of the activity itself rather than for some external goal. Researchers have found not only that this construct we call intrinsic motivation is essential for creativity but also that it is especially ephemeral. In other words, while an individual's creativity skills (e.g., familiarity with brainstorming and related techniques or the ability to temporarily suspend judgment) or domain skills (e.g., knowledge of chemistry, physics or engineering or facility with a paint brush) may be fairly stable, motivational orientation is highly variable, and largely situation-dependent. None of us is always intrinsically motivated under all conditions. And there are few social conditions more damaging to intrinsic interest than situations in which evaluations have been linked with task completion.

INTRINSIC MOTIVATION AND CREATIVITY: SOME DEFINITIONS AND OPERATIONALIZATIONS

Intrinsic motivation is not an easily defined concept. An examination of the literature reveals that, over the years, a variety of different (although largely compatible) conceptualizations of this construct have been offered. Hebb (1955) and Berlyne (1960) proposed that enjoyable (intrinsically motivating) activities are those that present an optimal level of novelty. White (1959) and Harter (1978) suggested that a sense of competence and mastery are central components of intrinsic motivation. Finally, deCharms (1968), Deci (1971) and Lepper and colleagues (Lepper et al., 1973) placed their emphasis on a sense of control: when a person perceives her task engagement as externally controlled, she is extrinsically rather than intrinsically motivated.

In sum, researchers tell us that a large number of features of task engagement contribute to an intrinsically motivated orientation. The individual may be curious about or in some other way stimulated by the presentation of the activity. With task engagement come feelings of competence, mastery or self-efficacy. And, perhaps most important, while engaging in the task, individuals feel that their involvement is free of strong external control: They get the sense that they are playing rather than working. Importantly, each of these hallmarks of intrinsic motivation focuses on the individual's inner phenomenological state. Whether prompted by just the right amount of novelty, feelings of competence, or a sense of control, the intrinsically motivated state comes about as the result of an internal, very individualized process.

Researchers and theorists interested in studying creativity have found that, like intrinsic motivation, this construct, too, is difficult to define, quantify or otherwise measure. The majority of creativity researchers and theoreticians believe that the key to understanding this phenomenon lies in the study of individual difference variables and the unique constellation of traits that make up the creative person. Others focus their attention on the creative process. A third group, including many investigators interested in the social psychology of creativity, has chosen to concentrate on the fruits of that process -- the creative product. This theoretical approach has been particularly helpful to researchers interested in assessing the impact of extrinsic constraints on performance.

But how are investigators to decide whether products produced by persons working under the expectation of evaluation are more or less creative than products made by persons in a control/no evaluation condition? Is it appropriate for such creativity criteria to be laid out by the researcher? Perhaps the creators themselves should have the final say? The Consensual Assessment Technique (CAT) (Amabile, 1982; Hennessey & Amabile, 1999) for assessing creativity is based on the assumption that a panel of independent expert raters, persons who have not had the opportunity to confer with one another and who have not been trained by the researcher, are best able to make such judgments. Over 20 years of research has clearly established that product creativity can be reliably and validly assessed based on the consensus of experts. Although creativity in a product may be difficult to characterize in terms of specific features, it is something that people can recognize and agree on when they see it.

The Consensual Assessment Technique (CAT) is grounded in two complementary definitions of creativity. The underlying conceptual definition that has been used in building a theoretical formulation of the creative process states that:

> a product will be judged as creative to the extent that (a) it is both a novel and appropriate, useful, correct or valuable response to the task at hand, and (b) the task is heuristic rather than algorithmic (Amabile, 1996, p. 35).

The operational definition upon which the CAT is based is readily applicable to empirical research:

> A product or response is creative to the extent that appropriate observers agree it is creative. Appropriate observers are those familiar with the domain in which the product was created or the response articulated (Amabile, 1996, p. 33).

Importantly, this consensual definition is based on the creative *product* rather than the creative process. Not only has a clear articulation of the creative process yet to be developed but, more importantly, any identification of a thought process as "creative" must finally depend on the fruit of that process -- a product or response.

Amabile and her colleagues have attempted to capture the essential characteristics of the conceptual definition of creativity in the Consensual Assessment Technique (CAT). First, participants are presented with tasks that leave room for considerable flexibility and novelty of response. Second, these are tasks for which the range of appropriate responses has been clearly identified in participants' instructions. Finally, the experimental activities employed are all heuristic in nature -- judges are only asked to make ratings of open-ended tasks, tasks with more than one solution and a variety of paths to those solutions.

Because it is essential for social psychological research that there not be large individual differences in baseline performance on the target experimental task, the CAT requires that the creativity task not depend heavily upon specialized skills such as drawing or verbal facility that some individuals will have undoubtedly developed more fully than others. At the same time, the task should be open-ended enough to permit considerable flexibility and allow for novelty in responses. In addition, of course, the task must be one that leads to some clearly observable response. In this way, the creativity assessment procedure is similar to real-world assessments of creativity where appropriate judges, experts in such widely disparate domains as the visual arts and the sciences, make ratings of products according to their own, subjective criteria.

Researchers deciding to utilize this consensual assessment procedure must make certain that a number of requirements are met. First, the judges should all have had some experience with the domain in question. However, they need not be experts, and the level of experience for all judges need not be identical. It is the judges' familiarity with the domain that is important, not the fact that they, themselves, may have produced work rated as highly creative. Second, the judges must make their assessments independently. They are not trained by the experimenter to agree with one another; are given no specific criteria for judging creativity; and are not allowed to confer in their assessments. Third, judges should be instructed to rate the products relative to one another, rather than rating them against some absolute standards they might hold for drawing, sculpture, poetry, etc. Finally, each judge should view the products in a different random order.

Given the consensual definition of creativity, the most important criterion for the results of this assessment procedure is that the product ratings be reliable. In most instances, a reliability figure of .70 (Cronbach's coefficient alpha as calculated by the "reliability" procedure in SPSS (Statistical Package for the Social Sciences)) or higher can be considered evidence of an acceptable level of agreement between judges. Once such a level is reached, it is then appropriate to compute a sum (or an average) across all ratings given each product. These sums (or averages) then constitute the unit of analysis for between-group comparisons (e.g., evaluation vs. no evaluation conditions).

EARLY EMPIRICAL INVESTIGATIONS OF THE IMPACT OF EVALUATION

There is little empirical research on the effects of expected evaluation that predates the advent of the CAT and related product-assessment techniques. However, as early as 1969, investigators were already finding some suggestive evidence in support of the Intrinsic Motivation Principle of Creativity. In one clinical interview study (Garfield, Cohen, & Roth, 1969), undergraduates who were judged to have an internal locus of evaluation scored higher on standard paper-and-pencil tests of creativity than did undergraduates with an external locus. In a similar investigation (Poole, Williams, & Lett, 1977), elementary school children who earned high scores on the Torrance Tests of Creativity (Torrance, 1966) performed significantly differently on a locus-of-evaluation test than did children with low creativity scores. Again in this instance, high creativity was associated with an internal locus of evaluation. Finally, in a more controlled, experimental investigation (White & Owen, 1970), boys assigned to a classroom setting stressing self-evaluation scored significantly more creative on a standardized test than did boys assigned to classrooms stressing peer evaluation or teacher evaluation.

Taken together, these early investigations lead to the conclusion that external evaluation will undermine creativity (and intrinsic motivation). However, other researchers offered evidence that contradicted this hypothesis. Most of the investigations showing a positive relation between evaluation and creativity of performance focused on competitive evaluation. Torrance (1964, 1965) found that competition (promising prizes for high scores) increased both the fluency and the flexibility of children's responses to his test items. Goetz (1981) conducted a prototypical behavior-modification study in which preschoolers who received verbal praise for novel block-building showed significant increases in innovation and creativity over baseline levels. And Raina (1968) assessed the effects of competition on children's performance on the Product Improvement and Unusual Uses Test (Torrance, 1966). Children assigned to the control group completed these tests without any mention of competition. In the experimental condition, however, study participants were told that their performance would be evaluated and that monetary prizes would go to the three highest scorers. In an effort to make this evaluative manipulation as salient as possible, the investigators prominently displayed the money during the testing session. In addition, the children expecting the evaluation were told that the names of the winners would be posted on the school bulletin board. Results indicated that the experimental-group children scored significantly higher on indices of both fluency and flexibility.

INTRINSIC MOTIVATION, CREATIVITY, AND TASK TYPE

At first glance the data presented here may appear to fall into two distinct and entirely contradictory camps. Nevertheless, there is a simple explanation for the fact that expected evaluation was shown both to enhance and severely undermine performance. These seemingly contradictory results can be reconciled with a consideration of the nature of the experimental tasks employed. Over the years, creativity researchers have come to distinguish between two distinct task types. Amabile explains:

> The conceptual definition of creativity states that a creative response is a novel and appropriate solution to a *heuristic* task. If the path to solution is clear and straightforward, the task is an algorithmic one, and responses to it simply cannot be considered creative. To allow response that may be considered creative, the task must be open-ended to some degree. Some search for solution paths is required (1996, p. 133).

Importantly, each of the studies demonstrating positive effects of evaluation employed tasks that are categorized as algorithmic. Creativity was operationalized in terms of a score earned on a paper-and-pencil test; and high scores, while they might reflect originality, were determined in large part by "fluency" (number of responses made) or "flexibility" (number of different categories of responses made). McGraw's (1978) model predicts that extrinsic motivation will undermine performance on heuristic tasks and enhance performance on algorithmic ones. According to this formulation, it should be expected that fluency and flexibility would improve under conditions of expected evaluation. Surely, individuals who are told that they can do well on a test by giving a large number of answers will give a large number of answers -- larger perhaps than the number given by individuals who are not competing for positive evaluations. Similarly, Wallach (1970) points out that high scores on a creativity test are to be expected if the test-takers have been explicitly told what they should do to perform well. Whether such performance should even be deemed "creative" is another issue.

In situations where the path to correct and positively evaluated solution(s) is straightforward, the promise of an evaluation can be predicted to enhance performance. However, this same facilitative effect should not be expected with heuristic, open-ended creativity-type tasks. Success at these types of activities requires sustained periods of intensely focused attention and a willingness to take risks; and the distractions brought by an impending evaluation are likely to make such a motivational orientation unlikely, if not impossible.

THE BASIC RESEARCH PARADIGM

Research investigating the impact of expected evaluation on intrinsic motivation and creativity of performance on truly heuristic tasks has been based on a modified version of the standard overjustification paradigm (e.g., Lepper, et al., 1973). In a typical research study, experimental subjects, who have been led to expect an evaluation of their performance, work at an interesting, open-ended and fairly complex task, whereas control subjects perform in the absence of any evaluation expectation.

While the classic overjustification studies focused on subsequent intrinsic interest in task engagement, the major dependent variable in the investigations to be reviewed in this section is creativity of products or responses. When experimenters do obtain a measure of intrinsic motivation, they either observe study participants to determine whether they freely choose to return to the evaluated task during a subsequent free-choice period, or they attempt to directly assess task motivation via interviews or with the aid of written questionnaires.

Importantly, subjects are not told that the experiment concerns intrinsic interest or creativity. Although target tasks are chosen specifically because there is no clear and straightforward path to correct (i.e., creative) solutions, if study participants knew that the researchers were interested in motivational orientation and creativity, they might be able to generate algorithms for producing creative solutions.

In an initial study of evaluation expectation (Amabile, 1979), the target task was a collage-making activity for which the path to a creative solution was neither clear nor straightforward. However, for some subjects in the constraint conditions, the task was rendered algorithmic, as they were given specific instructions as to how to make a collage that would be judged creative. This manipulation was included in an effort to test the possible differential effects of evaluation on heuristic and algorithmic tasks.

Amabile predicted that subjects working under an evaluation expectation on the heuristic collage-making task would evidence lower levels of both creativity and intrinsic interest than would no evaluation control group members. Further, in accordance with McGraw's (1978) theory, it was expected that the group working under an evaluation constraint but given explicit instructions on "how to be creative" would show higher levels of creativity but lower levels of intrinsic interest than would the controls.

In addition to these evaluation constraint and instructions variables, a "focus" variable was also introduced. Some subjects within each of the design groups were asked to focus on the creativity of their art works. Some were asked to focus on the technical aspects and others were not given any particular focus. This variable was included in an effort to determine whether subjects might generate algorithms for producing creative collages simply by knowing that the task called for creativity.

Study participants were 95 college-aged women enrolled in an introductory psychology course at Stanford University. To ensure that subjects would be unaware of the study's focus on creativity, a cover story was employed. Participants were told that they were pretesting a variety of measures that would be used in investigations the following semester. It was explained that one of five different activities would be randomly chosen and that after engaging in that activity, the subject would complete a mood questionnaire. Of course, in each instance, the collage activity was selected by the experimenter, at which point the subject was asked whether she was an artist or had done much collage work. An affirmative answer to either of these questions terminated the session. When explaining the art task to subjects, the experimenter stressed that they had complete freedom as to how they might use the materials to make a design; however, they were reminded that only the materials provided could be used.

Upon completion of this general introduction, the instructions given to subjects diverged to produce eight treatment groups. Subjects in the control conditions (nonevaluation-no focus, nonevaluation-technical focus and nonevaluation creativity focus) were told:

> There is one more important point that I should make clear before you begin. We won't be using your design as a source of data. We are not interested at all in the activity itself or what you do with the activity. We are only interested in the mood you report on the questionnaire. So we do not care about the design itself at all -- its only purpose is to provide you with this experience so we can see how it affects your mood.

In addition to hearing this introduction, subjects in the nonevaluation-technical focus group were instructed to concentrate on the technical aspects of the activity and subjects in the nonevaluation-creativity focus condition were asked to focus on the creative aspects.

The instructions for the five experimental (evaluation) groups (evaluation-no focus, evaluation technical focus, evaluation-creativity focus, evaluation-specific technical focus and evaluation-specific creativity focus) were:

> There is one more important point that I should make clear before you begin. In addition to your questionnaire, we will be looking at your finished design as an important source of data. We have five graduate artists from the Stanford Art Department working with us, and when this experiment is over, we will have them come in to judge each art work. They will make a detailed evaluation of your designs, noting the good points and criticizing the weaknesses. And since we know that our subjects are interested in how they are evaluated, we will send you a

> copy of each judge's evaluation of your design in about two weeks.

In addition, subjects in the evaluation-technical focus condition were told that the judges would base their evaluations on how technically good the designs were. Subjects in the evaluation-creativity focus condition were told that the judges would base their ratings on how creative the designs were. Participants in the evaluation-specific technical focus condition were told that the judges would base their technical evaluation of the designs on six elements: neatness, balance, amount of planning evident, level of organization, presence of actual recognizable figures or objects, and the degree to which the design expressed something to them. Subjects in the evaluation-specific creativity focus condition were told that the judges would base their evaluation on seven elements: novelty of idea, novelty shown in the use of materials, amount of variation in shapes used, asymmetry of design, amount of detail, complexity, and amount of effort evident. Importantly these lists of six and seven elements were those that had clustered closely with judges' actual ratings of technical goodness and creativity in a pretest.

After working alone for 15 minutes on the collage, subjects were asked to complete a "Mood Questionnaire," in keeping with the experimental cover story. In addition, an "Art Activity Questionnaire" was administered in an effort to assess subjects' interest in and attitudes toward the collage task.

The 95 collages were rated by 15 artists according to the provisions of the CAT (Amabile, 1982; Hennessey & Amabile, 1999). Rater's assessments of the technical goodness of the art works revealed that for the no focus groups (nonevaluation-no focus and evaluation-no focus) and the creativity focus groups (nonevaluation-creativity focus, evaluation-creativity focus, and evaluation-specific creativity focus), evaluation groups were rated lower on technical goodness than were their nonevaluation controls. Paired comparisons revealed that: the nonevaluation-no focus group was rated significantly higher on technical goodness than the evaluation-no focus group; and the nonevaluation-creativity focus group was rated significantly higher than both the evaluation-creativity focus and the evaluation-specific creativity focus group. Importantly, this pattern was reversed for the three technical focus groups, with the nonevaluation control (nonevaluation-technical focus) condition receiving the lowest ratings of the three conditions. These data support the premise that the technical quality of artwork resulting from an algorithmic process is not severely undermined by the expectation of evaluation; whereas the heuristic processes leading to creativity are severely impaired.

Interjudge reliability on the creativity dimension was .79. An overall analysis of variance of creativity scores was conducted. Results of this ANOVA were statistically significant. A planned contrast designed to test the hypothesis that control (nonevaluation) groups would be higher than experimental (evaluation) groups was highly significant ($p < .001$).

In addition, McGraw's (1978) hypothesis that extrinsic constraints like evaluation will have differential effects on algorithmic and heuristic tasks was also supported by a series of paired comparisons between control groups and their respective evaluation conditions. As predicted, the expectation of evaluation only boosted the creativity of persons who had been given specific instructions as to how to make a creative design. This between-group comparison was significant. In all other cases, the creativity of the nonevaluation group was significantly higher than that of the comparable evaluation group (see Table 1).

Table 1. Creativity Results: Paired Comparisons Between Control Groups and Their Relevant Experimental Groups. Amabile (1979)

	Instruction			
	No Focus	Technical Focus	Specific Technical Focus	Specific Creativity Focus
Evaluation Expectation				
Absent	+	+	+	
Present				+

Note: + indicates which of two groups (evaluation present or absent) was higher in mean creativity within each of the four instructional conditions. All comparisons were statistically significant ($p < .05$).

Six items on the "Art Activity Questionnaire" were specifically constructed to measure participants' attitudes toward the collage-making activity. It was expected that, as a group, subjects in the control (nonevaluation) groups would be higher in self-rated interest than would subjects in the experimental (evaluation) conditions. In particular, Amabile predicted that even though subjects in the specific creativity focus group might exhibit high levels of creativity as a result of having been given specific task instructions, their intrinsic interest would still be undermined by the expectation of evaluation. In sum, all eight design groups were expected to fit a pattern of lowered interest under conditions of evaluation. This general pattern was, in fact, observed. An analysis of variance involving all six groups yielded a significant main effect, as did a planned contrast of nonevaluation groups with evaluation groups.

While these between-group (evaluation/nonevaluation) differences were not as strong as with the creativity data, results clearly indicated that intrinsic interest was undermined by evaluation expectation. Of particular significance was the fact that while the specific technical focus group was high on technical goodness and the specific creativity focus group was high on creativity, both groups were quite low on intrinsic interest. In other words, the participants who received specific creativity instructions did not indicate a high level of intrinsic interest to match their high level of creativity.

In sum, these data demonstrate a negative effect of evaluation expectation on intrinsic motivation and creativity. While there did appear to be a positive effect of evaluation expectation for persons who had been given specific instructions as to how to produce a creative product, realistically speaking it is unlikely that creativity could be enhanced by telling people exactly what will be deemed a creative product or performance. In a real-world setting, we cannot know beforehand how to produce a novel and appropriate response. In this study, the specific creativity instructions that were given rendered the collage activity algorithmic. Yet for the nonevaluation groups, the collage making remained a heuristic task.

FURTHER EXPLORATIONS OF THE NEGATIVE EFFECTS OF EVALUATION ON INTRINSIC MOTIVATION AND CREATIVITY

Expected Evaluation

In an effort to further explore the finding that evaluation expectation has a negative effect on creativity, Amabile undertook two experimental replications. In both studies, a two-way factorial design was employed: Subjects either expected or did not expect an evaluation of their performance and they worked either alone or in the presence of others.

In a study focused on artistic creativity (Amabile, Goldfarb, & Brackfield, 1990, Study 2), 40 undergraduate women who were enrolled in an introductory psychology course were randomly assigned to one of four conditions: nonevaluation-no audience, nonevaluation audience, evaluation-no audience, evaluation-audience. In this investigation, no subjects were instructed to focus on particular aspects of their collage-making; they were simply told that the experiment examined the effects of performing various activities on mood.

Participants in the evaluation groups were told that their art works would be used as an important source of data. Evaluation was not mentioned to the subjects in the two nonevaluation conditions, and post-test interviews confirmed that they did not believe that their collages would be viewed as data. Those in the evaluation-audience condition were told that on the other side of a one-way mirror in the experimental room were four student-artists who had been hired to watch subjects and make expert evaluations of the collage-making and the finished products. It was explained that these judges would note the good points and criticize the weaknesses, and that subjects would see these evaluations before leaving the experimental session. Subjects in the nonevaluation-audience group also were led to believe that there were students on the other side of the one-way mirror. However, study participants in this condition were told that these people were waiting in the dark for a vision experiment. Subjects in the no audience conditions were told nothing about an audience, and the one-way mirror was covered. All study participants, regardless of the condition to which they had been assigned, were run individually.

The reliability for 10 artist-judges' ratings of the collages was .93 for creativity. These data lent strong support to the intrinsic motivation principle, as an analysis of variance yielded a significant main effect of evaluation on creativity. Nonevaluation subjects produced products that were judged significantly more creative than products produced by subjects expecting an evaluation of their work. There was a nonsignificant trend for the audience variable to undermine creativity, and there was no significant interaction between the two variables. In sum, these results parallel nicely the findings of the earlier study on artistic creativity (Amabile, 1979). When given no particular focus for their artwork, adult subjects who expected an evaluation produced less creative products than did subjects unconcerned with evaluation. Importantly, there was no undermining effect of evaluation expectation on technical goodness in this study. This result is in keeping with the premise that technical goodness involves largely algorithmic processes, while creative aspects of products are largely heuristic (Amabile, 1996).

When asked to rate the extent to which they felt anxious while making their collages, study participants assigned to the evaluation conditions made significantly higher ratings than did nonevaluation subjects. A similar main of evaluation effect was found on an item asking how concerned subjects felt about possible evaluations of their performance. Finally, evaluation subjects reported feeling significantly more distracted while making their collages than did nonevaluation subjects; and there was a significant negative correlation between subjects' rated concern with evaluation and the creativity of their products ($r = -.41$).

In a related investigation, Amabile and colleagues (Amabile, Goldfarb, & Brackfield, 1990, Study 1) again crossed evaluation expectation with the presence or absence of others. In this study, however, the audience was composed of coacting subjects participating in the same target activity and the target experimental task was designed to examine verbal, rather than artistic, creativity.

Subjects in this investigation were 48 female undergraduates enrolled in an introductory psychology course. All participants were told that the experiment in which they were participating involved an analysis of handwriting, and they were asked to compose an American haiku poem that would be used as a handwriting sample with "original content." Subjects in the evaluation condition were told that the experimenter wished to examine the relation between handwriting features and poem content and that both would be evaluated by expert judges. In addition, these subjects believed that they would receive a copy of the judges' evaluations of their poems. Participants in the nonevaluation conditions were told that the experimenter was only interested in their handwriting, and evaluation was not mentioned. As a cross variable, subjects worked either alone or in a room with three others. In addition, each participant completed a postexperimental questionnaire to assess intrinsic interest.

Poem creativity was again assessed via the consensual assessment technique. The interrater reliability for 10 poet-judges was .87. Once again there emerged a significant main effect of evaluation expectation on the creativity ratings. Nonevaluation subjects produced poems that were judged to be significantly more creative than those written by evaluation subjects. There was no main effect of the audience variable and no significant interaction. On the postexperimental questionnaire, nonevaluation subjects reported greater satisfaction with their poems than did evaluation subjects. In addition, evaluation subjects reported higher levels of concentration on the "rules" of American haiku, and they were more likely to report that the haiku task was more like work than like leisure. Again, these results point to the importance of attention variables (attention focused on the task itself rather than on task constraints) for creative performance.

Finally, in a third investigation, Hennessey (1989) set out to explore the possible differential effects of expected evaluation delivered by a teacher compared to a nonhuman (computer) source. Participants in this investigation were 29 elementary school students ranging in age from 7 to 13 years who had been specifically selected because they were relatively inexperienced with computers. After participating in a brief session which allowed them to become acquainted with the workings of an Apple computer, children were randomly assigned to one of three experimental conditions: evaluation-computer, evaluation-experimenter or nonevaluation-control.

All subjects met individually with the experimenter and were asked to produce a simple geometric design. This task required only that the children choose between 16 clearly marked keys corresponding to line color choices and the points of a grid appearing on the computer screen. It was explained to the children in the evaluation-experimenter condition that after they had finished their design, the experimenter would fill out a report card according to how well she felt they had completed the computer activity. A sample report card bearing a fictitious child's name and a grade of *Very Good* and the experimenter's and classroom teacher's signatures were then shown.

For a subject assigned to the evaluation-computer condition, the experimenter explained that after the design task had been completed, the computer would figure out how well the child had done and register a grade for the activity. A sample report card in the same format as the written version employed in the experimenter-evaluation condition was then displayed on the computer screen. For a subject assigned to the nonevaluation-control condition, no mention was made of a report card or evaluation contingency.

The creativity of the computer products produced was rated by seven judges and reliability was high (.87). Design creativity scores revealed that children assigned to the evaluation conditions produced products that were judged lower in creativity than those produced by children who did not expect an evaluation. However, a one-way ANOVA of these creativity ratings failed to reveal a main effect for the evaluation manipulation. When only the 16 older subjects (ages 10-13) were considered separately, the deleterious effects of evaluation was particularly pronounced. An ANOVA comparing the three design groups showed a significant main effect for evaluation (p = .05). A planned comparison between the evaluation-computer and the evaluation-experimenter groups was not statistically significant. In other words, evaluation expected from a computer source was as detrimental as was expected evaluation coming from an experimenter or teacher figure (Figure 1).

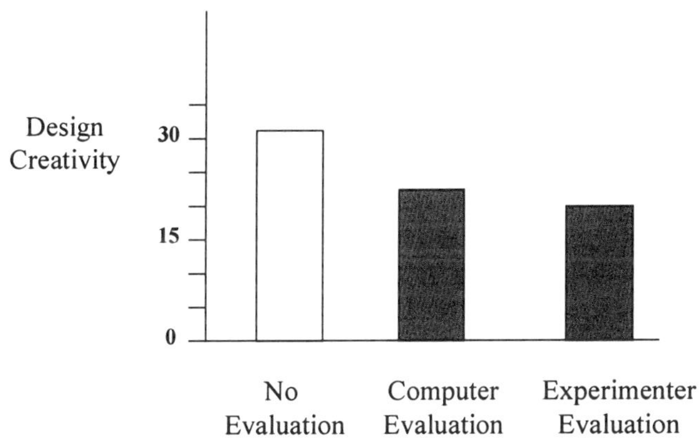

Figure 1. Design creativity (Hennessey, 1989).
Note: Highest possible score is 49, lowest possible score is 0.

Actual Evaluation

The work of a number of theorists interested in the effect of expected reward on intrinsic motivation can also be readily applied to situations of evaluation. Edward Deci (1975) demonstrated that when the offer of an extrinsic reward conveys external control over a person's work, intrinsic motivation will be undermined. However, to the extent that the receipt of a reward conveys competence, intrinsic motivation can be expected to be enhanced. Research conducted by Karniol and Ross (1977) revealed that while performance-contingent rewards did not enhance intrinsic motivation above levels shown by nonrewarded controls, persons receiving informative rewards were able to maintain baseline levels of intrinsic task motivation. Subjects in a task-contingent reward condition (where rewards were both nonevaluative and noninformative) showed the expected motivational decrements. Further, in several experiments, Deci and colleagues (Deci, 1971, 1972a; Deci, Cascio, & Krusell, 1973) have demonstrated that male subjects had higher levels of intrinsic motivation after receiving positive information about their performance than after receiving no feedback. (As expected, negative feedback was found to decrease intrinsic motivation.)

Importantly, however, Deci (1972b) also found that performance-contingent rewards which convey external control through the use of evaluation can often undermine intrinsic motivation. Harackiewicz (1979) reported data that supports this finding. Her results showed that while both task-contingent and performance-contingent rewards both undermine task motivation, performance-contingent rewards can be particularly detrimental. In addition, subjects receiving performance-contingent rewards in the Harackiewicz study recalled fewer aspects of the task that were not obviously relevant to solving the problem; and positive feedback (whether expected or unexpected) was found to enhance intrinsic motivation, independent of the effect of reward.

In sum, the effects of evaluation on intrinsic motivation appear to be especially complex. Like rewards, evaluations can be perceived as either controlling or competence affirming. When evaluation conveys external control over task engagement, intrinsic motivation can be expected to decrease. Evaluation conveying positive competence information, however, can increase intrinsic motivation; and according to the Intrinsic Motivation Principle of Creativity, creativity of performance should show a similar pattern. Importantly, these data underscore a fundamental difference between expected and actual evaluation. As reported earlier in this chapter (Amabile, 1979, 1982a; Amabile, Goldfarb, & Brackfield, 1990), expected evaluation, evaluation which has not yet been delivered, can only convey external control over performance and must be predicted to undermine intrinsic interest and creativity. On the other hand, actual evaluation of performance can affect subsequent task motivation and creativity either negatively or positively, depending upon the nature of the information given.

In one particularly elegant experiment, Amabile and colleagues (Berglas et al., 1979) investigated the effects of actual prior evaluation on children's subsequent creativity of performance. Ninety-seven second through sixth graders participated in individual sessions in a 2 x 2 factorial design with a separate control group. Half the students were told that their doing "well" on a spin-art activity would help to determine the potential job status of the experimenter (who was posing as a student teacher). For others, nothing was made contingent on their performance.

All children made art works. Children assigned to the experimental group were given positive evaluations after producing their spin-art product, with half receiving *task-based* information (which physical aspects of their product were good and why) and half receiving *person-based* feedback (information that they, themselves, appeared to be good artists). They then made a second art work -- a collage. Control-group subjects simply produced the two art works, without evaluation or information about possible external contingencies of their performance.

Six judges employing the standard CAT rated the collage products. Reliability was .77 for creativity and .72 for technical goodness. An examination of mean creativity scores indicated that feedback based on specific information about task performance did, in fact, lead to somewhat higher levels of creativity. In addition, there was some tendency for children who believed that the experimenter's professional future was dependent on their performance to produce less creative collages. However, neither of these main effects was significant, nor was there a significant interaction.

A planned contrast between the control and the experimental condition revealed a clear superiority of the collages produced by control subjects over all four experimental groups. There were no significant between-group differences on the technical goodness ratings of the collages. Thus, while some types of positive evaluation may at times be found to enhance motivation and qualitative aspects performance, the overall negative effects of prior evaluation appear to be much more influential. While all of the experimental group children had received positive competence information about their earlier performance, it is likely that they came to expect that their performance on the second, collage-making, activity would also be evaluated by the experimenter. It appears that this controlling aspect was more salient than the particular task-based or performance-based feedback they had received.

In fact, Amabile (1996) hypothesizes that information on artistic performance may be especially likely to be perceived as external control. Activities such as drawing or collage-making are usually intrinsically interesting in their own right, and feedback is likely to be seen as superfluous. As Harackiewicz (1979) suggests, however, activities such as games are intrinsically motivating partly due to the feelings of competence they produce, and feedback about one's performance at these nonartistic type tasks is far more likely to be intrinsically motivating.

Competitive Evaluation

In each of the investigations reviewed thus far, study participants worked individually and were led to expect that the evaluation of their work would not be affected by the performance of other individuals. However, in the real world, the evaluation of an individual's performance is often based, at least in part, on comparisons with the work of others. Situations of expected evaluation often contain elements of competition, and sometimes expected reward as well.

In a 1982 study, Amabile set out to investigate the impact of a competitive evaluation situation on the creativity of girls, ages 7-11. These elementary-school aged study participants were randomly selected to attend either a Saturday or a Sunday "Art Party" held in the common room of their apartment complex. Girls attending the Saturday (noncompetition-control) session were greeted at the entrance by a table of desirable toys and gifts which they were told would be raffled off at the end of the party. They then spent the afternoon engaged in a variety of fun activities, including a collage-making task that they completed without any expectation of evaluation. Girls attending the Sunday (competition) session had an identical experience, with one important exception. They played the same games and were given the same materials with which to make their art works, but when they arrived at the party and saw the table of prizes, they were told that these items would be awarded to those children who made the "best" collages.

Following the procedures outlined in the Consensual Assessment Technique, artist-judges assessed the collage designs on creativity and a variety of other product dimensions. Interrater reliability on the creativity measure was .77, and analyses revealed that those collages made by girls in the noncompetition condition were significantly more creative than those made by girls in the competition condition.

In a second study, adults worked on a set of water-jar problems (Amabile, 1987). These problems at first appear to be rather complicated, but they are all solved by the same equation -- except for the final problem (see Luchins, 1942). The final problem can be solved either with the familiar equation or by employing a second equation that is considerably simpler. Although participants in this investigation worked alone, they attempted these problems in a large group setting. Half were given competitive instructions promising a prize to the individual who "did the best job." The other half received instructions that encouraged them to have fun with the problems. Results revealed that participants in the competition condition were less likely to discover the novel solution for the final problem, and they were more likely to make errors overall. In addition, those subjects exposed to this competitive atmosphere were less likely to try to solve some riddles that were included at the end of the session "to amuse themselves before time is called."

PROPOSED MECHANISMS

Researchers have found it all too easy to undermine task motivation and creativity of performance with the promise or delivery of an evaluation. Demonstrating how to kill motivation and creativity has been the straightforward part. What has not been as easy is understanding why evaluation can have such a negative impact. What are the internal mechanisms that bring about the undermining effects of evaluation and under what circumstances can they be expected to surface?

In recent years, researchers have come to learn that most of us are not all that in touch with our own motivations. We do not always know why it is that we do the things we do. Almost as if we were outside observers of even our own actions, we seem to use essentially the same rubrics for explaining our own behaviors as we do for explaining why others behave in the ways that they do. In situations where both a plausible internal and external (intrinsic and extrinsic) cause of behavior are present, we tend to *discount* the internal cause in favor of the external cause. A young girl in Amabile's (1979) "Art Party" study thinks to herself, "I must be making this collage not because it's fun and I want to but because this woman has told me that the adults are going to decide which children have made the best designs and those girls will win a prize." And a university student participating in an experiment reasons, "I am putting my best effort into this poem not because I was intrigued by the assignment but because I know that expert judges, poets, are going to evaluate my work." In these examples, when multiple explanations for their behavior are available, the undergraduate and the elementary school student discount their own intrinsic interest in favor of a purely external explanation for their task engagement.

In fact, some social psychologists have come to refer to this process as the "discounting principle" (e.g., Kelley, 1973). Other theorists turn to the "overjustification" hypothesis, a formulation derived from the attribution theories of Bem (1972), Kelley (1967, 1973), and deCharms (1968). According to this model, when a behavior is overjustified (when there exists both a possible internal and external cause for one's own or another's behavior), each of us will tend to overlook the internal cause (the presence of intrinsic task motivation) in favor of the external cause (an evaluation was at stake). In effect, we discount the excess justification for explaining why we did something.

Whatever the particulars of the theoretical explanation evoked, the fact remains that in the face of expected evaluation and often after the receipt of an actual evaluation, intrinsic motivation is bound to suffer. And without high levels of intrinsic motivation, creative performance is highly unlikely. Why is intrinsic motivation so necessary to creative performance?

Researchers in the area of cognitive psychology offer empirical evidence and models that have proven useful in understanding how the type of motivation brought to a task can influence performance on that task. Simon (1967) has proposed that the most important function of task motivation is the control of attention. He postulates that task motivation determines which of many goal hierarchies will be activated and goes on to suggest that the more intense the motivation to achieve a goal, the less attention will be paid to environmental aspects that are seemingly irrelevant to achieving that goal. This formulation can be used to explain the finding that incidental or latent learning is impaired when an extrinsic constraint, like evaluation, is placed upon task completion (e.g., Kimble, 1961; Spence, 1956). More specifically, it can also help to explain the negative effects of expected evaluation on creativity.

Success at the types of activities targeted in the research reported earlier (e.g., Amabile, 1979; Amabile, Goldfarb, & Brackfield, 1990) very much depends on sustained, focused attention. Amabile (1998) offers a maze metaphor that is helpful in illustrating this point. She asks that we think of an open-ended "creativity-type" task as a maze. There is one starting point, one entrance, into this maze but there are a variety of exit points and many different paths to those exits. Most importantly, some of those exits, or solutions, are more "elegant" or creative than others. In the face of an expected performance evaluation, the goal is to get in and out of the maze as quickly and efficiently as possible. The "safest," most straightforward route is chosen, and experimentation with unexplored pathways is viewed as too dangerous. All behavior is narrowly directed toward attaining a passing evaluation. In order for a creative idea to be generated, however, it is often necessary to temporarily "step away" from the evaluation, to become immersed in the maze itself, to test alternative pathways, and to direct attention toward more seemingly incidental aspects of the task and the environment. The more focused an individual is about an impending evaluation, the less likely it is that risks will be taken and that these alternative paths to solution will be explored.

When working under the expectation of evaluation, people may indeed pay less attention to a task or less attention to aspects of their environment that might prove useful in generating a response to that task. However, this shift in focus need not always occur simply because they are distracted by the evaluative feedback they are to receive or by their worries about what they have to do to attain a positive evaluation. Under evaluation conditions, people may simply *feel* less intrinsically involved. They may feel less positively toward the task and less inclined to devote their energy and attention to it.

There is good reason to believe, in fact, that affective processes can and do play an important role in the mediation of the impact of evaluation on interest and creativity. Earlier in this chapter, explanations of cognitive mechanisms such as discounting and overjustification were offered. While these models have proven useful for understanding the negative effects of expected evaluation in adults, they fail to adequately explain the undermining effects of actual evaluation that has already been delivered as well as the fact that young children working under an evaluation expectation have also been observed to suffer decreases in intrinsic motivation and creativity.

Simply stated, children under the age of 7 or 8 years have consistently been shown to lack the cognitive capabilities necessary for weighing multiple sufficient causes and employing discounting (e.g., Shultz, Butkowsky, Pearce, & Shanfield, 1975; Smith, 1975). How is it that, when working under the expectation of evaluation, young children also frequently demonstrate decreases in intrinsic motivation and creativity of performance yet they seem cognitively incapable of engaging in the thought processes that underlie the overjustification paradigm?

One viable alternative to the discounting explanation is that the reduction of intrinsic interest in young children (and perhaps all of us) is driven primarily by the learned expectation that evaluations are usually paired with activities that need to be done -- activities that are often not fun and sometimes even aversive. The undermining of intrinsic interest may result as much from emotion or affect as it does from thoughts or cognitive analysis. Children may learn to react negatively to a task as "work" when their behavior is controlled by socially imposed factors (such as evaluations), and they may react positively to a task as "play" when there are no constraints imposed. Negative affect resulting from socially learned stereotypes or scripts of work (see Lepper, Sagotsky, DaFoe, & Greene, 1982; Morgan, 1981; Ransen, 1980) may be what leads to decrements in intrinsic interest (see Hennessey, 1999).

REFINING THE MODEL

Must intrinsic motivation and creativity always suffer when evaluations are expected or delivered? Not necessarily. When investigations into what has come to be known as the "social psychology of creativity" were begun some 25 years ago, it was thought that the determinants of motivational orientation were pretty much the same for everyone. Intrinsic and extrinsic motivation were believed to combine in a sort of hydraulic fashion. In other words, high levels of extrinsic motivation were thought to preclude high levels of intrinsic motivation -- as evaluations were imposed, intrinsic motivation (and creativity) would necessarily be decreased.

Now, a good many years and countless investigations later, most researchers taking a social-psychological approach to the study of creativity have come to appreciate the many complexities of both motivational orientation and the evaluation process. They have come to supplement their original hydraulic conceptualization with an additive model that recognizes that under certain specific conditions, both the delivery of a competence-affirming evaluation and the expectation of an impending evaluation can sometimes increase levels of extrinsic motivation without having any negative impact on intrinsic motivation or performance. In fact, some types of extrinsic motivation can actually enhance creativity of performance.

Recent Research: Individual Differences and Interaction Effects

This complexity of evaluation effects is demonstrated in several recent publications (e.g., Jussim, Soffin, Brown, Ley, & Kohlhepp, 1992; Harackiewicz, Abrahams, & Wageman, 1991). Creativity research conducted over the past decade has yielded some replications of the negative effect of expected evaluation on creativity, some failures to replicate, some partial replications, and occasionally some evidence of positive effects of evaluation under certain specific conditions.

Cheek and Stahl (1986) preassessed subjects' shyness and then experimentally manipulated evaluation expectation. While they found no main effect of evaluation on poem-writing creativity, they did uncover an intriguing interaction. When faced with the knowledge that they would receive evaluative feedback, shy subjects performed significantly less creatively than did those who were not shy. Thus, the effects of evaluation expectation may be mediated, at least in part, by certain personality characteristics.

In two studies in which children were asked to make collages in competitive or noncompetitive settings, the detrimental effects of competitive evaluation were found to apply to girls but not to boys (Conti, Collins, & Picariello, 1995). In fact, in both of these investigations, boys appeared to demonstrate higher levels of artistic creativity under competitive conditions.

In another investigation (Conti, Amabile, & Pollak, 1995), half of the participants engaged in a creative preactivity related to the target experimental task and half engaged in a noncreative preactivity. All participants then completed an open-ended creativity task either with or without the expectation of evaluation. Results revealed that the impact of this evaluation expectation was dependent on participants' preactivity condition. Only those nonevaluation persons who had participated in the creative preactivity condition produced products that were judged more creative than those made by participants expecting an evaluation. All participants who had been exposed to the noncreative preactivity exhibited relatively low creativity on the target task, even those who performed without the expectation of evaluation.

When Conti and Amabile (1995) examined the creativity of computer science students, they found that participants' skill levels mediated the impact of evaluation. Once again, no main effect of evaluation expectation was found. Instead, low-skill students wrote more creative programs when expecting an evaluation, and high-skill students wrote better programs in the no evaluation condition. Similar effects are also reported by Pollak (1992) in a study where advanced art students were asked to produce a drawing; and Hill, Amabile, Coon, and Whitney (1994) also reported a skill level-evaluation interaction pattern. In this investigation, introductory psychology students composed a brief passage after undergoing a separate assessment of their prose writing skills. Half the participants expected that their work would be subject to immediate public evaluation, while the other half completed the writing activity without any evaluation expectation. No main effect of evaluation expectation was found. In fact, low-skill participants were *more* creative under evaluation conditions. High-skill participants were more creative under nonevaluative conditions.

Nonexperimental Research Evidence

Nonexperimental (field) research carried out over the past several years has also uncovered some evidence that evaluation need not always undermine intrinsic interest and creativity. As would be predicted from the Intrinsic Motivation Principle of Creativity, interview studies reveal that, in the workplace, the prospect of impending, critical evaluation often co-occurs with low levels of creativity (Amabile & S. Gryskiewicz, 1987). However, this same research shows that when employees were asked to describe the circumstances surrounding high-creativity events, it was found that informative evaluation that conveyed positive recognition of creative work often contributed to highly creative workplace performance. Similarly, in studies employing questionnaire measures to assess the presence or absence of specific social factors in the work environment (e.g., Amabile, Conti, Coon, & Lazenby, 1996; Amabile & N. Gryskiewicz, 1989), constructive feedback has also been associated with high levels of creativity.

These and other studies like them reveal that, just as is the case in the laboratory, in real-world settings evaluation need not always undermine intrinsic interest and creative performance. Based on these data, it is reasonable to expect that creativity will be undermined by evaluation that conveys incompetence or threatens perceptions of self-determination. As Amabile (1998) explains:

> A culture of evaluation leads people to focus on the external rewards and punishments associated with their output, thus increasing the presence of extrinsic motivation and its potentially negative effects on intrinsic motivation... such a culture creates a climate of fear, which again undermines intrinsic motivation (1998, p. 83).

But evaluations (whether positive *or negative*) that are work-focused and that provide useful information about performance improvement or recognition of competence and hard work can, under certain circumstances, serve to *enhance* creativity.

Motivational Synergy

Amabile's (1993) discussion of "motivational synergy" is helpful in reconciling these more recent laboratory and field study results with the findings reported in the earlier evaluation literature. This model proposes that extrinsic constraints such as evaluations can sometimes serve as "synergistic extrinsic motivators." In other words, rather than detract from initial interest, they can, under certain specific circumstances, combine in an *additive* fashion with intrinsic motivation and actually enhance task enjoyment and involvement. A revision of the Intrinsic Motivation Principle of Creativity (Amabile, 1996) explains the process this way:

> Intrinsic motivation is conducive to creativity; controlling extrinsic motivation is detrimental to creativity, but informational or enabling extrinsic motivation can be conducive, particularly if initial levels of intrinsic motivation are high (p. 119).

The important element here seems to be the preservation of a sense of self-determination (Deci & Ryan, 1985b). Any extrinsic factors that support a sense of competence without undermining self-determination should positively contribute to intrinsic motivation. Thus, evaluations that are perceived as useful and informative rather than as instruments of coercion can serve to increase involvement in the task at hand and should not be expected to have detrimental effects. In keeping with Bem's (1972) suggestion that individuals' internal attitudes and states will be most subject to external influences when their initial internal states are vague or ambiguous, this synergistic effect has been found to occur only under circumstances in which initial task intrinsic motivation is especially strong and salient. In what can be seen as an "extrinsics in service of intrinsics cycle" (Amabile, 1993, p. 194), the receipt of an evaluation can combine positively with intrinsic motivation and enable study participants or research and development scientists in the workplace to do exciting work.

CONCLUSIONS AND FUTURE DIRECTIONS

Research evidence gathered over the past two decades has generally supported the contention that intrinsic motivation is conducive to creativity. We now understand, however, that the impact of extrinsic motivation on performance is much more complex than we once believed. Whatever an individual's particular talents, domain skills, and creative thinking abilities, the conditions under which she works can significantly impact her motivational orientation and the level of creativity produced. Investigators interested in specifying the link between motivation and creativity initially focused on experimental settings. They directly manipulated subjects' evaluation expectations or delivered actual evaluations and looked for accompanying changes in intrinsic motivation and the creativity of the ideas and products produced. More recent investigations have also included nonexperimental methods such as surveys, interviews, and an examination of archival sources. This broadening of focus convinced researchers that the original Intrinsic Motivation Principle of Creativity and related models had to be revised to reflect a more comprehensive "systems" approach. The impact of evaluation -- either expected or actually delivered -- is far too complex to be summarized in terms of absolutes. Individual difference variables such as shyness and skill level must also be considered.

In addition, many theorists and researchers have come to believe that it is no longer reasonable to conceptualize motivation as a transitory and very much situation-specific state. They argue instead for a consideration of both environmentally-induced states and enduring motivational orientations or "traits." Deci and Ryan (1985a), for example, use the concept of causality orientations, or characteristic ways that each of us develop for understanding and orienting to inputs. More specifically, they hypothesize that individuals vary in the degree to which they exhibit "autonomy," "control" and "impersonal" orientations, and they argue that these individual differences have important implications for how an impending evaluation or an actual evaluation that has already been delivered will be viewed.

Amabile, Hill, Hennessey, and Tighe (1994) have also advocated for the examination of stable traitlike motivational orientations. They have developed and administered a personality inventory, The Work Preference Inventory (WPI), to hundreds of college students and working adults; and a number of important differences between respondents have been revealed. While there has consistently emerged a positive relation between intrinsic motivation and creativity, it is clear that for some people certain extrinsic constraints in the workplace, including evaluation, can serve as positive motivators that provide information value or facilitate task engagement. Not all of us define the optimal work environment in the same way.

Clearly, a great deal of work remains to be done if researchers are to understand the complex effects of evaluation and expected evaluation on intrinsic motivation and creativity. The role of attentional mechanisms and the hypothesis that a concern with an impending evaluation leads one to focus on more obvious, or algorithmic, task aspects must be explored. In addition, future research must concentrate on the role of skill and test the possibility that evaluation is more likely to be perceived as informational by persons at low levels of skill and as controlling by individuals at higher levels of skill. Gender differences in response to situations of competition must be examined, and investigators must set out to discover the critical components of evaluative messages that render them either supportive of or detrimental to intrinsic motivation and creativity. Finally, investigations will have to be carried out to determine which individual traits and motivations might immunize individuals against the potential negative effects of evaluation on creativity. Only with these understandings can we hope to structure classroom and workplace environments that are truly conducive to creative performance.

REFERENCES

Amabile, T. M. (1979). Effects of external evaluation on artistic creativity. *Journal of Personality and Social Psychology, 37*, 221-233.

Amabile, T. M. (1982a). Children's artistic creativity: Detrimental effects of competition in a field setting. *Personality and Social Psychology Bulletin, 8*, 573-578.

Amabile, T. M. (1982b). Social psychology of creativity: A consensual assessment technique. *Journal of Personality and Social Psychology, 43*, 997-1013.

Amabile, T. M. (1983). *The social psychology of creativity.* New York: Springer-Verlag.

Amabile, T. M. (1987). The motivation to be creative. In S. Isaksen (Ed.), *Frontiers in creativity research: Beyond the basics.* Buffalo, NY: Bearly Limited.

Amabile, T. M. (1993). Motivational synergy: Toward new conceptualizations of intrinsic and extrinsic motivation in the workplace. *Human Resource Management Review, 3*, 185-201.

Amabile, T. M. (1996). *Creativity in context.* Boulder, CO: Westview.

Amabile, T. M. (September-October 1998). How to kill creativity. *Harvard Business Review*, 76-87.

Amabile, T. M., Conti, R., Coon, H. M., Lazenby, J., & Herron, M. (1996). Assessing the work environment for creativity. *Academy of Management Journal, 39*, 1154-1184.

Amabile, T. M., Goldberg, N., & Capotosto, D. (1982). *Effects of Reward and Choice on Adults' Artistic Creativity.* Unpublished manuscript, Brandeis University.

Amabile, T. M., Goldfarb, P., & Brackfield, S. C. (1990). Social influences on creativity: Evaluation, coaction, and surveillance. *Creativity Research Journal, 3*, 6-21.

Amabile, T. M., & Gryskiewicz, N. (1989). The creative environment scales: The work environment inventory. *Creativity Research Journal, 2*, 231-254.

Amabile, T. M., & Gryskiewicz, S. (1987). *Creativity in the R&D laboratory.* Technical report no. 30. Greensboro, N.C.: Center for Creative Leadership.

Amabile, T. M., Hill, K., Hennessey, B. A., & Tighe, E. (1994). The Work Preference Inventory: Assessing intrinsic and extrinsic motivational orientations. *Journal of Personality and Social Psychology, 66*, 950-967.

Amabile, T. M., Phillips, E. D., Collins, M. A. (1993). *Creativity by Contract: Social Influences on the Creativity of Professional Artists.* Unpublished manuscript, Brandeis University.

Bem, D. (1972). Self-perception theory. In L. Berkowitz (Ed.), *Advances in experimental social psychology* (Vol. 6). New York: Academic Press.

Berglas, S., Amabile, T. M., & Handel, M. (1981). *Effects of Evaluation on Children's Artistic Creativity.* Unpublished manuscript, Brandeis University.

Berlyne, D. E. (1960). *Conflict, arousal, and curiosity.* New York: McGraw-Hill.

Cheek, J. M., & and Stahl, S. (1986). Shyness and verbal creativity. *Journal of Research in Personality, 20*, 51-61.

Conti, R., Amabile, T. M., & Pollak, S. (1995). The positive impact of creative activity: Effects of creative task engagement and motivational focus on college students' learning. *Personality and Social Psychology Bulletin, 21*, 1107-1116.

Conti, R., & Amabile, T. M. (1995). *Problem solving among computer science students: The effects of skill, evaluation expectation and personality on solution quality.* Paper presented at the annual meeting of the Eastern Psychological Association, Boston, MA.

Conti, R., Collins, M. A., & Picariello, M. (1995). *Differential effects of competition on the artistic creativity of girls and boys.* Unpublished manuscript, Brandeis University.

deCharms, R. (1968). *Personal causation.* New York: Academic Press.

Deci, E. L. (1971). Effects of externally mediated rewards on intrinsic motivation. *Journal of Personality and Social Psychology, 18*, 105-115.

Deci, E. L. (1972a). Intrinsic motivation, extrinsic reinforcement, and inequity. *Journal of Personality and Social Psychology, 22*, 113-120.

Deci, E. L. (1972b). The effects of contingent and noncontingent rewards and controls on intrinsic motivation. *Organizational Behavior and Human Performance, 8*, 217-229.

Deci, E. L. (1975). *Intrinsic motivation.* New York: Plenum.

Deci, E. L., Cascio, W. F., & Krusell, J. (1973). *Sex differences, positive feedback, in intrinsic motivation.* Paper presented at the meeting of the Eastern Psychological Association.

Deci, E. L., & Ryan, R. M. (1985a). The general causality orientations scale: Self-determination in personality. *Journal of Personality and Social Psychology, 19*, 109-134.

Deci, E. L., & Ryan, R. M. (1985b). *Intrinsic motivation and self-determination in human behavior.* New York: Plenum.

Garbarino, J. (1975). The impact of anticipated reward upon cross-age tutoring. *Journal of Personality and Social Psychology, 32*, 421-428.

Garfield, S. J., Cohen, H. A., & Roth, R. M. (1969). Creativity and mental health. *Journal of Educational Research, 63*, 147-149.

Goetz, E. M. (1981). The effects of minimal praise on the creative blockbuilding of three year olds. *Child Study Journal, 11*, 55-67.

Greene, D., & Lepper, M. (1974). Effects of extrinsic rewards on children's subsequent interest. *Child Development, 45*, 1141-1145.

Harackiewicz, J. M. (1979). The effects of reward contingency and performance feedback on intrinsic motivation. *Journal of Personality and Social Psychology, 37*, 1352-1363.

Harackiewicz, J. M., Abrahams, S., & Wageman, R. (1991). Performance evaluation and intrinsic motivation: The effects of evaluative focus, rewards and achievement orientation. *Journal of Personality and Social Psychology, 63*, 1015-1029.

Harter, S. (1978). Effectance motivation reconsidered: Toward a developmental model. *Human Development, 21*, 34-64.

Hebb, D. O. (1955). Drives and the CNS. *Psychological Review, 62*, 243-254.

Hennessey, B. A. (1999). Intrinsic motivation, affect and creativity. In S. Russ (Ed.), *Affect, creative experience and psychological adjustment* (pp. 77-90). Philadelphia: Taylor & Francis.

Hennessey, B. A. (1989). The effect of extrinsic constraint on children's creativity while using a computer. *Creativity Research Journal, 2*, 151-168.

Hennessey, B. A., & Amabile, T. M. (1999). Consensual assessment. In M. Runco & S. Pritzker (Eds.), *Encyclopedia of creativity.* New York: Academic Press.

Hill, K., Amabile, T. M., Coon, H. M., & Whitney, D. (1994). *Testing the componential model of creativity.* Unpublished manuscript, Brandeis University.

Hughes, T., & McCullough, F. (Eds.) (1982). *The journals of Sylvia Plath.* New York: Dial.

Jussim, L. S., Soffin, S., Brown, R., Ley, J., & Kohlhepp, K. (1992). Understanding reactions to feedback by integrating ideas from symbolic interactionism and cognitive evaluation theory. *Journal of Personality and Social Psychology, 62*, 402-421.

Karniol, R., & Ross, M. (1977). The effects of performance relevant and performance irrelevant rewards on children's intrinsic motivation. *Child Development, 48*, 482-487.

Kelley, H. (1967). Attribution theory in social psychology. In D. Levine (Ed.), *Nebraska symposium on motivation*, Vol. 15. Lincoln: University of Nebraska.

Kelley, H. (1973). The processes of causal attribution. *American Psychologist, 28*, 107-128.

Kernoodle-Loveland, K., & Olley, J. (1979). The effect of external reward on interest and quality of task performance in children of high and low intrinsic motivation. *Child Development, 50*, 1207-1210.

Kimble, G. (1961). *Hilgard and Marquis' conditioning and learning* (2nd ed.). New York: Appleton-Century-Crofts.

Kruglanski, A. W., Friedman, I., & Zeevi, G. (1971). The effects of extrinsic incentive on some qualitative aspects of task performance. *Journal of Personality, 39*, 606-617.

Lepper, M., Greene, D., & Nisbett, R. (1973). Undermining children's intrinsic interest with extrinsic rewards: A test of the "overjustification" hypothesis. *Journal of Personality and Social Psychology, 28*, 129-137.

Lepper, M., Sagotsky, G., Dafoe, J. L., & Greene, D. (1982). Consequences of superfluous social constraints: Effects on young children's social inferences and subsequent intrinsic motivation. *Journal of Personality and Social Psychology, 42*, 51-65.

Luchins, A. (1942). Mechanization in problem solving: The effect of Einstellung. *Psychological Monographs, 54* (6, Wiole No. 248).

McGraw, K. (1978). The detrimental effects of reward on performance: A literature review and a prediction model. In M. Lepper & D. Greene (Eds.), *The hidden costs of reward.* Hillsdale, NJ: Lawrence Erlbaum Associates.

McGraw, K., & McCullers, J. (1979). Evidence of a detrimental effect of extrinsic incentives on breaking a mental set. *Journal of Experimental Social Psychology, 15*, 285-294.

Morgan, M. (1981). The overjustification effect: A developmental test of self-perception interpretations. *Journal of Personality and Social Psychology, 40*, 809-821.

Pittman, T. S., Emery, J., & Boggiano, A. K., (1982). Intrinsic and extrinsic motivational orientations: Reward-induced changes in preference for complexity. *Journal of Personality and Social Psychology, 42*, 789-797.

Pollak, S. (1992). *The effects of motivational orientation and constraint on the creativity of the artist.* Unpublished manuscript, Brandeis University.

Poole, M. E., Williams, A. J., & Lett, W. R. (1977). Inner-centeredness of highly creative adolescents. *Psychological Reports, 41*, 365-366.

Raina, M. K. (1968). A study into the effect of competition on creativity. *Gifted Child Quarterly, 12*, 217-220.

Ransen, D. (1980). The mediation of reward-induced motivation decrements in early and middle childhood: A template matching approach. *Journal of Personality and Social Psychology, 35*, 49-55.

Shapira, Z. (1976). Expectancy determinants of intrinsically motivated behavior. *Journal of Personality and Social Psychology, 39*, 1235-1244.

Shultz, T., Butkowsky, I., Pearce, J., & Shanfield, H. (1975). The development of schemes for the attribution of multiple psychological causes. *Developmental Psychology, 11*, 502-510.

Simon, H. (1967). Motivational and emotional controls of cognition. *Psychological Review, 74*, 29-39.

Smith, M. C. (1975). Children's use of the multiple sufficient cause schema in social perception. *Journal of Personality and Social Psychology, 32*, 737-747.

Spence, K. (1956). *Behavior theory and conditioning.* New Haven: Yale University Press.

Torrance, E. P. (1964). *Role of evaluation in creative thinking.* Cooperative Research Project No. 725, University of Minnesota.

Torrance, E. P. (1966). *The Torrance Tests of Creative Thinking: Norms-technical manual.* Lexington, MA: Personal Press.

Torrance, E. P. (1965). *Rewarding creative behavior: Experiments in classroom creativity.* Englewood Cliffs, N.J.: Prentice Hall.

Wallach, M. A. (1970). *Creativity.* In P.H. Mussen (Ed.), *Carmichael's manual of child psychology* (Vol. 1). New York: Wiley.

White, K., & Owen, D. (1970). Locus of evaluation for classroom work and the development of creative potential. *Psychology in the Schools, 7*, 292-295.

White, R. W. (1959). Motivation reconsidered: The concept of competence. *Psychological Review, 66*, 297-333.

Chapter 4

EVALUATION AND INTRINSIC MOTIVATION: THE DOUBLE-EDGED SWORD

John M. Tauer
University of St. Thomas

Judith M. Harackiewicz
University of Wisconsin-Madison

Each summer, one of us runs a basketball camp for youths, and is always astounded at the spirit of young athletes. They possess endless optimism, and the majority of the campers play basketball simply for the love of the game. Within the camp, different structured activities stress a variety of fundamentals. For example, some drills focus on skill improvement and developing competence at specific skills (e.g., dribbling, passing, shooting). Other drills are more competitive in nature (e.g., shooting contests), and focus on outperforming others. Both types of activities are focused on developing competence, and both involve some degree of evaluation in this instructional context. However, the competitive activities are particularly evaluative, and provide an opportunity for campers to demonstrate their competence compared to others. Campers know that a coach may be evaluating their performance, and typically the kids anticipate receiving performance feedback as a result of this evaluation. The coaches frequently comment on the markedly different reactions that campers have to these evaluative activities. Some kids thrive in competition, but do not appear to enjoy themselves as much in the absence of it, and even express boredom with skill-development activities. Other kids tend to withdraw when they are being evaluated, and seem to really enjoy the activities that are not as competitive.

Competition is prevalent in our society, and our success is frequently based on how we perform compared to others. As a result, our performance in a wide range of activities is under constant evaluation, and people seem to have markedly different reactions to this evaluation. Whether it is a student being graded on a curve, an athlete in competition, or an employee being evaluated by a supervisor, we often expect our performance to be evaluated. Moreover, even our favorite leisure activities can take on a competitive flavor. Whether it is a family game of

Scrabble or a friendly game of chess, rare is the game in which we are not trying to outdo one another. Whenever we compete, our performance is compared with others, and this comparison process is inherently evaluative. What are the effects of this type of interpersonal evaluation? Other chapters in this book discuss the effects of evaluation on performance, and clearly these are crucial lines of research. However, we believe an equally important outcome is the development of intrinsic motivation in an activity. This unique type of motivation involves the desire to take part in an activity for its own sake (Deci & Ryan, 1985), and should help people develop long-lasting interest in an activity. In turn, developing intrinsic motivation may promote increased performance over an extended period of time.

Early research on intrinsic motivation found that external rewards undermined intrinsic motivation (Deci, 1971; Lepper, Greene, & Nisbett, 1973). Deci and Ryan (1985) went on to propose cognitive evaluation theory (CET), which stated that whenever an activity was perceived as externally controlled, intrinsic motivation should be negatively affected. Moreover, they argued that external performance evaluation was very controlling and should undermine interest in activities. However, they also argued that positive feedback could enhance intrinsic motivation to the extent that it increases perceived competence. If evaluation eventually results in positive performance information, then this feedback could help offset the negative effects of evaluation by increasing perceptions of competence.

One particularly common type of evaluation involves competition, but surprisingly little research has tested the effects of competition on intrinsic motivation. In the first study of face-to-face competition and intrinsic motivation, Deci, Betley, Kahle, Abrams, and Porac (1981) found that competition undermined intrinsic motivation. Participants who had competed against another participant were less likely to return to the activity during a free-choice period than those who had not competed. Deci et al. did not assess variables that may have mediated this relationship, but they speculated that the competition was perceived as controlling. In addition, they argued that participants' focus on winning, rather than on the activity itself, was responsible for this undermining of intrinsic motivation.

More recently, Reeve and Deci (1996) tested CET in a study of competition that included five experimental conditions. Participants were assigned to either a more or less controlling competition where they won, or to a less controlling competition where they lost, or to a no-feedback condition that was either competitive or noncompetitive. In the controlling competition, participants were instructed to focus all of their attention on winning, whereas in the less controlling competition participants were told simply to try to solve puzzles more quickly than their opponent. In support of CET, Reeve and Deci found that among participants who received positive feedback, the controlling competition reduced intrinsic motivation. In addition, they found that participants who won showed higher levels of intrinsic motivation than those who had lost, replicating previous research (McAuley & Tammen, 1989; Reeve, Olson, & Cole, 1985, 1987; Vallerand & Reid, 1984; Weinberg & Ragan, 1979). They found no differences between competition and noncompetition when participants were not provided feedback. In sum, they did not find evidence of consistently negative effects for competition. Rather, their results support CET, showing that specific aspects of competition can enhance (e.g., positive feedback) or decrease (e.g., a particularly controlling competition or negative feedback) intrinsic motivation. Taken together, these findings indicate that the effects of competition depend on specific aspects of the situation, including the evaluative context and the performance feedback provided.

Our research has examined the effects of different types of evaluative contingencies on intrinsic motivation. By an evaluative contingency, we mean a situation in which an individual anticipates evaluation from another person. Typically, these evaluative contingencies also entail the provision of performance feedback, but it is important to distinguish the *expectation of evaluation* from the *receipt of feedback* (Harackiewicz, 1989). At times, this feedback may be expected, and the comparison standard for the evaluation may be quite clear. For example, in competition, people know that their performance will be evaluated, they know what it will be compared against (i.e., their opponent's performance), and they know they will receive feedback as soon as the winner is announced. Other types of evaluative contingencies may establish contexts in which people expect evaluation, but don't have clear standards for evaluation or strong expectations for performance feedback. For example, a coach may announce a drill and suggest that everyone work on improving their dribbling skills. Players know that they are being evaluated by the coaches, but they don't necessarily expect a specific type of feedback.

We have examined a wide range of evaluative contexts, including those where people expect external feedback (e.g., competition) and those where they may not (e.g., goal setting). In this chapter, we will review our recent experimental work that examines the effects of evaluative contingencies on intrinsic motivation and explores the motivational dynamics underlying these effects. We believe an analysis of the effects of evaluation on motivation requires a close examination of moderator variables that help identify individuals for whom evaluation may have particularly positive or negative effects, as well as mediator variables that help identify the motivational processes responsible for these effects.

A PROCESS MODEL OF INTRINSIC MOTIVATION

Harackiewicz and Sansone (1991, 2000; see also Harackiewicz, Barron,

& Elliot, 1998; Sansone & Harackiewicz, 1996) proposed a process model of intrinsic motivation that identifies situational and personality variables that may moderate the effects of evaluative contingencies, as well as the motivational processes responsible for these effects. This model enables us to separate processes that are initiated by evaluative contingencies at the outset of an activity from those initiated by feedback at the end of an activity. We have adapted this model to characterize the processes involved in a competition (see Figure 1), and it is important to recognize that there are two distinct paths to intrinsic motivation. First, evaluative contingencies may have powerful effects on the way individuals approach and experience an activity, and these processes can influence subsequent intrinsic motivation. Second, within these evaluative contingencies, the performance feedback that individuals eventually receive may also affect intrinsic motivation. In examining the effects of evaluative contingencies, it is important to consider the unique and combined effects that each of these paths may have on subsequent motivation.

Harackiewicz and Sansone (1991) hypothesized that evaluative contingencies (e.g., competition) and personality variables may affect the goals an individual adopts in a given situation. In Figure 1, these effects are represented by solid paths from evaluative contingencies and individual differences to perceived goals. In addition, the model predicts that individual differences (e.g., achievement motivation) may moderate the effects of the evaluative situation (represented by a dashed path). In other words, individual differences in achievement motivation may lead people to have different goals in the same situation. Murray (1938) defined achievement motivation as a desire to master tasks, seek challenge, outperform others, and attain a high level of competence. Individuals high in achievement motivation (HAMs) desire objective ability feedback (McClelland, 1961) and seek out activities that provide the opportunity for self-evaluation (Greenwald, 1982). On the other hand, those low in achievement motivation (LAMs) do not place the same emphasis on competence, and typically avoid evaluation. Thus, LAMs should find evaluative situations particularly aversive, and they may be unlikely to be intrinsically motivated in these situations. Harackiewicz and Sansone (1991) argue that HAMs should approach and experience evaluative situations more positively than LAMs. Specifically, HAMs should enter these situations with the goal of attaining competence, whereas LAMs should not. In turn, HAMs should show higher levels of subsequent intrinsic motivation in evaluative situations than LAMs, and these different effects on motivation should be the result of the different ways in which HAMs and LAMs approach and experience evaluative situations.

Harackiewicz and Sansone (1991) identified three motivational processes that are particularly relevant to the way that individuals approach and experience tasks (see Figure 1). Competence valuation concerns an individual's emotional commitment to attaining competence, or the extent to which he or she cares about doing well in that situation.

Task involvement concerns an individual's absorption in the task during performance. Perceived competence reflects the person's sense of competence as she or he performs the task. Intrinsic motivation can be enhanced to the extent that individuals care about doing well, become involved in a task, and develop a sense of competence while performing an activity. These processes are typically measured during the course of task engagement, and are hypothesized to mediate the effects of evaluative

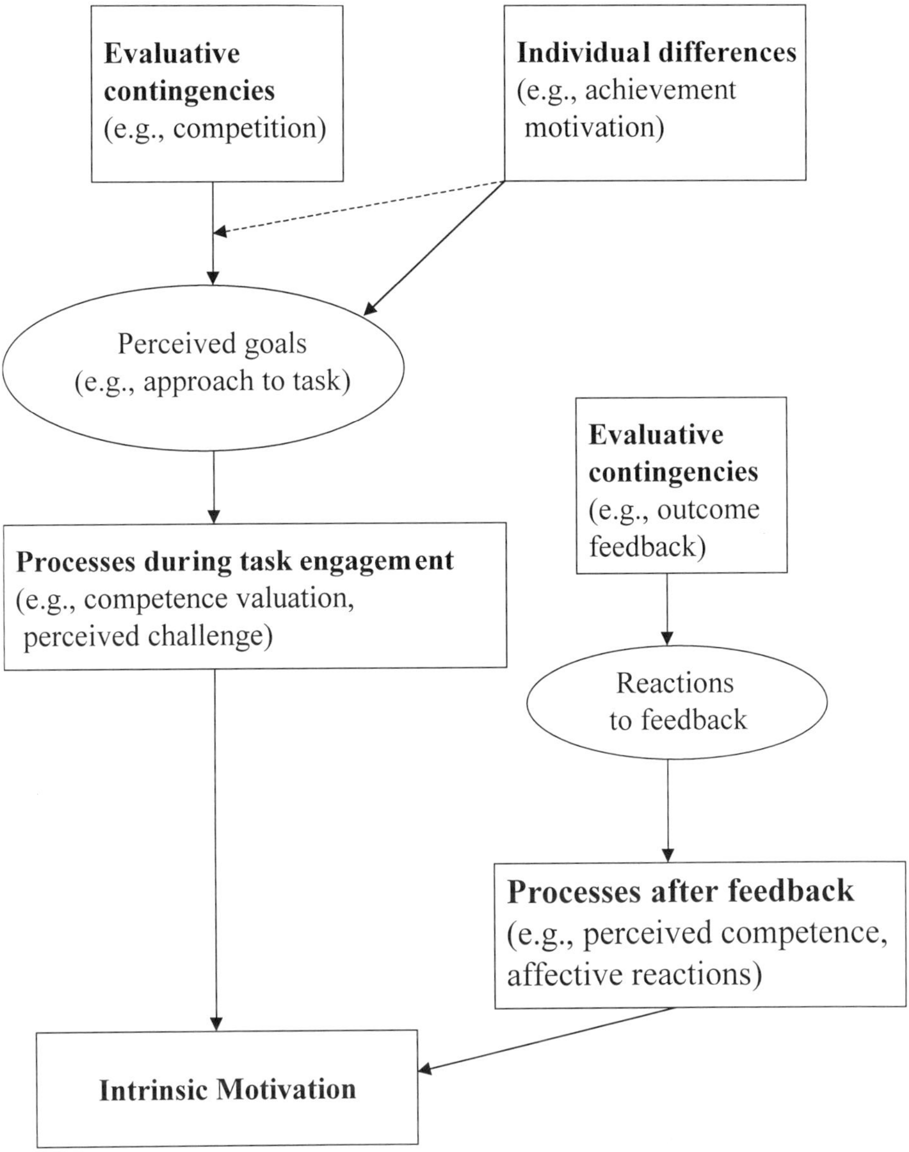

Figure 1. This figure is based on Harackiewicz and Sansone's (1991) process model of intrinsic motivation.

contingencies and perceived goals on intrinsic motivation. Evaluative contingencies can promote these processes (for example, competition might make people care more about doing well at an activity than they otherwise would) and thus facilitate the development of intrinsic motivation. Alternatively, evaluative contingencies might interfere with task involvement or make people feel incompetent, thereby reducing intrinsic motivation.

Another determinant of subsequent motivation is the feedback that participants eventually receive in evaluative situations. Positive feedback should promote perceived competence and affective reactions, and in turn this should increase intrinsic motivation. Perceived competence has been a central aspect of both Deci and Ryan's (1985) CET, as well as Harackiewicz and Sansone's (1991) process model, and it can be examined at several points in the motivational process. Thus, evaluative contingencies have the potential to foster positive (or negative) processes at two distinct points in the motivational process: at the outset when the evaluative context is established, and at task conclusion, when feedback is provided. These effects can be separated by designing experiments that manipulate both the evaluative context and the valence of feedback provided.

OUR RESEARCH ON COMPETITION AND INTRINSIC MOTIVATION

Recent studies of competition have been designed to test the moderating effect of achievement motivation in competition, as well as the effects of feedback in competitive situations. In line with Harackiewicz and Sansone's (1991) model, Epstein and Harackiewicz (1992) predicted that individuals high in achievement motivation (HAMs) would demonstrate higher levels of intrinsic motivation in competition than those low in achievement motivation (LAMs), whereas in noncompetition LAMs would show higher levels of intrinsic motivation than HAMs. Participants who had completed a measure of achievement motivation (Jackson, 1974) at the beginning of the semester played an enjoyable word game (Boggle) along with another participant (actually a confederate). The object of Boggle is to find words in a 4 x 4 letter matrix. In competition, participants were told to try to find more words than their opponent, whereas in a noncompetition participants were simply told to find as many words as possible. All participants received feedback that they had outperformed the other participant. That is, in a competition participants were told that they had won the competition; in a noncompetition they were simply informed that they had scored more points than the other participant. As predicted, Epstein and Harackiewicz found an interaction between competition and achievement motivation, such that HAMs enjoyed the activity more in competition, whereas competition undermined enjoyment for LAMs (see Table 1).

Table 1. Adjusted means for enjoyment (1-7 scale) as a function of competitive context and achievement motivation. Epstein & Harackiewicz (1992)

	No Competition	Competition
Low Achievement motivation	5.07	4.78
High Achievement motivation	4.50	4.90

Examining the competitive context in conjunction with an individual difference variable allowed Epstein and Harackiewicz (1992) to conclude that the effects of competition cannot be summarized with a single, main effect conclusion. Rather, this study provided initial evidence that individuals may experience competition differently as a function of achievement motivation, and that competition can have both positive and negative effects. Nonetheless, it is important to remember that all participants received positive feedback in this study, leaving us to consider several possible reasons why achievement motivation moderates the effects of competition.

One possibility is that because HAMs value competence more than LAMs in evaluative settings, they should value positive, winning feedback more highly. In Epstein and Harackiewicz's study (1992), everyone eventually received positive feedback, and this feedback should have promoted feelings of competence among all participants. If HAMs valued this positive competence feedback more than LAMs, we would expect HAMs to show higher levels of intrinsic motivation than LAMs (Harackiewicz, Abrahams, & Wageman, 1987; Harackiewicz & Manderlink, 1984). However, according to this explanation, we should see a different pattern of results in the presence of negative feedback. If HAMs care more about doing well than LAMs, they should be much more disappointed and enjoy an activity less than LAMs when they *lose* a competition. In sum, competence valuation may intensify reactions to feedback, leading HAMs to enjoy an activity in competition when they win, but to dislike the same activity when they lose.

A second possibility is that HAMs and LAMs approach competition differently from the outset, and this may explain why the effects of competition are moderated by achievement motivation. Recall that Harackiewicz and Sansone's (1991) model outlines a process that begins to unfold as soon as an evaluative contingency is initiated. The effects of competition and achievement motivation may take hold immediately, and have powerful effects throughout the competition, rather than only at the conclusion when feedback is provided. According to this analysis, we would expect HAMs to respond positively to competition as soon as they learn they will be competing, whereas LAMs should immediately demonstrate a negative reaction to competition, and these initial reactions should influence their experience while competing as well as their subsequent intrinsic motivation.

Several theorists have highlighted the positive effects that optimal challenge can have on intrinsic motivation (Csikszentmihalyi, 1990; Deci & Ryan, 1985; Harter, 1981; White, 1959), and competition may increase levels of perceived challenge (Csikszentmihalyi, 1990; Reeve & Deci, 1996). In this case, HAMs may respond positively to competition because of the challenge associated with trying to outperform another person, and these initial perceptions of challenge should promote intrinsic motivation. Although not included in Harackiewicz and Sansone's (1991) original process model, this variable may be especially helpful in documenting the affective process responsible for changes in intrinsic motivation in competitive settings. If HAMs respond positively to challenge, we should see differential reactions among HAMs and LAMs as soon as they learn whether or not they are competing, and these reactions should carry through the entire course of the competition, regardless of the feedback eventually received.

Although each of these explanations for the differential reactions of HAMs and LAMs to competition involves unique motivational processes, any combination of these could also exist. That is, we may see HAMs and LAMs respond differently at the outset of the competition, and also observe that HAMs and LAMs respond in different ways to the feedback they receive. A process analysis allows us to consider the separate effects due to either the evaluative contingency or feedback, and should allow us to clarify the mechanisms responsible for these effects. Testing these two possibilities requires that we manipulate both the competitive context (i.e., competition vs. noncompetition) and feedback (i.e., win vs. lose), and measure key motivational processes during task engagement and following feedback.

Accordingly, we conducted an experiment in which we manipulated competitive condition (competition vs. noncompetition); outcome feedback (outperform another person vs. be outperformed by another person); and performance pattern (ascending performance vs. descending performance), in a 2 x 2 x 2 design (Tauer & Harackiewicz, 1999, Experiment 1). We asked participants to play two games of Boggle, and they were randomly assigned to either a competition or noncompetitive condition. We manipulated the difficulty of the two Boggle puzzles in order to control whether or not participants improved their performance from the first puzzle to the second. If we gave participants the "easy" puzzle first, their performance would deteriorate; if we gave them the "hard" puzzle first, their performance would improve. We provided all participants with feedback about their own performance after each game, and this is how they learned whether or not they had improved their performance. Finally, all participants were randomly assigned to receive feedback after the second game that they had either outperformed or been outperformed by the other participant by eight points. This is how participants in the competition conditions learned whether they had won or lost the competition (and it also ensured that participants in noncompetitive conditions received identical performance feedback). We assessed potential mediating variables throughout the session, and measured our dependent variable, task enjoyment, at the conclusion of the session.

We found an interaction between competition and achievement motivation on task enjoyment, indicating that HAMs enjoyed the activity more than LAMs in competition, whereas LAMs enjoyed the activity more than HAMs in noncompetition (see Table 2). We found this effect across conditions of positive and negative feedback, indicating that positive feedback was not the reason HAMs enjoyed the activity in competition more than LAMs. In addition, participants who received positive outcome feedback reported higher levels of task enjoyment than those participants who were told they had been outperformed by the other participant. Interestingly, this effect was found across competitive conditions, indicating that the benefits of positive feedback were similar in competitive and noncompetitive conditions.

Table 2. Predicted values for enjoyment (1-7 scale) as a function of competitive context and achievement motivation. Exp. 1, Tauer & Harackiewicz (1999)

	No Competition	Competition
Low Achievement motivation	5.15	4.80
High Achievement motivation	5.00	5.05

To test our process model, we measured perceived challenge and competence valuation before the session began. We found a main effect indicating that competition increased competence valuation. It was more important for participants to do well in a competition than in a noncompetition, demonstrating one positive feature of competition -- it can make people care more about doing well. In addition, on perceived challenge, we found an interaction between competitive condition and achievement orientation similar to the one we observed on enjoyment. HAMs perceived the activity as more challenging in competition than LAMs (see Table 3). This finding highlights the different approaches HAMs and LAMs take to competitive activities, and demonstrates that these processes are initiated even before an activity begins.

After we provided participants with outcome feedback, we measured perceived competence and positive affect. On perceived competence, we found a main effect indicating that participants who were told that they had outperformed the other participant felt more competent than those participants who were told that they had been outperformed. In addition, we found a main effect indicating that participants whose performance

Table 3. Predicted values for perceived challenge (1-7 scale) as a function of competitive context and achievement motivation. Exp. 1, Tauer & Harackiewicz (1999)

	No Competition	Competition
Low Achievement motivation	4.97	4.70
High Achievement motivation	4.60	4.91

improved from the first puzzle to the second reported higher levels of perceived competence than those participants whose performance had deteriorated. Finally, we also found a main effect for actual performance, such that participants who scored more points in the game felt more competent. In sum, we found that three different types of positive feedback (outcome feedback, improvement over time, and actual scores) each had unique positive effects on perceived competence.

When we measured positive affect, we also found positive effects of feedback. Participants who had outperformed the other person reported more positive affect than those who had been outperformed, and we observed a similar pattern for participants who had improved their performance. Finally, we also found an interaction between competition and achievement motivation on positive affect. This was the same interaction that we observed on task enjoyment and perceived challenge, which indicated that HAMs reported more positive affect than LAMs in competition, whereas LAMs reported more positive affect than HAMs in noncompetition (see Table 4). Again, this effect was across conditions of positive and negative feedback, suggesting that regardless of feedback, HAMs and LAMs experienced competition quite differently.

Table 4. Predicted values for positive affect (1-7 scale) as a function of competitive context and achievement motivation. Exp. 1, Tauer & Harackiewicz (1999)

	No Competition	Competition
Low Achievement motivation	5.03	4.62
High Achievement motivation	4.75	4.82

Finally, to test whether these process variables mediated the direct effects on task enjoyment, we conducted a mediational analysis according to the guidelines set forth by Judd and Kenny (1981). To establish mediation, it is necessary to show that (a) the independent variable had an effect on the outcome variable, (b) the independent variable had an effect on the process variable, and (c) when both the independent variable and the process variable are tested simultaneously, only the process variable is a significant predictor of the outcome variable. To test this, we added perceived challenge, competence valuation, perceived competence, and positive affect, first individually, and then simultaneously, to our regression model on task enjoyment. Individually, each of these four variables was a significant predictor of task enjoyment, providing support for Harackiewicz and Sansone's (1991) process model. If participants felt a sense of challenge, cared about doing well, felt competent, or expressed positive affect, they were more likely to enjoy the activity. When tested simultaneously, perceived challenge, competence valuation, and positive affect were all significant predictors of task enjoyment (perceived competence was not). In addition, the interaction between competition and achievement motivation was rendered nonsignificant, as was the main effect of outcome, meeting the final requirement for evidence of mediation.

Taken together, these results provide strong support for Harackiewicz and Sansone's (1991) process model, highlighting two unique routes (competitive context and feedback) to intrinsic motivation. One route (via competitive context) was evident throughout the course of the competition, and was initiated at the outset of the competition. HAMs and LAMs approached competition differently, and this affected their perceptions of challenge and values going into the task, as well as their affect at task conclusion. Most compelling was that the interaction between competition and achievement motivation on task enjoyment was not dependent on outcome feedback. In competition, HAMs enjoyed the activity more than LAMs regardless of whether they won or lost.

We outlined two possible explanations for the interaction between competition and achievement orientation first observed by Epstein and Harackiewicz (1992) in positive feedback conditions. The current design and results allow us to evaluate each of these explanations. The first possibility we considered was that because HAMs value competence more than LAMs, they might be more responsive to outcome feedback in competition. This would have resulted in a 3-way interaction between competition, achievement motivation, and outcome feedback. Specifically, HAMs would have enjoyed the activity more in competition than LAMs when they received positive feedback, but they would have disliked the activity when they lost the competition. Instead, we found a 2-way interaction between competition and achievement motivation, indicating that *regardless* of the outcome, and even when they lost, HAMs enjoyed the activity more in competition than LAMs. We found this same interaction on perceived challenge measured at the outset of the competition.

These findings support the second possibility that we considered, suggesting that the experience of performing a task in competition is a critical determinant of subsequent intrinsic motivation, independent of the feedback eventually received in competition. Our results shed light on the different approaches HAMs and LAMs take to competition, and the mediation analyses support our theoretical analysis. We found evidence that HAMs and LAMs approached competition differently, with HAMs finding competition more challenging than LAMs, and perceived challenge mediated the interaction between competition and achievement motivation on task enjoyment.

We also observed a second route to intrinsic motivation, and this was through feedback. As a result, this process was not observed until the end of the competition. Positive feedback (outcome, improving one's score, or actually scoring many points on the Boggle puzzles) had beneficial effects for perceived competence, positive affect, and task enjoyment. It is important to note that we observed these positive feedback effects in both competitive and noncompetitive contexts, suggesting that feedback effects are generally independent of competition effects.

In sum, the results of this study provide compelling evidence that the effects of competition can be positive or negative, and that this is partially determined by individual differences in achievement motivation. In addition, three types of positive feedback led to numerous positive outcomes (on task enjoyment, perceived competence, and positive affect). By measuring process variables, we obtained evidence for two routes to task enjoyment. The first route is initiated immediately, with HAMs perceiving more challenge in competition than LAMs, and this effect mediated task enjoyment. In addition, both HAMs and LAMs cared more about doing well in competition than in noncompetition, and competence valuation also mediated effects on task enjoyment. The second route is contingent on feedback, and therefore is initiated later in the process when feedback is provided. These two routes are relatively independent, with each providing a unique path to task enjoyment.

It is important to note that we did not find any main effects of competition on task enjoyment. Instead, a more complex analysis demonstrated that the effects of competition are moderated by achievement motivation, and we identified competence valuation, perceived challenge, and positive affect as mediators of this relationship. The interaction between competition and achievement motivation was not dependent on feedback, but positive feedback did provide a second route to task enjoyment. These results support Harackiewicz and Sansone's (1991) process model, and highlight the importance of considering both moderator and mediator variables to understand the differential reactions of HAMs and LAMs in competition. Our findings allow us to rule out positive feedback as the sole explanation for this interaction between competition and achievement motivation. However, it is still possible that the reason HAMs enjoy activities more in competition than LAMs is because they simply enjoy receiving any type of outcome feedback, whether it be positive or negative.

To test this, we conducted a subsequent study (Tauer & Harackiewicz, 1999, Experiment 2), in which we did not provide participants with feedback about their performance compared to the other participant. By removing outcome feedback, we were better able to investigate the effects of competitive context on task enjoyment, without these effects being obscured by powerful feedback effects. Participants were again assigned to compete or not, and also informed that they would be working on either easy or difficult puzzles (in this study, the puzzles they actually worked on did not differ in difficulty). Manipulating perceived difficulty allowed us to examine the early processes initiated by competition in more depth. We measured how eager participants were to engage in the activity in addition to their levels of perceived challenge and competence valuation.

In this 2 (competition vs. noncompetition) x 2 (easy vs. difficult puzzles) design (Tauer & Harackiewicz, 1999, Experiment 2), we measured task enjoyment immediately after the second puzzle and again found the predicted interaction between competition and achievement motivation, indicating that HAMs enjoyed the activity more than LAMs in competition, even when they did not receive any feedback (see Table 5).

Table 5. Predicted values for enjoyment (1-7 scale) as a function of competitive context and achievement motivation. Exp. 2, Tauer & Harackiewicz (1999)

	No Competition	Competition
Low Achievement motivation	4.64	4.12
High Achievement motivation	4.47	4.86

To further explore the basis for this interaction, we assessed potential mediators of this relationship. On competence valuation, we found that HAMs cared more about doing well than LAMs, and that competition also increased competence valuation for all participants. On perceived challenge, we found that participants who thought they were working on the difficult puzzles felt more challenged, and that this was particularly true for those in a competition. On eagerness, we found an interaction between competition and achievement motivation. Once again, we observed that HAMs and LAMs were approaching competition differently from the outset, with HAMs looking forward to the activity more in competition than LAMs (see Table 6).

Table 6. Predicted values for eagerness (1-7 scale) as a function of competitive context and achievement motivation. Exp. 2, Tauer & Harackiewicz (1999)

	No Competition	Competition
Low Achievement motivation	4.49	4.12
High Achievement motivation	4.51	5.00

We added these three terms (competence valuation, perceived challenge, and eagerness) individually, and then simultaneously, to our regression model, and found that each of these three variables independently predicted task enjoyment. In addition, the interaction between competition and achievement motivation was no longer significant, meeting the final criterion for mediation. Even when provided with no feedback, HAMs enjoyed the activity more than LAMs in competition, and this process was initiated at the beginning of the competition.

Taken together, these studies (Epstein & Harackiewicz, 1992; Tauer & Harackiewicz, 1999) provide strong support for Harackiewicz and Sansone's process model (1991), and demonstrate the positive potential of competition for certain individuals. This was true both on task enjoyment measured at the end of the session, as well as on process variables measured before the session began. We saw this pattern of findings in the case of positive feedback (Epstein & Harackiewicz, 1992), across conditions of positive and negative feedback (Tauer & Harackiewicz, 1999, Experiment 1), and in the absence of feedback (Tauer & Harackiewicz, 1999, Experiment 2). In sum, it is clear that the differential reactions of HAMs and LAMs to competition do not depend on the availability or the valence of outcome feedback.

We would also like to note that in all of these studies, we found no overall differences between noncompetition and competition. Had we not measured achievement motivation, we would have concluded that competition had no effect on intrinsic motivation. By considering this moderating personality variable, we uncovered a consistent relationship between competition, achievement motivation, and intrinsic motivation, indicating that the effects of competition can be positive or negative, depending on individual differences in achievement motivation. Moreover, our mediational findings highlight the different approaches HAMs and LAMs take to evaluative contingencies such as competition, and demonstrate that these different approaches have powerful effects on subsequent task enjoyment.

RELATIONSHIP BETWEEN COMPETITION AND ACHIEVEMENT GOAL RESEARCH

To this point, we have focused on one type of evaluative contingency, and observed that the effects of competition on intrinsic motivation are moderated by achievement motivation. However, the type of competition we have studied involves a rather explicit type of evaluation, where the goal of winning a face-to-face competition is an integral component of the evaluative contingency. There are other evaluative situations in which goals are more implicitly suggested. For example, at large universities, grades are often assigned based on a normative curve, creating a competitive climate. Students come to understand that their performance will be evaluated, and that they must outperform a certain percentage of students (e.g., 85%) to receive an "A" in the class. This type of goal, labeled a performance goal, is more implicit, but as in explicit competition, the focus is on demonstrating one's competence (Dweck & Leggett, 1988). Performance goals have been associated with negative outcomes on important achievement behaviors such as reduced challenge seeking, surface level cognitive processing (as opposed to deep processing of educational materials), and decreased performance (Dweck & Leggett, 1988; Elliott & Dweck, 1988; Nolen, 1988).

Typically, performance goals have been contrasted with mastery goals, where the focus is on learning and developing competence. Mastery goals have been linked with positive outcomes such as increased challenge-seeking and deeper levels of cognitive processing (Ames & Archer, 1988; Nicholls, Cheung, Lauer, & Patashnick, 1989; Nolen & Haladyna, 1990). Not surprisingly, many theorists have advocated mastery goals over performance goals, which are more evaluative in nature. However, based on Harackiewicz and Sansone's process model (1991), we would predict that performance goals, and the evaluation that accompanies them, need not have negative effects (Harackiewicz, Barron, & Elliot, 1998). Indeed, our work on competition leads us to expect that performance goals might have positive effects for some people.

Harackiewicz and colleagues (Barron & Harackiewicz, 2000; Elliot & Harackiewicz, 1994; Harackiewicz & Elliot, 1993) have conducted a series of studies examining the effects of achievement goals on intrinsic motivation. Harackiewicz and Elliot (1993, Experiment 1) had participants play pinball, an activity generally regarded as enjoyable by college students. Their basic design compared mastery and performance goals, while considering the potential moderating role of achievement motivation. In the performance goal condition, participants were told that their performance would be compared to others, whereas in the mastery goal condition, participants were told to try to learn to play pinball and improve their skills. So, although participants in the performance goal condition knew they were being evaluated, it was not

Table 7. Predicted values for task enjoyment (1-7 scale) as a function of goal type and achievement motivation. Exp. 1, Harackiewicz & Elliot (1993)

	Mastery Goal	Performance Goal
Low Achievement motivation	4.79	4.77
High Achievement motivation	4.52	5.53

explicit whether or not they would receive feedback. In fact, none of the participants received feedback about their performance. Findings from this study parallel those in our competition studies, and support Harackiewicz and Sansone's (1991) process model of intrinsic motivation. Harackiewicz and Elliot found that achievement motivation moderated the effects of goal type, such that HAMs enjoyed an activity more than LAMs when assigned a performance goal, whereas LAMs enjoyed the activity more than HAMs when assigned a mastery goal (see Table 7).

Harackiewicz and Elliot (1993, Experiment 2) went on to replicate and extend these results by again manipulating goal type, and then providing half of the participants with positive performance feedback. This feedback manipulation would help rule out the possibility that the pattern of results in their first study was dependent on the absence of feedback. After playing the pinball games, participants were provided either positive or no feedback, and asked to complete a measure of task enjoyment. The results revealed an interaction between goal type and achievement motivation, indicating that HAMs enjoyed the activity more than LAMs when assigned a performance goal, whereas LAMs enjoyed the activity more than HAMs when working under conditions of a mastery goal (see Table 8). Across these two studies, we see that the effects of a more implicitly evaluative contingency are also moderated by achievement motivation.

Table 8. Predicted values for task enjoyment (1-7 scale) as a function of goal type and achievement motivation. Exp. 2, Harackiewicz & Elliot (1993)

	Mastery Goal	Performance Goal
Low Achievement motivation	5.12	4.73
High Achievement motivation	4.93	5.23

In another study, Elliot and Harackiewicz (1994) provided a more explicit goal for all participants, giving them a specific score to try to surpass for each of two pinball games (29,750 and 31,430 points, respectively). This allowed participants to evaluate their own performance, and performance was experimentally controlled to ensure that all participants actually attained these goals. Participants in the performance goal condition learned beforehand that only 35% of students were able to surpass these scores. Participants in the mastery goal condition were told that these standards should help them develop their skills, but were provided no normative information about the scores. Participants also completed measures of competence valuation and task involvement, two mediators in Harackiewicz and Sansone's (1991) process model.

On task enjoyment, Elliot and Harackiewicz (1994) found the same interaction between goal type and achievement motivation, indicating that HAMs enjoyed the pinball game under conditions of a performance goal more than a mastery goal. On the other hand, LAMs enjoyed playing pinball under conditions of a mastery goal more than a performance goal (see Table 9). In addition, they found the same interaction between goal type and achievement motivation on both competence valuation and task involvement, and each of these variables mediated the significant interaction on task enjoyment.

Table 9. Predicted values for task enjoyment (1-7 scale) as a function of goal type and achievement motivation. Elliot & Harackiewicz (1994)

	Mastery Goal	Performance Goal
Low Achievement motivation	4.91	4.48
High Achievement motivation	4.91	5.62

Although the effects of mastery and performance goals are typically evaluated relative to one another, it is possible that both types of goals could be recommended in a situation. For example, teachers want students to learn *and* perform well, and thus might emphasize both mastery and performance goals in the same situation. People may therefore adopt both goals simultaneously, or they may adopt a mastery goal in some situations, and a performance goal in others (Harackiewicz, Barron, & Elliot, 1998; Harackiewicz, Barron, Tauer, Carter, & Elliot, 2000). Barron and Harackiewicz (2001) examined the effects of mastery and performance goals in a learning environment, but also included a multiple goal condition. They had students work on either easy or difficult math problems, and assigned students either a mastery goal, a performance goal, or both goals. Providing people with both goals may allow them more flexibility in the way that they approach the activity, given that some individuals enjoy activities more under a mastery goal, but others show more enjoyment under a performance goal. The multiple goal condition might optimize motivation for everyone. In fact, Barron and Harackiewicz found a very similar pattern of results to the studies we have reviewed to this point. Across conditions of easy and difficult problems, HAMs showed higher levels of intrinsic motivation when given a performance goal, whereas LAMs were more motivated under a mastery goal. Interestingly, both HAMs and LAMs showed *intermediate* levels of motivation when assigned both a mastery and a performance goal. This linear effect indicates that as the situation became more evaluative, HAMs enjoyed the activity more and LAMs enjoyed the activity less. As a result, the multiple goal condition provided somewhat of a compromise for HAMs and LAMs, allowing HAMs to enjoy the activity more than in the pure mastery goal condition, and LAMs to enjoy the activity more than in the pure performance goal condition (see Table 10). In sum, the results of these studies on achievement goals provide strong support for the process model, and correspond nicely to our findings in studies of competition.

Table 10. Predicted values for task enjoyment (1-7 scale) as a function of goal type and achievement motivation. Barron & Harackiewicz (2001)

	Mastery Goal	Both Goals	Performance Goal
Low Achievement motivation	5.45	5.17	4.85
High Achievement motivation	5.13	5.26	5.40

SUMMARY OF EXPERIMENTAL WORK ON EVALUATIVE CONTINGENCIES

We have reviewed the results of seven studies that provide evidence across a wide range of contexts and activities that the effects of evaluative contingencies are complex, but consistently moderated by achievement motivation. We observed this interaction across conditions of positive, negative, and no feedback, as well as across conditions of varied difficulty. It is clear that evaluative contingencies need not undermine intrinsic interest in an activity for everyone. Our results indicate that competition and performance goals are experienced quite differently by HAMs and LAMs, and that these differential reactions are initiated before, during, and after the activity. This is as true in our studies of more implicitly evaluative contingencies (i.e., achievement goals) as it is of our competition studies, and our results are remarkably consistent across these very different types of evaluative contingencies. HAMs and LAMs approach evaluative contingencies differently, and these approaches have powerful effects throughout the entire course of the activity.

These findings are in contrast to conventional wisdom that argues that the effects of evaluation, competition, and performance goals are uniformly negative (Kohn, 1992; see also Hidi & Harackiewicz, 2000). In none of the studies that we have reviewed was there ever a main effect (positive or negative) of either competition or goal type. Rather, each study found evidence that the effects of evaluative contingencies on intrinsic motivation were moderated by individual differences in achievement motivation. These findings are consistent with a hallmark of social psychology: behavior is a function of both the environment and personality (Lewin, 1935). We believe a consideration of both situational and personality variables is crucial in understanding the effects of evaluative contingencies on intrinsic motivation. Harackiewicz and Sansone's (1991) process model highlights the complexities involved in understanding the separate effects of evaluative contingencies and the feedback they provide, as well as the motivational processes these contingencies invoke, and our experimental work offers strong support for this model.

CONCLUSIONS

Based on our experimental work, we are left to conclude that although evaluative contingencies have the potential to undermine intrinsic motivation, these effects are quite complex and require a careful analysis of a number of variables. In addition to considering overall effects of variables such as competition and performance goals, we encourage researchers to consider individual difference variables that may moderate these effects. Harackiewicz and Sansone's (1991) process model is particularly useful in our analysis, both in identifying the moderating effects of achievement motivation, as well as identifying process variables that help us understand the effects of evaluation on intrinsic motivation. This model affords three levels of analysis of evaluative situations. First, the model considers the overall effects of an evaluative contingency over time, separating the anticipation of evaluation from the receipt of feedback. Second, the model identifies the moderating effect of personality variables. Third, it identifies the mediating effects of variables such as competence valuation, perceived challenge, task involvement, and perceived competence. This model outlines different processes that can lead to intrinsic motivation, some that begin immediately and depend on the interplay between an evaluative contingency and personality variables, and others that depend on feedback that comes at the end of task performance.

It appears that the intuitions of the coaches at the basketball camp were correct: different individuals *do* respond quite differently to evaluative contingencies. So what should they do to structure activities at basketball camp to motivate all of their campers? We believe it is not realistic to avoid all evaluation, as this is a part of our society that children will eventually encounter. Kids will encounter evaluation, and one goal should be to maximize intrinsic motivation within these evaluative contexts. At the same time, being sensitive to the preferences of individuals should help coaches tailor activities in a way that leads to a positive experience for everyone. Continued research should help us better understand these differential reactions to evaluation, and ultimately will provide us the guidance to devise creative methods to foster intrinsic motivation in all individuals. The process model highlights general variables that should promote intrinsic motivation across a wide range of evaluative contingencies. To the extent that we can structure activities so that they promote competence valuation, feelings of optimal challenge, task involvement, and perceptions of competence, we will be doing a service to all of our students and athletes.

The study of evaluative contingencies is a challenging one, and is relevant to many aspects of our lives. As teachers, coaches, and parents strive to foster motivation in their students, athletes, and children, it is important to arm them with a complete picture of the effects of evaluation. Our studies of evaluative contingencies, competition, and achievement goals demonstrate that individuals may respond quite differently to the same evaluative contingency. Rather than conclude that evaluation has uniformly positive or negative effects on intrinsic motivation, our results encourage us to consider the separate and combined effects of evaluative contingencies and the feedback that they provide. We believe that evaluation effects are best understood using the Harackiewicz and Sansone (1991) process model because it highlights contextual and personality variables that moderate these effects, as well as the mechanisms underlying these effects. After all, the effects of evaluative contingencies may only be as powerful as the motivational processes they initiate. The findings we have obtained to date begin to shed light on the complex effects of evaluative contingencies. Although this analysis does not lead to simple conclusions about the effects of evaluation on motivation, this is precisely what makes the study of evaluation so challenging and intrinsically motivating!

REFERENCES

Ames, C., & Archer, J. (1988). Achievement goals in the classroom Students' learning strategies and motivation processes. *Journal of Educational Psychology, 80*, 260-267.

Barron, K. E., & Harackiewicz, J. M. (2001). Achievement goals and optimal motivation: Testing multiple goal models. *Journal of Personality and Social Psychology, 80*, 706-722.

Csikszentmihalyi, M. (1990). *Flow: The psychology of optimal experience.* New York: Harper & Row.

Deci, E. L. (1971). Effects of externally mediated rewards on intrinsic motivation. *Journal of Personality and Social Psychology, 18*, 105-115.

Deci, E. L., Betley, G., Kahle, J., Abrams, L., & Porac, J. (1981). When trying to win: Competition and intrinsic motivation. *Personality and Social Psychology Bulletin, 7*, 79-83.

Deci, E. L., & Ryan, R. M. (1985). *Intrinsic Motivation and self-determination in human behavior.* New York: Plenum.

Dweck, C. S., & Leggett, E. L. (1988). A social-cognitive approach to motivation and personality. *Psychological Review, 95*, 256-273.

Elliot, A. J., & Harackiewicz, J. M. (1994). Goal setting, achievement orientation, and intrinsic motivation: A mediational analysis. *Journal of Personality and Social Psychology, 66*, 968-980.

Elliott, E. S., & Dweck, C. S. (1988). Goals: An approach to motivation and achievement. *Journal of Personality and Social Psychology, 54*, 5-12.

Epstein, J. A., & Harackiewicz, J. M. (1992). Winning is not enough: The effects of competition and achievement orientation on intrinsic interest. *Personality and Social Psychology Bulletin, 18*, 128-139.

Greenwald, A. G. (1982). Ego task analysis: An integration of research on ego-involvement and self-awareness. In A. H. Hastorf & A. M. Isen (Eds.), *Cognitive social psychology* (pp. 109-147). New York: Elsevier North Holland.

Harackiewicz, J. M. (1989). Performance evaluation and intrinsic motivation processes: The effects of achievement orientation and rewards. In D. M. Buss & N. Cantor (Eds.), *Personality psychology: Recent trends and emerging directions* (pp. 128-137). New York: Springer-Verlag.

Harackiewicz, J. M., Abrahams, S., & Wageman, R. (1987). Performance evaluation and intrinsic motivation: The effects of evaluative focus, rewards, and achievement orientation. *Journal of Personality and Social Psychology, 53*, 1015-1023. (Special issue: Integrating personality and social psychology).

Harackiewicz, J. M., Barron, K. E., Tauer, J. M., Elliot, A. J., & Carter, S. M. (2000). Short-term and long-term consequences of achievement goals in the college classroom. *Journal of Educational Psychology, 92*, 316-330.

Harackiewicz, J. M., & Elliot, A. J. (1993). Achievement goals and intrinsic motivation. *Journal of Personality and Social Psychology, 65*, 904-915.

Harackiewicz, J. M., & Manderlink, G. (1984). A process analysis of the effects of performance-contingent rewards on intrinsic motivation. *Journal of Experimental Social Psychology, 20*, 531-551.

Harackiewicz, J. M., & Sansone, C. (1991). Goals and intrinsic motivation: You can get there from here. In M. L. Maehr & P. R. Pintrich (Eds.), *Advances in motivation and achievement* (Vol. 7, pp. 21-49). Greenwich, CT: JAI Press.

Harackiewicz, J. M., & Sansone, C. (2000). Rewarding competence: The importance of goals in the study of intrinsic motivation. In C. Sansone & J. M. Harackiewicz (Eds.), *Intrinsic Motivation: Controversies and New Directions.* New York: Academic Press.

Harter, S. (1981). A model of mastery motivation in children: Individual differences and developmental change. In W. A. Collins (Ed.), *Aspects of the development of competence: The Minnesota symposium on child psychology* (Vol. 14, pp. 215-255). Hillsdale, NJ: Lawrence Erlbaum Associates, Inc.

Hidi, S., & Harackiewicz, J. M. (2000). Motivating the academically unmotivated: A critical issue for the 21st century. *Review of Educational Research, 70*, 151-179.

Jackson, D. N. (1974). *Personality Research Form Manual.* Goshen, NY: Research Psychologists Press.

Judd, C. M., & Kenny, D. A. (1981). Process analysis: Estimating mediation in treatment evaluations. *Evaluation Review, 5*, 602-619.

Kohn, A. (1992). *No Contest: The Case Against Competition.* New York: Houghton Mifflin.

Lepper, M. R., Greene, D., & Nisbett, R. E. (1973). Undermining children's intrinsic interest with extrinsic reward: A test of the overjustification hypothesis. *Journal of Personality and Social Psychology, 28*, 129-137.

Lewin, K. (1935). *Dynamic theory of personality.* New York: McGraw-Hill.

McAuley, E., & Tammen, V. V. (1989). The effects of subjective and objective competitive outcomes on intrinsic motivation. *Journal of Sport and Exercise Psychology, 11*, 84-93.

McClelland, D. C. (1961). *The achieving society.* Princeton, NJ: Van Nostrand.

Murray, H. A. (1938). *Explorations in personality.* New York: Oxford University Press.

Nicholls, J. G., Cheung, P. C., Lauer, J., & Patashnick, M. (1989). Individual differences in academic motivation: Perceived ability, goals, beliefs, and values. *Learning and Individual Differences, 1*, 63-84.

Nolen, S. B. (1988). Reasons for studying: Motivation orientations and study strategies. *Cognition and Instruction, 5*, 269-287.

Nolen, S. B., & Haladyna, T. M. (1990). Personal and environmental influences on students' beliefs about effective study strategies. *Contemporary Educational Psychology, 15*, 116-130.

Reeve, J., & Deci, E. L. (1996). Elements of the competitive situation that affect intrinsic motivation. *Personality and Social Psychology Bulletin, 22*, 24-33.

Reeve, J., Olson, B. C., & Cole, S. G. (1985). Motivation and performance: Two consequences of winning and losing in competition. *Motivation and Emotion, 9*, 291-298.

Reeve, J., Olson, B. C., & Cole, S. G. (1987). Intrinsic motivation in competition: The intervening role of four individual differences following objective competence information. *Journal of Research in Personality, 21*, 148-170.

Sansone, C., & Harackiewicz, J. M. (1996). "I don't feel like it": The function of interest in self-regulation. In L. L. Martin & A. Tesser (Eds.), *Striving and feeling: Interactions among goals, affect, and self-regulation* (pp. 203-228). Mahwah, NJ: Lawrence Erlbaum Associates.

Stanne, M. B., Johnson, D. W., & Johnson, R. T. (1999). Does competition enhance or inhibit motor performance: A meta-analysis. *Psychological Bulletin, 125*, 133-154.

Tauer, J. M., & Harackiewicz, J. M. (1999). Winning isn't everything: Competition, achievement orientation, and intrinsic motivation. *Journal of Experimental Social Psychology, 35*, 209-238.

Vallerand, R. M., & Reid, G. (1984). On the causal effects of perceived competence on intrinsic motivation: A test of cognitive evaluation theory. *Journal of Sport Psychology, 6*, 94-102.

Weinberg, R. S., & Ragan, J. (1979). Effects of competition, success/failure, and sex on intrinsic motivation. *Research Quarterly, 50*, 503-510.

White, R. W. (1959). Motivation reconsidered: The concept of competence. *Psychological Review, 66*, 297-333.

Chapter 5

THE ROLE OF TASK COMPLEXITY, AND SOURCES AND CRITERIA OF EVALUATION IN MOTIVATING TASK PERFORMANCE

Stephen G. Harkins
Northeastern University

In the first four chapters of this text, work in each of four research traditions has been described: social loafing, goal setting, intrinsic motivation, and achievement goal theory. Each of these traditions incorporates the notion that the potential for evaluation affects task performance, and provides a theoretical rationale for these effects. I will describe a fifth tradition, social facilitation, which also incorporates the notion that evaluation affects performance, but I will do so in the context of a first attempt to integrate these areas.

This first attempt at integration can be accomplished in a simple, straightforward way. It suggests that the performance findings from each of these traditions can be represented by taking into account only three factors: (a) Whether or not the participants' outputs can be evaluated by an external source (e.g., the experimenter); (b) the level of performance the participants are asked to achieve. Specifically whether the experimenter simply asks the participants to do their best, or s/he sets a stringent goal, and (c) task complexity. Crossing these three variables yields the three-way design depicted in Table 1.

Table 1. Three-Way Design

	Simple Task		Complex Task	
	Do Your Best	Stringent Goal	Do Your Best	Stringent Goal
Experimenter Evaluation				
No Experimenter Evaluation				

Central to this analysis is the thesis that within the research paradigms used in these traditions, the potential for evaluation by external sources (i.e., the experimenter) is more powerful than the potential for self-evaluation. For example, we argue that although the potential for self-evaluation alone can motivate participants as much as the potential for experimenter evaluation, as performance requirements are increased, concern over the potential for experimenter evaluation spurs greater effort than the potential for self-evaluation. In addition, when there is the potential for evaluation by both sources, concern over the potential for evaluation by a social source supersedes interest in the potential for self-evaluation. This thesis is not part of the theoretical accounts of any of these traditions, and, in fact, directly contradicts some of them (e.g., Locke and Latham's [1990a] account of goal setting effects). Nonetheless, I will argue that the ascendancy of external evaluation in combination with the effects of task instructions (do your best versus goal setting instructions) and task complexity accounts for the findings of each of these traditions.

In the current chapter, I will first describe the research that makes the case for the ascendancy of external evaluation. In so doing I will show how social loafing and goal setting research fit in the three-way design. Then I will extend this analysis to research on social facilitation and to research on intrinsic motivation and achievement goals. Finally, I will report an experiment that shows that the typical findings from each of these traditions can be replicated in this design, and consider the implications of these findings.

SOCIAL LOAFING

Social loafing refers to the finding that people put out less effort when working together than when working alone (Latané, Williams, & Harkins, 1979). Although Latané et al.'s (1979) description implies that social loafing is simply a consequence of participants "working together," Harkins (1987) has suggested that this reduction in effort is a consequence of the fact that, in loafing experiments, when participants work together their outputs are pooled (combined). Thus, individual outputs are "lost in the crowd," and participants can receive neither credit nor blame for their performances. Harkins (1987) argued that it was this lack of evaluation potential that led to loafing in these experiments.

Consistent with this argument are the findings of Williams, Harkins, and Latané (1981; see also Kerr & Bruun, 1981), who led participants to believe that their outputs could always be monitored whether they shouted individually or with others. Under these conditions, participants worked as hard in groups as when alone. Also, when participants were led to believe that the experimenter's interest was focused on group performance, and that individual outputs were to be pooled, the participants loafed as much when they performed individually as when they performed together. Williams et al. (1981) concluded on the basis of these findings that identifiability of individual outputs was an important mediator or social loafing.

However, Williams et al. (1981) did not manipulate identifiability alone. When performances were identifiable, because the participants all worked on exactly the same task, the performance of any given participant could be directly compared with the performances of the other participants. This combination of conditions provided the two pieces of information that we would argue are necessary for evaluation: (a) a measure of the participant's output (in this case, the shouting score); and (b) an evaluative criterion against which this output can be compared (in this case, the shouting scores of the other participants). Thus, it could have been the potential for evaluation, not identifiability alone, that motivated performance in Williams et al.'s (1981) research.

To test this notion, Harkins and Jackson (1985) manipulated identifiability and evaluation potential orthogonally, using a use-generation task in which participants were asked to generate as many uses for an object as they could. To manipulate identifiability participants were led to believe that their uses would be pooled with those of other participants (not identifiable) or would be counted individually by the experimenter (identifiable). To manipulate the potential for evaluation, one-half of the participants were led to believe that they were generating uses for the same object, whereas the other half were led to believe that each participant in the experiment was generating uses for a different object. Of course, the participants actually all generated uses for the same object, but if they believed they were generating uses for different ones, there would be no evaluative criterion against which their performance could be compared, and regardless of identifiability, they should loaf.

Consistent with previous loafing research (e.g., Harkins & Petty, 1982), participants generated more uses for an object when outputs were identifiable than when outputs were pooled. However, this difference emerged only when participants believed that their outputs could be compared to those of their coworkers'. When participants believed that they were generating uses for different objects, and, as a result, their outputs could not be compared, identifiability made no difference. Participants whose outputs were identifiable generated as few uses as participants whose outputs were pooled, because, in each case, there was no evaluative criterion against which their output could be compared. Consistent with this analysis, based on the findings of their meta-analysis, Karau and Williams (1993) report that: "In fact, social loafing was eliminated when evaluation potential was not varied across coactive (*individual outputs identifiable*) and collective (*individual outputs pooled*) conditions" (p. 696, italicized text added).

Clearly, the potential for evaluation is central to the loafing effect, but evaluation by whom? In early loafing research, the role of the experimenter as evaluator was emphasized. So, for example, Harkins, Williams, and Latané (1980) argued that their results could be explained by a minimizing strategy that led participants to work only when the experimenter could monitor their individual performances. However, there are three potential sources of evaluation in the loafing paradigm: the experimenter, the coactor(s), and the participant. In this research (e.g., Harkins et al., 1980), it appears that when the participants performed together, no one could evaluate individual performance. The experimenter had no measure of the participants' outputs, and the participants had no access to a criterion. When participants performed individually, participants could have believed that the experimenter could evaluate them. The experimenter had access to their output and the outputs of the other participants (evaluative criterion), and so could compare them. They also could have believed that they would have access to the same information, and so, could evaluate themselves and/or be evaluated by their coparticipants.

Given the types of tasks typically used in loafing research, it is not clear that the potential for self-evaluation would be sufficient to motivate performance. That is, it is quite easy to imagine research participants eagerly testing their skills on tasks that appear interesting and challenging whether or not the experimenter can monitor their performances. However, the tasks used in loafing research have been described as "noncompetitive, boring, tiring" (Harkins et al., 1980), and "unlikely to be personally involving for students, providing intrinsic importance, personal meaning, or significant consequences for one's life" (Brickner, Harkins, & Ostrom, 1986).

To test the possibility that the opportunity for self-evaluation would be sufficient to eliminate the loafing effect even when participants performed an uninteresting task, we (Szymanski & Harkins, 1987) asked participants to generate as many uses as they possibly could for a common object, regardless of the creativity of these uses. Pilot work had shown that, after completing the task, participants felt that they knew how many uses they had generated, a measure of their output. Therefore, to manipulate the potential for self-evaluation, we provided an evaluative criterion by telling one-third of the participants that at the end of their performance they would be given the average number of uses generated by participants in a previous version of the experiment (criterion). We told another third of the participants that to ensure confidentiality, we would not be able to give them this average (no criterion), and a final third were told nothing about the criterion (no information). When the participants were provided with the evaluative criterion, they were presented with the opportunity for self-evaluation by social comparison. This manipulation of the potential for self-evaluation was crossed with a manipulation of the potential for experimenter evaluation. One-half of the participants were told that at the end of the experimental session, the experimenter would come in and count the number of uses that they had generated (experimenter evaluation), whereas the other half were told that the experimenter was interested in average performance, and so their individual outputs would be pooled with those of the others and would not be examined (no experimenter evaluation).

As can be seen in Table 2, consistent with previous loafing research (e.g., Latané et al., 1979), participants subject to experimenter evaluation produced more uses than those who were not subject to this evaluation, and this outcome was obtained both when participants were given no information about the criterion and when they were explicitly told that they would not be given the criterion. In previous research, it is possible that participants in the "experimenter evaluation" condition were motivated by the potential for evaluation by any of three sources: experimenter, coactor, self. However, in response to a question asking them by whom their performance could be evaluated, participants reported that the experimenter could evaluate them to a greater extent than the self or coactors. In fact, participants indicated that the self and coactors were as unable to serve as sources of evaluation as all the sources were rated in the "no experimenter evaluation" condition. Thus, it appears that in the basic loafing paradigm, it is the experimenter that is the salient source of evaluation. This pattern of results was replicated in the no criterion condition in which the experimenter told the participants that they could not be provided with average performance on this task, because it had to be held in confidence.

Table 2. Mean uses for a "knife": Exp. 2, Szymanski & Harkins (1987)

	No Information	No Criterion	Criterion
Experimenter Evaluation	28.5_a	25.4_a	25.9_a
No Experimenter Evaluation	20.0_b	18.2_b	27.3_a

Means that do not share a subscript are significantly different, $p < .05$

Descriptions of the tasks used in loafing research (Brickner et al., 1986; Harkins et al., 1980) would suggest that taking part in these tasks would be sheer drudgery and that, in the absence of external evaluation pressures, there would be little reason to perform well since the tasks are devoid of inherent interest. Nonetheless, we found that the opportunity for self-evaluation alone (no experimenter evaluation/criterion) was sufficient to motivate participants to produce more uses than the number found in the no experimenter evaluation/no criterion and no experimenter evaluation/no information conditions. In fact, the opportunity for self-evaluation led to performance equivalent to that produced when participants were subject to experimenter evaluation.

We (Harkins & Szymanski, 1988) replicated this pattern of results using a simple vigilance task, which required participants to try to detect as many signals as they could while minimizing false alarms (i.e., do your best). The evaluative criterion used in this case was objective; participants performed the task knowing that, at its conclusion, they would be told how many signals had been presented, or that this information would be withheld. As noted previously, at the conclusion of the use-generation task, participants think that they know how many uses they have generated. However, on the vigilance task, pilot testing indicated that participants do not think that they know how many signals they have detected. Thus, in this experiment, we were able to manipulate the two components of evaluation -- task output and evaluative criterion -- independently. The participants could be evaluated by the experimenter or could not, the task output was displayed or not, and participants were told that the objective criterion would be provided at the end of the task or not.

Table 3. Number of Errors: Harkins & Szymanski (1988)

	Evaluative Criterion		No Evaluative Criterion	
	Output Feedback	No Output Feedback	Output Feedback	No Output Feedback
Experimenter Evaluation	2.4_a	2.4_a	2.5_a	2.3_a
No Experimenter Evaluation	2.7_a	3.3_a	6.1_b	6.7_b

Means that do not share a subscript are significantly different, $p < .05$

As Table 3 shows, analysis of the performance data showed that the potential for experimenter evaluation motivated performance; however, when the experimenter could not evaluate individuals, but they could evaluate themselves (task output plus the objective criterion), the same level of performance was achieved, a self-evaluation effect. When participants who were not subject to experimenter evaluation were missing one or both of the necessities for evaluation (output & criterion), performance fell significantly with one interesting exception: no experimenter evaluation participants who were provided only with the criterion performed as well as the experimenter evaluation participants. Even though these participants were missing one of the pieces of information required for evaluation (output feedback), they achieved the same level of performance as participants subject to experimenter evaluation. Follow-up research (Szymanski, 1988) showed that these participants were so motivated by the prospect of self-evaluation that they went to the trouble of keeping track of the number of signals that they had detected in order to do so.

Thus, both Szymanski and Harkins (1987) and Harkins and Szymanski (1988) showed that when participants were asked to do their best, the potential for self-evaluation motivated participants to the same extent as the potential for evaluation by the experimenter. Each of these designs incorporated orthogonal manipulations of the potential for evaluation by the experimenter and the self, and, in each experiment, we found that the joint action of these sources produced performance no better than that achieved by either source taken alone. This failure of motivation stemming from the two sources to summate could have resulted from a ceiling effect. The potential for evaluation by either source could have put the participants at peak motivation, eliminating the possibility of greater output. After all, the "motivated" participants detected 86% of the signals in the vigilance task. However, the same pattern of findings was produced on the use-generation task for which there is no meaningful ceiling. In addition, in follow-up research Szymanski (1988) showed that participants were able to generate more uses and detect more signals when offered a financial incentive, demonstrating that they were not at a performance ceiling.

Instead of a ceiling effect, we argue that the combination of these sources does not produce greater output than the potential for evaluation by either taken alone because concern over the potential for experimenter evaluation supersedes interest in the potential for self-evaluation. Thus, the effect of the combination of the two sources is no greater than either taken alone, because, in effect, there is no combination. We are seeing the effect of experimenter evaluation alone. In the vigilance task, participants in the no experimenter evaluation condition went to the trouble of keeping track of the number of signals that were presented so that they could self-evaluate. Participants in the experimenter evaluation counterpart of this condition were presented with this very same opportunity but they did not take advantage of it. That is, they would have had the opportunity for self-evaluation had they kept track of the signals, but they did not, suggesting that their concern over the impending evaluation by the experimenter may have supplanted their interest in self-evaluation.

Szymanski and Harkins (1993) generated additional evidence consistent with this argument in a choice paradigm in which participants selected the conditions under which they would work. Participants were randomly assigned to one of three experimental conditions. In the first condition, participants were given a choice between working on a task that was arranged so that participants could be evaluated by the experimenter only, or working on a task that was arranged so that no one could evaluate them. The participants chose reliably more often to be evaluated by no one. Thus, participants avoided the potential for experimenter evaluation. In a second condition participants could choose between an experiment that afforded the opportunity for self-evaluation alone or no one. Consistent with our earlier findings, participants chose the former, the opportunity for self-evaluation. In a third condition, participants chose between evaluation by both experimenter and self or no one. They opted for the latter, evaluation by no one.

This pattern of findings both reinforces and extends the interpretation of the previous research (Harkins & Szymanski, 1988; Szymanski, 1988). The overall pattern of data suggests that the dominance of experimenter over self-evaluation stems from apprehension regarding evaluation by the experimenter, rather than interest in impressing the experimenter. In fact, as shown in condition three, the prospect of experimenter evaluation was so distasteful that participants chose to pass up the opportunity for self-evaluation, rather than to submit themselves to the scrutiny of the experimenter. These findings suggest that although the two sources, experimenter and self, can produce the same level of performance, when there is the potential for evaluation by both, concern over the evaluative potential of the experimenter supplants interest in the potential for self-evaluation.

Table 4. Three-Way Design

	Simple Task		Complex Task	
	Do Your Best	Stringent Goal	Do Your Best	Stringent Goal
Experimenter Evaluation	SL			
No Experimenter Evaluation	SL			

SL = Social Loafing

Thus, as shown in Table 4, in the basic loafing paradigm, it is the opportunity for experimenter evaluation that is responsible for the elimination of the loafing effect. In the absence of information to the contrary, participants assume that the experimenter will be able to evaluate their performance, and that neither evaluation by the self or a coactor will be possible. Even if there were the potential for self-evaluation, interest in this source is supplanted by concern over the potential for experimenter evaluation. In this research, participants are asked to produce as much as possible (i.e., do your best), and for the most part, simple tasks have been used. Thus, as shown in Table 4, the basic conditions in the social loafing paradigm fall in the simple task/do your best/experimenter evaluation and no experimenter evaluation cells of the three-way design.

GOAL SETTING

In the research described thus far, participants have been asked to "do their best" (e.g., generate as many uses as you can, detect as many signals as you can). Locke and Latham (1990a) report that participants urged to strive to attain a specific, difficult level of performance do even better than participants asked to do their best. They argue that this goal setting effect is the result of the potential for self-evaluation. Just as Szymanski and Harkins (1987) argued that for self-evaluation to be possible, participants must have access to some measure of output and a criterion, Locke and Latham (1990b) argue that the goal setting effect requires that participants have knowledge of their output (feedback in Locke & Latham's terminology). Goals then "provide them with a yardstick for determining whether the feedback they are given reveals acceptable or unacceptable performance. Without a goal or standard, people do not appraise feedback as significant and thus do not take action in response to it" (p. 241). Thus, it is the opportunity for self-evaluation provided by comparing the performance to a specific, difficult criterion that is supposedly responsible for the goal setting effect.

If the potential for self-evaluation were responsible for producing goal setting effects, it would suggest that interest in the potential for self-evaluation is not superseded by concern over social evaluation when, instead of only being asked to do one's best, one is asked to strive to reach a stringent criterion. However, the potential for self-evaluation is not responsible for the goal setting effect. White, Kjelgaard, and Harkins (1995) used the social loafing paradigm to test the contribution of self-evaluation processes to the goal setting effect by giving participants 12 minutes to generate as many uses as possible for a "knife." They were told either that their uses would be individually counted by the experimenter (experimenter evaluation), or that their uses would be combined with those of the previous participants because the researchers were interested in average performance (no experimenter evaluation). Crossed with this manipulation, in the conditions on which we will focus, participants were asked to "do your best;" or were told to strive to achieve a goal of 40 uses which they were told was based on the performance of participants in a prior version of the experiment (goal). Prior studies using "do your best" instructions revealed that approximately 10% of participants produced 40 uses. Thus, 40 uses was chosen in accord with Locke and Latham's suggestion that a goal attainable by only 10% of participants would be difficult enough to produce the goal setting effect (1990a, p. 349).

The "do your best" conditions correspond to the basic conditions included in social loafing research. That is, in loafing research, participants are told to produce as much as they can (i.e., to do their best). In these conditions, the social loafing effect was replicated: Participants subject to experimenter evaluation outperformed participants who are not subject to experimenter evaluation (Latané, Williams, Harkins, 1979). In the goal setting literature (Locke & Latham, 1990a) to test for goal setting effects the performance of participants in the goal condition is compared to the performance of participants who are asked to do their best. In this research, the experimenter typically has access to the participants' outputs. Replicating the goal setting effect reported in the literature (Locke & Latham, 1990a), White et al. (1995) found that participants who were subject to the evaluation of the experimenter and were provided a stringent goal produced more uses than participants who were subject to experimenter evaluation and asked to do their best.

Table 5. Mean uses for a "knife": Exp. 1, White et al. (1995)

	Do Your Best	Goal-40
Experimenter Evaluation	25.1_a	35.6_b
No Experimenter Evaluation	17.6_c	26.5_a

Means that do not share a subscript are significantly different, $p < .05$

Locke and Latham (1990a) suggest that it is the potential for self-evaluation that produces goal setting effects. White et al.'s (1995) finding does not support or refute this view, because (as in almost all goal setting research) the potential for experimenter evaluation was confounded with the potential for self-evaluation. In White et al.'s (1995) paradigm, the effect of experimenter evaluation was removed in the no experimenter evaluation/goal condition. If the potential for self-evaluation alone is sufficient to produce a goal setting effect, then it should be seen here, but, as can be seen in Table 5, it was not.

However, providing a goal did have some effect on the performance of participants in the no experimenter evaluation/goal condition -- their performance exceeded that of participants in the no experimenter evaluation/do your best condition (i.e., exceeded the "loafing" level), and equaled the performance of participants subject to experimenter evaluation who were asked to do their best. Thus, even though the potential for self-evaluation alone may not have been sufficient to produce a goal setting effect, one could argue that the goal setting effect found in the experimenter evaluation/goal condition was produced by the combination of the motivation produced by the potential for experimenter and self-evaluation. That is, the potential for experimenter evaluation alone provided one source of motivation, as shown by the difference between performance in the experimenter evaluation/do your best condition and performance in the no experimenter evaluation/do your best condition. Providing a goal to participants in the no experimenter evaluation condition provided another source of motivation (i.e., better performance under goal instructions than under do your best instructions), and the two sources of motivation combined to produce the goal setting effect (an additive model). Consistent with the argument that an additive model can account for these results, an overall 2 (experimenter evaluation vs. no experimenter evaluation) x 2 (do your best vs. goal instructions) analysis of variance yielded two robust main effects and no interaction.

White, Mitchell, and Bell (1977) also manipulated the potential for experimenter evaluation (experimenter evaluation versus no experimenter evaluation) and goal (goal instructions versus no goal instructions). Like White et al., (1995), they found main effects for experimenter evaluation and goal instructions, results that are consistent again with the interpretation that goal setting effects are produced by the additive effects of the potential for experimenter evaluation and self-evaluation. But based on our previous research (e.g., Harkins & Szymanski, 1988; Szymanski & Harkins, 1993), we argue that an additive model does not account for the goal setting effect, because concern over the potential for experimenter evaluation overpowers interest in the potential for self-evaluation. Thus, the goal setting effect is produced by the potential for experimenter evaluation alone.

We do not mean to suggest that the potential for self-evaluation does not motivate performance. To the contrary, we argue exactly that. We (Harkins, White, & Utman, 2000) propose that these participants "did their best" to see how this level of performance compared to the stringent goal. That is, they used the stringent goal as a "yardstick" against which they could compare their do-your-best performance. Thus, finding that the no experimenter evaluation participants performed at about the same level as the participants in the experimenter evaluation condition who were asked to do their best was no accident. In fact, we saw the same do-your-best level of performance produced by participants in the no experimenter evaluation/goal condition in several pilot studies, as well as twice more in Experiment 2 of White et al.'s research.

If no experimenter evaluation/goal participants were motivated to do their best so they could compare their performance to a stringent criterion, neither the striving instructions nor the fact that the criterion was delivered before performance should matter. The striving instructions should not matter because it is the potential for self-evaluation that motivates the participants, not the experimenter's instructions to strive. And when the criterion is delivered (before versus after performance) should not matter either, because the participants are simply doing their best to see how their performance compares to the criterion. Thus, a stringent criterion should serve as a yardstick in Szymanski and Harkins' (1987) "social comparison paradigm," just as it did in White et al.'s (1995) goal setting research.

Harkins, White, and Utman (2000) tested this hypothesis in an experiment (Experiment 1) in which participants were asked to generate as many uses as possible for a common object (e.g., Szymanski & Harkins, 1987; White et al., 1995). They were told either that the experimenter would count the number of uses that they had generated at the end of the session (experimenter evaluation), and then add these uses to a box containing the uses generated by previous participants, or that they should add their uses to this box before the experimenter entered the room (no experimenter evaluation). Participants were then given one of three instructional sets. One-third of the participants were asked simply to generate as many uses as possible (do your best). In the other two conditions, a criterion was provided. One-third of the participants were told that at the end of the experiment, they would be informed how many uses were generated in a previous experiment by someone at the 90th percentile of this distribution (stringent criterion). The final one-third of the participants were told that at the end of the experiment, they would be informed how many uses were generated by someone at the 30th percentile of this distribution (lenient criterion).

The choice of these stringent and lenient criteria was based on the results of a preliminary study. In that study, participants were given the use-generation instructions described above, after which the concept of percentile rankings was explained to them. Thinking they were about to perform the task, participants then estimated what their percentile rank would be if the other participants were students at their school. The results revealed no differences between the percentile ranks assigned by participants given experimenter evaluation and no experimenter evaluation instructions. The overall mean was 60%, with a range from the 30th percentile to the 100th percentile. The 30th percentile was chosen as the lenient criterion, and the 90th percentile was chosen as the stringent criterion, because these percentile ranks were equidistant from the mean percentile rank.

As can be seen in Table 6, the results of this experiment showed that when experimenter evaluation was possible, participants performed at the same level when they were given no criterion, a lenient criterion, or a

Table 6. Mean uses for a "knife": Exp. 1, Harkins et al. (2000)

	Do Your Best	Stringent Criterion (90th%)	Lenient Criterion (30th %)
Experimenter Evaluation	28.5_a	26.8_a	29.5_a
No Experimenter Evaluation	20.5_b	29.2_a	17.8_b

Means that do not share a subscript are significantly different, $p < .05$.

stringent criterion. When experimenter evaluation was not possible, participants who were promised the score at the ninetieth percentile (stringent criterion) performed at the same level as participants subject to experimenter evaluation, whereas participants who were promised no criterion, or who were promised the score at the thirtieth percentile (lenient criterion), generated significantly fewer uses. Thus, we replicated the social loafing effect, and we also supported White et al.'s (1995) proposal that a lenient criterion would be rejected as a valid means of self-evaluation. But we were most interested in the fact that participants in the no experimenter evaluation/stringent criterion (90th percentile) condition performed at the same level as participants in the experimenter evaluation/do your best condition (a do-your-best level of performance). Thus, consistent with the yardstick hypothesis, providing a stringent criterion appeared to motivate participants to the same extent as no experimenter evaluation participants were motivated by White et al.'s stringent goal.

One could argue, perhaps, for another interpretation of the no experimenter evaluation/stringent criterion (90th percentile) finding. Instead of using the stringent criterion as a yardstick, participants in this condition may have felt that their performance was at the ninetieth percentile. But, after performing the task, these participants were asked the number of uses they believed would correspond to performance at the ninetieth percentile. They reported a mean of 52.17 uses, a level significantly higher their actual level of performance ($p < .05$). This suggests that they did not believe their performance was at the ninetieth percentile.

In addition, in another experiment (Utman & Harkins, 1994), instead of providing the score as information in which they might be interested, we asked participants to strive to reach the score represented by performance at the 90th percentile. We found that participants subject to experimenter evaluation performed significantly better when asked to strive to reach this level of performance than when the score was to be provided as information in which they might be interested. In fact, these experimenter evaluation/striving participants performed significantly better than participants in the experimenter evaluation/do your best condition, a "goal setting effect." If these participants believed that their performance was already at the 90th percentile, there would be no reason for them to work harder when asked to strive than when promised the score as a piece of information. No experimenter evaluation/striving participants once again performed at the same level as participants in the experimenter evaluation/do your best condition. Thus, these findings are consistent with the yardstick interpretation.

However, a more convincing case for the yardstick interpretation could be made if we directly manipulated whether or not the yardstick (criterion) provided a valid means of self-evaluation, and showed that the do-your-best effect occurred when the criterion was informative, but did not occur when it was not. Hypothesis III of Festinger's (1954) theory of social comparison proposes that "the tendency to compare oneself with some other specific person decreases as the difference between his opinion or ability and one's own increases" (p. 120). This hypothesis suggests that criteria based on the performances of individuals whose abilities differ greatly from our own are seen as uninformative (e.g., a person whose score falls at the 90th percentile as in the previous experiment). However, Wood (1989) reviewed work showing that people are interested in comparing themselves to high scoring others, because high-scorers provide information about the entire range of performance. Thus, even though participants in our experiment were promised a score high above the average (ninetieth percentile), Wood's (1989) review suggests that they should have found this stringent criterion informative.

In our research, whether the criteria were stringent (e.g., previous experiment; White et al., 1995) or "average" (e.g., Szymanski & Harkins, 1987), participants believed those criteria were based on the performance of other students at the same university, taking the same course, at about the same time. Thus, the students on whose performances the criteria were based should have seemed highly similar to the participants themselves. According to Wood's (1989) review, people prefer to compare their abilities to those of others that are generally similar to them in just this way. As Wood wrote: "people choose to compare themselves with others who are similar on even unrelated surrounding dimensions and the degree of similarity on surrounding dimensions determines the impact of comparisons that are presented by the environment" (p. 238). If the yardstick explanation accounts for the do-your-best effect, then comparison of one's performance to criteria based on the performances of others that are dissimilar would not provide a meaningful criterion for comparison. Consequently, there would be no valid basis for self-evaluation and the do-your-best effect should be eliminated.

To test this hypothesis, participants in this experiment (Harkins, White, & Utman, 2000, Experiment 2) performed the same task as before, but were promised criteria based on the performance of similar or dissimilar others. For similar others, as in our previous research, we used the participants' fellow students. For dissimilar others, we selected two groups, namely 9th graders and 3rd-year Ph.D. students. The former group fell below the undergraduates in both age and academic accomplishment, whereas the latter fell above. Pretesting showed that participants believed that 9th graders could generate significantly fewer uses, and that 3rd-year Ph.D. students could generate significantly more uses, than the participants themselves could generate in twelve minutes. However, these performance differences were not what made criteria involving these groups uninformative. After all, the previous experiment showed that participants found the performance of a person whose score fell at the ninetieth percentile informative. But that criterion was based on the performance of a fellow undergraduate, taking the same class, etc., and it was this general similarity that made the criterion informative. It is the lack of general similarity that makes criteria based on the performance of 9th graders and 3rd-year Ph.D. students uninformative, whether they seem capable of generating fewer (9th graders) or more (3rd-year Ph.D. students) uses than the participants.

Once again participants were led to believe that their performances either would (experimenter evaluation) or would not (no experimenter evaluation) be evaluated by the experimenter. Crossed with this manipulation, participants were asked to do their best (do your best), or they were asked to do their best and told that afterwards they would learn the average performance of other undergraduates at their university (similar-undergraduate criterion), the average performance of 9th graders (dissimilar-9th grader criterion), or the average performance of 3rd-year Ph.D. students (dissimilar-Ph.D. criterion).

In this experiment, we replicated the social loafing effect: Participants in the experimenter evaluation/do your best condition produced more uses for the knife than did participants in the no experimenter evaluation/do your best condition. We also replicated Szymanski and Harkins' (1987) do-your-best finding: No experimenter evaluation participants who could self-evaluate by comparing their performances to the average performance of their fellow undergraduates (similar) produced as many uses as did the experimenter evaluation/do your best participants.

However, this do-your-best level of performance was produced by participants in the no experimenter evaluation condition only when the criterion was based on the performance of similar others. When the criterion was based on the performance of dissimilar others, whether 9th graders or 3rd-year Ph.D. students, the performance of no experimenter evaluation participants dropped significantly below that of experimenter evaluation/do your best participants. We believe that the participants were not motivated to do their best because criteria based on the performance of dissimilar others did not provide a valid means of self-evaluation. Performances were not affected by the validity of the criterion when the participants were subject to experimenter evaluation. The experimenter asked participants to do their best and they followed those instructions, producing a do-your-best level of performance whether the criterion was based on the performance of similar or dissimilar others.

Taken together, the results from these experiments support the argument that participants in White et al.'s (1995) no experimenter evaluation/goal condition used the stringent criterion as a yardstick against which they could compare their do-your-best level of performance rather than as a level of performance that they were to try to achieve. If the criterion were used as a yardstick, neither the fact that it was delivered before performance, nor the striving instructions should matter. Consistent with this interpretation, in the first experiment participants in the no experimenter evaluation condition produced a do-your-best effect despite the fact that the criterion was presented after performance and only as a piece of information in which they might be interested. In the second experiment, we directly manipulated whether or not the yardstick provided a valid means of self-evaluation. Comparison of one's performance to a criterion based on the performances of others that are dissimilar should not provide a valid basis for self-evaluation, and, thus, the do-your-best effect should be eliminated. Consistent with this argument, we found a do-your-best effect when the criterion was valid (based on the performance of similar others), but not when the criterion was invalid (based on the performance of dissimilar others).

Thus, these experiments suggest that the potential for self-evaluation motivated the do-your-best performance of White et al.'s no experimenter evaluation/goal participants. These findings are consistent with the notion that goal setting effects are produced by the additive effects of experimenter evaluation and self-evaluation. That is, experimenter evaluation represents one source of motivation, and supplying a goal to participants represents another source (the potential for self-evaluation). It is the additive effect of these two motivation sources (experimenter plus self) that is responsible for the goal setting effect. However, once again we (Harkins, et al., 2000) argue that the potential for self-evaluation does not contribute at all to White et al.'s goal setting effect. Instead, based on the research that suggests that concern over the potential for evaluation by the experimenter supersedes interest in the potential for self-evaluation (e.g., Harkins & Szymanski, 1988; Szymanski & Harkins, 1993), we argue the goal setting effect was produced by the potential for experimenter evaluation alone.

We reasoned that if experimenter evaluation alone is important, then the validity of the criterion (the goal) should not matter. If the experimenter has directed them to strive to reach the goal, participants should attempt to do so. So, whether participants in the experimenter evaluation condition were given an invalid criterion (goal based on the performance of dissimilar others) or a valid criterion (goal based on the performance of similar others), they should produce a goal setting effect (i.e., performance greater than that found in the experimenter evaluation/do your best condition). In contrast, if the goal setting effect requires motivation stemming from the potential for self-evaluation (additive model), then there should be a goal setting effect when the criterion is valid, but not when it is invalid, because in the latter case the contribution of self-evaluation has been eliminated.

We pitted the experimenter evaluation only interpretation against the additive model in a second way. Participants in the experimenter evaluation/do your best condition outperform participants in the no experimenter evaluation/do your best condition because of the potential for experimenter evaluation. There is no opportunity for self-evaluation, because the participants have no criterion against which to compare their performance. The additive model would suggest that the improvement from this "do best" level of performance to the level required for a goal setting effect reflects the influence of motivation stemming from the potential for self-evaluation provided by the goal. No striving instruction should be required. Whether or not the experimenter asks the participants to strive, the goal provides a criterion for self-evaluation. In contrast, the experimenter evaluation only interpretation suggests that it is simply the experimenter's instruction to strive to reach the stringent goal that produces the additional performance. Without this striving instruction, there can be no goal setting effect, only a "do best" effect.

To test these predictions, we (Harkins, White, & Utman, 2000, Experiment 3) crossed a manipulation of the experimenter's demands (striving instructions) with a manipulation of the potential for self-evaluation (criterion validity). Once again, participants were asked to generate uses for an object. The basic design for the experiment was a 2 (striving vs. no striving) x 2 (criterion based on the performance of similar vs. dissimilar others) x 2 (experimenter evaluation vs. no experimenter evaluation) + 2 (experimenter evaluation/do your best vs. no experimenter evaluation/do your best). Participants in the 2 x 2 x 2 design were provided a criterion of 40 uses before they began performing. Half of them were asked to strive to achieve this criterion (striving instructions), whereas the other half were merely told that they might be interested in knowing that our prior research showed that this number of uses could be produced (no striving instructions). Crossed with this manipulation, half of the participants were told that the criterion was based on the performance of other undergraduates at their university (similar others), whereas the other half were told that the criterion was based on the performance of 3rd-year Ph.D. students (dissimilar others). Crossed with these manipulations, half of the participants were led to believe that they would be evaluated by the experimenter, whereas the other half were led to believe that they would not be evaluated.

Participants in the two do your best conditions were not provided with a criterion. They simply were asked to do their best to generate as many uses as they could on the task. Half of these participants were led to believe that they would be evaluated by the experimenter, whereas the other half were led to believe that they would not be evaluated. As shown in Table 7, these participants replicated the social loafing effect: Participants in the experimenter evaluation condition outperformed participants in the no experimenter evaluation condition (e.g., Latané, Williams, & Harkins, 1979).

In both the striving and the no striving conditions, we predicted a replication of our previous finding that participants in the no experimenter evaluation condition who were given a criterion based on the performance of similar others (valid criterion) would produce a do-your-best effect (performance equivalent to that found in the experimenter evaluation/do your best condition), whereas participants who were given a criterion based on the performance of dissimilar others (invalid criterion)

Table 7. Mean uses for a "knife": Exp. 3, Harkins et al.

	Do Your Best	Striving Instructions Similar	Striving Instructions Dissimilar	No Striving Instructions Similar	No Striving Instructions Dissimilar
Experimenter Evaluation	31.6	39.32‡	39.32‡	32.90*	32.58*
No Experimenter Evaluation	19.7	32.05*	22.53	30.21*	22.90

* = do-your-best effect ‡ = goal setting effect

would perform significantly worse. Consistent with this prediction, no experimenter evaluation participants who were given striving instructions and a valid criterion performed at the same level as did participants in the experimenter evaluation/do your best condition, whereas no experimenter evaluation participants who were given striving instructions and provided an invalid criterion produced significantly fewer uses than did participants in the experimenter evaluation/do your best condition. The same pattern of results was obtained in the no striving conditions. No experimenter evaluation participants who were given a valid criterion performed at the same level as participants in the experimenter evaluation/do your best condition, whereas participants provided an invalid criterion performed significantly worse than the do-your-best level.

These findings set the stage for our tests of the experimenter evaluation only versus the additive model explanations for White et al.'s (1995) goal setting effect. In the striving conditions, the experimenter evaluation only explanation predicted significant goal setting effects regardless of criterion validity, whereas the additive model predicted a goal setting effect only when the criterion was valid. Our findings support the former interpretation: Participants who were urged to reach a stringent criterion produced goal setting effects regardless of criterion validity. In fact, the means for the valid and invalid criterion conditions were identical, and each was significantly greater than the mean for the experimenter evaluation/do your best condition.

In the no striving conditions, the experimenter evaluation only interpretation predicted that participants subject to the potential for experimenter evaluation would perform at the level of participants in the experimenter evaluation/do your best condition (do-your-best effect) regardless of criterion validity, whereas the additive model predicted a do-your-best level of performance when the criterion was invalid, but a goal setting effect when it was valid. Once again, the results favored the former interpretation. Whether the criterion was valid or invalid, participants produced no more than the do-your-best level.

Thus, when participants were asked to strive to reach the criterion, whether the goal was based on the performance of similar or dissimilar others, participants subject to the evaluation of the experimenter produced the same level of performance, a goal setting effect. Eliminating the potential for self-evaluation through the use of an invalid criterion left the goal setting effect unaffected. In the no striving conditions, participants subject to experimenter evaluation who were provided a criterion based on the performance of similar others (valid criterion) performed at the same "do your best" level as participants provided an invalid criterion. In this case, adding the potential for self-evaluation had no effect. These findings provide strong support for the argument that concern over the potential for experimenter evaluation supplants interest in self-evaluation.

Taken together, these results suggest that three conditions must be met to produce goal setting effects: Participants must anticipate external evaluation, they must be given a stringent criterion, and they must be urged to strive to achieve that criterion. Unless all of these conditions are met, no goal setting effects will be obtained. In addition, in the overwhelming majority of goal setting research, simple tasks have been used. Given these features, the conditions incorporated in the goal setting paradigm fall in the three-way design as depicted in Table 8.

Table 8. Three-Way Design

	Simple Task		Complex Task	
	Do Your Best	Stringent Goal	Do Your Best	Stringent Goal
Experimenter Evaluation	SL,GS	GS		
No Experimenter Evaluation	SL			

SL = Social Loafing GS = Goal Setting

Thus, when participants are asked to do their best or are urged to strive for stringent goals on simple tasks, it is the potential for experimenter evaluation that eliminates social loafing and produces goal setting effects, respectively. To incorporate performance on complex tasks in our analysis, we next turn to research on social facilitation.

SOCIAL FACILITATION

Given that Triplett published the first experiment on social facilitation in 1898, one might imagine that the relevant issues in this area would have long since been settled. However, this is far from the case. In the years following Triplett's work, researchers found that the presence of others sometimes facilitated performance, and other times debilitated it. In 1952 Asch summarized the research in this area by noting that the so-called explanations represented only restatements of the results, explaining nothing. In 1965 Zajonc brought some order to the muddle by suggesting that the "mere presence" of others leads to increased drive, which enhances the tendency to emit dominant responses. If correct, as in the case of simple or well-learned tasks, the facilitation of the dominant response leads to improved performance. If incorrect, as in the case of complex or unlearned tasks, performance is debilitated.

Over the next decade, this drive account was seen as the most parsimonious theoretical explanation of facilitation effects (e.g., Geen & Gange, 1977), although there was controversy over whether it was the mere presence of the others that increased drive (Zajonc, 1965, 1980) or the fact that these others were associated with evaluation and/or competition (Cottrell, 1972). However, in a review of the facilitation literature since 1977, Geen (1989) concluded that "today such a confident assertion of the primacy of the drive theoretical approach is not warranted. Instead, several sophisticated alternatives have found considerable support in experimental studies" (p. 17).

Geen (1989) organized these theoretical approaches into three broad classes. One class of theories incorporated those approaches that continue to rely on the notion that the presence of others increases drive (e.g., distraction/conflict, Baron, 1986; evaluation apprehension, Cottrell, 1972; social monitoring, Guerin & Innes, 1982; compresence, Zajonc, 1980). The second class of theories included those approaches that suggest that "the presence of others creates either explicit or implicit demands on the person to behave in some specific way" (Geen, 1989, p. 31) (e.g., self-presentation, Bond, 1982; self-awareness, Carver & Scheier, 1981), whereas the third class consisted of Baron's (1986) information processing view of distraction/conflict, which proposes that the presence of others affects focus of attention and information processing.

None of these theories "appears to command the high ground as drive theory did in the 1960s and 1970s" (Geen, 1989, p. 43), and the exact mechanism(s) through which social facilitation works remain(s) unknown. Nonetheless, each of these theories focuses on the effects of one or both of the same two features of the facilitation paradigm: the mere presence of others, and/or the potential for evaluation that these others represent. Harkins (1987) argued that the findings not only from research on social facilitation but also from research on social loafing (e.g., Latané, Williams, & Harkins, 1979) can be represented in the 2 x 2 that results from the crossing of these two variables. In the 2 x 2 design, mere presence is manipulated by asking participants to work alone, or along side another person working independently on the same task (coaction). Evaluation is manipulated by arranging the situation so that the participant's performance either can or cannot be compared to that of others. In virtually all loafing research, the performances of participants in a coaction/evaluation cell have been compared to the performances of coacting participants whose outputs were pooled (coaction/no evaluation). In facilitation research (e.g., Klinger, 1969; Sanders, Baron, & Moore, 1978), the performances of coactors whose outputs can be evaluated (coaction/evaluation) are compared against the performances of single participants whose outputs can also be evaluated (alone/evaluation). Viewed in this way, the experimental conditions that have been included in loafing and facilitation research fall into three cells of the 2 x 2 design. The fourth cell, alone/no evaluation, had been run in no coaction study using either the facilitation or loafing paradigms before Harkins's (1987) research.

Using two different, simple tasks (use-generation and vigilance), Harkins (1987) found main effects for both mere presence and evaluation in this design. Coactors outperformed participants working alone, a "mere presence" effect, and participants whose outputs could be evaluated outperformed participants whose outputs could not be. Though mere presence and concern about evaluation have often been pitted against each other as rival explanations for facilitation effects, Markus (1981) pointed out that both factors could contribute to facilitation effects. In these experiments, both did, and in an additive fashion.

These experiments suggest that loafing and facilitation effects are complementary. In social facilitation research, when participants coact, their outputs can be compared and they work harder than participants working alone. In social loafing research, when participants coact, their outputs cannot be evaluated, and they put out less effort than participants whose outputs can be compared. In both cases, evaluation is central. In social facilitation, working together enhances evaluation potential; in social loafing, working together reduces it.

This research (Harkins, 1987) was limited to the simple, well-learned tasks that have been used in most loafing research. On tasks like rope pulling, shouting, pumping air, and vigilance, the potential for evaluation leads to better performance. However, when complex tasks are used in facilitation research (e.g., Martens & Landers, 1972; Seta, Paulus, & Schkade, 1976), the potential for evaluation leads to poorer performance. This suggests that if, instead of the simple tasks typically used in loafing research, a complex task were used, participants in the coaction/no evaluation (loafing) condition should perform better than participants in the coaction/evaluation condition, and this is exactly what was found by Jackson and Williams (1985). Participants in a coaction/evaluation condition performed better on simple mazes than participants whose outputs were pooled (coaction/no evaluation), a loafing effect, but when the mazes were complex, the pattern was reversed. Participants whose outputs were pooled performed better than participants whose individual outputs could be evaluated. Sanna (1992) found the same pattern of results using the "Remote Associate Test" (RAT), which requires participants to examine sets of three words (e.g., "elephant," "lapse," and "vivid") and to generate a fourth word that is somehow related to each word of the triad ("memory"). On simple RAT items, Sanna (1992) found that participants in a coaction/evaluation condition solved more items correctly than participants in a coaction/no evaluation condition, a loafing effect. However, on complex RAT items, Sanna (1992) found that participants in the coaction/no evaluation condition solved more items than coaction/evaluation participants.

This work suggests that the same evaluation-mediated process produces social loafing and social facilitation effects. The potential for evaluation improves performance on simple tasks and debilitates it on complex tasks. But evaluation by whom? Social facilitation researchers have referred to each of the potential sources of evaluation in their accounts of coaction effects (e.g., coactor evaluation, Klinger, 1969; self-evaluation, Sanders, Baron, & Moore, 1978; experimenter evaluation, Seta, Paulus, & Schkade, 1976). However, there is no compelling evidence that these accounts have captured the motivational structure of the experiments that they were meant to describe. For example, although Sanders et al.'s (1978) explanation relies on the potential for self-evaluation, there was also the potential for evaluation by the experimenter. Our research suggests that, under these circumstances, concern over the potential for evaluation by the experimenter would supersede interest in self-evaluation. Thus, we would argue that, at the least, the potential for experimenter evaluation is sufficient to produce social facilitation effects.

In facilitation research, as in loafing research, participants are asked to do their best. Thus, social facilitation fits in the three-way design as depicted below. Social loafing and social facilitation are paired in the table to reflect their complementary relationship.

Table 9. Three-Way Design

	Simple Task		Complex Task	
	Do Your Best	Stringent Goal	Do Your Best	Stringent Goal
Experimenter Evaluation	GS,SL&SF	GS	SL&SF	
No Experimenter Evaluation	SF&SF		SL&SF	

SL = Social Loafing SF = Social Facilitation GS = Goal Setting

INTRINSIC MOTIVATION AND ACHIEVEMENT GOAL THEORY

In a recent paper, Utman (1997) noted that researchers "involved with intrinsic motivation (e.g., Deci & Ryan, 1987), ego involvement (e.g., DeCharms, 1968; Nicholls, 1984), and achievement goal theories (e.g., Elliott & Dweck, 1988) have all proposed theories which describe how the induction of different motivational states may lead to disparate responses to task demands and consequently to different performance outcomes." These theories propose a distinction between two major classes of motivational states:

> "an intrinsic motivation state in which individuals are focused on learning and mastering task skills;" and
> "an extrinsic motivational state, in which individuals feel pressure and focus on demonstrating that they have high ability" (Utman, 1997, p. 170).

These theories suggest that "intrinsic or learning motivation leads to flexible, creative responding that allows a focus on the task at hand, and consequently to better performance" (p. 170). On the other hand, the theories suggest that the extrinsic motivational state "leads to feelings of pressure, distraction from task engagement, and deteriorated performance" (p. 170).

Consistent with this theorizing, in his meta-analysis, Utman (1997) found that learning (mastery) goals led to better performance than did performance goals. However, the results also indicated that this learning goal advantage was limited to relatively complex tasks. This finding suggests that these research traditions fall in the complex half of the three-way design. In addition, the participants in these research traditions are given "do your best" instructions. The terms, learning and performance goals, refer to orientations toward performance, not to specific levels of attainment that the participants are urged to achieve.

Finally, I would argue that, at the least, manipulations of the potential for external evaluation provide one means of inducing performance goals (extrinsic motivation). In fact, many of the studies in Utman's meta-analysis explicitly incorporate manipulations of the potential for external evaluation. For example, in the experiment that produced the single largest effect size in the analysis, Amabile (1979) told participants in an extrinsic motivation condition that their collages would be evaluated in detail by five artists, whereas participants in the intrinsic motivation condition were told that their collages would not be used as a source of data. Elliott and Dweck (1988) told children in the performance goal condition that their performance was being taped and would be normatively evaluated by experts, whereas in the learning goal condition, nothing was said about evaluation of their performance.

Thus, the role of the potential for external evaluation seems quite clear in these manipulations. However, the role of the learning goal manipulation is not. All that may be required to produce the "learning goal" advantage is the absence of the potential for external evaluation. For example, Bartis, Szymanski and Harkins (1988) asked one-half of their participants to generate as many uses as possible without regard to creativity, whereas the other half of the participants were asked to generate uses that were as creative as possible without regard to number. Replicating previous findings (e.g., Harkins & Jackson, 1985), when given number instructions, participants who were subject to experimenter evaluation generated more uses than participants who were not. However, when given creativity instructions, participants who were subject to experimenter evaluation generated uses that were less creative than participants who were not.

Thus, manipulating the potential for experimenter evaluation alone produced a pattern of results that is consistent with the findings of the achievement goal/intrinsic motivation literature (e.g., Amabile, 1979). The findings of the Bartis et al. (1988) research are also consistent with findings in the social facilitation/social loafing literature. That is, Jackson and Williams (1985) and Sanna (1992) found that the potential for experimenter evaluation improved performance on a simple task (simple mazes and easy RAT items), but debilitated performance on a complex one (complex mazes and difficult RAT items). Likewise, Bartis et al. (1988) found that performance on a simple task (number instructions) was improved by the potential for experimenter evaluation, whereas performance on a complex task (creativity instructions) was debilitated. Viewed in this way, the findings in the intrinsic motivation/achievement goal literature are simply replications of the findings for complex tasks in the social facilitation literature. Thus, I would argue that these lines of research can be represented in the three-way design as shown in Table 10.

Table 10. Three-Way Design

	Simple Task		Complex Task	
	Do Your Best	Stringent Goal	Do Your Best	Stringent Goal
Experimenter Evaluation	SL&SF,GS	GS	SL&SF EM,PG	
No Experimenter Evaluation	SL&SF		SL&SF IM,LG	

SL = Social Loafing SF = Social Facilitation GS = Goal Setting
EM = Extrinsic Motivation PG = Performance Goal
IM = Intrinsic Motivation LG = Learning Goal

As can be seen, this account suggests that none of the traditions has provided findings definitive enough to claim that its paradigm encompasses the complex task/goal conditions in the three-way design. Researchers in the goal setting tradition have examined the effects of goal setting on what they termed complex tasks and found improved performance, although the effects were attenuated compared to those found on simple tasks (Locke & Latham, 1990a). However, in the main, data for these complex tasks were collected in real world settings in which participants had extensive experience with the tasks. Given a great deal of experience, the tasks may not have been "complex" for the participants. In addition, other goal setting researchers have suggested that setting goals on complex, laboratory tasks may not improve performance, and, in fact, may lead to decrements in performance. For example, DeShon, Brown, and Greenis (1996) have argued "that setting difficult, specific performance goals on complex tasks often has little positive effect on performance and has even resulted in performance decrements (Earley, Connolly, & Ekegren, 1989; Kanfer & Ackerman, 1989; Latham & Locke, 1991; Wood, Bandura, & Bailey, 1990)" (p. 595). It is certainly the case that researchers in the achievement goal/intrinsic motivation tradition would argue strongly that stringent goals should undermine performance on complex tasks, because, if anything, goals would produce greater feelings of pressure than "do best" instructions. However, there is no research published in these traditions that demonstrates this effect.

REPLICATION EXPERIMENT

To demonstrate that the pattern of findings predicted in the three-way design by these different research traditions can be replicated in this three-way design, we conducted an experiment using the Remote Associates Task (RAT) described previously (Sanna, 1992). This experiment also allowed us to examine the effects of goal setting on performance on complex tasks like those used in the social facilitation and the achievement goal literatures. Half of the participants were told that the experimenter would determine how well they had performed at the end of the experimental session (experimenter evaluation). The other half were told that, at the end of the experimental session, they would be adding their booklets to an envelope containing the booklets of all of the previous participants (no experimenter evaluation). Crossed with the potential for experimenter evaluation, one-half of the participants were instructed to "do their best," whereas the other half were assigned a stringent goal. Participants in the goal conditions were told that their goals were based on the performances of previous participants in the same research, and so, the goals were valid. Crossed with experimenter evaluation and instructions, one-half of the participants were given 20 triads that pretesting how shown to be relatively simple, whereas the other half of the participants were given 20 triads that pretesting had shown to be difficult to solve.

The goals for the simple (solve 16) and difficult (solve ten) tasks were also selected on the basis of pretesting, so that equivalent proportions of the participants in the two conditions (simple, difficult) could be expected to achieve them. The triads were presented in booklets, one triad per page, and the participants were allowed to allocate the ten minutes they had to work on the task in any manner they saw fit. That is, they could spend as much of the time allotted as they wished on any single triad; they could skip triads; and they could go back later to work on a given triad. At the end of the ten minutes, the experimenter knocked on the door and either came in and scored their performance (experimenter evaluation) or waited for them to open the door after they put their booklet in the envelope supposedly containing the booklets of prior participants.

Each of the effects produced in the research paradigms of these traditions is replicated in this design, as shown in Table 11. The social loafing effect was replicated. Participants in the experimenter evaluation/do your best/simple condition solved more RAT items than participants in the no experimenter evaluation/do your best/simple condition. The typical goal setting effect (Locke & Latham, 1990a) was replicated. Participants in the experimenter evaluation/goal/simple condition solved significantly more RAT items than participants in the experimenter evaluation/do your best/simple condition. In addition, as

Table 11. Three-Way Design: Replication Experiment

	Simple Task		Complex Task	
	Do Your Best	Stringent Goal	Do Your Best	Stringent Goal
Experimenter Evaluation	12.7_a	16.0_b	3.1_c	3.1_c
No Experimenter Evaluation	9.0_d	12.5_a	5.9_e	3.1_c

Means that do not share a subscript are significantly different, $p < .05$

found by Harkins, White, and Utman (2000), the potential for self-evaluation alone (no experimenter evaluation/goal/simple) led only to a "do your best" effect (i.e., performance equal to that found in the experimenter evaluation/do your best/simple condition).

On the complex version of the RAT task, we see that the findings of Utman's (1997) meta-analysis are replicated. Participants in the experimenter evaluation/do your best/complex condition solved reliably fewer RAT items than participants who could not be evaluated by the experimenter (no experimenter evaluation/do your best/complex). Thus, a manipulation of the potential for experimenter evaluation alone was sufficient to produce the effect described in the intrinsic motivation/achievement goal literatures. The mere absence of the potential for external evaluation improved performance, at least in this paradigm. Finally, consistent with predictions from the achievement goal/intrinsic motivation literatures, providing goals on a complex task did not produce a goal setting effect in the experimenter evaluation condition. There is not the slightest hint of better performance by participants in the experimenter evaluation/goal/complex condition than by participants in the experimenter evaluation/do your best/complex condition. In fact, providing a goal to participants in the no experimenter evaluation/complex task condition significantly reduced the number of items that they solved, $p < .05$. A floor effect may account for the fact that a similar reduction was not seen in the experimenter evaluation/goal/complex task condition.

CONCLUSIONS

There are at least five research traditions that suggest that the potential for evaluation affects task performance: social loafing, goal setting, social facilitation, intrinsic motivation, and achievement goal theory. For the most part, these traditions do not take into account the findings obtained within the other traditions, nor the processes hypothesized to produce these findings. Our analysis suggests that the basic findings of each of these research traditions can be produced by manipulating only three variables: whether or not there is the potential for evaluation by the experimenter, whether the experimenter asks participants to do their best or to strive to achieve a stringent goal, and whether the task is simple or complex. Consistent with this analysis, in the RAT experiment in which we manipulated these three variables, we replicated the basic findings of each of the traditions.

Each of the traditions provides a theoretical account for the findings generated within the context of that particular tradition. In some cases, the three-variable account suggests an alternative process. For example, Locke and Latham's (1990a) theory of goal setting would suggest that goal setting effects stem from the potential for self-evaluation provided by the opportunity to compare one's performance to the stringent criterion represented by the goal. The current analysis suggests that the potential for self-evaluation does not contribute at all to goal setting effects. Instead, goal setting effects depend on the potential for experimenter evaluation. In addition, the present analysis suggests that goal setting effects will be obtained only on simple tasks. On complex tasks, stringent goals do not facilitate performance, and, in fact, may debilitate it.

In other cases, the current account reduces the ambiguity about which source(s) is (are) responsible for the production of the performance effects. So, for example, although it has been clear that the potential for evaluation was involved in the elimination of social loafing effects and the production of social facilitation effects, it was not clear which source(s) of evaluation produced these effects. The current analysis shows that it is the potential for experimenter evaluation that is responsible for the elimination of social loafing in the original paradigm (e.g., Latané, et al., 1979; Williams, et al., 1980; Harkins et al., 1981), and that, at the least, the potential for experimenter evaluation is sufficient to produce social facilitation effects in the coaction paradigm (e.g., Jackson & Williams, 1985; Sanna, 1992).

Finally, in the case of intrinsic motivation and the achievement goal literature, this analysis suggests that the accounts of performance effects provided by these theories require elaboration. For example, although researchers in the intrinsic motivation tradition have conducted a great deal of research that examines the effects of extrinsic/intrinsic motivation on task interest, they have conducted much less research on their effects on task performance. In those cases in which they have examined performance effects, they have had little to say about the process involved. For example, Flink, Boggiano, and Barret (1990) write: "To the extent that students feel controlled to achieve a given performance standard, their sense of self-determination should be lowered, thereby producing performance deterioration" (p. 916). Exactly how this happens is left unspecified. Other researchers suggest that intrinsic motivation leads to an active learning process, whereas extrinsic motivation leads to passive learning (e.g., Benware & Deci, 1984; Conti, Amabile, & Pollak, 1995; Grolnick & Ryan, 1987). Exactly how these differences in learning style are translated into performance differences is left unspecified. Not only do these accounts have little to say about the process, they also leave us with the following problem: At the same time that the loss of one's sense of self-determination or a passive learning style apparently debilitates performance on complex tasks, it facilitates performance on simple ones.

Researchers in the achievement goal tradition have provided more detail about the process intervening between manipulation of the potential for evaluation and the task outcome on complex tasks. For example, Dweck and her colleagues argue that performance goals lead individuals to seek to "maintain positive judgments of their ability and avoid negative judgments by seeking to prove, validate, or document their ability and not discredit it" (Elliott & Dweck, 1988, p. 5). On the other hand, a focus on learning goals leads individuals to seek to "increase their ability or master new tasks" (Elliott & Dweck, 1988, p. 5). Thus learning goals "which focus individuals on increasing their ability over time, will promote the mastery-oriented response to obstacles: strategy formulation, positive affect, and sustained performance" (p. 5).

The achievement goal approach distinguishes between two types of goals, learning versus performance, but does not explicitly address the issue of the source of evaluation. Of course, we argue that the potential for external evaluation motivates participants to focus on performance goals, undermining their performance on complex tasks. However, Szymanski and Harkins (1992) have shown that the potential for self-evaluation also debilitates performance on complex tasks. Like Bartis, Szymanski, and Harkins (1988), we (Szymanski & Harkins, 1992) asked participants either to generate as many uses as possible for an object without regard to their creativity, or to generate uses that were as creative as possible without regard to their number, but, in this experiment, we eliminated the potential for experimenter evaluation. Crossed with the creativity/number manipulation, participants were either promised a criterion at the end of their performance (number: the average number of uses generated by previous participants; creativity: a list of uses produced by previous participants ranked in order of creativity) or were told that a criterion would not be forthcoming.

Consistent with previous research (Szymanski & Harkins, 1987), we found that participants asked to generate as many uses as possible produced more uses when promised a criterion (self-evaluation) than when they were not. However, when asked to be as creative as possible, the uses were more creative when people were not promised a criterion than when they were. Thus, as in the RAT experiment, the potential for self-evaluation improved performance on the simple task (number), but damaged it on the complex one (creativity).

Of course, these findings are not inconsistent with achievement goal theory. The results suggest that other-referenced criteria focus participants on performance goals even though the source of evaluation is the self and the criterion is provided only as a piece of information. Perhaps the fact that the criterion was based on the performance of previous participants led the participants to feel pressured and to focus on demonstrating to themselves that they had high ability. Achievement goal theory focuses specifically on the positive effects of the opportunity for participants to monitor their progress across time. That is, while social criteria lead participants to focus on performance goals, the opportunity to compare one's performance on one trial to one's performance on previous trials leads to the adoption of learning goals, yielding improved performance. However, once again, achievement goal theory does not specify the source of evaluation. Our research would suggest that it is unlikely that this improvement would occur if the potential for evaluation by an external source were salient whether the criterion was self-referenced or other-referenced.

In addition, any explanation that relies solely on self-improvement to account for learning goal effects will be incomplete. In our research such comparisons were not available because the participants performed only a single trial which did not allow participants to track their progress across time. In fact, in at least eight of the 24 papers that Utman (1997) reviewed in his meta-analysis, participants took part in single trial experiments in which they were not provided with any means of self-evaluation. Nonetheless, participants in the "learning goal" conditions outperformed participants in the "performance goal" conditions (unweighted d for complex tasks = .71). And once again, this approach also must account for the finding that the potential for evaluation (whether by experimenter or self) facilitates performance on simple tasks.

Whether or not the present analysis ultimately proves capable of accounting for the findings of these five research traditions, at the least it can serve a useful heuristic function by providing a common starting point for our effort to integrate these areas. In addition, this analysis has already identified considerable areas of overlap, which suggests that there is substantial potential for a successful integration. It remains to be seen whether or not this potential will be realized.

REFERENCES

Amabile, T. (1979). Effects of external evaluation on artistic creativity. *Journal of Personality and Social Psychology, 37*, 221-233.

Asch, S. (1952). *Social Psychology*. New York: Holt, Rinehart & Winston.

Bandura, A. (1986). *Social foundations of thought and action: A social cognitive theory*. Englewood Cliffs, NJ: Prentice-Hall.

Baron, R. (1986). Distraction-conflict theory: Progress and problems. In L. Berkowitz (Ed.), *Advances in experimental social psychology* (Vol. 19, pp. 1-40). New York: Academic Press.

Bartis, S., Szymanski, K., & Harkins, S. (1988). Evaluation of performance: A two-edged knife. *Personality and Social Psychology Bulletin, 14*, 242-251.

Benware, C., & Deci, E. (1984). Quality of learning with an active versus passive motivational set. *American Educational Research Journal, 21*, 755-765.

Bond, C. (1982). Social facilitation: A self-presentational view. *Journal of Personality and Social Psychology, 42*, 1042-1050.

Brickner, M. A., Harkins, S. G., & Ostrom, T. M. (1986). Effects of personal involvement: Thought-provoking implications for social loafing. *Journal of Personality and Social Psychology, 51*, 763-769.

Carver, C., & Scheier, M. (1981). The self-attention-induced feedback loop and social facilitation. *Journal of Experimental Social Psychology, 17*, 545-568.

Conti, R., Amabile, T., & Pollak, S. (1995). The positive impact of creative activity: Effects of creative task engagement and motivational focus on college students' learning. *Personality and Social Psychology Bulletin, 2*, 1107-1116.

Cottrell, N. (1972). Social facilitation. In C. McClintock (Ed.), *Experimental social psychology* (pp.185-236). New York: Holt, Rinehart & Winston.

DeCharms, R. (1968). *Personal causation: The internal affective determinants of behavior*. New York: Academic Press.

Deci, E., & Ryan, R. (1987). The support of autonomy and the control of behavior. *Journal of Personality and Social Psychology, 53*, 1024-1037.

DeShon, R., Brown, K., & Greenis, J. (1996). Does self-regulation require cognitive resources? Evaluation of resource allocation models of goal setting. *Journal of Applied Psychology, 81*, 595-608.

Earley, P., Connolly, T., & Ekegren, G. (1989). Goals, strategy development, and task performance: Some limits on the efficacy of goal setting. *Journal of Applied Psychology, 74*, 24-33.

Elliott, E., & Dweck, C. (1988). Goals: An approach to motivation and achievement. *Journal of Personality and Social Psychology, 54*, 5-12.

Festinger, L. (1954). A theory of social comparison processes. *Human Relations, 7*, 117-140.

Flink, C., Boggiano, A., & Barrett, M. (1990). Controlling teaching strategies: Undermining children's self-determination and performance. *Journal of Personality and Social Psychology, 59*, 916-924.

Geen, R. (1989). Alternative conceptions of social facilitation. In P. Paulus (Ed.), *Psychology of group influence* (pp. 15-51). Hillsdale, NJ: Erlbaum.

Geen, R., & Gange, J. (1977). Drive theory of social facilitation: Twelve years of theory and research. *Psychological Bulletin, 84*, 1267-1288.

Grolnick, W., & Ryan, R. (1987). Autonomy in children's learning: An experimental and individual difference investigation. *Journal of Personality and Social Psychology, 52*, 890-898.

Guerin, B., & Innes, J. (1982). Social facilitation and social monitoring: A new look at Zajonc's mere presence hypothesis. *British Journal of Social Psychology, 7*, 81-90.

Harkins, S. (1987). Social loafing and social facilitation. *Journal of Experimental Social Psychology, 23*, 1-18.

Harkins, S., & Jackson, J. (1985). The role of evaluation in eliminating social loafing.

Personality and Social Psychology Bulletin, *11*, 457-465.
Harkins, S., Latané, B., & Williams, K. (1980). Social loafing: Allocating effort or taking it easy? *Journal of Experimental Social Psychology*, *16*, 456-465.
Harkins, S., & Petty, R. (1982). Effects of task difficulty and task uniqueness on social loafing. *Journal of Personality and Social Psychology*, *43*, 1214-1229.
Harkins, S., & Szymanski, K. (1988). Social loafing and self-evaluation with an objective standard. *Journal of Experimental Social Psychology*, *24*, 354-365.
Harkins, S., White, P., & Utman, C. (2000). The role of internal and external sources of evaluation in motivating task performance. *Personality and Social Psychology Bulletin*, *26*, 100-117.
Jackson, J., & Williams, K. (1985). Social loafing on difficulty tasks: Working collectively can improve performance. *Journal of Personality and Social Psychology*, *49*, 937-942.
Kanfer, R., & Ackerman, P. (1989). Motivational and cognitive abilities: An integrative/aptitude-treatment interaction approach to skill acquisition. *Journal of Applied Psychology*, *74*, 657-690.
Karau, S., & Williams, K. (1993). Social loafing: A meta-analytic review and theoretical integration. *Journal of Personality and Social Psychology*, *65*, 681-706.
Kerr, N., & Bruun, S. (1981). Ringelmann revisited: Alternative explanations for the social loafing effect. *Personality and Social Psychology Bulletin*, *7*, 224-231.
Klinger, E. (1969). Feedback effects and social facilitation of vigilance performance: Mere coaction versus potential evaluation. *Psychonomic Science*, *14*, 161-162.
Latané, B., Williams, K., & Harkins, S. (1979). Many hands make light the work: The causes and consequences of social loafing. *Journal of Personality and Social Psychology*, *37*, 823-832.
Latham, G., & Locke, E. (1991). Self-regulation through goal setting. *Organizational Behavior and Human Decision Processes*, *50*, 212-247.
Locke, E., & Latham, G. (1990a). *A theory of goal setting and task performance.* Englewood Cliffs, N.J.: Prentice Hall.
Locke, E., & Latham, G. (1990b). Work motivation and satisfaction: Light at the end of the tunnel. *Psychological Science*, *1*, 240-246.
Markus, H. (1981). The drive for integration: Some comments. *Journal of Experimental Social Psychology*, *17*, 257-261.
Martens, R., & Landers, D. (1972). Evaluation potential as a determinant of coaction effects. *Journal of Experimental Social Psychology*, *8*, 347-359.
Nicholls, J. (1984). Achievement motivation: Conceptions of ability, subjective experience, task choice, and performance. *Psychological Review*, *91*, 328-346.
Sanders, G., Baron, R., & Moore, D. (1978). Distraction and social comparison as mediators of social facilitation effects. *Journal of Experimental Social Psychology*, *14*, 291-303.
Sanna, L. (1992). Self-efficacy theory: Implications for social facilitation and social loafing. *Journal of Personality and Social Psychology*, *62*, 774-786.
Seta, J., Paulus, P., & Schkade, J. (1976). Effects of group size and proximity under cooperative and competitive conditions. *Journal of Personality and Social Psychology*, *34*, 47-53.
Szymanski, K. (1988). *Social loafing and self-evaluation.* Unpublished doctoral dissertation, Northeastern University, Boston, MA.
Szymanski, K., & Harkins, S. (1987). Social loafing and self-evaluation with a social standard. *Journal of Personality and Social Psychology*, *53*, 891-897.
Szymanski, K. & Harkins, S. (1992). Self-evaluation and creativity. *Personality and Social Psychology Bulletin*, *18*, 259-265.
Szymanski, K., & Harkins, S. (1993). The effect of experimenter evaluation on self-evaluation within the social loafing paradigm. *Journal of Experimental Social Psychology*, *29*, 268-286.
Triplett, N. (1898). The dynamogenic factors in pacemaking and competition. *American*

Journal of Psychology, *9*, 507-533.

Utman, C. (1997). Performance effects of motivational state: A meta-analysis. *Personality and Social Psychology Review*, *1*, 170-182.

Utman, C., & Harkins, S. (1994). *Acceptance of performance standards: The effects of perceptions of criterion stringency*. Paper presented at Midwestern Psychological Association, Chicago, IL.

White, P., Kjelgaard, M., & Harkins, S. (1995). Testing the contribution of self-evaluation to goal setting effects using the social loafing paradigm. *Journal of Personality and Social Psychology*, *69*, 69-79.

White, S., Mitchell, T., & Bell, C. (1977). Goal setting, evaluation apprehension, and social cues as determinants of job performance and job satisfaction in a simulated organization. *Journal of Applied Psychology*, *62*, 665-673.

Williams, K., Harkins, S., & Latané, B. (1981). Identifiability as a deterrent to social loafing: Two cheering experiments. *Journal of Personality and Social Psychology*, *40*, 303-311.

Wood, J. (1989). Theory and research concerning social comparisons of personal attributes. *Psychological Bulletin*, *106*, 231-248.

Wood, R. E., Bandura, A., & Bailey, T. (1990). Mechanisms governing organizational productivity in complex decision-making environments. *Organizational Behavior and Human Decision Processes*, *46*, 181-201.

Zajonc, R. (1965). Social facilitation. *Science*, *149*, 269-274.

Zajonc, R. (1980). Compresence. In P. Paulus (Ed.), *Psychology of group influence* (pp. 35-60). Hillsdale, NJ: Lawrence Erlbaum Associates.

Chapter 6

PERFORMANCE AMONG INDIVIDUALS AND GROUPS: THE IMPLICATIONS OF PARALLEL RESEARCH TRADITIONS FOR SOCIAL LOAFING

James A. Shepperd
University of Florida

Research on social loafing began with a simple question: Why are individual effort and productivity less when people work in groups compared with when they work individually? That is, a common consequence of collective effort tasks is that the combined effort of group members falls short of the sum of the efforts of an equivalent number of people working individually. Although nonpsychological factors such as poor coordination of efforts (Kravitz & Martin, 1986) may account for some of the decline in effort productivity, the decline persists even when poor coordination of effort is eliminated. Indeed, one of the most striking findings from the social loafing literature is that the mere belief that individual efforts will be combined to produce a group product can lead to lower productivity. Chapter 1 places the phenomenon squarely within an expectancy-value framework. Accordingly, people will work provided three conditions hold. First, they must perceive a relationship between their efforts and their performance (e.g., high effort will lead to a good performance). Second, they must perceive a relationship between performance and the outcome (e.g., a good performance will be rewarded). Third, they must value the outcome such that the value must exceed the costs associated with contributing.

The other topics discussed in this volume (i.e., intrinsic and extrinsic motivation, goal setting, creativity, achievement motivation, social facilitation) raise a variety of important issues and questions. For example, one way to increase the value of contributing is to make the task an individual one rather than a group one. In a sense, this means *degrouping* individual efforts and contributions, and the most straightforward means of achieving this degrouping is to make individual efforts identifiable. When individual efforts can be identified, they can be evaluated and outcomes (i.e., rewards and punishments) can be tied directly to individual efforts. However, the research on intrinsic and extrinsic motivation reveals that external evaluation can undermine intrinsic motivation and diminish the enjoyment of the task and may ultimately produce a decline in performance (Tauer & Harackiewicz, Chapter 4). In a similar vein, whereas external evaluation can increase the quantity of contributions, it can be devastating to creativity (Hennessey, Chapter 3). This finding raises the intriguing question of whether an expectancy-value approach is applicable when the goal is quality rather than quantity.

The present chapter explores how research on intrinsic and extrinsic motivation, goal setting, creativity, and achievement motivation contribute to our understanding of motivation and productivity and groups and the extent to which an expectancy-value theoretical framework is able to account for issues and problems raised by these parallel research traditions. The chapter begins with a discussion of how goal setting informs our understanding of social loafing. Second, I address the issue of creativity and the extent to which solutions to low motivation and productivity in groups are applicable when quality rather than quantity is the objective of the group. Third, I discuss the relationship between intrinsic and extrinsic motivation, the achievement motivation and productivity in groups. Fourth, I address findings from social facilitation and how they can be understood alongside the results from research on social loafing. In each section, I explore the extent to which an expectancy-value framework provides a useful vehicle for understanding motivation and productivity in groups in light of findings from these related research traditions.

SOCIAL LOAFING AND GOAL SETTING

The Goal Specificity and Goal Difficulty Hypotheses

The chapter on goal setting (Chapter 2) describes two goal setting hypotheses: the goal specificity hypothesis and the goal difficulty hypothesis. According to the goal specificity hypothesis, specific, difficult, assigned goals lead to higher performance than more vague "do your best" goals. According to the goal difficulty hypothesis, difficult assigned goals lead to higher performance than easy assigned goals. Most research on goal setting focuses on individual behavior. The question the goal setting research poses for social loafing is whether the goal specificity hypothesis and the goal difficulty hypothesis hold true in collective settings where individuals pool their efforts.

Examination of the literature suggests that both the goal specificity hypothesis and the goal difficulty hypothesis find support in collective settings. For example, in a study described earlier in this volume (White, Kjelgaard, & Harkins, 1995; see also White, Mitchell, & Bell, 1977), participants generated uses for a knife for 12 minutes. Some participants believed their efforts would be individually evaluated (experimenter evaluation condition), whereas other participants believed their efforts would be pooled to produce a group product (no experimenter evaluation). In addition, participants received instructions either to generate as many uses as possible ("do your best"), or to work to achieve a specific, difficult goal of 40 uses. The results are presented in Table 5 of Chapter 5 of this volume. Participants generated more uses in the specific goal condition than in the "do your best" goal condition. More importantly, the specific goal led to better performance even when individual efforts presumably could not be evaluated. In short, the goal specificity hypothesis enjoys support in group settings where contributions are pooled.

The goal difficulty hypothesis also enjoys empirical support in group settings. Specifically, in a study by Harkins, White and Utman (2000; see a full description in Chapter 5 of this volume), participants again worked on a use-generation task and believed their efforts would be pooled to form a group product (no experimenter evaluation) or would not be pooled (experimenter evaluation). In addition, participants received one of three sets of instructions. Some participants merely received instructions to generate as many uses as possible. Other participants believed that at the end of the experiment they would be told how many uses had been generated by the participant falling at the 90th percentile of the distribution. Still other participants believed that at the end of the experiment they would be told how many uses had been generated by the participant falling at the 30th percentile of the distribution. Although participants who anticipated feedback about another participant whose performance fell either at the 30th or 90th percentile did not receive a specific goal to strive toward, the anticipated feedback functioned as an implicit easy (30th percentile) or difficult (90th percentile) goal. The results are presented in Table 6 of Chapter 5 of this volume. The anticipation of experimenter evaluation led to high effort regardless of the instructions (do your best, implicit easy goal, implicit difficult goal) participants received. In the no evaluation condition, where efforts presumably would not be evaluated, participants generated more uses in the difficult goal condition than in the "do your best" and easy goal conditions.

In sum, research in social loafing provides support for both the goal specificity and the goal difficulty hypotheses. Providing people with specific, difficult goals leads to greater effort, eliminating social loafing even when efforts are pooled and individual efforts presumably cannot be evaluated. The implication is the leaders or managers do not need to threaten or impose evaluation on group or team members to insure high effort. They merely need to establish a specific, difficult or challenging goal and participants will respond with higher effort, even though their individual efforts may be anonymous.

Goal Setting and Expectancy-Value Theory

Why do specific goals lead to better performance than "do your best" goals, and why do difficult assigned goals lead to better performance than easy assigned goals? And, more importantly from the current perspective, can an expectancy-value theoretical framework account for these findings? I believe the answer is "yes" and suspect that goal specificity and goal difficulty influence individual and collective performance most directly by affecting the value component of the model, but also indirectly by affecting the expectancy component of the model. I consider each of these in turn.

Effort Expectations

Specific, difficult goals can influence performance subtly and indirectly by influencing the perceived dispensability of individual efforts to achieving a good group performance. When facing difficult goals, people may come to perceive their efforts as indispensable for two reasons. First, difficult goals may lead people working collectively to exert higher effort because they come to believe that a good group performance is dependent on all group members working hard. As such, all efforts are regarded as indispensable and free-riding on the efforts of others is not an option if the group is to reach the goal.

Second, difficult goals may lead people working collectively to exert higher effort because they egocentrically believe that they alone, or at least more so than others, have the requisite skills to insure a good group performance. That is, research on the better-than-average effect documents a pervasive belief among people that they are above average on positive attributes and below average on negative attributes. Thus, people universally appear to believe they are above average on such dimensions as in honesty, friendliness and intelligence (Dunning, 1993). When undertaking a difficult goal, the better-than-average belief may lead people to reason that the success of the group falls inordinately on their shoulders. That is, because of their self-perceived better-than-average skills and abilities, people may come to infer that they must work harder when facing difficult goals rather than easy goals because they believe that their efforts are uniquely essential to achieving a good group performance. Consistent with this reasoning is the research by Harkins and Petty (1982) described in Chapter 1. Participants working on an easy or difficult task believed that their personal efforts could or could not be evaluated. Whereas participants working on an easy task worked hard when their efforts could be evaluated and loafed when they could not, participants working on a difficult task worked hard regardless of whether their efforts could or could not be evaluated.

It is noteworthy that difficult goals are likely to lead to greater effort provided the goal seems realistic. To the extent that the goal seems excessively high, exceeding what the person thinks is possible, then the person is likely to withhold effort. As noted in Chapter 1, people will work hard provided they perceive relationship between effort and performance. That is, they must perceive the high effort will lead to a good performance. Goals define what is a good performance. If group members perceive that the goal is unattainable regardless of how hard the group works, then they will withhold efforts. Such was the case in Study 1 of research by Shepperd and Taylor (1999) described in Chapter 1. In that study, participants faced a high performance criterion and came to believe, based on feedback from practice trials, that their group was unlikely to reach the criterion on the crucial test trial. Consistent with expectancy-value theory, participants exerted less effort when they believed that the criterion was unreachable than when they believed that criterion was within reach.

Performance Expectations

It seems unlikely that specific, difficult goals affect performance by influencing performance expectations. Recall that performance expectation refers to the extent to which the person believes that a good performance will be rewarded. With specific, difficult goals, achieving the goal and being rewarded are one and the same because achieving the goal is presumably rewarding in its own right in that the person can take pleasure in performing at or above the standard. Moreover, to the extent that the person attaches particular pleasure or value to achieving challenging goals, then the more difficult or challenging the goal, the greater personal reward the person will garner from accomplishing the goal.

Outcome Value

Specific, difficult goals potentially can affect outcome value, and thus performance, in two ways. The first, most obvious way is by providing a standard or "yardstick" against which people can compare and evaluate personal performance (Harkins, Chapter 5; Locke & Latham, 1990). As noted in Chapter 5 of this volume, people are concerned not only that others evaluate them favorably, but also with evaluating themselves favorably. Goals provide people with a criterion against which to evaluate their performance, and people will work hard to insure a good performance and thus favorable self-evaluation. Moreover, it seems apparent that difficult goals need not be explicitly provided by a manager or team leader to be effective. As noted in the Harkins et al. (2000) study, merely having a standard against which one can evaluate performance, or even the merely anticipation of information that will provide a standard for evaluating performance will elicit greater effort. The standard leads people to set personal (high) goals for performance. For example, learning that the an opponent trains by running 50 miles a week is likely to lead a runner to evaluate his or her own training program and perhaps set a personal goal of running 50 miles a week.

In collective settings where efforts are pooled, providing people with a goal, such as "strive to generate 40 uses," shifts the focus of the task from the group to the individual. That is, the focus of the task moves from generating a good group effort to generating a favorable self-evaluation, and a favorable self-evaluation is one in which one's personal performance compares favorably with the goal or standard. For example, telling a group of five workers that they must construct 10,000 widgets a week is tantamount to setting for each individual worker a goal of constructing 2,000 widgets a week. Workers can evaluate their individual productivity by how it compares with the implicit 2,000 widget individual goal.

The second way specific, difficult goals can affect value is by increasing the value associated with performance. Specifically, more difficult goals offer more of a challenge, and people may attach greater value to achieving a difficult challenging goal than an easy goal. People may thus work harder when working toward a difficult goal because achieving a difficult goal means more to them, and thus is presumably more intrinsically rewarding than achieving an easy goal.

Viewing the implications of the goal setting literature on motivation and effort in groups through the lens of expectancy-value theory reveals a gap in the literature. Specifically, will a specific, difficult goal lead to greater individual effort when the goal is specified at the group level and the group goal cannot be broken down to permit either external or personal evaluation of individual performance? Prior studies have not examined the effect of goal setting on contributing in groups, but rather have examined the effects of goal setting when contributions are ostensibly anonymous and presumably cannot be externally evaluated. Thus, for example, participants are instructed to strive toward generating 40 uses for an object. The goal of 40 uses leads to greater performance than the vague goal of working as hard as you can. But what if the goal was specified at the group level rather than the individual level and individual efforts were difficult or impossible to evaluate either externally or internally? For example, what if the goal was to build the road or bridge in two weeks? Presumably, if expectancy, instrumentality and value were high, group members would work hard to achieve a specific, difficult group goal. In a laboratory setting, a test of this hypothesis would require a design in which participants receive instructions to achieve a specific, difficult goal. The goal would need to be specified in such a way that participants could not evaluate their personal efforts nor could their efforts be externally evaluated. Rather, all that could be evaluated is the extent to which the collective effort of group members approximated the group goal.

One final comment on goal setting and outcome value deserves mention. Tubbs (Chapter 2) noted that the goal specificity hypothesis, and presumably also the goal difficulty hypothesis, hold provided the individual accepts and is committed to the goal. From the perspective of expectancy-value theory, acceptance and commitment of the goal imply that the person values the goal and believes the benefits of pursuing and achieving the goal outweigh any material or psychological costs associated with striving toward the goal. Stated otherwise, consistent with expectancy-value theory, goal specificity and goal difficulty produce greater performance provided the individual values the goal.

Summary

Specific, difficult goals lead to greater effort and better performance in collective settings than easy goals or vague, "do your best" goals. Moreover, specific, difficult goals produce an increase in effort and performance even when individual efforts cannot be individually evaluated. The increased effort and performance may stem indirectly from higher effort expectations. When the goal is difficult, group members may perceive that personal efforts are more necessary to achieve a good group performance. This perception may arise from group members perceiving all efforts as essential to reaching the goal. Alternatively, the perception may arise from an egocentric perception among individual group member that achieving the goal rests inordinately on their shoulders because they alone have the requisite skills to insure a good performance. The increased effort and performance may also stem directly from higher value attached to the outcome. Specifically, group members may work harder when provided a specific, difficult goal because such goals provide a yardstick or standard against which to evaluate personal performance and people attach value to meeting or exceeding such standards. For example, if left to their own devices, a group of workers might dig 60 feet of trench a day. If, however, they learn that they are expected to dig 90 feet of trench a day and 90 feet is a challenging but not unreasonable goal, then the workers are likely to rise to the occasion, digging 90 feet instead of 60 feet. Alternatively, the greater effort and performance may result from group members attaching greater value to achieving a difficult goal. Group members may thus work harder because achieving a difficult goal is more personally rewarding.

SOCIAL LOAFING AND THE QUALITY OF CONTRIBUTIONS

The research on social loafing provides ample evidence that people exert less effort when efforts are pooled to produce a group product than when efforts are considered individually. The result is that the whole is *less* than the sum or its parts; individuals produce less when working as part of a group than when working alone. It is important to note, however, that most research on social loafing has examined the quantity rather than the quality of performance. This raises an interesting question. Does the decline in performance appear when performance is defined in terms of quality? Quality can be a somewhat nebulous commodity. It is difficult to quantify quality and thus difficult to operationalize it in a laboratory experiment. Perhaps the most successful attempts to study quality come from research on creativity by Amabile and others (Amabile, 1982, 1996; Hennessey & Amabile, 1999). Studies of creativity suggest that being creative demands long periods of isolation and that creative achievements typically result from individual mental efforts or activity (Ochse, 1990; Simonton, 1988; Sternberg, 1988). Moreover, there is little evidence that people are particularly creative in groups (Kasof, 1995; Paulus et al., 1999).

This leads to a second question. As noted in Chapter 1, interventions that increase the contingency between personal efforts and performance (effort expectancy), the contingency between the performance and the outcome (performance expectancy), and the importance of the outcome relative to its cost (outcome value) increase the quantity of contributions. People work harder and contribute more when effort expectancy, performance expectancy and outcome value are high than when these components of expectancy-value theory are low. But what is the impact of these three components on the *quality* of contributions? There is reason to believe that these interventions may actually undermine the quality of performance. As Hennessey noted in Chapter 3 of this volume, intrinsic motivation is conducive to creativity. More importantly, as evident across a series of studies described by Hennessey, external evaluation diminishes intrinsic motivation and creativity in most settings. Apparent in this line of research is the fact that creativity is a fragile and elusive entity that is easily undermined. In addition, and certainly more challenging to researchers examining social loafing, the most consistent way researchers have found to increase the quantity of contributions in groups, i.e., making individual contributions identifiable, can undercut the quality of contributions. Thus, whereas experimenter evaluation eliminates social loafing, it appears disastrous for creativity.

How does expectancy-value theory explain performance in groups when quality rather than quantity is the commodity of interest? To answer this question, I consider effort expectations, performance expectations, and outcome value separately.

Effort Expectations

As noted in Chapter 1, effort expectation refers to the relationship between effort and performance. It answers the question "Will high effort yield a good performance?" When performance is defined in terms of quantity, the central concern is whether high effort will yield high quantity (e.g., will high effort yield more mousetraps than low effort). When performance is defined in terms of quality, the central concern is whether high effort will yield high quality (i.e., will high effort yield better mousetraps than low effort). At one level the distinction between quantity and quality seems purely semantic, particularly when people work in teams or groups, or when efforts are otherwise pooled. To the extent that people perceive that their efforts as unnecessary or redundant with the contributions of other people (i.e., the group will generate a good performance or product regardless of their personal contributions), then effort will be low. This relationship seems equally true both when performance is defined in terms of quantity and quality. If a person perceives that the group can produce a high quality product regardless of whether he or she personally makes a high quality or creative contribution, then effort will be low.

This point aside, when people are working in teams or groups and efforts are pooled, there is good reason to believe that a focus on quality will lead to an increase in effort and greater quality in contributions. Specifically, people overwhelmingly perceive themselves as "better than average" on positive traits such as responsibility and creativity (Dunning, 1993). People are thus egocentrically inclined to perceive themselves as uniquely creative, responsible or talented, and in group settings, more creative, responsible and talented than their average fellow group member. When efforts are pooled and a good group performance is defined in terms of quality or creativity, the belief that one is more creative, responsible, and talented than fellow group members is likely to prompt the conclusion that the performance of the group rests disproportionately on one's own shoulders. As noted in the discussion of difficult goals, people may thus work harder in a group setting because they perceive the success of the group as primarily their responsibility. In other words, individual group members may perceive a strong contingency between their personal efforts or contributions and the group's performance even when efforts are pooled and the responsibility for a good group performance is shared.

It is also possible, however, that the perception that the group's performance is dependent on personal efforts may backfire, leading on the one hand to a greater quantity of effort, but on the other hand to a lower quality in the final contributions. Specifically, the perception that the success of the group rests disproportionately on one's personal shoulders may create added pressure to generate a good group effort. The added pressure may shift the motivation from working on the task because it is intrinsically enjoyable to working hard because to do otherwise would spell disaster for the group. The added pressure may undermine intrinsic motivation. More importantly, the added pressure may produce anxiety or other interfering cognitions that tax cognitive capacity and divert attention away from generating a creative product.

These possible outcomes for the quality of group performance are, of course, largely speculative. No study has examined how effort expectations affect creativity or the quality of contributions. Clearly, the consequences of effort expectations for performance quality remains an important direction for future research.

Performance Expectations

It seems unlikely that the decline in effort or contributing observed when performance is defined in terms of quality or creativity arises from low performance expectations. As a reminder, performance expectancy refers to the relationship between performance and outcome (see Chapter 1). It answers the question "Will a good performance be rewarded?" When performance is defined in terms of quality or creativity, the central concern with regard to performance expectation is whether a high quality or creative performance will be rewarded. In many instances and for many people, the mere act of producing a high quality contribution is reward in itself because people find being creative intrinsically reinforcing. Thus, when performance is defined in terms of quality or creativity, performance expectancy may naturally be high, because the reward (satisfaction or pleasure in having produced a creative or high quality product) is largely inseparable from the performance.

Often, however, the decision of quality or creativity is not decided or determined personally, but rather is determined by a third party or evaluator. In these instances, performance expectancy may be low to the extent that group members believe that the evaluator may not reward quality or creativity, or may believe that the evaluator is a poor judge of quality. For example, members of an architectural firm may believe that a city contract for a new building or bridge will not go to the best design, but rather will be decided by some factor unrelated to quality such as the cost of the project (the city will accept the lowest bid), or the relationship of the competing firms have with the city manager (e.g., the architects may believe that a "good-old-boys" network exists, such that the city manager will choose a design proposed by a friend or relative). While such instances would undoubtedly lead people to exert less effort, because high effort would be regarded as futile, it is likely that such instances are relatively rare and do not account for the decline in effort when contributions are pooled.

Outcome Value

Outcome value refers to the value (minus any costs) placed on generating a good performance. Generally speaking, if value is high, then performance should be high. As noted in Chapter 1, people are concerned with (i.e., place a high value on) how others perceive and think about them. This concern leads people to work harder when personal efforts can be evaluated than when they cannot be evaluated. Indeed, when personal efforts can be evaluated, the goal typically shifts away from producing a good group performance to producing a favorable personal evaluation. Similarly, when personal efforts can be evaluated, group members can no longer hide in the crowd, leading people to work hard, not just to attain a favorable evaluation, but to avoid an unfavorable one. In short, as evident from two decades of research across a variety of studies examining both cognitive and physical tasks, introducing the prospect of evaluation eliminates social loafing.

Virtually every prior study of social loafing, however, has examined the quantity rather than the quality of performance. While introducing evaluation leads people to work harder, resulting in an increase in the quantity of performance, the research by Amabile and her colleagues (see Chapter 3 for a summary) reveals that it can undermine the quality of performance.

The decline in quality is illustrated in a study by Bartis, Szymanski, and Harkins (1988). Participants received instructions to generate uses for an object for a set time period. Participants in the *quality* condition received instructions to generate creative uses for the object and not to worry about the quantity of uses. Participants in the *quantity* condition received instructions to generate as many uses as they could for the object and not to worry about the quality of the uses. In addition, all participants believed that their performance (defined either in terms of quality or quantity) would or would not be evaluated by the experimenter at the end of the time period. At the end of the trials the experimenter determined the quantity of performance by counting the number of uses generated by each participant. The experimenter determined the quality of performance by having judges rate the creativity of each use and then computed for each participant a creativity score by averaging the creativity ratings for each of the uses that the participant generated. The results revealed that in the quantity condition, quantity was significantly higher when contributions could be evaluated than when contributions ostensibly could not be evaluated. In the quality condition, quality was significantly higher when contributions ostensibly could not be evaluated than when contributions could be evaluated.

Why does creativity decline when contributions can be evaluated? In Chapter 3, Hennessey suggests three explanations. According to the *overjustification* explanation, the evaluation provides an alternative explanation for engaging in the behavior. The person concludes that s/he is engaging in the behavior not for its own sake, but to achieve a favorable evaluation. While it is clear that such a shift in focus might undermine intrinsic motivation, it is less clear according to this explanation why creativity should suffer as a consequence of evaluation. That is, while people may enjoy the task less when the motivation shifts externally to creating a favorable evaluation, the decline in enjoyment does not explain why people are less creative.

According to the *conditioned association* explanation, evaluation transforms the task from play to work. Work, which is typically evaluated, comes to be viewed as drudgery; play, which is typically not evaluated, comes to be viewed as fun. However, while this explanation would again explain why evaluation might undermine intrinsic motivation, it does not explain why evaluation produces a decline in creativity. People might come to enjoy the task less, but that does not necessarily mean they will be less creative as a consequence.

According to the *attention* explanation, creative responses required sustained attention to the task. Evaluation distracts the person from the task as the person shifts attention back and forth between the evaluator (and perhaps what has to be done to achieve a favorable evaluation) and the task. The shifting attention may not only mean less time devoted to the task, but also less feeling of intrinsic involvement in the task.

The attention explanation seems to provide the most satisfactory explanation for the decline in creativity when contributions can be evaluated. Moreover, the attention explanation comes closest to the explanation offered by the expectancy-value framework. According to expectancy-value theory, the decline in performance stems from the fact that the shift to achieving a favorable personal evaluation often changes the motivation driving behavior from performing well for its own sake (an intrinsic motivation) to performing well to secure a favorable evaluation (an extrinsic motivation). The change in value introduces a cost to the task. The cost stems from the perception that the evaluator may view the quality as inadequate or may disapprove of a performance that diverges excessively from the status quo. The concern with a negative evaluation may undermine creativity for two reasons. First, it may lead to excessive caution and self-censorship, stifling creativity. Second, it may lead to excessive distracting or interfering thoughts about possible disapproval, diverting precious cognitive resources away from performing the task.

We are quick to note that working in a group where efforts are unidentifiable offers no insurance that the group product will be more creative than when contributions can be evaluated. Being creative, after all, is hard work. Although people may attach intrinsic value to quality and being creative, or find creative process intrinsically interesting, and although there may even be an external reward for a creative group performance, being creative is still taxing, requiring the expenditure of resources. People may reason that the effort required to produce a truly clever or creative performance is not justified by the benefits, intrinsic or otherwise. Similarly, while the finished product of the creative process may be rewarding or gratifying to the creator, getting to that finished product can be tedious or frustrating. Finally, as noted earlier, creativity seems primarily to involve sustained periods of individual work in isolation (Ochse, 1990; Simonton, 1988; Sternberg, 1988), suggesting that expecting creativity in groups may be futile.

However, there is some hope for increased creativity in group settings. Specifically, several recent studies by Paulus suggests that people can be productive in groups, even more productive than individuals working individually, provided certain conditions hold (e.g., Dugosh, Paulus, Roland, & Yang, 2000; Paulus & Yang 2000). These conditions included attending to the ideas generated by others, having a facilitator present to keep the group moving and on task, introducing an element of competition to the task, and having an alone period following the group meeting where group members can continue to work on the task alone. According to Paulus and his colleagues, working in teams or groups can increase creativity by providing both social and cognitive stimulation. The social stimulation comes from competition and from fellow group members providing a standard against which a group member can match his or her own performance. The cognitive stimulation comes from hearing the ideas of others which can prime group members to generate new ideas they otherwise would not have thought of (see Paulus, Larey, & Dzindolet, 2001, for a review).

Summary

When people work individually and individual efforts can be evaluated, quality (e.g., creativity) tends to suffer. Although researchers have offered various explanations for the decline in quality, from the perspective of expectancy-value theory, the most likely reason is that evaluation introduces a cost to contribution. The cost stems from the possibility that the evaluator may disapprove of the quality of the performance. Concerns with disapproval may lead to self-censorship or may produce distracting thoughts that reduce the cognitive resources available for generating a high quality performance. When people work collectively, the quality of individual group members' contributions may improve or may suffer. On the one hand, consistent with an expectancy-value framework, quality may improve to the extent that group members perceive that a creative group performance is dependent on their efforts. The perceived dependency would perhaps arise from an egocentric view shared by each member that he or she is uniquely more talented or creative than fellow group members. On the other hand, quality may decline to the extent that group members regard their efforts as dispensable in achieving a creative group product. It also may decline if group members feel added pressure to produce a good group performance and the added pressure produces anxiety or other interfering cognitions that divert attention away from generating a creative product. The reasons offered for why people may be less creative when efforts are pooled to form a group product suggest that eliminating individual evaluation is no guarantee that contributions will be more creative. These reasons, however, await empirical test.

INTRINSIC MOTIVATION AND THE ACHIEVEMENT MOTIVE

The simple message from research on intrinsic and extrinsic motivation is that situational factors (such as outside rewards, competition and evaluation) that are considered externally controlling (i.e., they provide the person an external incentive or reason for performing a task), undermine intrinsic motivation. They alter the goal from performing the task because doing so is personally gratifying to performing the task to achieve some external outcome (a reward, a win, a positive evaluation). As a consequence, people find the task less intrinsically interesting and enjoyable. For example, introducing competition in a task shifts the focus of the task from performing it well because it is enjoyable or satisfying to do so, to performing it well to defeat or outperform the competition. As noted in Chapter 5 of this volume, many of the tasks examined in research on social loafing (e.g., pumping air, making paper chains, generating uses for an object) are not intrinsically interesting to begin with. The tasks are generally not difficult, challenging or interesting, and thus there is little in the way of intrinsic interests to undermine.

Importantly, Tauer and Harackiewicz argue in Chapter 4 that the relationship between motivation and situational factors that imply external control is not quite so simple. They propose, for example, that competition does not automatically undermine intrinsic motivation. Instead the effect of competition on intrinsic motivation depends on the person's level of achievement motivation. Whereas people low in the achievement motive respond to competition with decreased intrinsic motivation, people high in the achievement motive respond to competition with increased intrinsic motivation. According to Tauer and Harackiwicz the achievement motive affects the way people approach and experiences activities. People high in the achievement motive (HAMs) approach performance settings that involve evaluation and competition more positively than do people low in the achievement motive (LAMs). For HAMs, it appears that competition and evaluation increase intrinsic motivation by adding an element of challenge to performance. They thus thrive in competitive and evaluative settings, approaching them eagerly. LAMs, by contrast, disdain evaluation and competition, and show a decline in intrinsic motivation in such settings.

The research on achievement motivation and performance raises an interesting question. How do intrinsic motivation and the achievement motive affect performance in teams or groups where efforts are pooled to produce a collective product? One recent study bears on this question (Hart, Karau, Stasson, & Kerr, 2001). Participants scoring in the upper or lower quartile of a measure of achievement motivation and working in pairs received instructions to generate as many uses as possible for a knife in 12 minutes. In addition, participants received information that performance on an idea-generation task was highly related to intelligence and achievement. Half of the participants believed that the experimenter was interested in their individual performance (coactive condition), whereas half believed that the experimenter was interested only in the performance of groups (collective condition).

Finally, participants received false information ostensibly from their coworker that he or she planned to work hard on the task or that he or she did not plan to work hard on the task. The purpose of this final manipulation was to vary performance expectations in the collective condition. In the coactive conditions where efforts would be monitored individually, the anticipated effort of the coworker would presumably have no bearing on participants' personal efforts. Participants would have to work hard to achieve a favorable personal evaluation regardless of how hard their coparticipant worked. However, in the collective condition where individual efforts presumably would not be evaluated and the focus was on the performance of the group, the belief that one's coworker would work hard would make personal efforts less important to achieving a good group performance (low effort expectation). The news that one's coworker in the collective condition would exert little effort would serve to make personal efforts more important to achieving a good group performance (high effort expectations).

Did HAMs work harder than LAMs? Or did the efforts of HAMs and LAMs depend on whether they believed the experimenter would monitor individual performance and on the anticipated efforts of their coworker? The results revealed that HAMs worked hard regardless of whether they believed their coworker would or would not work hard, and regardless of whether they believed the experimenter would monitor their individual efforts. In short, the HAMs were unresponsive to the performance conditions; they always worked hard. LAMs, by contrast, were more sensitive to the performance conditions. Like HAMs, LAMs worked hard coactively (i.e., when individual efforts could be evaluated). When working collectively, LAMs worked hard only when they anticipated that their coworker would exert low effort, making their personal efforts necessary for a good group performance. When they anticipated that their coworker would exert high effort, making their personal contributions unnecessary, LAMs working collectively loafed.

The effort allocation of LAMs is straightforward and sensible. They responded to the situational demands, working hard when efforts could be evaluated and when their efforts were necessary to achieve a good group performance, and loafing when their efforts could not be evaluated and when their coworker would presumably work hard. The effort allocation of HAMs, i.e., the fact that they worked hard regardless of the situational demand, is more intriguing. Their behavior offers hints about how HAMs perceive contingencies and what they value. Examining the behavior of HAMs through the lens of expectancy-value theory offers several possible explanations for the results.

Effort Expectations

The consistently high efforts of HAMs may reflect a difference between HAMs and LAMs in effort expectations. HAMs may have regarded their efforts as essential regardless of the situational manipulations. That is, whereas LAMs viewed their efforts as dispensable in the coactive/hard working coworker condition, HAMs did not. The question that begs answering is why did HAMs regard their efforts as indispensable. Perhaps HAMs believed that high effort on the part of their coworker would be insufficient to achieve a good group performance. They may have believed that a good group performance was dependent on their efforts with or without their coworkers' inputs. This belief may arise from prior experience working in groups in which coworkers loafed and the group outcome depended on the HAM's personal efforts. Or perhaps HAMs believed they were simply more capable than their coworker at achieving a good group performance regardless of how hard their coworker reported s/he would work. Counter to this explanation are the findings from manipulation check items. These items revealed that in the hardworking coworker condition (compared with the loafing coworker condition), both HAMs and LAMs reported believing that their coworker would work harder and was higher in ability. An alternative explanation is that HAMs have a higher standard of performance. Their criterion for what meets the definition of a good group performance is rigorous, requiring that they work hard irrespective of the efforts of their coworker.

Performance Expectations

An alternative explanation for the consistently high effort of HAMs rests in the possibility of a difference between HAMs and LAMs in their performance expectations. The explanation here is quite simple and thus needs little elaboration. HAMs may perceive a tighter link between performance and evaluation than do LAMs. Stated otherwise, HAMs may be more inclined than LAMs to believe that a poor group performance would reflect poorly on them and that a good group performance would reflect well on them. This belief may stem from the perception among HAMs that they are contributing more to the group performance than their coworker and a belief that the experimenter will recognize this fact.

Outcome Value

The most compelling explanation for the high effort among HAMs in the coaction/hard working coworker condition is that HAMs and LAMs differed in the value they attached to performing well. HAMs may attach greater value than LAMs to the performance or outcome. The greater value may come from several sources. First, HAMs may simply enjoy working hard and value hard work regardless of whether their individual efforts can be evaluated. Second, HAMs may have found the task more enjoyable and intrinsically interesting than LAMs. Thus, they worked harder because they were more inclined to see the task as fun. This second explanation is consistent with research by Harackiewicz showing that HAMs approach and experience evaluative situations (and perhaps in the present case, situations in which the group rather than the individual is the target of evaluation) more positively than LAMs (see Chapter 4 for a summary).

Third, HAMs may define themselves in terms of high achievement. That is, their self-worth may be contingent on being at or near the best. As a consequence, HAMs may be motivated to compete and excel on all tasks, even mundane task like generating uses for an object. Accordingly, all tasks provide an opportunity to achieve and affirm their identity. Fourth, HAMs may have become so accustomed to working hard (and their identity so closely linked with high effort and achieving), that they exhibit an almost reflexive or conditioned response of high effort when presented with performance tasks. They work hard regardless of the situational demands because that is what they have become conditioned to do.

At first blush, the findings of Hart et al. (2000) and Harackiewicz and her colleagues (see Chapter 4 of this volume) might seem inconsistent. Harackiewicz and her colleagues found that LAMs fare better in situations with minimal evaluation (e.g., in noncompetitive settings), whereas HAMs fare better in situations in which evaluation pressures are high (i.e., in competitive settings). On the other hand, Hart et al. find that LAMs are more productive when they can be evaluated than when they cannot be evaluated, whereas HAMs are highly productive regardless of whether they can or cannot be evaluated.

While these findings may seem contradictory, the two studies differed in what they assessed. Hart et al., focused on performance (i.e., the number of uses generated for an object), whereas the series of studies described by Tauer and Harackiewicz in Chapter 4 focused on responses to the task -- responses such as enjoyment, positive affect, eagerness, and perceived challenge. These latter responses were used to infer participants' level of intrinsic motivation. It is tempting to infer performance outcomes based on levels of intrinsic motivation. Accordingly, HAMs will be more productive in competition or when evaluated, whereas LAMs will be more productive when there is no competition or evaluation, a finding contrary to Hart et al. (2000). However, making such an inference is quite a leap and may in no way reflect actual performance levels. HAMs, for example, might enjoy a task more when under evaluation or competition than when not. However, they might nevertheless work hard regardless of whether external evaluation is present or absent. Likewise, LAMs, might enjoy a task more when competition and evaluative pressures are absent. However, they nevertheless may be more productive when these pressures are present.

Summary

The effect of evaluation on intrinsic motivation depends on the person's level of achievement motivation, with HAMs displaying greater intrinsic motivation when evaluated and LAMs showing lower intrinsic motivation when evaluated. Effort and productivity, however, do not correspond to level of intrinsic motivation for either HAMs or LAMs. HAMs appear to work hard regardless of evaluation concerns (and presumably their level of intrinsic motivation) and regardless of the presumed effort of a fellow group member. LAMs, by contrast, work hard only when the external circumstances dictate that they must, i.e., when they are evaluated or when their efforts are necessary for a good group performance. The uniformly high effort of HAMs irrespective of the situational contingencies may stem from differences form LAMs in their perception of effort expectations, performance expectations or in the value they attach to high effort.

SOCIAL LOAFING AND SOCIAL FACILITATION

A problem that vexed group researchers for close to a decade was the inconsistent findings from research on social loafing and research on social facilitation. Whereas research on social loafing typically finds that motivation and productivity suffer in group settings, research on social facilitation typically finds that the motivation and productivity improve in group settings, at least on the simple tasks, the same sort of tasks examined in most social loafing research. How can researchers account for these inconsistent findings?

Harkins (1987) proposed an elegant solution by suggesting that research on social loafing and social facilitation can be represented within a 2 x 2 design that emerges from crossing an evaluation manipulation (evaluation vs. no evaluation) with a mere presence manipulation (working alone vs. coacting -- i.e., performing the same task alongside yet independently of others). As discussed in greater detail in Chapter 5 of this volume, the typical social loafing study and the typical social facilitation study each manipulate two cells in the 2 x 2 design. In social loafing research, the two cells are the coaction/evaluation and the coaction/no-evaluation cells. In social facilitation research, the two cells are the coaction/evaluation and the alone/evaluation cells. Moreover, part of the inconsistency in findings resulted from a different use of language by social loafing and social facilitation researchers when describing their research. Among social loafing researchers, the coaction/evaluation condition was considered an "individual" condition because individual efforts could be evaluated, whereas the coaction/no evaluation condition was considered a "group" condition because individual efforts ostensibly could not be evaluated but instead were pooled to produce a collective or group performance. By contrast, among social facilitation researchers, the alone/evaluation condition was considered an "individual" condition because the participant performed alone, whereas the coaction/evaluation condition was considered a "group" condition because participants worked alongside others.

When Harkins included all four cells within a single study, the inconsistency in terminology and findings was resolved. Specifically, Harkins found that working coactively led to greater productivity than working alone and that evaluation led to greater productivity than no evaluation. Or, more to the point, the coaction/evaluation condition led to greater productivity than did either the alone/evaluation condition or the coaction/no evaluation condition. Moreover, other studies lend support to these findings (Jackson & Williams, 1985; Sanna, 1992).

From the perspective of expectancy-value theory, the findings are best viewed in terms of the value component of the model. Regarding the greater productivity in the coaction/evaluation than in the coaction/no evaluation condition, the opportunity for evaluation increases the value associated with contributing. Regarding the greater productivity in the coaction/evaluation than in the alone/evaluation condition, the presence of a coactor performing the same task provides a standard against one's personal efforts can be judged. Participants work harder in the coactor/evaluation condition to insure favorable (or avoid an unfavorable) evaluation relative to the coactor. In the alone/evaluation condition, the absence of a coactor means there is no standard against which to compare the participant's efforts. In sum, rather than being inconsistent, the findings from social loafing research and social facilitation research are really complementary.

CONCLUSIONS

As noted in the Preface and Chapter 5 of this volume, several research traditions in psychology (i.e., goal setting, intrinsic motivation, creativity and achievement motivation) have explored the effect that situational forces have on motivation and performance among individuals and in groups. These research traditions, however, have operated largely independently with little cross communication. Examining social loafing in light of what we know about these parallel research traditions (and conversely, examining these parallel research traditions in light of what we know about social loafing) leads to two broad conclusions about motivation and performance. First, while evaluation generally undermines intrinsic motivation (at least for people low in the achievement motive) and creativity, it appears not to undermine effort. People work even harder when evaluation is present than when it is absent. Second, expectancy-value theory remains a useful framework for understanding motivation and performance in groups, explaining a diverse set of findings from a wide array of research traditions. Regardless of whether researchers focus on goals vs. motivations, efforts that are pooled vs. efforts that are considered individually, or the quantity vs. the quality of those efforts, people can be expected to work hard provided (a) they believe high effort will lead to a good performance, (b) they believe a good performance will be rewarded, and (c) the value of the outcome exceeds the costs incurred in producing that outcome.

Perhaps more importantly, examining these parallel research traditions together reveals important gaps in the research. For example, why do specific, difficult goals lead to an increase in effort and performance even when individual efforts cannot be individually evaluated? Does evaluation lead to a decline in creativity even though the group effort rather than individual efforts is the target of the evaluation? Why do people high in the achievement motive (HAMs) work hard irrespective of external situational forces? And, are there circumstances in which even HAMs will loaf? Addressing these and other questions will moved us still closer to integrating the divergent research traditions exploring motivation and performance among people working individually and in groups.

REFERENCES

Amabile, T. M. (1982). Children's artistic creativity: Detrimental effects of competition in a field setting. *Personality and social Psychology Bulletin, 8*, 573-578.

Amabile, T. M. (1996). *Creativity in context.* Boulder, CO: Westview.

Bartis, S., Szymanski, K., & Harkins, S. G. (1988). Evaluation and performance: A two-edged knife. *Personality and Social Psychology Bulletin, 14*, 242-251.

Dugosh, K. L., Paulus, P. B., Roland, E. J., & Yang, H. (2000). Cognitive stimulation in brainstorming. *Journal of Personality and Social Psychology, 79*, 722-735.

Dunning, D. (1993). Words to live by: The self and definitions of social concepts and categories. In J. M. Suls, et al., (Eds.). *The Self in Social Perspective: Psychological Perspectives on the Self, Vol. 4* (pp. 99-126). Hillsdale, NJ: Erlbaum.

Harkins, S. (1987). Social loafing and social facilitation. *Journal of Experimental Social Psychology, 23*, 1-18.

Harkins, S. G., & Petty, R. E. (1982). Effects of task difficulty and task uniqueness on social loafing. *Journal of Personality and Social Psychology, 43*, 1214-1229.

Hart, J., Karau, S. J., Stasson, M. F., & Kerr, N. L. (2001). *Achievement motivation, expected coworker performance, and collective task motivation: Working hard or hardly working?* Unpublished manuscript, Stephen F. Austin State University.

Hennessey, B. A., & Amabile, T.M. (1999). Consensual assessment. In M. Runco & S. Pritzker (Eds.), *Encyclopedia of creativity.* New York: Academic Press.

Jackson, J. M., & Williams, K. D. (1985). Social loafing on difficult tasks: Working collectively can improve performance. *Journal of Personality and Social Psychology, 49*, 937-942.

Kasof, J. (1995). Explaining creativity: The attributional perspective. *Creativity Research Journal, 8*, 311-366.

Kravitz, D. A., & Martin, B. (1986). Ringelmann rediscovered: The original article. *Journal of Personality and Social Psychology, 50*, 936-941.

Locke, E., & Latham, G. (1990). *A theory of goal setting and task performance.* Englewood Cliffs, NJ: Prentice Hall.

Ochse, R. (1990). *Before the gates of excellence: The determinants of creative genius.* New York: Cambridge University Press.

Paulus, P. B., & Yang, H. (2000). Idea generation in groups: A basis for creativity in organizations. *Organizational Behavior and Human Decision Processes, 82*, 76-87.

Paulus, P. B., Brown, V., & Ortega, A. H. (1999). Group creativity. In R. E. Purser & A. Montuori (Eds.), *Social creativity: Vol. 2* (pp. 151-176). Cresskill, NJ: Hampton.

Paulus, P. B., Larey, T. S., & Dzindolet, M. T. (2001). Creativity in groups and teams. In M. E. Turner (Ed.), *Groups at work: Theory and research* (pp. 319-338). Mahwah, NJ: Erlbaum.

Sanna, L. (1992). Self-efficacy theory: Implications for social facilitation and social loafing. *Journal of Personality and Social Psychology, 62*, 774-786.

Shepperd, J. A., & Taylor, K. M. (1999). Social loafing and expectancy-value theory. *Personality and Social Psychology Bulletin, 25*, 1147-1158.

Simonton, D. K. (1988). *Scientific genius: A psychology of science.* New York: Cambridge University Press.

Sternberg, R. J. (Ed.). (1988). *The nature of creativity: Contemporary psychological perspectives.* Cambridge, England: Cambridge University Press.

White, P., Kjelgaard, M., & Harkins, S. (1995). Testing the contribution of self-evaluation to goal-setting effects using the social loafing paradigm. *Journal of Personality and Social Psychology, 69*, 69-79.

White, S., Mitchell, T., & Bell, C. (1977). Goal setting, evaluation apprehension, and social cues as determinants of job performance and job satisfaction in a simulated organization. *Journal of Applied Psychology, 62*, 665-673.

Chapter 7

EXTERNAL PERFORMANCE EVALUATIONS AND TASK MOTIVATION: SOME SUGGESTIONS

Mark E. Tubbs
University of Missouri - St. Louis

Our purpose in this volume is to consider the role of external evaluations in individual motivation and performance. In the most basic (and oversimplified) terms possible, it seems that the central issues are these: What are the effects of external performance evaluation? Is it a good or a bad thing? When does it work best/worst? The first four chapters in this volume describe different research traditions, all of which share the common theme of investigating motivated task behavior and, in one way or another, the effects of performance evaluation. Each tradition has of course been shaped by parochial concerns, resulting in many methodological differences, including the choice of independent and dependent variables, level of analysis, and experimental tasks. Overall, in my opinion, while there is some overlap in these literatures, they are more often complementary, representing special, particularly salient, cases of task motivation. It is quite understandable why these particular variables and contexts have been examined and, for the most part, they do represent rather different cases involving rather different concerns.

My focus in this chapter will be to briefly summarize the features of the four areas (goal setting, social loafing, achievement motivation, creativity) in order to identify the key facets on which they differ. Given my background, I will concentrate on the degree of overlap and complement of the other three areas with the goal setting tradition in industrial/organizational psychology, leaving more detailed comparisons between the social psychological perspectives to my colleagues. Following this I will revisit Harkins' initial integration of the areas from Chapter 5 in the context of my analysis of the chapters, and then conclude with some suggestions for future research on task motivation in social and organizational psychology.

FOUR DIFFERENT RESEARCH TRADITIONS

Considering that our focus is on the effects of evaluation, I think that the single biggest difference in these traditions is a philosophical one regarding the view taken of evaluation. Perhaps this goes without saying, but external evaluation of task performance seems to sometimes be viewed in a less-than-positive light in the social psychological traditions described in the previous chapters. The position that evaluation can have a detrimental impact is quite evident, although some recent findings do appear to indicate that this may not be true for all individuals in all situations. This somewhat skeptical orientation regarding evaluation is perhaps linked to the study of task contexts where the possibility of not being evaluated actually exists, or at least where the use of evaluation remains open for debate. For example, when painting or poetry is the "task" of interest, as in the creativity studies, it is easy to imagine contexts (e.g., pursuing one's hobby) where it might be possible to completely avoid any meaningful external evaluations for extended periods of time.

But in the workplace (or the classroom), evaluation is a fact of life and avoiding it for long is rarely possible. In fact, "employees continually have their job performance appraised, whether on a formal or an informal basis" (Muchinsky, 2000, p. 206). As noted in my previous chapter, the workplace differs from the other contexts in which evaluation is studied in that adults have willingly entered into contractual agreements with an organization to provide services for a certain amount of compensation (Rousseau & Parks, 1993). They may not always look forward to the prospect, but they naturally expect that their performance will have to meet acceptable standards and that their adherence to those standards will be examined in some manner. This is not to say that I/O psychologists, or business managers, themselves necessarily think performance evaluation is always a good thing and has only positive effects on people. I think it is safe to say that everyone has experienced the stress that being evaluated can create. But given the reality of the workplace (which is where even laboratory research in the applied literature is expected to be relevant), I/O psychologists have tended to focus on the often beneficial performance-enhancing effects of evaluation rather than on possible detrimental effects on other variables.

Not surprisingly, the basic purpose of goal setting research seems different from that underlying the social psychological traditions. Though not atheoretical, the goal setting literature is ultimately applied in nature. It represents a deliberate attempt to understand how to increase subjects' extrinsic task motivation and performance, and clearly takes an advocate's role in recommending the use of the procedure. In contrast, the evaluation treatments in the social psychological research traditions are often described and used in a far more neutral way. The effects are of interest, but far from advocating evaluation, the feeling is more one of tolerance. In many ways this difference in orientation reflects the difference between an applied and a more basic field of endeavor. More specifically, it reflects the reality that social psychologists often study people in contexts where they have more control over their behavior than do people in work contexts, and, as a result, external performance evaluation is not always a necessary and expected component of life.

Beyond this basic distinction in perspective, there are several more specific, but related, differences which are relevant for understanding the findings: independent and dependent variables, tasks, levels of analysis, and individual difference variables.

Independent Variables

At an operational level, the most important difference in the traditions is in the exact nature of the independent variable manipulated by the researchers. In the social psychological approaches, either anticipated or actual evaluation of subjects' task performance has been the treatment investigated. In the former case, subjects have simply been made aware that their results will be or can be evaluated, whereas in the latter, an actual evaluation (e.g., of creative quality) took place. In the goal setting approach as commonly operationalized by I/O psychologists, actual evaluation is only part of what is experimentally manipulated. The procedure does include what could be called an evaluative component but, more importantly, goal setting also has a more proactive motivational component.

Although it has been said in different ways, the basic perspective espoused in the goal setting literature is that setting specific goals (most often quantity, but also quality goals or time deadlines) can increase performance by giving direction to one's efforts (Locke & Latham, 1990; Naylor & Ilgen, 1984). That is, goals encourage one to develop some specific intentions for task completion: How many?, Of what quality?, Made how?, By when? Effort allocations and strategy development may occur as well. This direction of attention is the primary purpose of goal assignment -- to encourage employees to adopt intentions consistent with organizational objectives. And well-known research in both the social and applied literatures has demonstrated that behavioral intentions are predictive of subsequent behavior (Fishbein & Ajzen, 1975; Locke & Latham, 1990).

The evaluation component of goal setting (if we want to call it that) is related to what is known as performance feedback in the applied literature, but what is perhaps more precisely called knowledge of results (KOR). This simply means providing subjects with their performance score on the task. Research findings are supportive, and it just makes common sense, that people will do better at tasks when they have access to information regarding their progress (Locke & Latham, 1990). Knowledge of results provides the information which helps direct future action, by indicating the need for the refinement of action plans ("need to speed up") or by encouraging the status quo ("things are going fine"). Cybernetic control theories (Campion & Lord, 1985; Carver & Scheier, 1982) describe these findings well. Especially when someone is succeeding, KOR can also serve to enhance task self-efficacy (Bandura, 1977) thus enabling future performance. But it is the initial setting of the goal, that is, the creation of a challenge, that advocates of performance goals would suggest is the motivational "spark" which starts it all (Locke & Latham, 1990).

The informational use of KOR, as described by control theory, is essentially an internal kind of evaluation process, but external evaluation is inherent in the collection and delivery of the performance data to the person by either an experimenter or a supervisor -- and also in the external assignment of the goal itself. Clearly, an assigned goal communicates an externally-derived standard of performance to which the person is being asked to adhere, and against which their performance will presumably be compared. In real-life contexts, it is inevitable that KOR will also be accompanied by more subjective evaluations (e.g., praise or criticism), which can have more unpredictable effects on motivation and performance, as can the influence of coworkers.

Given that the greatest interest in goal setting has come from industry, the focus on formally assigned goals in the applied psychology literature is understandable. However, the finding that specific intentions are more easily monitored and enacted does not necessarily rely on some external intervention, such as a supervisor formally assigning a goal. In nonwork contexts, or in work contexts with much autonomy, self-set specific objectives can also help to direct behavior.

Reflecting the different purposes evident in these research traditions, the goal setting treatment was deliberately designed as a way to motivate task performance, whereas the expected evaluation manipulation in the social psychology literature was, at least in my opinion, never really intended to be a practical motivational treatment. Again, it seems that the purpose in the latter case was simply to (in a more pure, detached, sense) investigate the effects of evaluation, not to attempt to improve performance by actually conducting performance evaluations.

But, ironically, using just the up-front warning of evaluation in effect retains only what is arguably the most "negative" part of what in realistic contexts is always a more complex procedure. The informational, confidence-building part -- that is, the (hopefully) "positive" part -- is missing. Amabile (1979, 1982, 1993, 1996) and Hennessey in her chapter have made similar observations. Given these differences, it is easy in retrospect to see why there is some evidence of a lack of generalizability between the expected evaluation and actual evaluation manipulations. If expected or anticipated evaluation was originally intended as a proxy manipulation for actual evaluation, perhaps this needs to be reconsidered, as actual evaluations clearly contain additional important elements. On the other hand, perhaps it truly is the specific construct of anticipated evaluation with which some have had interest. If so, the differing findings reflect not a lack of generalizability but evidence pertaining to different questions.

Tasks

Experimental tasks have varied in many ways. The task context (work, learning, or play) examined basically reflects the subject matter of interest to the researchers. Task complexity has varied from simple to complex, but also has included creative tasks like painting or creative writing. Such creative tasks seem somehow different from technically complex tasks. For example, piloting an airliner must be considered a complex task, but it would under normal circumstances probably not be considered a creative one. Tasks examined have also varied in terms of repetitiveness. Most production-type tasks are highly repetitive, with performance measured as the quantity of some tangible outcome product ("widgets") produced. The creative tasks studied tend instead to be 1-shot in nature (e.g., one painting is to be produced), although there are exceptions (e.g., the number of ideas produced in brainstorming tasks). Whether the 1-shot format is an unintentional consequence of the time it ordinarily takes to complete a single product like a painting, or an indication of the inherently nonproduction-oriented nature of the creative context, or both, is unclear. Tasks have also varied in terms of novelty. Tasks in most laboratory studies by their very nature are fairly novel, whereas, especially in the applied literature, many field studies involve people's real-life, well-learned, jobs.

Dependent Variables, Level of Analysis, Individual Difference Variables

Another obvious difference is in outcome variables, where performance quantity, performance quality, task enjoyment or intrinsic motivation, and learning have all been used. Again these choices have made sense given the areas of interest. In terms of level of analysis, social loafing research is inherently group level, whereas the others typically have addressed individual-level motivational concerns. Various individual difference variables have been investigated, usually as moderators of the evaluation or goal treatment. The common theme is that there are some people for whom the interaction with external evaluations, competition, and goals is a positive or effective one, and is sometimes even sought out. For others the experience is less satisfactory.

BOUNDARIES, OVERLAP, AND COMPLEMENT

Goal Setting

Although there have been a number of exceptions, the literature on performance goal setting consists mostly of studies of assigned performance goals on repetitive "widget-making" tasks, where both goal level and dependent variable are based on some easily quantifiable performance index. In the work task context, extrinsic motivation and rewards have been emphasized for practical reasons. And as noted in my previous chapter, quantitative performance is generally enhanced by goal assignment, except when tasks are complex where the evidence is more mixed.

Organizations, and, as a result, industrial-organizational psychologists, have tended to focus on extrinsic motivation and performance for at least three reasons. First, it is a lot easier to have impact on extrinsic motivation. Although conditions in the United States have on the whole changed for the better since the days of assembly lines and sweatshops, the fact remains that the majority of real-life work tasks are probably not all that intrinsically interesting to a lot of people. Would people really be, for example, accountants, janitors, insurance salespeople, shop workers, or business executives, if they didn't need the money? Some surely would, but many people would no doubt do something different if they could. Of course, there are a few lucky individuals who are able to earn their living at something they truly love, but these are the exceptions rather than the rule. Efforts to enhance the intrinsic appeal of work (e.g., job enrichment, Turner & Lawrence, 1965; the job characteristics model, Hackman & Oldham, 1976; empowerment, Spreitzer, 1997) come and go, but the base rate is probably still that most jobs are relatively uninvolving to many job incumbents. Second, extrinsic rewards are important in the workplace. Surviving in the modern world does usually mean accepting a position with some organization and performing some task(s) in order to earn money for the necessities of life (Rousseau, 1995). People, whether they are intrinsically motivated by it or not, want and need to be paid for their work (Greenberg, 1990). A third reason is that organizations often tend to take a short-term view of productivity. Immediate production and profit is often emphasized over issues which might have more long-term, but less predictable, impact on organizational effectiveness, such as job attitudes and intrinsic motivation.

As noted earlier, although assigned goals have been the most common treatment investigated (again as a function of the extrinsic focus of the workplace), a self-set goal can have the same directing effect on one's intentions and actions, as long as commitment to the goal remains strong. The "advantage" of assigned goals, and definitely a factor in their empirical success, is that people are more likely to stick to a goal when it is linked to important external consequences (e.g., yearly performance reviews, job security, bonuses, promotions, peer approval). External commitments to goals are particularly motivating (Hollenbeck & Klein, 1987; Locke & Latham, 1990).

There is evidence that goal setting does seem to be moderated by individual differences. Several studies have indicated that subjects with either higher need for achievement or the Type A pattern set higher goals for themselves (Matsui, Okada, & Kakuyama, 1982; Taylor, Locke, Lee, & Gist, 1984). Likewise, achievement-oriented subjects have reported stronger commitment to difficult goals (Hollenbeck, Williams, & Klein, 1989). More recently, research on goal orientation (Button, Mathieu, & Zajac, 1996) and conscientiousness (Barrick, Mount, & Strauss, 1993) indicate similar findings. Goals tend to be more effective for conscientious (i.e., hard working, diligent) individuals and those with a learning orientation, that is, those who take goals (and perhaps other evaluative treatments) as a challenge rather than a threat. Although not a major focus in the applied literature, there is also some evidence (Ivancevich, 1982; Sales, 1970) of negative affective consequences of goal setting (e.g., job dissatisfaction and stress). As Locke and Latham (1990) observed, "It should not be surprising if goal setting, at least in some circumstances, led to greater anxiety and stress" (p. 241).

Social Loafing Research

The social loafing tradition as described in Shepperd's chapter investigates the issue of individual contributions to group efforts, particularly the question of when individuals will "loaf" in a group setting. Typical studies involve fairly simple laboratory tasks with quantifiable outcome measures. Shepperd offers an expectancy theory explanation for individuals' choices to contribute to group efforts or not, and the key social loafing finding, that individuals tend to loaf when their personal contributions cannot be distinguished or evaluated by others, is explained as a function of outcome value. Everything else being equal, when individual efforts can be evaluated, the negative outcomes of loafing tend to lead people to choose more cooperative behaviors. When evaluation is not possible, and there are thus no negative consequences, loafing is more likely. So in this research tradition, the potential for external evaluation tends to result in increased motivation and task performance.

The perspective offered by Shepperd is very compatible with theoretical perspectives offered in the goal setting and work motivation literatures. The expectancy theory model has often been used to explain goal setting effects (Klein, 1989; Reidel, Nebeker, & Cooper, 1988; Tubbs, Boehne, & Dahl, 1993) and choices of work behaviors in general (Mitchell, 1974; Naylor, Pritchard, & Ilgen, 1980; Vroom, 1964). In fact, the social psychology literature on social loafing itself is often cited in applied psychology journals. Although there have been exceptions (Klein & Mulvey, 1995), work motivation and goal setting researchers have tended to focus on individual-level rather than group-level behavior, and have often relied heavily on the social psychological research on group behavior. However, with the increasing prevalence of work teams in organizations (Guzzo & Shea, 1992), there has been a new emphasis on group level productivity, accountability, and outcome interdependence (Lawler, 1990; Motowidlo & Schmit, 1999; Wageman, 1995).

Achievement Motivation Research

The research described in the Tauer and Harackiewicz chapter involves manipulations of expected evaluation, competition, and goal type (mastery vs. performance) and their effects on intrinsic motivation, task enjoyment, and positive affect. Tasks were games such as Boggle and pinball. Perhaps the most interesting aspect of their work is their use of achievement motivation as a moderator variable. Basically, their results showed that evaluation, competition, and performance goals, all typically thought to hurt intrinsic motivation, actually were positively related to that outcome for subjects who scored high in achievement motivation. Their findings are, as they put it, "in contrast to conventional wisdom that argues that the effects of evaluation, competition, and performance goals are uniformly negative" (Chapter 4, pp. 94-95). They suggest that further study of personality moderators is warranted in order to better understand differential reactions to evaluative influences and to enhance the intrinsic motivation of all individuals.

The achievement motivation perspective is well known in the applied literature as a model for task motivation, and these particular findings are consistent with the previously mentioned findings in the goal setting literature related to motivational types. The common thread in these various results is that individuals who work hard, like to work, and view work as a challenge may react more positively to goals, evaluation, and competition than do others. As Tauer and Harackiewicz note, person by situation interactions are common in psychology and should probably be expected in the case of motivational and evaluative treatments.

Research on Creativity and Intrinsic Motivation

Hennessey reviews research on creativity on heuristic tasks, that is, those requiring novel solutions every time. The other literatures have primarily dealt with algorithmic tasks, where the path to completion is more straightforward and evaluation is consequently predicted to be more effective. Another difference in tasks is that those examined in this literature were not repetitive in nature. Typically, a single painting, poem, collage, or geometric design was to be created during an experiment. Intrinsic motivation and performance (assessed as the creative quality of the subjects' work) were dependent variables.

One key issue involves the independent variable. In many studies, evaluation was only anticipated by subjects, whereas in others an actual evaluation of each subject's creative performance was conducted. An expected evaluation can indeed be motivating, but mostly in a threatening way. And though that manipulation has led to increased performance in some cases, sometimes it has not. One wonders to what extent the "1-shot" nature of the creative tasks contributes to such findings, in that the pressure created by the expected evaluation might be exacerbated. That is, a subject might (correctly) feel that everything would depend on that one painting. In contrast, effects on task performance have been more positive when an actual evaluation took place, and this makes sense. An actual evaluation provides everything an anticipated one does, but, as noted earlier, adds actual task relevant information (KOR) that may encourage subjects, build task self-efficacy, and perhaps even increase motivation. Amabile's (1993, 1996) recent discussions have dealt with these issues at length.

On creative tasks like those examined in this literature it is easy to see why there is a philosophical opposition to evaluation, goals, and competition -- all factors which do seem in a way contrary to the basic nature of the creative process. However, even in these contexts there apparently can be some positive benefits of extrinsic influences. Similar to the trend noted by Tauer and Harackiewicz, the initial position that evaluation can only have negative consequences has begun to give way to a middle ground, where evaluation is sometimes predicted to have positive effects depending on the person involved, with shyer people, females, and high-skill subjects reacting more negatively to expected evaluations than others. As Hennessey put it, "We now understand...that the impact of extrinsic motivation on performance is much more complex than once believed" (Chapter 3, p. 71).

Future research may provide more clues to the nature of any moderating effect of individual differences in creative task environments. But in general, aren't feedback from peers and experts on one's style and technique, and suggestions for future efforts necessary, unavoidable, even desirable things for one's growth as an artist? No doubt some people in creative endeavors work in complete isolation, but others often (and of their own free will) seek out a friend or mentor's opinion. Isn't it just really mostly an issue of how and when these evaluative events should occur, not if they should ever occur? Perhaps it is the autocratic, top-down, mandatory type of evaluation that has the most negative implications for people, not necessarily the fact that the information comes from an external source. I do not suggest that seeking feedback from an esteemed colleague, an expert, or even a friend, is without its stressful side, but just that perhaps the mechanism and the source of the evaluation should be considered separately.

In general, these findings are not inconsistent with the goal setting literature. Tasks like these have rarely been examined by I/O psychologists, but given the findings with other complex tasks (Wood, Mento, & Locke, 1987) relatively weak goal setting effects would probably be predicted. Are performance goals even compatible with creative tasks? Certainly the typical quantity goal setting would seem relatively useless in this context. Time deadline goals might be more applicable, but I don't really mean to suggest that artists should necessarily create more structure for their creative behavior -- or that others (instructors, patrons, etc.) should do it for them. That is an issue for art school faculty (or whomever) to decide. However, such goals would almost certainly be effective for some people in some circumstances, and are no doubt used spontaneously all the time. For example, when a painting must be completed prior to an art opening, it is inevitable that the artist has at some level incorporated that external deadline into her intentional structure (i.e., adopted it as a time goal). To not have done so -- at some level of awareness -- would require an odd kind of mental discipline for someone who actually wanted the opening to take place. It would be interesting to know how often people in creative contexts do spontaneously set specific goals (time or otherwise) for themselves and the nature of their consequences.

INTEGRATING THE AREAS

In Chapter 5, Harkins presented a model for integrating the four research traditions (along with that of social facilitation) along three dimensions: evaluation, goal, and task complexity. This is an interesting and useful summary which helps to, in a different way than I did earlier, make the point that these research areas do not overlap so much as they cover distinct conceptual space. And I generally concur with the categorizations and conclusions reached. However, there are two minor issues which, from the perspective of the goal setting literature (if I can presume to represent that viewpoint), might be interpreted differently, so they are mentioned here in the hopes of aiding in the refinement of the model.

One consideration is the manner in which a goal setting effect is defined in the discussion of the tables of results. Rather than defining a goal setting effect as some specific mean difference between particular cells in the design, goal setting researchers would probably consider any significant mean difference attributable to a goal manipulation to be a goal setting effect. For example, the significant mean difference in the no evaluation condition would probably be interpreted as being a goal setting effect, in that performance was increased as a result of the specific goal. A larger mean difference is indeed observed in the experimenter evaluation condition, due to the added motivation of an external review, but because both performance effects are due to goal assignment they would probably both be considered goal setting effects. It is true that goal setting, as typically studied, does not occur in the absence of some external evaluation. But not calling the effect of an assigned goal a goal setting effect in that case seems to somehow imply that goal setting cannot be effective (i.e., there can't be "a goal setting effect") in the absence of some external evaluation. People set their own, very effective, goals all the time. In fact, an advocate of goal setting might suggest that results in the no evaluation conditions provide evidence that goal setting can be somewhat effective even in the absence of external evaluations, at least in the short term. This issue may be mostly one of semantics.

Another issue is that even though goal setting has sometimes been successful with some fairly complex tasks, this is not represented in the model because in the field studies in question the complex tasks were the subjects' real-life well-learned jobs. Should a complex task (e.g., piloting an airliner) not be considered complex once it is no longer novel? This seems debatable. It may be premature to completely exclude goal setting from the complex-task side of the matrix, especially when some evidence from the creativity and achievement motivation areas suggests that certain individuals may respond positively to evaluations even on highly creative tasks.

CONCLUSIONS AND SUGGESTIONS

Several conclusions seem relevant regarding the effect of evaluation on motivation and performance. The most important consideration, in my opinion, is that of how evaluation is defined. Some researchers have actually conducted 1-on-1 performance feedback sessions. Most others have instead manipulated expected or anticipated evaluation in short-term lab studies, in essence letting subjects know that evaluation is possible or probable, rather than actually following through with the evaluation. From the perspective of an industrial/organizational psychologist, the distinction between a real and a potential performance evaluation seems extremely important.

For example, in laboratory goal setting research actual KOR is normally always given, as it is virtually axiomatic that KOR is a necessary condition for effective goal setting to occur (Locke & Latham, 1990). However, that is usually the extent of the formal evaluation; any further evaluative information (e.g., praise or criticism) is usually avoided as the purpose of the research is to assess, as purely as possible, the effects of goal setting per se. But in real-life work tasks, a much more extensive evaluation of an employee's performance usually takes place: what is known as a performance appraisal.

A major subdiscipline of the industrial branch of I/O field focuses on the topic of performance appraisal. The need for effective performance evaluation and feedback is recognized as being so important to the success and well-being of organizations that decades of research has investigated such questions as: Who should give feedback?, When/how often should it occur?, What dimensions of performance should be discussed?, What corrective action is needed?, What constitutes a "fair" evaluation?, What recourse does the employee have?, and so on (e.g., see Campbell, McCloy, Oppler, & Sager, 1993; Cardy, 1998; Meyer, Kay, & French, 1965; Pulakos, 1997). Of course the threatening and aversive aspect of evaluation is present; that will unfortunately always exist when people perform tasks and are evaluated by others. But from an organization's perspective, that aspect of the process goes hand in hand with the (hopefully) positive rewarding and corrective aspects of evaluation.

My point is that it may be worthwhile for social psychologists to take a fresh look at the concept of performance evaluation and how it relates to the kind of task contexts they examine. Amabile and her colleagues' work has clearly already taken that path. The applied psychology literature on performance appraisal may also have something to offer. We in I/O psychology have borrowed so much from social psychology; perhaps this is one area where the applied literature can return the favor.

Although the applied literature may have the advantage regarding techniques for directing task behavior and administering performance evaluation, the social psychology literature is clearly more advanced in terms of examining negative consequences of evaluation. Sometimes given a back seat, the impact of goals and feedback on attitudes, intrinsic motivation, anxiety and stress deserve greater attention in the applied literature.

Recent findings suggest that the study of individual difference moderator variables may be one of the keys to further understanding these issues. Trends beginning to emerge suggest (not surprisingly in retrospect) that different things motivate different people. Some are spurred on by competition, accountability, and reward; others are petrified by the same factors. The latter is perhaps especially true on complex, creative tasks where extrinsic influences may be most detrimental in general. Further efforts on this issue, in all of the literatures, appear warranted.

Another issue is the standard concern over external validity and generalizability. Many of the studies in both the applied and the social literature were conducted in the laboratory with tasks that were highly novel to subjects. As I noted in my earlier chapter, the most successful instances of goal setting with complex tasks have involved workers performing well-learned activities, where adequate task strategies would allow even very complex tasks to be performed more predictably. In contrast, the evidence for reduced goal setting effects with complex tasks were all obtained with very novel laboratory tasks. Similar arguments could be made regarding some of the social psychological research with short-term lab studies and 1-shot creativity tasks. Although field research is inefficient, that may be the best context for experiments which can truly untangle the novelty and complexity dimensions of tasks.

A final issue that deserves mention is the base rates of particular task types in the real world. Of all the tasks which people do and on which they might be evaluated, it seems to me that most are either work tasks or academic tasks, and are generally the kind of tasks on which evaluation and goals have been at least somewhat effective. The very complex, creative tasks Hennessey discusses are certainly of great interest, but they are also of relatively low base rate overall. My point is that externally-based goals and evaluations may well be effective, efficient, and, if carried out intelligently and humanely, tolerable to all concerned, on many of the tasks that are done in the world. Such procedures will of course sometimes be ineffective, and perhaps even detrimental, depending on task, context, and person. In some of these cases (perhaps on certain tasks where intrinsic motivation is crucial) it may make sense to avoid some external contingencies or at least temper them (e.g., by using learning rather than performance goals). In other cases, perhaps where only a few people react negatively, it may be most efficient to continue the external procedures and deal with the problems on an individual basis.

Goals and evaluation may always be most effective in formal work contexts, as a result of both the behavioral expectations which accompany organizational membership and the repetitive nature of many common work tasks. I personally share the gut feeling that evaluation and creative task performance are inherently somewhat incompatible. But the trend in the creativity area, as well as in achievement motivation, has begun to swing from a mostly negative view of evaluation to an initial acceptance of a contingency approach. In the goal setting literature, ironically, almost the opposite trend exists, with recent evidence on task and personality moderators qualifying what originally seemed to be a more generally positive effect (DeShon, Brown, & Greenis, 1996; Earley, Connolly, & Ekegren, 1989). That both basic and applied researchers are, from different directions, reaching this same, more moderate, conclusion perhaps affords some degree of confidence in its merit.

A FINAL THOUGHT

Sometimes when I talk to psychologists not familiar with industrial/organizational psychology, I get the feeling that they think that the sole purpose of that field is to assist the business world in the creation of control and evaluation systems which ultimately take away freedom and individuality. As a way of concluding, I would like to relate what a colleague said long ago in response to a similar concern. He said that our role as psychologists studying the workplace is not just to help make the organization more effective, but also to help make it more fair and rewarding for the people who make up the organization. Hirings, firing, layoffs, evaluations, goals, performance appraisals, all will occur (often unsystematically and inequitably) whether psychologists are asked to intervene or not. Our role is to, when given the opportunity, improve on past techniques with the goal of increasing both organizational and personal health and well-being. Perhaps my friend's view represents an idealistic perspective, and one to which our field may not always live up, but it is a viewpoint with which I agree and which underlies the suggestions offered here. If formal performance evaluations and goals are indeed to increasingly occur in the various contexts discussed in this volume, a similar perspective regarding the design and implementation of those procedures would be beneficial.

REFERENCES

Amabile, T. M. (1979). Effects of external evaluation on artistic creativity. *Journal of Personality and Social Psychology*, *37*, 221-233.
Amabile, T. M. (1982). Children's artistic creativity: Detrimental effects of competition in a field setting. *Personality and Social Psychology Bulletin*, *8*, 573-578.
Amabile, T. M. (1993). Motivational synergy: Toward new conceptualizations of intrinsic and extrinsic motivation in the workplace. *Human Resource Management Review*, *3*, 185-201.
Amabile, T. M. (1996). *Creativity in context.* Boulder, CO: Westview.
Bandura, A. (1977). Self-efficacy: Toward a unifying theory of behavioral change. *Psychological Review*, *84*, 191-215.
Barrick, M. R., Mount, M. K., & Strauss, J. P. (1993). Conscientiousness and performance of sales representatives: Test of the mediating effects of goal setting. *Journal of Applied Psychology*, *78*, 715-722.
Button, S., Mathieu, J., & Zajac, D. (1996). Goal orientation in organizational behavior research: A conceptual and empirical foundation. *Organizational Behavior and Human Decision Processes*, *67*, 26-48.
Campbell, J. P., McCloy, R. A., Oppler, S. H., & Sager, C. E. (1993). A theory of performance. In N. Schmitt & W. C. Borman (Eds.), *Personnel selection in organizations* (pp. 35-70). San Francisco: Jossey-Bass.
Campion, M. A., & Lord, R. G. (1982). A control systems conceptualization of the goal-setting and changing process. *Organizational Behavior and Human Performance*, *30*, 265-287.
Cardy, R. L. (1998). Performance appraisal in a quality context: A new look at an old problem. In J. W. Smither (Ed.), *Performance appraisal* (pp. 132-162). San Francisco: Jossey-Bass.
Carver, C. S., & Scheier, M. F. (1982). Control theory: A useful conceptual framework for personality-social, clinical, and health psychology. *Psychological Bulletin*, *92*, 111-135.
DeShon, R. P., Brown, K. G., and Greenis, J. L. (1996). Does self-regulation require cognitive resources? Evaluation of resource allocation models of goal setting. *Journal of Applied Psychology*, *81*, 595-608.
Earley, P. C., Connolly, T., and Ekegren, G. (1989). Goals, strategy development, and task performance: Some limits on the efficacy of goal setting. *Journal of Applied Psychology*, *74*, 24-33.
Fishbein, M., & Ajzen, I. (1975). *Belief, attitude, intention, and behavior: An introduction to theory and research.* Reading, MA: Addison-Wesley.
Greenberg, J. (1990). Employee theft as a reaction to underpayment inequity: The hidden costs of pay cuts. *Journal of Applied Psychology*, *75*, 561-568.
Guzzo, R. A., & Shea, G. P. (1992). Group performance and intergroup relations in organizations. In M. D. Dunnette & L. M. Hough (Eds.), *Handbook of industrial and organizational psychology* (Vol. 3, pp. 269-313). Palo Alto, CA: Consulting Psychologists Press.
Hackman, J. R., & Oldham, G. R. (1976). Motivation through the design of work: Test of a theory. *Organizational Behavior and Human Performance*, *16*, 250-279.
Hollenbeck, J. R., & Klein, H. J. (1987). Goal commitment and the goal-setting process: Problems, prospects, and proposals for future research. *Journal of Applied Psychology*, *72*, 212-220.
Hollenbeck, J. R., Williams, C. R., & Klein, H. J. (1989). An empirical examination of the antecedents of commitment to difficult goals. *Journal of Applied Psychology*, *74*, 18-23.
Ivancevich, J. M. (1982). Subordinates' reactions to performance appraisal interviews: A test of feedback and goal-setting techniques. *Journal of Applied Psychology*, *67*, 581-587.

Klein, H. J. (1989). An integrated control theory model of work motivation. *Academy of Management Review*, *14*, 150-172.

Klein, H. J., & Mulvey, P. W. (1995). Two investigations of the relationships among group goals, goal commitment, cohesion, and performance. *Organizational Behavior and Human Decision Processes*, *61*, 44-53.

Lawler, E. E. (1990). *Strategic pay: Aligning organizational strategies and pay systems.* San Francisco: Jossey-Bass.

Locke, E. A., & Latham, G. P. (1990). *A theory of goal setting and task performance.* Englewood Cliffs, NJ: Prentice-Hall.

Matsui, T., Okada, A., & Kakuyama, T. (1982). Influence of achievement need on goal setting, performance, and feedback effectiveness. *Journal of Applied Psychology*, *67*, 645-648.

Mento, A. J., Steel, R. P., & Karren, R. J. (1987). A meta-analytic study of the effects of goal setting on task performance: 1966-1984. *Organizational Behavior and Human Decision Processes*, *39*, 52-83.

Meyer, H. H., Kay, E., & French, J. R. (1965). Split roles in performance appraisal. *Harvard Business Review*, *43*, 123-129.

Mitchell, T. R. (1974). Expectancy models of job satisfaction, occupational preference, and effort: A theoretical, methodological, and empirical appraisal. *Psychological Bulletin*, *81*, 1053-1077.

Mitchell, T. R. (1997). Matching motivational strategies with organizational contexts. In B. M. Staw & L. L. Cummings (Eds.), *Research in Organizational Behavior*, *19*, 57-149.

Motowidlo, S. J., & Schmit, M. J. (1999). Performance assessment in unique jobs. In D. R. Ilgen & E. D. Pulakos (Eds.), *The changing nature of job performance* (pp. 56-86). San Francisco: Jossey-Bass.

Muchinsky, P. M. (2000). *Psychology applied to work.* Belmont, CA: Wadsworth.

Naylor, J. C., & Ilgen, D. R. (1984). Goal setting: A theoretical analysis of a motivational technology. In B. M. Staw & L. L. Cummings (Eds.), *Research in organizational behavior*, *6*, (pp. 95-140). Greenwich, CT: JAI.

Naylor, J. C., Pritchard, R. D., & Ilgen, D. R. (1980). *A theory of behavior in organizations.* New York: Academic Press.

Pulakos, E. D. (1997). Ratings of job performance. In D. L. Whetzel & G. R. Wheaton (Eds.), *Applied measurement methods in industrial psychology* (pp. 291-318). Palo Alto, CA: Consulting Psychologists Press.

Reidel, J. A., Nebeker, D. M., & Cooper, B. L. (1988). The influence of monetary incentives on goal choice, goal commitment, and task performance. *Organizational Behavior and Human Decision Processes*, *42*, 155-180.

Rousseau, D. M. (1995). *Psychological contracts in organizations.* Thousand Oaks, CA: Sage.

Rousseau, D. M., & Parks, J. M. (1993). The contracts of individuals and organizations. In B. M. Staw & L. L. Cummings (Eds.), *Research in organizational behavior* (Vol. 15, pp. 1-43). Greenwich, CT: JAI Press.

Sales, S. M. (1970). Some effects on role overload and role underload. *Organizational Behavior and Human Performance*, *5*, 592-608.

Spreitzer, G. M. (1997). Toward a common ground in defining empowerment. In W. A. Pasmore & R. W. Woodman (Eds.), *Research in organizational change and development* (Vol. 10, pp. 31-62). Greenwich, CT: JAI Press.

Taylor, M. S., Locke, E. A., Lee, C., & Gist, M. E. (1984). Type A behavior and faculty research productivity: What are the mechanisms? *Organizational Behavior and Human Performance*, *34*, 402-418.

Tubbs, M. E., Boehne, D. M., & Dahl, J. G. (1993). Expectancy, valence, and motivational force functions in goal setting research: An empirical test. *Journal of Applied Psychology*, *78*, 361-373.

Turner, A. N., & Lawrence, P. R. (1965). *Industrial jobs and the worker: An investigation of response to task attributes.* Cambridge, MA: Harvard University Press.

Vroom, V. (1964). *Work and motivation.* New York: Wiley.

Wageman, R. (1995). Interdependence and group effectiveness. *Administrative Science Quarterly*, *40*, 145-180.

Wood, R. E., Mento, A. J., & Locke, E. A. (1987). Task complexity as a moderator of goal effects: A meta-analysis. *Journal of Applied Psychology*, *72*, 416-425.

Chapter 8

ATTENDING TO THE DETAILS

Beth A. Hennessey
Wellesley College

Details. We must now pay closer attention to the details. This is the underlying message behind each of the initial five chapters contained in this volume. Most of the theoretical traditions outlined in these pages have been around for quite some time. As Tubbs explains, there is voluminous empirical research to support the traditional goal setting paradigm, and the same could be said for social loafing, social facilitation, cognitive evaluation theory, or the social psychology of creativity. Years ago, when these models were just being developed, it made sense to make sweeping generalizations about the effect of evaluation on motivation and performance. Out of necessity, researchers and theorists exploring these relatively uncharted waters began at the macro level and sought to develop general "laws" of behavior that would apply to the majority of persons the majority of the time. But now our level of understanding is much more sophisticated, much more in depth. We have advanced to the point where we must refine our models and look at the subtleties behind the impact of evaluation.

While each of the contributors to this book would probably agree with these statements up to this point, our ideas about which details merit consideration are not as congruent. Along with myself, Tauer and Harackiewicz argue that we must focus more of our attention on the inner experience of the individual expecting an evaluation and the differences in motivational orientation between individuals. Shepperd recommends that particular attention be paid to the contingencies of the evaluative situation. Tubbs turns his attention to the impact of evaluation in real-world industrial/organizational settings. And Harkins weighs in with a valiant attempt to subsume all of our theoretical orientations, models and literatures under one, single rubric.

In the pages that follow, I will attempt to outline what have I learned, how my own theorizing has benefited, from my reading of these authors. In recent years, my colleagues and I have been faced with the daunting task of revising the Intrinsic Motivation Principle of Creativity (Amabile, 1996), the theoretical model underlying the bulk of our work. The data we have collected over the last 5 or 10 years have revealed an increasingly complex picture and have raised a great many important issues. Although I cannot claim that the chapters contained in this volume have allowed me to resolve these issues, they have given me a great many new insights: Insights which have enabled me to at least reframe a number of research questions that up until now had appeared virtually intractable.

As explained in my previous chapter, our understanding of the interface between motivational orientation and environmental influences has grown considerably. It has become increasingly clear that a relatively simplistic model which proposes that, as extrinsic motivation increases, intrinsic motivation must necessarily decline cannot sufficiently explain the behavior of all individuals under all circumstances. Under some conditions in both the laboratory and the workplace, intrinsic and extrinsic motivation have been found to combine in a complementary fashion. In response to this realization, my colleagues and I have come to supplement our original hydraulic conceptualization with an additive model that recognizes that under certain specific conditions, both the delivery of a competence-affirming evaluation and the expectation of an impending evaluation can sometimes increase levels of extrinsic motivation without having any negative impact on intrinsic motivation or performance.

Revising the Intrinsic Motivation Principle of Creativity to include the caveat that under certain circumstances extrinsic incentives need not be detrimental to intrinsic motivation or creativity of performance was only the first step. We still must specify the circumstances that produce these additive motivational effects, and we must also work to uncover the specific individual difference variables or personality traits that make some people less susceptible to the deleterious effects of extrinsic constraints than others. Most important of all, we have yet to identify the mechanism behind the undermining of intrinsic motivation.

As outlined in my earlier chapter, Amabile's (1993) discussion of "motivational synergy" has proven somewhat helpful in reconciling our more recent laboratory and field study results with the findings reported in the earlier evaluation literature. This model proposes that extrinsic constraints such as evaluations can sometimes serve as "synergistic extrinsic motivators." In other words, rather than detract from initial interest, they can, under certain specific circumstances, combine positively in an *additive* fashion with intrinsic motivation and actually enhance task enjoyment and involvement. The major problem with this model is that it does not provide an explanation of the underlying mechanisms.

MEDIATORS, MODERATORS AND A FOCUS ON INDIVIDUAL DIFFERENCES

What are the specific conditions under which this synergistic process can be expected to occur? How can we predict whether an individual's motivation and creativity of performance will be undermined, enhanced, or remain relatively impervious to the expectation of an evaluation? In my efforts to answer this highly complex question, I have found the work of Harackiewicz and Tauer and their colleague Sansone to be particularly helpful. Their focus is not just on the effect of evaluation (and other extrinsic constraints) on qualitative aspects of performance. Instead, they also concentrate on the impact of evaluation on motivational orientation. In fact, like my colleagues and myself, Tauer and Harackiewicz believe that it is the motivational orientation brought about by the expectation of evaluation that is responsible for changes in performance.

Despite the fact that one particularly common type of evaluation involves competition, few investigations have tested the effects of competition on intrinsic motivation. In an effort to fill this research void, Tauer and Harackiewicz have carried out a series of studies focused on the effects of evaluations promised and delivered in competitive situations. In their chapter appearing in this volume, they report the results of these investigations and argue that that the effects of competition cannot be summarized with a single, main effect conclusion. Instead, they make the case that "an analysis of the effects of evaluation on motivation requires a close examination of moderator variables that help identify individuals for whom evaluation may have particularly positive or negative effects, as well as mediator variables that help identify the motivational processes responsible for these effects" (Chapter 4, p. 79). While many investigators have tended to focus on the self-regulation of behavior rather than intrinsic motivation *per se*, Tauer and Harackiewicz have worked to bridge intrinsic motivation and performance-based approaches with a concentration on the individual's phenomenological experience while working under the expectation of evaluation. As they explain, the effects of evaluative contingencies may only be as powerful as the internal processes they initiate.

THE ROLE OF AFFECT

My colleagues and I have also come to be especially concerned with the internal processes that result from the introduction of an extrinsic constraint such as evaluation. For the most part, the internal processes upon which my own work has focused have involved affective response. As explained in my previous chapter, I have spent a number of years trying to understand the mechanism behind the undermining of intrinsic motivation in young children Over the years, a number of cognitively-based explanations have been offered. The "discounting principle" (Kelley, 1973), the "overjustification hypothesis" (Bem, 1972; Kelley, 1967, 1973; deCharms, 1968) and "cognitive evaluation theory" (Deci, 1975; Deci & Ryan, 1980) have all proven useful for understanding the negative effects of extrinsic, environmental constraints (such as evaluation) on adults, yet they fail to adequately explain why young children have also been observed to suffer decreases in intrinsic motivation and creativity. Simply stated, children under the age of 7 or 8 years have consistently been shown to lack the cognitive capabilities necessary for weighing multiple sufficient causes of behavior and employing discounting (e.g., Shultz, Butkowsky, Pearce, & Shanfield, 1975; Smith, 1975). How is it, then, that when working under the expectation of evaluation young children frequently demonstrate decreases in intrinsic motivation and creativity of performance yet seem cognitively incapable of engaging in the thought processes believed to underlie the overjustification paradigm?

I hypothesize that the reduction of intrinsic interest in young children (and perhaps in all of us) is driven primarily by the learned expectation that evaluations are usually paired with activities that need to be done -- activities that are often not fun and sometimes even aversive. The undermining of intrinsic interest may result as much from emotion or affect as it does from cognitive analysis. Children may learn to react negatively to a task as "work" when their behavior is controlled by socially imposed factors (such as evaluations), and they may react positively to a task as "play" when there are no constraints imposed. Negative affect resulting from socially learned stereotypes or scripts may be what leads to decrements in intrinsic interest (see Hennessey, 1999).

Tauer and Harackiewicz offer a synthesis of the literature coupled with original empirical data that do much to support this affectively-based view. Turning their attention to personality variables, they review research that reveals significant, systematic individual differences in participants' responses to evaluation and competition. The results of these investigations provide compelling evidence that the effects of competition (and evaluation) can be positive or negative, and that this outcome is at least partially determined by individual differences in affective response. Simply stated, studies conducted by Tauer and Harackiewicz and others reveal that not everyone reacts to the prospect of evaluation in the same way.

THE PROCESS MODEL

In an earlier exploration of the means by which situational and personality variables may moderate the effects of evaluative contingencies, Sansone and

Harackiewicz (1996) contend that we must think about intrinsic or extrinsic motivation not only as an end-state but as a *process*. In other words, while outcome-derived motivation resulting from the expectation of an evaluation may pull one into an activity, a self-regulated, process-derived motivation (e.g., cognitive and affective absorption in the task) may be necessary to maintain performance over time. Sansone and Harackiewicz (1996) believe that this self-regulation of behavior requires that the individual actively maintain both internal and external sources of motivation. If a task is to be brought to successful completion, expectancy and valuation processes must be oriented at compatible outcomes. This melding of the these two goal types, the individual's own goals for task engagement and the incentives introduced into the environment, is seen as critical to the self-regulatory process. In other words, like Amabile, these authors argue that creativity and other hallmarks of successful task performance will only come about when task motivation and extrinsic incentives like evaluation combine in a synergistic, additive or complementary fashion.

In their present chapter, Tauer and Harackiewicz consider the role played by achievement motivation in an evaluative situation. Although not included in the original process model (Harackiewicz & Sansone, 1991), the achievement motivation variable appears to be especially helpful in documenting the affective processes responsible for changes in intrinsic motivation in competitive settings. Tauer and Harackiewicz report that individuals high in achievement motivation (HAMs) tend to respond positively to competition because of the challenge involved. They "desire objective ability feedback (McClelland, 1961) and seek out activities that provide the opportunity for self-evaluation (Greenwald, 1982). On the other hand, those low in achievement motivation (LAMs) do not place the same emphasis on competence, and typically avoid evaluation" (Chapter 4, p. 80).

Importantly, while it may be desirable, the prospect of receiving performance feedback does not appear to be a major motivator for HAMs faced with a competitive situation. Regardless of the feedback they receive or whether they win or lose, HAMs report more positive affect than do LAMs; whereas LAMs report more positive affect than do HAMs in noncompetitive (nonevaluative) situations. In their discussion of these findings, Tauer and Harackiewicz demonstrate how their model makes it possible to separate processes that are initiated by evaluative contingencies at the outset of an activity from those prompted by feedback at the end of an activity.

According to their analyses, there are two distinct paths to intrinsic motivation in competitive situations. The imposition of evaluative contingencies has the potential to exert a powerful influence on the way that individuals approach and experience an activity and also can strongly influence subsequent intrinsic motivation. In addition, the performance feedback that individuals eventually do receive may also affect task motivation. Tauer and Harackiewicz report that we can expect to see HAMs and LAMs respond differently at the outset of a competition, and they also observe that HAMs and LAMs react in different ways to the feedback they later receive. In examining the effects of evaluative contingencies, Tauer and Harackiewicz argue that it is important to consider the unique and combined effects that each of these distinct paths may have on subsequent task motivation and affective response.

Within their chapter, Tauer and Harackiewicz report the results of seven studies designed to investigate the effect of competition on task motivation and enjoyment. Importantly, in none of these investigations did they find a main effect of competition. In fact, as they point out, had they not measured achievement motivation, they would have concluded that competition had no effect on intrinsic motivation. In their consideration of this moderating personality variable, they uncover a consistent relation between competition, achievement motivation, and intrinsic motivation and demonstrate that competitive situations can engender either positive or negative affect, depending on individual differences in achievement motivation. HAMs and LAMs react differently to evaluative contingencies, and their different approaches have powerful effects on subsequent affective response and task enjoyment. As Tauer and Harackiewicz remind us, "These findings are consistent with a hallmark of social psychology: behavior is a function of both the environment and personality (Lewin, 1935)" (Chapter 4, p. 95).

THE ROLE OF INDIVIDUAL DIFFERENCES

Like myself, Tauer and Harackiewicz believe that in situations of expected evaluation, it is alterations in motivational orientation that are largely responsible for changes in performance. Given this orientation, it makes sense that these researchers would focus their attention on differences in achievement motivation and ask whether everyone is likely to respond to evaluation in the same way. In our own investigations of evaluation contingencies, my colleagues and I are beginning to appreciate the role played by other personality differences as well.

Although the research waters are still considerably "muddied," it seems that a number of individual difference variables, many of which appear to be entirely separate from issues of motivation, may play an important part in determining whether the prospect of an impending evaluation will have a positive, a negative or no appreciable impact on performance. As outlined in my previous chapter, Cheek and Stahl (1986) offer data that suggest that the effects of evaluation may be moderated by characteristics such as shyness. Conti, Collins, and Picariello (1995) found that the detrimental effects of competitive evaluation held for girls but not for boys. And Conti and Amabile (1995) reported that individuals' skill levels mediated the impact of evaluation. Low-skill students produced more creative products (and demonstrated higher levels of intrinsic motivation) when expecting an evaluation, and high-skill students were more creative in the no-evaluation condition. Similar effects were also observed by Pollak (1992) and Hill, Amabile, Coon, and Whitney (1994).

Nonexperimental research carried out over the past several years has also uncovered some evidence that expected reward or evaluation need not always undermine intrinsic interest and creativity. For example, in a study of commissioned and noncommissioned works done by professional artists, the extrinsic incentive of a commission was seen by some artists as a highly controlling constraint; and the creativity of their work plummeted. Yet for those who looked at the commission as an opportunity to achieve recognition or a confirmation of their competence by respected others, creativity was enhanced (Amabile, Phillips, & Collins, 1994). As mentioned previously, interview studies in the workplace have also revealed that the prospect of impending, critical evaluation often leads to low levels of intrinsic motivation and creativity (Amabile & Gryskiewicz, 1987). However, these same studies show that informative evaluation that conveyed positive recognition of creative work often contributed to highly creative performance.

My reading of the chapter authored by Tauer and Harackiewicz has added to my conviction that motivational orientation in situations of expected evaluation and other extrinsic constraints must be seen not as a dichotomy (intrinsic vs. extrinsic) but as a highly complex and multi-layered continuum -- a continuum very much dependent upon differences in causality orientation (see Deci & Ryan, 1985a, 1985b), personal history, and previous experience. Extrinsic motivation must not be viewed simply as the absence of intrinsic motivation. Both the content and the *process* of motivational orientation must be considered, and the work of Tauer, Harackiewicz and colleagues does much to bring us closer to this goal.

THE EXPECTANCY-VALUE AND SOCIAL LOAFING FRAMEWORKS

At first glance, Shepperd's application of the expectancy-value framework to the phenomenon of social loafing appears to have little relevance to the social psychology of creativity. The bulk of investigations coming from the intrinsic motivation/creativity literature concentrates on solitary task performance; while social loafing almost always occurs in group situations. In addition, Shepperd's review of the literature reveals that the majority of tasks presented in the expectancy-value/social loafing research traditions are physical -- involving a tug of war, clapping, typing speed and the like. Even the studies employing more cerebral activities present subjects with algorithmic tasks having only one solution (e.g., maze completion) or evaluate performance on the basis of quantity rather than quality of response (e.g., unusual uses tests).

Yet researchers like myself would do well to take a lesson from Shepperd and colleagues. Once again, we must learn to pay attention to the details. All too often we are guilty of making assumptions about our study participants' motivation to take part in the activities placed before them. We pretest our target tasks to make certain that subjects will find them intrinsically interesting; but rarely do we assess participants' expectations that their performance will be contingent on effort or probe their perceptions of the costs (psychological and material) associated with achieving a creative solution. Rarely, in other words, do we consider (much less test) subjects' effort motivation. How can we be certain that they will put forth their best effort? How are we to be sure that our study participants believe that there is a good probability that they will be able to perform up to our standards? In fact, as creativity researchers, we make every effort to preserve the open-ended nature of our target tasks and go to great lengths *not* to specify any sort of performance criteria. The potential for subject loafing in our studies looms large and deserves our attention.

Goal Setting in I/0 Environments

Focusing his sights on performance in industrial/organizational environments, Tubbs too advocates that we attend to the details. The details with which he is most concerned involve task complexity and the moderating effect of this factor on goal setting. As is the case with the social loafing literature, Tubbs reports that the majority of tasks used in goal setting research are fairly simple (see Wood, Mento, & Locke, 1987). Tubbs questions whether research findings can be generalized across task types; yet he is also quick to point out that a sizeable minority of studies have focused on moderately complex activities performed in the context of real-life settings. Generally speaking, effect sizes tend to be somewhat larger on less complicated tasks, yet the impact of goal setting remains moderate even on the most complex tasks examined (Wood et al., 1987).

There are a great many similarities between the work that Tubbs reviews and the investigations carried out by myself and my colleagues. In recent years we too have turned much of our attention to the workplace as we have set out to discover which social and environmental factors are particularly conducive to (or detrimental to) real-world creative performance. The moderately complex activities of which he speaks are not unlike some of the tasks targeted in the intrinsic motivation/creativity literature.

For the most part, investigations of creative performance in industrial/organizational settings have been nonexperimental (field) studies. These naturalistic investigations have taken a variety of forms. In some cases, research and development scientists whose job it is to be creative were interviewed using the critical incident technique (Amabile & Gryskiewicz, 1987; Amabile, 1988). Under this system, study participants were asked to describe in detail two significant events from their work experience: one an attempt to solve a problem or complete a task that exemplified high creativity, and one that exemplified low creativity. Detailed content analyses of both classes of stories were then conducted to determine the personal characteristics of the main "players" and the features of the environment in which they found themselves. This methodology has been supplemented with questionnaire studies that ask employees to rate their perceptions of their work environment and most recently with investigations that allow for the actual assessment of and comparison of products and ideas that have been developed in a variety of real-world work environments (e.g., Amabile, 1994).

Results from these nonexperimental studies "fit" nicely with many of the research outcomes reported by Tubbs. In fact, many of the parallels between these two lines of research are quite striking. Despite conventional wisdom that underscores the importance of personal characteristics in creative performance, naturalistic studies of creativity in business indicate that the context, the work environment, may play an equal, if not more influential, role. Similarly, a review of the goal setting literature reveals that a major factor in the typical success of goal setting in work contexts is the context itself. As Tubbs explains, I/O psychology, as a field, examines human behavior in what must be viewed as especially strong situations relative to those typically studied in social psychological research. After all, the very purpose of an organization is to organize and control human behavior in order to produce some "product" and, eventually, a profit (Bedeian & Zammuto, 1991; Etzioni, 1964).

Another commonality between the goal setting and intrinsic motivation/creativity research findings is that both bodies of work reveal the significant role played by individual difference variables in determining performance. And, in fact, Tauer and Harackiewicz also come to essentially this same conclusion in their own discussion of the achievement motivation literature. Whereas investigators interested in goal setting have emphasized goal orientation (learning goal orientation vs. performance goal orientation) and conscientiousness, motivational theorists have focused on individuals with high and low levels of achievement motivation, and creativity researchers have underscored the importance of initial skill level and trait-like affective tendencies. As revealed in our earlier chapters, the data have forced not only myself and Tauer and Harackiewicz, but also Tubbs to come to the conclusion that no one theoretical model can carry the day. The realization that not everyone will react to environmental constraints in the same way has prompted all of us to turn our attentions to the *process* underlying the behaviors that we study. Each of us believes that it is essential that the *mechanism underlying subjects' performance* be examined. In Tubb's words, "One can either avoid such speculation or cautiously embrace it" (p. 38). But deeper understanding will only come about if the latter course is followed and potential explanations for behavior are sought.

A variety of other important parallels between these different research traditions also deserve mention. For instance, in an attempt to examine process as well as outcome, some investigators from each of these three theoretical camps have proposed that a diffusion of attention away from the target task may be at least partially responsible for performance decrements. Kanfer and Ackerman's (1989) model, cited by Tubbs, hypothesizes that, because of the presence of a specific performance goal, attentional resources that would better be spent on skill acquisition are instead expended on self-regulation activities like performance monitoring, resulting in poor performance (Kanfer, Ackerman, Murtha, Dugdale, & Nelson, 1994). Similarly, a distraction hypothesis put forth by some motivation theorists proposes that performance may be undermined when energies that might be devoted toward task engagement are instead consumed by concerns about impending evaluation (e.g., Reiss & Sushinsky, 1975).

Lest we become too comforted by these similarities in orientation and investigative outcome, I must also point out that not all of our findings can be so neatly packaged. Take for example the question of expertise. In our respective chapters, both Tubbs and I speculate about the role played by experience and familiarity with the task at hand. I report that skill level has been found to mediate the impact of evaluation, with low-skill participants exhibiting higher creativity when expecting an evaluation, and high-skill participants performing better in the absence of evaluation (Conti & Amabile, 1995; Hill, Amabile, Coon, & Whitney, 1994; Pollak, 1992). Yet Tubbs reveals that assigned goals are somewhat less effective, at least initially, with complex and novel tasks and reasons that it is no surprise that adding the pressure of an assigned goal into a situation where someone is trying to learn a new and difficult task can hurt performance. Here again we see the complexity that comes from attending to the details. But how are we to decide which of the many details deserve our attention, and which, for the time being at least, will just serve to confuse the issues without adding anything significant to our understanding?

SORTING THROUGH THE DETAILS FROM A SOCIAL FACILITATION PERSPECTIVE

Contributing the final chapter in the first portion of this volume, Harkins makes a valiant attempt to resolve these thorny issues. Perhaps much better than the rest of us, he sees the points of overlap in the literatures upon which our various theoretical orientations have been based and sets out to integrate our findings via a fairly simple and straightforward three-way factorial model. He argues that perhaps the picture is not nearly as complex as we have feared. As we have been striving to uncover the details (and yes, at times, perhaps even the minutiae), Harkins has been working from the other end, to streamline and simplify our understanding of the impact of expected evaluation on task performance.

It is Harkins's argument that the performance findings from the social loafing, goal setting, intrinsic motivation, achievement goal theory and social facilitation traditions can be explained by taking into account only three factors: (a) whether participants' outputs can be evaluated by the experimenter; (b) the level of performance participants are asked to achieve (stringent goal vs. do your best); and (c) task complexity. He theorizes that external evaluation is probably the most powerful of these three components. He presents data to show that a subject's concern over the potential for experimenter evaluation supersedes interest in the potential for self-evaluation. Yet Harkins is also careful to point out that, in the absence of experimenter evaluation, the potential for self-evaluation is in and of itself sufficient to eliminate social loafing even when the target experimental task is relatively uninteresting (Szymanski & Harkins, 1987).

I have found many aspects of Harkins's argument to be compelling. His reconceptualization of these literatures has, in fact, forced me to take a new look at features of my own work. For example, never have my colleagues or I paid any real attention to the issue of self-evaluation; yet the open-ended target tasks employed in our investigations are exactly the sort that Harkins reports are most likely to engender this tendency to evaluate one's own performance. In our efforts to measure creativity, we make every effort to present research participants with activities that they will find personally involving, interesting and challenging. In our studies of the impact of expected evaluation on intrinsic motivation and creativity of performance, it has been our assumption that subjects in the no evaluation condition were working in the complete absence of extrinsic constraints. But what if they were engaging in self-evaluation? Is it possible that this research paradigm has provided a contrast between two sources of evaluation (experimenter vs. self) rather than a comparison of an evaluation and a true control-no evaluation group? And how might we go about testing this possibility?

Investigators who probe the relation between motivational orientation and creativity of performance would also do well to examine whether participants in their studies perceive that they are being or will soon be evaluated by the experimenter. Unlike the majority of studies reviewed by Harkins, investigations in this genre typically do not employ tasks that can be scored on the spot. On these open-ended, creativity tasks there are no right or wrong answers, no time limits and no behavioral norms. In studies focused on the impact of expected evaluation on motivational orientation and creativity, it is made clear to participants that their performance will be evaluated *after the fact* by a group of expert judges; and for subjects in the control group, no mention is made of evaluation. As a researcher, I have never stopped to consider whether our subjects are participating with the expectation that the product they produce (story, collage, poem, etc.) will also be evaluated by the experimenter. And yet data reported by Harkins reveals that across a variety of experimental situations and tasks, study participants show a profound concern over the potential for experimenter evaluation. This concern, this apprehension about what the experimenter might think about one's performance is so powerful, in fact, that it supplants interest in self-evaluation or feedback from a coactor and also surpasses the desire to impress the experimenter. Might our subjects in the evaluation condition be working under the expectation of immediate experimenter evaluation rather than (or in addition to) evaluation from a distant and nameless group of raters? And is it possible that subjects in our control (no evaluation) condition were also expecting some sort of implicit evaluation on the part of the experimenter?

Along similar lines, both Szymanski and Harkins (1987) and Harkins and Szymanski (1988) showed that when participants were asked to do their best, the potential for self-evaluation motivated them to the same extent as did the potential for evaluation by the experimenter. Once again, the experience of our no evaluation/control group is called into question. Although, in our own investigations, we do not explicitly ask participants to "do their best," it might be argued that there is an implicit expectation that they will put real effort into the experimental task. Importantly, however, it is most likely that, in our studies, participants' efforts to produce their best work are driven by genuine interest in and even excitement about the task rather than by any directive (implied or explicit) from an experimenter. Because they have been designed as measures of creativity, the activities we present are entirely open-ended and have been selected precisely because subjects find them to be intrinsically interesting. Rather than push a button, clap their hands or come up with a one-word answer, participants are asked to produce a collage, a poem, a story or some other tangible product. Few, if any, guidelines are provided; there are no specific goals, no standards or yardsticks, no right or wrong answers, shortcuts, no rote responses.

At first glance, Harkins in his chapter appears to have carefully addressed these issues of task type and task complexity. Like Tubbs and myself, he underscores the fact that social loafing studies have concentrated mainly on noncompetitive, boring, or tiring activities. And his review of the goal setting literature reveals that for the most part, simple tasks that require nothing more than sheer drudgery have been used in this genre of studies as well. As Harkins points out, in the absence of external evaluation pressures, there would be little reason to perform well on such tasks since they are entirely devoid of inherent interest. While this observation makes a lot of sense, his characterizations of the experimental activities targeted in the majority of achievement goal theory or intrinsic motivation studies are not nearly as insightful. He carefully examines the nature of the expectations communicated by the experimenter or the feedback and task information given to study participants, but he fails to look carefully at the experimental tasks themselves.

According to Harkins, the findings in the intrinsic motivation and the achievement goal literatures are simply replications of findings for complex tasks in the social facilitation literature. The problem with this reasoning is that it lumps together studies of intrinsic and achievement goal motivation and ignores important differences in task type. While both experimental traditions utilize complex activities, achievement goals are simply not compatible with open-ended, creativity type activities -- tasks like story-telling or poetry composition for which there is no one right answer or no one best path to solution. Any model designed to subsume these various literatures must classify tasks in terms of more than just how complicated or difficult they appear.

The problem-solving or pinball tasks employed by Tauer and Harackiewicz were chosen as much for their inherent interest as for their complexity. So too the collage-making or story-telling activities employed by my colleagues and me were selected *both* because they allow for creativity of performance and because they are intrinsically interesting. Harkins appears to miss or gloss over this interest component and mistakenly equates task complexity with task interest. He reports investigations contrasting simple and difficult mazes or simple and more challenging RAT items and concludes that the potential for evaluation improves performance on simple tasks and debilitates it on complex tasks. But he does not seem to consider the possibility that it is level of task interest rather than (or in addition to) level of task complexity that drives such research results.

In addition, the definitions of intrinsic and extrinsic motivation offered by Harkins (borrowed from Utman, 1977) are devoid of interest or affective components. He defines an intrinsic motivational state as one in which individuals are focused on learning and mastering task skills, while an extrinsic motivational state is seen as one in which individuals feel pressure and focus on demonstrating that they have high ability. Importantly, operationalizations offered in the mainstream intrinsic motivation literature emphasize the fact that with intrinsic motivation come positive *feelings*. For example, Amabile's (1996) definition reads: "We define as intrinsic any motivation that arises from the individual's positive *reaction* to qualities of the task itself; this reaction can be experienced as interest, involvement, curiosity, satisfaction or positive challenge." And extrinsic motivation is seen as arising "from sources outside of the task itself" (p. 115). Harkins's (and Utman's) tendency to equate extrinsic motivation with perceptions of constraint ignore recent research and theorizing by Deci, Ryan and others that demonstrates that while extrinsic motivation is often perceived as controlling, it can under some circumstances be seen instead as informational (Deci & Ryan, 1985b; Amabile, 1996).

Harkins is to be credited both with carrying out some elegant experiments and subsuming a variety of highly complex findings within a single paradigm. Pitting one explanation against another or eliminating the potential for self-evaluation through the use of an invalid criterion, he presents a theoretical model that can and does explain a variety of heretofore seemingly disparate findings. Harkins's three-way account is partially successful in that it suggests an alternative process to goal setting and adds clarity to the social loafing paradigm. Unfortunately, despite his claims to the contrary, intrinsic motivation/creativity studies are not well served by his conceptualization. Investigations of this type simply do not "fit" his model.

Harkins seems surprised that he can find no research that falls in the complex task/goal conditions in his three-way design. Once again, some of this lack of fit may be due to Harkins's tendency to ignore the important theoretical and methodological differences between the achievement motivation and intrinsic motivation traditions. For example, he comments that although researchers of motivation have conducted a great deal of research which examines the effects of extrinsic/intrinsic motivation on task interest, they have conducted much less research on their effects on task performance. While this observation may hold for the achievement motivation literature, it is by not an accurate representation of the creativity literature. The entire purpose of this line of inquiry is to look at the impact of motivational orientation on quality of performance -- creativity of performance.

The real crux of the problem stems from the fact that, due to their very nature, open-ended creativity tasks are not and cannot be combined with specific goal requirements. The complex RAT items or unusual uses exercises used by Harkins may, in fact, measure some skill, some facility related to creativity, but they do not simulate real-world creative performance. As explained earlier, investigations of the impact of expected evaluation on intrinsic motivation and creativity of performance rely on the production of a real world product. There is no one formula for producing a successful story, poem or collage. There is no one path to solution, and it makes no sense to think in terms of specific goal requirements for these heuristic activities.

The question to be addressed now is "where do we go from here"? In putting together this volume, the contributors have opened a dialogue across seemingly disparate traditions. Each of us, but perhaps most especially Harkins, has done much to contribute to our growing understanding of the impact of evaluation on task interest and performance. It is time now that we listen to our own advice and return to an examination of the details.

REFERENCES

mabile, T. M. (1983). *The social psychology of creativity*. New York: Springer-Verlag.

mabile, T. M. (1988). A model of creativity and innovation in organizations. In B. M. Staw & L. L. Cummings (Eds.), *Research in organizational behavior* (Vol. 10, pp. 123-167). Greenwich, CT: JAI Press.

mabile, T. M. (1993). Motivational synergy: Toward new conceptualizations of intrinsic and extrinsic motivation in the workplace. *Human Resource Management Review, 3*, 185-201.

mabile, T. M. (1994). The "atmosphere of pure work": Creativity in research and development. In W. R. Shadish & S. Fuller (Eds.), *The social psychology of science. Conduct of science series* (pp. 316-328). New York: The Guilford Press.

mabile, T. M. (1996). *Creativity in context*. Boulder, CO: Westview.

mabile, T. M., & Gryskiewicz, S. (1987). *Creativity in the R&D laboratory*. Technical report no. 30. Greensboro, N.C.: Center for Creative Leadership.

mabile, T. M., Phillips, E. D., & Collins, M. A. (1993). *Creativity by Contract: Social Influences on the Creativity of Professional Artists*. Unpublished manuscript, Brandeis University.

edeian, A. G., & Zammuto, R. F. (1991). *Organizations: Theory and design*. Chicago: Dryden.

em, D. (1972). Self-perception theory. In L. Berkowitz (Ed.), *Advances in experimental social psychology* (Vol. 6). New York: Academic Press.

heek, J. M., & and Stahl, S. (1986). Shyness and verbal creativity. *Journal of Research in Personality, 20*, 51-61.

onti, R., & Amabile, T. M. (1995). *Problem solving among computer science students: The effects of skill, evaluation expectation and personality on solution quality*. Paper presented at the annual meeting of the Eastern Psychological Association, Boston, MA.

onti, R., Collins, M. A., & Picariello, M. (1995). *Differential effects of competition on the artistic creativity of girls and boys*. Unpublished manuscript, Brandeis University.

eCharms, R. (1968). *Personal causation*. New York: Academic Press.

eci, E. L. (1975). *Intrinsic motivation*. New York: Plenum.

eci, E. L., & Ryan, R. M. (1980). The empirical exploration of intrinsic motivational processes. In L. Berkowitz (Ed.), *Advances in experimental social psychology* (pp. 39-80). New York: Academic Press.

eci, E. L., & Ryan, R. M. (1985a). The general causality orientations scale: Self-determination in personality. *Journal of Personality and Social Psychology, 19*, 109-134.

eci, E. L., & Ryan, R. M. (1985b). *Intrinsic motivation and self-determination in human behavior*. New York: Plenum.

iVitto, B., & McArthur, L. Z. (1978). Developmental differences in the use of distinctiveness, consensus and consistency information for making causal attributions. *Developmental Psychology, 14*, 474-482.

zioni, A. (1964). *Modern organizations*. Englewood Cliffs, NJ: Prentice-Hall.

reenwald, A. G. (1982). Ego task analysis: An integration of research on ego-involvement and self-awareness. In A. H. Hastorf & A. M. Isen (Eds.), *Cognitive social psychology* (pp. 109-147). New York: Elsevier North Holland.

arackiewicz, J. M., & Sansone, C. (1991). Goals and intrinsic motivation: You can get there from here. In M. L. Maehr & P. R. Pintrich (Eds.) *Advances in motivation and achievement* (vol. 7, pp. 21-49). Greenwich, CT: JAI Press.

arkins, S., & Szymanski, K. (1988). Social loafing and self-evaluation with an objective standard. *Journal of Experimental Social Psychology*, 24, 354-365.

ennessey, B. A. (1999). Intrinsic motivation, affect and creativity. In S. Russ (Ed.), *Affect, creative experience and psychological adjustment* (pp. 77-90). Philadelphia: Taylor & Francis.

ill, K., Amabile, T. M., Coon, H. M., & Whitney, D. (1994). *Testing the componential model of creativity*. Unpublished manuscript, Brandeis University.

anfer, R., & Ackerman, P. L. (1989). Motivational and cognitive abilities: An integrative/aptitude-treatment interaction approach to skill acquisition. *Journal of Applied Psychology, 74*, 657-690.

Kanfer, R., Ackerman, P. L., Murtha, T. C., Dugdale, B., & Nelson, L. (1994). Goal setting, conditions of practice and task performance: A resource allocation perspective. *Journal of Applied Psychology*, *79*, 826-835.

Kelley, H. (1967). Attribution theory in social psychology. In D. Levine (Ed.), *Nebraska symposium on motivation*, Vol. 15. Lincoln: University of Nebraska.

Kelley, H. (1973). The processes of causal attribution. *American Psychologist*, *28*, 107-128.

Lepper, M., Sagotsky, G., Dafoe, J. L., & Greene, D. (1982). Consequences of superfluous social constraints: Effects on young children's social inferences and subsequent intrinsic motivation. *Journal of Personality and Social Psychology*, *42*, 51-65.

Lewin, K. (1935). *Dynamic theory of personality*. New York: McGraw-Hill.

McClelland, D. C. (1961). *The achieving society*. Princeton, NJ: Van Nostrand.

Morgan, M. (1981). The overjustification effect: A developmental test of self-perception interpretations. *Journal of Personality and Social Psychology*, *40*, 809-821.

Pollak, S. (1992). *The effects of motivational orientation and constraint on the creativity of the artist.* Unpublished manuscript, Brandeis University.

Ransen, D. (1980). The mediation of reward-induced motivation decrements in early and middle childhood: A template matching approach. *Journal of Personality and Social Psychology, 35*, 49-55.

Reiss, S., & Sushinksy, L. W. (1975). Overjustification, competing responses, and the acquisition of intrinsic interest. *Journal of Personality and Social Psychology*, *31*, 1116-1125.

Sansone, C., & Harackiewicz, J. M. (1996). "I don't feel like it": The function of interest in self-regulation. In L. Martin & A. Tesser (Eds.) *Striving and feeling: Interactions among goals, affect and self-regulation* (pp. 203-228). Mahwah, NJ: Erlbaum.

Shultz, T., Butkowsky, I., Pearce, J., & Shanfield, H. (1975). The development of schemes for the attribution of multiple psychological causes. *Developmental Psychology, 11*, 502-510.

Smith, M. C. (1975). Children's use of the multiple sufficient cause schema in social perception. *Journal of Personality and Social Psychology, 32*, 737-747.

Szymanski, K., & Harkins, S. (1987). Social loafing and self-evaluation with a social standard. *Journal of Personality and Social Psychology*, *53*, 891-897.

Utman, C. (1997). Performance effects of motivational state: A meta-analysis. *Personality and Social Psychology Review*, *1*, 170-182.

Wood, R. E., Mento, A. J., & Locke, E. A. (1987). Task complexity as a moderator of goal effects: A meta-analysis. *Journal of Applied Psychology*, *72*, 416-425.

Chapter 9

JUST DO IT: REMAINING TASK FOCUSED WHEN PERFORMANCE OUTCOMES LOOM LARGE

Amanda M. Durik
University of Wisconsin-Madison

John M. Tauer
University of St. Thomas

Judith M. Harackiewicz
University of Wisconsin-Madison

Plastering billboards, flashing across TV screens, and lettering sport cups and T-shirts, "Just Do It" has become a household phrase. Perhaps this slogan resonates with so many because it emphasizes the process of engaging in athletic activities, rather than any specific outcome or achievement. Excellence in sport is admirable, and many ads for sporting equipment and shoes try to link their products with athletic superstars who have achieved excellence. The "Just Do It" campaign is different, and seems to focus instead on the process of sport without concern for evaluative outcomes. Of course, performance evaluation is implicit in many of the activities we undertake, and it can be difficult to ignore the potential outcomes that are an integral part of these activities. For example, most athletes in competition are focused on success with the hopes of winning. However, we believe that something may be lost if the desired end state eclipses the steps taken to reach that end. Our discussion of performance evaluation will consider both the process of task engagement and the outcomes of task engagement, and we will discuss the implications of our model for performance and intrinsic motivation. In particular, we hope to consider how the quality of an individual's experience is related to the quality of his or her performance under evaluation contingencies. By evaluation contingency, we refer to any social interaction that imposes or implies performance evaluation for an individual's task performance (e.g., assigned goals, experimenter evaluation, competition).

The authors of the previous chapters of this book (Harkins, Tubbs, Hennessey, Shepperd, this volume) have identified different types of evaluation contingencies, and carefully articulated the motivational dynamics through which evaluation affects performance. These chapters afford a comprehensive analysis of numerous factors that affect performance by influencing how a task is framed and experienced. Our goal for the present chapter is to integrate these factors with our process model of intrinsic motivation (Harackiewicz & Sansone, 1991). As detailed in earlier chapters, evaluation contingencies can influence performance by changing an individual's approach to a task, as well as his or her experience during task engagement. For example, an individual's approach to a task may vary depending on the source of evaluation, the information contained in the evaluation contingency, and whether he or she is evaluated in terms of individual or group performance. In addition, the type of task can also affect an individual's motivation and performance in response to evaluation contingencies. Properties of the task (e.g., open versus closed-ended, task difficulty) may influence the way performance is defined, and therefore impact how individuals approach task performance.

Evaluation contingencies can mobilize skill and effort, which may translate into trying hard, completing a task quickly, or performing a task successfully. This will have performance payoffs in many tasks. Most notably, these include closed-ended and simple tasks, in which there are limited, but direct paths to successful performance (Harkins, Shepperd, this volume). However, mobilized effort and skill should not necessarily lead to high performance on tasks that are open-ended, or those that have multiple paths to successful performance (Hennessey, Chapter 3). Thus the effects of evaluation contingencies will depend on both properties of the evaluative context *and* characteristics of the task. Moreover, our own research suggests another class of variables may be important to consider -- characteristics of the individual may also moderate the effects of evaluation contingencies. We will situate the factors found to impact performance (as discussed in chapters by Harkins, Hennessey, Shepperd, Tubbs, this volume) alongside those theorized to affect intrinsic motivation (as discussed in Tauer & Harackiewicz, Chapter 4), in order to develop an analysis of task experience that will track the convergence of task enjoyment and performance.

We agree that performance quality is an important variable to examine, but we view it as only one measure of success. The experience of an activity as enjoyable and fulfilling is also an important outcome. In our first chapter (Tauer & Harackiewicz, Chapter 4) we considered the implications of evaluation contingencies for intrinsic motivation, defined as the desire to engage in an activity for the value inherent in doing it. Intrinsic motivation is important because it is essential to some of the most enriching and satisfying life experiences. In addition to being important for its own sake, intrinsic motivation is integral to the study of performance because these two variables often affect each other. For example, intrinsic motivation can be both a predictor of future performance and an outcome of past performance. Young musicians who enjoy practicing their instruments because they like the soothing sounds that result are likely to become better musicians. However, it is also likely that their previous skill development and musical prowess spurred on their interest and enjoyment. In this way, performance and enjoyment reciprocally affect each other.

Although performance and intrinsic motivation may prove difficult to disentangle, they are far from completely overlapping. The individual who loves to sing in the shower may have first-hand experience that intrinsic motivation does not always lead to high performance, just as the burnt-out CEO might concur that high performance is not always accompanied by intrinsic motivation. Thus, there are instances where performance and intrinsic motivation may be related and others where they are not related.

As discussed in Tauer and Harackiewicz (Chapter 4) we argue that different motivational processes unfold over the course of an individual's performance of an activity. Some processes are relevant at the outset and reflect individuals' motivational orientation as they begin a task, such as their degree of competence valuation and their desire to seek challenge. Others are related to their experience during a task, such as ongoing performance quality, perceived competence, and task involvement. Still other processes come into play only after individuals have completed the task and received feedback about their performance, such as perceived competence and affective reactions to feedback. We have concentrated on the implications of these processes for subsequent intrinsic motivation, measured after task completion and feedback. In contrast, the authors of the previous chapters have examined performance quality during the experimental session. This has resulted in theoretical analyses emphasizing aspects of the motivational processes involved in evaluative situations that have immediate consequences for task performance, rather than sustained effects that emerge over time.

In this chapter, we begin with the models of motivated performance presented in earlier chapters, and consider how the properties of evaluation contingencies shown to affect performance might also relate to an individual's task experience and subsequent intrinsic motivation. Specifically, we argue that specific features of evaluation contingencies discussed in earlier chapters (Harkins, Hennessey, Tubbs, Shepperd, this volume) such as the degree to which performance is identifiable, the source of evaluation, and the stringency of performance criteria can influence an individual's approach to a task. As we have discussed (Tauer & Harackiewicz, Chapter 4), an individual's approach to a task (see Figure 1, Chapter 4) may influence how he or she experiences it, and thus, these factors that influence performance may also affect intrinsic motivation.

We will first consider how these evaluation contingencies affect an individual's approach to a task and the implications for intrinsic motivation. In particular, we will consider the possibility that these contingencies lead individuals to focus on the potential outcomes that might result from their performance, to the exclusion of focusing on the task. We will discuss how specific properties of these evaluation contingencies influence effort expenditure, competence valuation, and perceived challenge. Second, we will consider the implications of these motivational approaches for task engagement and performance, and explain how they unfold given varied task qualities and difficulty levels. Finally, we will discuss the effects of performance and performance feedback on subsequent intrinsic motivation.

EVALUATION CONTINGENCIES: HOW INDIVIDUALS APPROACH TASKS

Evaluation contingencies straddle a fine line between promising information about competence, theorized to promote intrinsic motivation (at least when positive), and instating what may feel like external pressure and control, theorized to undermine intrinsic motivation (Deci & Ryan, 1985). Because these properties are not mutually exclusive, both can be produced by an evaluation contingency and then can act simultaneously in a situation to affect intrinsic motivation. We argue that the presence of evaluation contingencies heightens the importance of achievement during task engagement. When confronted with external performance evaluation, individuals may redefine the purpose of the task in terms of their achievement and competence. For example, a basketball player practicing on her own may view the same shooting activity differently when a group of friends join her to start a shooting contest. The value of making baskets or the costs of missing baskets takes on new meaning because the activity has become refocused in terms of achievement. Achievement situations allow individuals to assess their competence and this may cause them to place more emphasis on the quality of their performance.

Defining task performance as an achievement situation may increase the importance of performing well, provide an opportunity for challenge, and focus effort and attention on task outcomes. The basketball player who was previously shooting baskets by herself may try harder now that she's competing with friends. She may even be thrilled by the challenge that accompanies competition and the prospect of winning. Or, she may be distracted and annoyed by the pressure to perform well, now that her performance is on the line. Among so many possibilities, one certainty is that her approach to shooting baskets is now bound up in her performance that will be evaluated at the end of the competition.

This heightened focus on the outcome of task performance may promote intrinsic motivation by focusing attention on performing well and shooting baskets. Alternatively, it may have deleterious effects on intrinsic motivation if it draws attention away from task engagement itself. Thus, the trick to promoting intrinsic motivation in the presence of evaluation contingencies may be to help individuals remain focused on the process of task engagement rather than having attention and affect tied up in the performance outcome.

Furthermore, because we are arguing that evaluation contingencies are the hallmark of achievement situations, it therefore follows that individual differences in achievement motivation are crucial to understanding how evaluation contingencies may be perceived and experienced. Given the variability in characteristic achievement striving, it seems likely that many different approaches to the task will be represented among the group of friends on the basketball court. In turn, these different approaches will influence enjoyment and performance during the shooting contest. Some of the players may be thoroughly drawn in by the challenge of competing and enjoy shooting free-throws in this context because it is a competition. For others, the competitive context may accentuate the potential outcome of the contest to such an extent that it diminishes task involvement and detracts from the enjoyment of shooting free throws. In addition, individual differences in achievement orientation that lead to variability in enjoyment, may also carry over to effects on performance in other contexts.

Evaluation contingencies change the way individuals approach a task by making their performance on the task salient. Several authors have suggested that expecting evaluation can lead to feelings of undue pressure and concerns about performance, and that these may have negative effects on task enjoyment (Amabile, 1983; Deci & Ryan, 1985; Harackiewicz, Manderlink, & Sansone, 1984; Hennessey, 1989). We contend that the patterns are more complex, and that caring about performance and challenging oneself to perform well can actually facilitate intrinsic motivation. Specifically, we will discuss how the factors known to affect performance can also affect the degree to which people value their competence on tasks and seek challenge during task performance. When people know their performance will be evaluated, they become more invested in their own competence and come to care more about their performance. Furthermore, the mere expectation of feedback is likely to lead individuals to challenge themselves to perform well so that they will come to evaluate themselves as competent. We argue that these processes can be triggered by several properties of the evaluation contingencies discussed in previous chapters (Harkins, Hennessey, Shepperd, Tubbs, this volume) and that these processes can affect performance and intrinsic motivation.

Competence Valuation

One of the mechanisms that may actively promote intrinsic motivation in evaluative circumstances is competence valuation. Caring about one's own competence can help people channel energy toward the task, and involve themselves in the task and their own performance (Harackiewicz & Sansone, 1991). Several factors influence the degree to which people care about doing well, including the opportunity for evaluation and the presence of performance criteria. Furthermore, individual differences in achievement orientation are also important because achievement oriented individuals seek out and respond to challenge, and therefore tend to value competence in a wide range of situations (Greenwald, 1982; McClelland, 1961).

A person working on a group task will perform better if his or her individual performance is made salient. Shepperd's (Chapter 1) expectancy-value model of effort motivation examines factors that influence social loafing on group tasks, and these factors may also influence competence valuation. We consider here the implications for intrinsic motivation as well as implications for group performance. This model takes into account the multiplicative effects of expecting one's effort to lead to successful performance and subsequent valued outcomes. The performance of individuals in a group is facilitated by manipulations of increasing identifiability and uniqueness of individual contributions as a result of greater effort (Harkins & Petty, 1982). When performance is identifiable, individuals may be more likely to value their competence. This is likely to promote intrinsic motivation because individuals who care about their performance are likely to become more invested in the task, and as a result, find the task more intrinsically motivating.

Shepperd (Chapter 1) describes the benefits of identification interventions in addressing the motivational problem of fostering participation in group tasks. He argues that spotlighting individual performance works to counter the anonymity typically experienced on group tasks. For example, participants who believed their contributions to a group task were important because the task was particularly challenging (Harkins & Petty, 1982), their contributions were unique (Harkins & Petty, 1982), or their performance was going to decide the group's fate in a conjunctive task (Kerr & Bruun, 1983), did not allow their effort to wane compared to participants in conditions led to believe their performances were anonymous. These positive effects of spotlighting on performance are due to increased effort. We hypothesize that another consequence of spotlighting would be increased competence valuation. Individuals in these conditions may have been willing to expend more effort because they valued their own competence at the task, and this may have drawn them into the task and increased their enjoyment. In this case, effort motivation and intrinsic motivation, although distinct, would have had similar origins.

Although effort motivation led to greater performance in this context, these effects may depend on the nature of the task. Because the tasks used in social loafing research are relatively simple ones such as generating uncommon uses for a knife, it seems likely that performance would be responsive to effort. Accordingly, individuals who care about doing well put forth more effort, which in turn enhances their performance and intrinsic motivation. When the behaviors necessary for high performance are straightforward and easy to execute, effort in response to competence valuation should prove highly effective. However, effort may not directly lead to elevated performance in situations where the task is difficult or the means to achieve competent performance are ambiguous.

Furthermore, it is essential to point out that not all effort motivation will promote intrinsic motivation. Theories of intrinsic motivation suggest that effort is not the most direct predictor of intrinsic motivation, but rather, that intrinsic motivation is dependent on perceptions that one's effort emanates from internal rather than external causes (DeCharms, 1968). Similarly, Shepperd (Chapter 1) explains that the value individuals place on performance varies widely, and can be either intrinsic or extrinsic. Expending effort in order to meet internal performance standards is most likely to lead to intrinsic motivation. For example, manipulations of identifiability that focus on unique individual contributions may be personally important (Harkins & Petty, 1982), and thus likely to promote intrinsic motivation. However, intrinsic motivation may be undermined as a result of manipulations that increase effort by motivating individuals to avoid being the lowest performer in a conjunctive task, wherein the group's outcome is dependent on the member who performs the worst. Although this latter condition is likely to lead to increased effort and enhanced performance on the task, it is also likely to undermine intrinsic motivation because it may lead to motivational orientations focused on avoiding failure rather than approaching success (Elliot & Harackiewicz, 1996; Higgins, 1997).

Furthermore, self-evaluation is likely to facilitate intrinsic motivation relative to other-evaluation. Individuals who expect to evaluate themselves, in contrast to those expecting to be evaluated by an experimenter, may have the best of both worlds. Not only does the ability to monitor and evaluate their own performance lead to competence valuation, but they can remain focused on the task itself because self-evaluation is likely to involve less pressure and distraction than more external evaluative pressure.

Perceived Challenge

Perceived challenge is the second process initiated at the outset of task engagement that can influence intrinsic motivation. Research on the effects of goal setting on performance consistently shows that difficult, specific goals promote performance (Tubbs, Chapter 2), and we believe that goals can also promote intrinsic motivation through their effects on perceived challenge. Understanding the motivational effects of goals requires a consideration of the meaningfulness attached to achieving them. Harkins (Chapter 5) has shown that a goal must have certain characteristics in order for it to promote performance. For example, the goal must be appropriately challenging and based on the performance of others who are from a self-relevant comparison group. Positive effects of goal setting on performance were found only when participants were assigned a goal that was not too lenient, and was based on norms of similar others (Harkins, White, & Utman, 2000). Therefore, upon reaching these goals, individuals were provided with useful information about their competence. In addition to the information about competence, we believe that the presence of goals at the start of a task can promote intrinsic motivation by inciting challenge. Therefore, we hypothesize that assigned goals promote intrinsic motivation as well as heightened performance, and this is because individuals are energized by the prospect of meeting goals that provide meaningful information about their competence.

However, all goals are not equal in the type of information they provide. This is important to acknowledge because individual differences in achievement orientation affect interpretations of and reactions to different kinds of goals. For example, the goals described by Tubbs (Chapter 2) all tended to define achievement in terms of relative standards of performance, rather than self-referenced progress and improvement. In the context of research on achievement goals discussed in our earlier chapter, the use of such normative standards suggests that the research cited by Tubbs may be more telling about the effects of performance goals than the effects of mastery goals. The Tauer and Harackiewicz chapter (Chapter 4) also highlighted the moderating role of achievement orientation in goal effects on intrinsic motivation. Recall that individuals' reactions to performance goals differed by individual levels of achievement orientation such that individuals high in achievement motivation (HAMs) responded to tasks involving performance goals with more intrinsic motivation than did those individuals low in achievement motivation (LAMs). Thus, it is very likely that although specific, difficult goals lead to higher performance among both HAMs and LAMs, HAMs are more likely to enjoy the task from the start as a result of these goals, relative to LAMs.

Furthermore, achievement orientation may also moderate individuals' responses to factors influencing effort motivation, such as those properties of evaluation in group tasks elaborated by Shepperd (Chapter 1). Because HAMs like challenge, seek evaluative feedback, and readily adopt goals, it is sensible to expect the effects of evaluative situational factors on intrinsic motivation to be moderated by achievement orientation. HAMs, in contrast to LAMs, are more likely to value competence and be excited by challenge at the outset of a task under conditions of expected evaluation (Epstein & Harackiewicz, 1992). Thus, whereas one person's response to experimenter evaluation is concern, worry and discomfort, another person's response is eagerness to receive diagnostic feedback. These responses have implications for intrinsic motivation, fostering intrinsic motivation for some (HAMs) but undermining it for others (LAMs). Moreover, it seems possible that performance could also be affected by individual differences in achievement orientation through these same processes. We recommend that performance researchers include these measures in future research because although evaluation contingencies may promote performance overall, these effects may be particularly strong among HAMs.

EVALUATION CONTINGENCIES: HOW INDIVIDUALS EXPERIENCE AND PERFORM TASKS

Intrinsic motivation is closely related to the degree to which individuals become absorbed into the task. Flow experiences, arguably the purest form of intrinsic motivation, are characterized by loss of sense of self and time, wherein the separation between the self and the activity dissolves (Csikszentmihalyi, 1990). Flow experiences are relatively rare, and the more typical experience of intrinsic motivation may be characterized by feelings of being caught up in the activity and focused on the task at hand, rather than distracted by peripheral or unrelated thoughts. Because task involvement is a key component of intrinsic motivation, evaluation contingencies that promote task involvement are also likely to promote intrinsic motivation. Furthermore, to the extent that active engagement in the activity promotes performance, task involvement will also relate positively to performance.

As we stated earlier, however, evaluation places emphasis on performance outcomes, and can therefore interfere with task involvement. This is especially likely if the importance of performing well overshadows the experience of performing it. Consistent with this analysis, research suggests that evaluation contingencies do not arrest the development of intrinsic motivation if the evaluation is conducive to focusing on the task. For example, participants who performed an enjoyable word game under evaluation that was focused on the task evidenced greater intrinsic motivation than those who performed the task under normative evaluation (Harackiewicz, Abrahams, & Wageman, 1987). Thus, evaluation contingencies had differential effects based on the focus of the evaluation, and this was reflected both in individuals' approach to and experience during the task.

Determining the direction of the effects of evaluation on intrinsic motivation depends not only on the properties of the evaluation contingency, but also on the nature of the task and characteristics of the individual. Because evaluation contingencies heighten the importance of performance and competence, an individual's sense of competence during task engagement will also be important for the development of intrinsic motivation. Individuals will be more intrinsically motivated in achievement situations when they perceive themselves as being capable of performing well. Thus, individuals' perceived competence is the final mediator of intrinsically motivated behavior, and it should be considered along with task involvement when considering individuals' enjoyment of tasks in which competence is focal.

The maintenance of perceived competence depends on the presence and type of competence information provided during the task. This information can be present in the evaluation contingency itself, as is the case when performance criteria are stated at the outset, and/or provided during the task as progress is made. For example, Tauer and Harackiewicz (1999) found that both intrapersonal feedback (improving one's performance) and interpersonal feedback (performing better than another) promoted perceived competence. This evidence indicates that individuals can experience evaluation from multiple sources (internal and external), and that these different sources of evaluation can independently affect perceptions of competence. Furthermore, the amount of task-based feedback about progress is dictated by the way performance is defined in the situation as well as by the tasks themselves. This is because tasks vary in the degree to which they inherently provide a clear route to successful performance. For example, in a use-generation task, individuals can easily gauge their own progress by monitoring the number of responses they generate, but the degree of creativity evidenced in those responses may be harder to assess. Focusing on the performance outcome during the task, particularly in the absence of ongoing feedback about competence, is likely to heighten evaluative threat, foster concerns about performance, and make it difficult to develop perceived competence. Evaluation contingencies might be particularly disruptive and annoying when the task does not provide a clear route to success, because individuals will be focused on the performance outcome, but have no means by which to gauge their progress. This analysis seems particularly relevant when considering open-ended tasks, in which both intrinsic motivation and creative performance have consistently been shown to suffer in the presence of evaluation contingencies.

Focusing on the means to achieve successful performance, if the means are known, can have positive effects on intrinsic motivation. For example, when performance criteria and ongoing progress feedback are available, individuals can develop feelings of competence as they work. The presence of performance criteria have been found to increase performance because participants focus on and are able to monitor their progress during task engagement. For example, participants in nonevaluation conditions who were provided performance criteria during a vigilance task showed facilitated performance relative to others who were not provided performance criteria (Harkins & Szymanski, 1988), presumably because they were able to evaluate their own performance during the task. It is likely that participants' monitoring of their successful progress was related to task involvement and intrinsic motivation, in addition to elevated performance. Therefore, we would predict that intrinsic motivation and performance would be strongly positively related under these conditions.

Task difficulty also affects the development of intrinsic motivation because evaluation contingencies may reduce task involvement if individuals' attention is occupied with concerns about performance (Harackiewicz, Manderlink, & Sansone, 1984; Harackiewicz, Abrahams, & Wageman, 1987). This can have negative effects on performance as well as intrinsic motivation. For example, participants' performance on a complex task decreased when they were given a stringent goal, in contrast to no goal. However, the reverse was found for participants working on a simple task (Harkins, Chapter 5). This pattern emerged even when individuals were working under self- rather than other-evaluation. Because task difficulty reversed the direction of the effect, it seems likely that concerns about performing well or misguided effort are responsible for these effects. Reduced task involvement may have mediated the reduction in performance for individuals completing the complex task.

However, focusing on competence is likely to promote task involvement and intrinsic motivation when competence is clearly defined and individuals can determine that they are being successful. This is the case for closed-ended tasks, in which competent responses require mere employment of set, programmatic behaviors. However, if evaluation contingencies focus individuals on the outcome of a task, then such contingencies may have negative effects on performance and intrinsic motivation during open-ended tasks, in which successful performance and the necessary steps to achieve it are unclear. Consistent with this, performance is facilitated when participants expect evaluation at the conclusion of closed-ended tasks, such as paper-and-pencil fluency tasks in which correct responses are fairly straightforward. However, performance is diminished when participants expect evaluation after open-ended tasks such as making collages and writing poems (Amabile, 1996). Furthermore, as reviewed by Hennessey (Chapter 3), the negative effects of evaluation on creativity during open-ended tasks are very robust. For example, creativity has been shown to suffer when evaluation is provided in the presence of an audience or alone, when other participants were present or not (Amabile, Goldfarb, & Brackfield, 1990), and even when the evaluation was provided by a computer rather than a human experimenter (Hennessey, 1989). Crucial to Hennessey's argument concerning the negative effects of evaluation on creativity, is evidence that performance on creative tasks is diminished because intrinsic motivation is diminished. Thus, the relationship between creativity and intrinsic motivation for open-ended tasks may be particularly strong.

Given the consistent and damaging effects of evaluation contingencies on creativity, it is interesting to consider how individuals' initial approach to a creativity task may have affected subsequent task involvement and intrinsic motivation via competence valuation. Importantly, competence valuation may not always lead to intrinsic motivation (Elliot & Harackiewicz, 1994). For example, caring a great deal about competence may place pressure on some individuals during task engagement that can subsequently interfere with intrinsic motivation. This may even be compounded by the provision of negative feedback at task conclusion, such that caring about competence and then receiving negative competence information may have particularly potent undermining effects on intrinsic motivation. Similarly, concern for competence that was elevated in response to evaluation contingencies may have dramatic effects on creative performance (Hennessey, Chapter 3). Valuing competence may exacerbate some individuals' tendency to focus on task outcome, and because creative, open-ended tasks provide little ongoing feedback about competence, concerns about competence can shift too much attention toward task outcome rather than task engagement.

Interesting results related to this point come from a study comparing computer science students who varied in ability on their creativity evidenced in writing computer programs. Students who were at a low skill level were actually more creative in response to evaluation than nonevaluation, whereas students who were at a high skill level showed the traditional effect of being less creative in response to evaluation than nonevaluation (Conti & Amabile, 1995, as cited in Hennessey, Chapter 3). One way to interpret these results involves considering different levels of competence valuation among the two groups of students. It is plausible that what interfered with the creativity of those with high skill was the personal investment and pressure they placed on themselves to perform well, and that this caused them to over-focus on the outcome of the task under evaluative conditions. In contrast, participants with low skill level may have not been fettered by such personal investment because the task was less ego-involving. They may have self-handicapped or made excuses for poor performance (Berglas & Jones, 1978; Deppe & Harackiewicz, 1996), thereby producing the ironic outcome of relieving performance pressure that led to heightened performance. Thus, the latter group may have been able to avoid being personally entangled by competence concerns because the domain was not as personally relevant.

Furthermore, achievement orientation may be a promising variable to consider in the investigation of evaluation on creativity. It is possible that expected evaluation might not undermine intrinsic motivation and creativity among HAMs. If intrinsic motivation is an important component of the conditions that lead to creativity, and HAMs' intrinsic motivation is heightened by evaluation, then creativity should not falter among these individuals, relative to HAMs in nonevaluative contexts. However, there are two caveats to this analysis. First, HAMs' responses to evaluation have been documented using tasks that have been almost exclusively closed-ended and algorithmic, and future research may find different patterns on open-ended tasks. Second, because HAMs are more likely to value competence in achievement situations, an alternative possibility is that increased competence valuation may undermine intrinsic motivation among HAMs, consistent with the previous hypothesis with regard to the computer programmers with high skill level.

EVALUATION CONTINGENCIES: RECEIVING FEEDBACK AT TASK CONCLUSION

Throughout this chapter, we have considered the parallel effects of performance and intrinsic motivation as they might occur simultaneously throughout task engagement. Naturally, performance can no longer be affected after the task is complete. However, the actual feedback expected throughout the task can still powerfully affect intrinsic motivation. Here we consider the effects of the presence or absence of feedback, and the valence of the feedback on intrinsic motivation and future performance. Recall the basketball player who became engaged in a free-throw contest with her friends. Perhaps she won the contest, or perhaps she finished somewhere in the middle. Regardless, her performance in that competition is complete. However, her enjoyment of free-throw shooting may have risen. This juncture presents a particularly rich opportunity to examine the effects of intrinsic motivation on performance directly, because performance and intrinsic motivation can be assessed in the absence of evaluation contingencies. We can examine whether or not she returns to shooting free-throws, a behavioral measure of intrinsic motivation, as well as how well she shoots them if she does return to the activity, another measure of performance.

Most research on intrinsic motivation involves controlling performance in order to consider other contextual factors. For example, Harackiewicz, Manderlink and Sansone (1984) experimentally controlled pinball scores so that all participants attained similar positive outcomes. This allowed the researchers to evaluate the effects of evaluation on motivation independently of performance effects, but of course limits efforts to integrate research across areas. It may be fruitful to measure performance quality once evaluative constraints are lifted. This would allow researchers to evaluate both subsequent performance and subsequent intrinsic motivation as outcomes of an evaluation contingency.

Although the valence of feedback is irrelevant to analyses of performance, it is critical to consider when predicting intrinsic motivation following task engagement. Not surprisingly, positive performance feedback leads to greater intrinsic motivation than negative feedback. For example, as previously reviewed by Tauer and Harackiewicz (Chapter 4), studies have shown that winning, in contrast to losing, a competition led to higher intrinsic motivation, and that this effect was independent of individual differences in achievement orientation. Thus, both LAMs and HAMs showed higher intrinsic motivation after winning, compared with losing. However, the effect of competition itself did interact with achievement orientation such that HAMs enjoyed the activity more in a competition than LAMs. Therefore, HAMs showed motivational benefits from both competition and successful performance feedback. LAMs, in contrast, only showed benefits from the positive feedback. Whereas evaluative contexts engage only HAMs from the start, both HAMs and LAMs benefit from positive performance feedback in this context.

Although we maintain that intrinsic motivation and performance are not perfectly correlated, they may be more interrelated in situations involving evaluation contingencies because they focus attention on competence. This is because both competence valuation and perceived competence would be particularly important in these situations, and these processes are known to enhance intrinsic motivation and performance. However, evaluation contingencies may be perceived as controlling even when they mobilize effort that actually leads to subsequent high performance. Furthermore, positive feedback may or may not promote intrinsic motivation, depending on the context (Sansone, 1989; Sansone, Sachau, & Weir, 1989) and the way in which the feedback is given (Fisher, 1978). Accordingly, it may not always remedy negative effects of evaluative contexts for LAMs. Several of the studies reviewed by Tauer and Harackiewicz (Chapter 4) suggest that LAMs respond negatively to assigned goals focused on their performance relative to others, even if they eventually receive positive feedback information (Harackiewicz & Elliot, 1993; Epstein & Harackiewicz, 1992). Performing well in a context that is perceived as a high-pressure situation may lead to greater concern about achieving such high performance again in the future. Furthermore, the differential responses to such feedback can have implications for self-protective strategies affecting individuals' approaches to subsequent task engagement in terms of their willingness to value competence, seek challenge, and expend effort (Elliot, Faler, McGregor, Campbell, Sedikides, & Harackiewicz, 2000). Thus, positive performance information may increase intrinsic motivation at task conclusion in some contexts and not others, and this is likely to affect the way individuals approach the task in the future. It is useful to divide the processes of intrinsic motivation into the sequential phases of task engagement because it highlights the points at which intrinsic motivation processes come into play.

Furthermore, in addition to the valence of feedback, the type of information about one's performance provided by feedback following task completion can affect both intrinsic motivation and future performance on the task through goal setting. Performance feedback may or may not contain information about normative standards, and this directly affects the type of achievement goal that can be set in the future. Information about one's own performance in the absence of normative information may lead to setting mastery goals because achievement is defined self-referentially. However, if normative information is provided as well as individual feedback, then performance goals may be set because achievement is defined in terms of relative standing. Importantly, if both types of information are provided, then presumably either or both goals can be set. This may be particularly useful given the moderating effects of achievement orientation on goal effects, such that LAMs and HAMs might be able to maximize their outcomes by self-setting the goal each prefers (Barron & Harackiewicz, 2001). Furthermore, because performance goals have been associated with higher performance, relative to mastery goals (Harackiewicz, Barron, Carter, Lehto, & Elliot, 1997; Harackiewicz, Barron, Tauer, Carter, & Elliot, 2000), information about normative standing might lead to setting performance goals and attaining higher performance. These effects might work through the process documented by Tubbs (Chapter 2) and Harkins (Chapter 5). In addition, the positive effects of mastery goals on intrinsic interest in the classroom suggest that both types of goals are beneficial and that adopting both goals can lead to both higher performance as well as intrinsic motivation (Harackiewicz, et al., 1997). Performance feedback can include various types of information, and the types of goals individuals set following receipt of feedback are dependent on that information. Because both performance and mastery goals have positive effects on performance and intrinsic motivation, respectively, providing feedback that allows individuals to set both goals is likely to facilitate both outcomes during subsequent task engagement.

SUMMARY

In summary it is clear that there are a plethora of variables that come together when considering the determinants of performance and intrinsic motivation in evaluative contexts. We hope that this chapter has provided a useful integration of some of these variables for researchers who study evaluation, performance, and motivation. By measuring process variables, we should gain a better understanding of how to achieve high levels of both of these critical indicators of success. We argue that a process approach is crucial to understanding the effects of evaluation because only then is it possible to identify the psychological mechanisms that influence performance and intrinsic motivation. For example, the amount of effort individuals devote to task performance may be a manifestation of competence valuation, perceived challenge, or both. It is necessary to measure these processes during task engagement in order to identify and track their development and subsequent effects on other processes such as task involvement and perceived competence, as well as performance and intrinsic motivation. In addition, we encourage researchers to consider both performance and intrinsic motivation as important outcomes, and to explore effects on these measures both during and after task performance.

Furthermore, we have attempted to identify variables that distinguish when performance and intrinsic motivation will converge. Specifically, we have argued that evaluation contingencies pose the threat of focusing attention on performance outcomes rather than the process of task engagement. Because focusing on task engagement is fundamental to intrinsic motivation, we have highlighted factors that can help maintain task focus when evaluation contingencies are present. However, these variables combine and interact in complex ways, and consideration of the processes depends not only on the evaluation contingencies themselves, but also on properties of the task as well as characteristics of the individual pursuing the activity. For example, competence valuation and perceived challenge are likely to lead to greater expenditures of effort. However, effort will only foster performance and intrinsic motivation when the route to competent performance is clear and simple so that focusing on competence during task performance can help individuals perform well and foster feelings of competence. Otherwise, focusing on potential outcomes during open-ended and complex tasks can have undermining effects on performance and intrinsic motivation because evaluation distracts individuals from focusing on the task itself.

Focusing on the outcome of task performance is a slippery slope when it comes to optimizing performance and intrinsic motivation. This is particularly the case when performance requires more than practiced skill and effort. Because important and meaningful life experiences are often encountered on slopes that are difficult to traverse or that require creativity, we suggest that the types of shoes one wears might actually make a difference. Maybe we should take the advice from the folks at Nike, focus on the task at hand, and, "Just Do It."

REFERENCES

Amabile, T. M. (1996). *Creativity in context.* Boulder, CO: Westview.
Amabile, T. M. (1983). *The social psychology of creativity.* New York: Springer-Verlag.
Amabile, T. M., Goldfarb, P., & Brackfield, S. C. (1990). Social influences on creativity: Evaluation, coaction, and surveillance. *Creativity Research Journal, 3*, 6-21.
Barron, K. E., & Harackiewicz, J. M. (2001). Achievement goals and optimal motivation: Testing multiple goal models. *Journal of Personality and Social Psychology, 80*, 706-722.
Barron, K. E., & Harackiewicz, J. M. (2000). Achievement goals and optimal motivation: A multiple goals approach. In C. Sansone & J. M. Harackiewicz (Eds.), *Intrinsic and extrinsic motivation: The search for optimal motivation and performance.* N.Y.: Academic Press.
Berglas, S., & Jones, E. E. (1978). Drug choice as a self-handicapping strategy in response to noncontingent success. *Journal of Personality and Social Psychology, 36*, 405-417.
Csikszentmihalyi, M. (1990). *Flow: The psychology of optimal experience.* New York: Harper & Row.
DeCharms, R. (1968). *Personal causation.* New York: Academic Press.
Deci, E. L., & Ryan, R. M. (1985). *Intrinsic Motivation and self-determination in human behavior.* New York: Plenum.
Deppe, R. K., & Harackiewicz, J. M. (1996). Self-handicapping and intrinsic motivation: Buffering intrinsic motivation from the threat of failure. *Journal of Personality and Social Psychology, 70*, 868-876.
Elliot, A. J., & Harackiewicz, J. M. (1994). Goal setting, achievement orientation, and intrinsic motivation: A mediational analysis. *Journal of Personality and Social Psychology, 66*, 968-980.
Elliot, A. J., & Harackiewicz, J. M. (1996). Approach and avoidance achievement goals and intrinsic motivation: A mediational analysis. *Journal of Personality and Social Psychology, 70*, 461-475.
Elliot, A. J., Faler, J., McGregor, H. A., Campbell, W. K., Sedikides, C., & Harackiewicz, J. M. (2000). Competence valuation as a strategic intrinsic motivation process. *Personality and Social Psychology Bulletin, 26*, 780-794.
Epstein, J. A., & Harackiewicz, J. M. (1992). Winning is not enough: The effects of competition and achievement orientation on intrinsic motivation. *Personality and Social Psychology Bulletin, 18*, 128-138.
Fisher, C. D. (1978). The effects of personal control, competence, and extrinsic reward systems on intrinsic motivation. *Organizational Behavior and Human Performance, 21*, 273-288.
Greenwald, A. G. (1982). Ego task analysis: An integration of research on ego-involvement and self-awareness. In A. H. Hastorf & A. M. Isen (Eds.), *Cognitive social psychology* (pp. 109-147). New York: Elsevier North Holland.
Harackiewicz, J. M., Abrahams, S., & Wageman, R. (1987). Performance evaluation and intrinsic motivation: The effects of evaluative focus, rewards, and achievement orientation. *Journal of Personality and Social Psychology, 53*, 1015-1023. (Special issue: Integrating personality and social psychology).
Harackiewicz, J. M., Barron, K. E., Carter, S. M., Lehto, A. T., & Elliot, A. J. (1997). Predictors and consequences of achievement goals in the college classroom: Maintaining interest and making the grade. *Journal of Personality and Social Psychology, 73*, 1284-1295.
Harackiewicz, J. M., Barron, K. E., Tauer, J. M., Carter, S. M., & Elliot, A. J. (2000). Short-term and long-term consequences of achievement goals in the college classroom. *Journal of Educational Psychology*, 92, 316-330.
Harackiewicz, J. M., & Elliot, A. J. (1993). Achievement goals and intrinsic motivation. *Journal of Personality and Social Psychology, 65*, 904-915.

Harackiewicz, J. M., Manderlink, G., & Sansone, C. (1984). Rewarding pinball wizardry: Effects of evaluation and cue value on intrinsic motivation. *Journal of Personality and Social Psychology*, *47*, 287-300.

Harackiewicz, J. M., & Sansone, C. (1991). Goals and intrinsic motivation: You can get there from here. In M. L. Maehr & P. R. Pintrich (Eds.), *Advances in motivation and achievement* (Vol. 7, pp. 21-49). Greenwich, CT: JAI Press.

Harkins, S. G., & Petty, R. E. (1982). Effects of task difficulty and task uniqueness on social loafing. *Journal of Personality and Social Psychology*, *43*, 1214-1229.

Harkins, S. G., & Szymanski, K. (1988). Social loafing and self-evaluation with an objective standard. *Journal of Experimental Social Psychology*, *24*, 354-365.

Harkins, S. G., White, P. H., & Utman, C. H. (2000). The role of internal and external sources of evaluation in motivating task performance. *Personality and Social Psychology Bulletin*, *26*, 100-117.

Hennessey, B. A. (1989). The effect of extrinsic constraint on children's creativity while using a computer. *Creativity Research Journal*, *2*, 151-168.

Higgins, E. T. (1997) Beyond pleasure and pain. *American Psychologist*, *52*, 1280-1300

Kerr, N. L., & Bruun, S. E. (1983). Dispensability of member effort and group motivation losses: Free-rider effects. *Journal of Personality and Social Psychology*, *44*, 78-94.

McClelland, D. C. (1961). *The achieving society*. Princeton, NJ: Van Nostrand.

Sansone, C. (1989). Competence feedback, task feedback and intrinsic interest: An examination of process and context. *Journal of Experimental Social Psychology*, *25*, 343-361.

Sansone, C., Sachau, D. A., & Weir, C. (1989). Effects of instruction on intrinsic interest: The importance of context. *Journal of Personality and Social Psychology*, *57*, 819-829.

Tauer, J. M., & Harackiewicz, J.M. (1999). Winning isn't everything: Competition, achievement orientation, and intrinsic motivation. *Journal of Experimental Social Psychology*, *35*, 209-238.

Chapter 10

THE THREE-VARIABLE MODEL: FROM OCCAM'S RAZOR TO THE BLACK BOX

Stephen G. Harkins
Northeastern University

In Chapter 5, I noted that there are five research traditions that suggest that the potential for evaluation affects task performance (social loafing, goal setting, social facilitation, intrinsic motivation/creativity, and achievement goal theory), and that, for the most part, these traditions do not take into account the findings obtained within the other traditions, nor the processes hypothesized to produce these findings. I then made a first attempt at an integration, suggesting that the performance findings from each of these traditions could be encompassed by taking into account only three variables: whether or not there is the potential for evaluation by an external source; whether the participants are asked to do their best or to strive to achieve a stringent goal; and whether the task is simple or complex.

After reading the chapters written by representatives of each of these traditions, I remain convinced that first, there are benefits to be gained by attempting to integrate these lines of research, and second, this three-variable model remains viable as a first approximation of this integration. In the current chapter, I continue to make the case for this three-variable model by addressing criticisms that could be raised by the proponents of the various traditions encompassed by the model. I then consider the issue of mediation, because, even if the model can successfully accommodate the performance effects of the various traditions, this tells us nothing about the process(es) through which these variables have their effects. Any explanation of the performance effects that fails to specify the contents of the black box that lies between the independent variables and the performance effects must remain incomplete. Because each of the traditions could provide a process model that explains these effects, I review these models, but then conclude that there is no compelling evidence that favors any of them. Finally, I present some preliminary data from a pilot experiment that may move us a small distance toward specifying the process.

PROCRUSTES'S BED VERSUS OCCAM'S RAZOR

One could argue that placing these traditions in the three-variable model is essentially a Procrustean enterprise. That is, researchers from each of these traditions could argue that their work has been forced into this three-fold classification, and that, in so doing, essential aspects of their conceptualizations have been lopped off. In the following section, we will consider three such arguments.

First, in the three-variable model, the "group" nature of the social loafing effect is discounted. That is, Latané, Williams, and Harkins (1979) described social loafing as the finding that people *working together* put out less effort than people working alone. This description of the loafing effects suggests that loafing is a "group versus individual" effect. In contrast, our analysis suggests that the basic loafing effect is simply an evaluation effect. Participants whose outputs are not subject to the evaluation of the experimenter put out less effort than participants whose outputs are subject to this evaluation (on simple tasks when the participants are asked to "do their best").

Second, the three-variable model argues that concern over the potential for external evaluation supersedes interest in the potential for self-evaluation, and as a result, it is the potential for external evaluation alone that is responsible for any performance effect. Researchers in the other traditions could question this claim for the primacy of the effects of external evaluation. For example, some traditions argue that self-evaluation alone produces the performance effect (e.g., goal setting, Locke & Latham, 1990b). Other traditions suggest that the performance effects can be produced by the potential for either self or external evaluation (e.g., social loafing, social facilitation).

Third, the three-variable model claims that the tasks that produce creativity and learning goal effects are nothing more than additional examples of the complex tasks used in social facilitation research. Creativity researchers (e.g., Hennessey, Chapter 3) could argue that this view leaves out task characteristics that are required to produce what they would define as a creative product. Likewise, proponents of the achievement goals perspective could argue that this view does not take into account the type of task required to produce learning goal effects.

Social Loafing: Group versus Individual Effect or an Evaluation Effect?

The argument that the basic social loafing effect is nothing more than an evaluation effect is key to our position, because we use the loafing paradigm (e.g., Latané, Williams, & Harkins, 1979) to distinguish among the joint and independent effects of the potential for self-evaluation and the potential for external (social) evaluation. We argue that two pieces of information are necessary for evaluation by any source: (a) a measure of the participant's task output; and (b) an evaluative criterion against which this task output can be compared. The "pooled output" condition of the typical loafing experiment provides a "no" or minimal evaluation baseline condition. Participants believe the experimenter will not know their output, and, even if the participants believe that they know their own, they have no evaluative criterion against which to compare it.

This analysis suggests that the basic loafing effect is a result of the fact that when participants "work together," their individual outputs cannot be evaluated, and it is the lack of evaluation potential, not the fact that they are "working together," that leads them to loaf. In fact, in their initial article Latané et al. (1979) suggested that it was the "information reducing" nature of the "group" trials (Davis, 1969) that was responsible for the loafing effect. They argued that when participants' performances were pooled, individual outputs were lost in the crowd, submerged in the total, and were not individually recoverable by the experimenter. Because participants could receive neither praise nor blame for their performances, they loafed. In support of this interpretation, Williams, Harkins, and Latané (1981) found that when participants were led to believe that their individual outputs could be monitored even when they performed "together" (i.e., pooled outputs), they worked as hard when they performed "together" as when they worked as individuals. Also, when participants were led to believe that interest centered on "group" performance and their individual outputs were to be summed, they loafed as much when they performed individually as when they performed "together."

These findings suggest that, in the basic loafing paradigm (e.g., Latané, Williams, & Harkins, 1979; Harkins, Latané, & Williams, 1980; Williams, Harkins, & Latané, 1981), it is not whether one works as an individual or in a group, but whether one's performance can be evaluated or not that determines one's level of performance. Consistent with this interpretation, in their meta-analysis, Karau and Williams (1993) found no difference in performance between participants who worked individually and "together" when evaluation potential was held constant.

Perhaps this should not be surprising. In the basic loafing paradigm, strangers come together for a brief time with no promise of future interaction. There is little in the procedure itself to make the participants feel that they are part of a group. The tasks used in the basic paradigm have been very simple and uninteresting (e.g., shouting, clapping, generating as many uses as possible for an object, vigilance), and so, there is nothing about the task itself that should motivate performance. There is no interaction during the experiment; the participants are not invited to compete with other groups, or even to try to outdo their own group's last effort. Thus, under these conditions, pooling the participants' outputs simply serves as a means of minimizing the extent to which the participants feel that their outputs can be evaluated. In addition, participants are not able to evaluate their own performances either by comparing them to the performances of other participants, or by comparing their performance on a given trial to their performance on a preceding one.

This argument is also supported by the responses of participants to the manipulation checks in this research (e.g., Harkins & Szymanski, 1989; Szymanski & Harkins, 1987). These measures show that, in the basic loafing paradigm, participants who work individually report that the experimenter can evaluate their performances, but they cannot, nor do they report that their performances can be evaluated by coactors. Participants who "work together" report that their individual performances can be evaluated by no one, and that they cannot compare their group's performance to the performances of other groups.

It is under these circumstances, we argue, that participants focus on the potential for evaluation by the experimenter. We certainly are not proposing that effects stemming from manipulations of evaluation potential account for all, or even most, motivation losses in groups. As demonstrated by Shepperd's review in Chapter 1, a large number of different variables affect performance in groups. In fact, even when our attention is limited to the social loafing paradigm, it is clear that other factors motivate performance when there is no potential for evaluation (see Shepperd, Chapter 1), but in these cases, we would argue that some aspect of the basic loafing paradigm has been changed. For example, Brickner, Harkins, and Ostrom (1986) found that when personal relevance was high, the social loafing effect was eliminated. But, of course, in the basic loafing paradigm personal relevance is low. Thus, it is certainly the case that there is more to social loafing research than the finding that participants subject to evaluation by the experimenter work harder than those who are not. However, we would argue that in the basic social loafing paradigm, the loafing effect is nothing more than this.

The Primacy of the Potential for External Evaluation

Given the minimal evaluation baseline provided by the "pooled" condition of the social loafing paradigm, to examine the effects of the potential for evaluation by a given source, one need only manipulate the availability of the information necessary for evaluation. In a series of experiments using this basic paradigm we have examined the effects of the potential for external and self-evaluation on task performance. It is this line of research that argues for the primacy of the potential for external evaluation under a wide range of conditions that, we would argue, encompass those incorporated in the various traditions included in this volume.

In our initial research, participants were asked to work on simple tasks by an experimenter who asked them to "do their best" (e.g., generate as many uses as you can, detect as many dots as you can). In this work, we found that the potential for self-evaluation alone led to performance better than that found in the "no evaluation" condition (i.e., no experimenter evaluation/no criterion). In fact, the potential for self-evaluation led to performance equivalent to that produced by the potential for experimenter evaluation (Harkins & Szymanski, 1988; Szymanski & Harkins, 1987).

However, we also found that when there was the potential for evaluation by *both sources*, concern over the potential for experimenter evaluation superseded interest in the potential for self-evaluation (Harkins & Szymanski, 1988). Follow-up research suggested that the dominance of experimenter over self-evaluation stemmed from apprehension regarding evaluation by the experimenter rather than interest in impressing him/her. In fact, Szymanski and Harkins (1993) showed that the prospect of experimenter evaluation was so distasteful that participants chose to pass up the opportunity for self-evaluation rather than to submit themselves to this scrutiny. Although these findings demonstrate that concern over the potential for evaluation by an external source supersedes interest in the potential for self-evaluation, this effect has been demonstrated under a limited set of conditions. We will now present additional research that demonstrates that the primacy of external evaluation holds across a variety of manipulations.

Power of the External Source

In our research (e.g., Szymanski & Harkins, 1993), it is concern over evaluation by the experimenter, a powerful source, that overpowers interest in self-evaluation. One could argue that the ascendancy of social evaluation depends on the power of the source of social evaluation. I would note that even if this were so, our findings would be relevant for the wide range of real world settings in which task performance is judged by powerful sources (e.g., teachers, coaches, supervisors). In addition, in each of the specific research traditions under consideration here, the source of external evaluation is powerful (e.g., the experimenter). In any event, Szymanski, Garczynski, and Harkins (2000) have found evidence that is consistent with the view that the potential for evaluation by a lower status source, a classmate, has the same effect on self-evaluation as the potential for evaluation by the experimenter. Szymanski et al. eliminated the potential for evaluation by the experimenter and then randomly assigned participants to one of four conditions in a 2 (self-evaluation vs. no self-evaluation) x 2 (coactor evaluation vs. no coactor evaluation) design. Just as has been the case in previous research in which the experimenter was the source of social evaluation (e.g., Szymanski & Harkins, 1987; Harkins & Szymanski, 1988), the potential for evaluation by each of the sources (self and coactor) led to better performance than was found in the "no evaluation" condition. And, just as in the previous research, the combination of the two sources led to no better performance than either one taken alone.

In a follow-up experiment, Szymanski et al. arranged matters so that participants could not self-evaluate and then randomly assigned participants to one of the four conditions in a 2 (experimenter evaluation vs. no experimenter evaluation) x 2 (coactor evaluation vs. no coactor evaluation) design. Replicating previous research, each of the sources taken alone led to better performance than was found in the "no evaluation" condition. However, unlike our past research in which one of the sources was always self, when there was the potential for evaluation by both external sources, performance was reliably better than that produced by either source taken alone. These findings suggest that the potential for evaluation by external sources, whether experimenter or coactor, have the same effect on the potential for self-evaluation.

Do Your Best versus Goal Setting Instructions

In the research reviewed so far, participants have only been asked to "do their best." For example, when asked to generate uses for a common object, they were asked to generate as many uses as they could (e.g., Szymanski & Harkins, 1987), but this level of output apparently does not actually represent the participants' "best" performance. In nearly 400 studies that have used 40,000 participants in eight countries, 88 different tasks, and time spans ranging from one minute to three years, it has been found that giving participants specific, difficult goals leads to better performance than instructing participants to do their best, whether the goals are self-set, participatively set, or set by an external source (Locke & Latham, 1990a).

Locke and Latham (1990b) argue that it is the potential for self-evaluation that produces goal setting effects. That is, the goal provides a stringent criterion against which participants can compare their performances. This claim, if supported, would suggest that concern over the potential for external evaluation does not supersede interest in the potential for self-evaluation in the goal setting paradigm. However, as noted in my first chapter (Harkins, Chapter 5), White, Kjelgaard, and Harkins (1995) have argued that although goal setting research does show that setting stringent goals produces better performance than do your best instructions, it does not tell us whether it is the potential for self-evaluation, the potential for external evaluation, or both that is (are) responsible for this effect. In virtually all goal setting research (for an exception, see White, Mitchell, & Bell, 1977), participants who had the potential to self-evaluate could also be evaluated by the experimenter who had access both to the goals and to the participants' outputs.

White, Kjelgaard, and Harkins (1995) used the social loafing paradigm to test the contribution of self-evaluation processes to the goal setting effect, and found that the potential for self-evaluation was not sufficient to produce a goal setting effect. However, it did motivate participants enough to exceed the performance of participants in the no experimenter evaluation/do your best condition (i.e., exceeded the "loafing" level). In fact, the performance of these participants equaled that of participants subject to experimenter evaluation who were asked to do their best (i.e., a do-your-best effect). Harkins, White, and Utman (2000) argued that the potential for self-evaluation motivated these participants enough to "do their best" so that they could see how this level of performance compared to the performance level represented by a stringent goal. That is, they used the stringent goal as a *yardstick* against which they could compare their do-your-best performance rather than as a level of performance that they were striving to achieve.

As summarized in Chapter 5, Harkins, White, and Utman (2000) tested this yardstick explanation by manipulating the validity of the evaluative criterion. That is, if the no experimenter evaluation participants were using the criterion as a yardstick, it should be of value only when it was based on the performance of similar others. Consistent with this argument, Harkins et al. (2000) showed that participants who were not subject to experimenter evaluation "did their best" only when the evaluative criterion was based on the performance of similar others (i.e., other college students). When the criterion was invalid (i.e., based on the performance of dissimilar others (9th graders or 3rd-year Ph.D. students)), the yardstick effect was eliminated.

Thus, even though the potential for self-evaluation alone was not sufficient to produce a goal setting effect, one could argue that the goal setting effect was produced by the combination of the motivation produced by the potential for experimenter and self-evaluation, an additive model. Of course, Harkins, White, and Utman (2000) argued that the potential for self-evaluation did not contribute at all to White et al.'s goal setting effect. Instead, based on previous research (e.g., Harkins & Szymanski, 1988; Szymanski & Harkins, 1993), Harkins et al. argued that the goal setting effect was produced by the potential for experimenter evaluation alone.

Harkins et al. (2000) tested the "experimenter evaluation alone" versus the additive explanations in two ways. First, they manipulated the potential for self-evaluation by providing participants with a criterion that was based on the performance of similar (valid criterion), or dissimilar others (an invalid criterion). Harkins et al. reasoned that if experimenter evaluation alone is important, then the validity of the criterion (the goal) should not matter. If the experimenter has directed them to strive to reach the goal, they should attempt to do so. In contrast, if the goal setting effect requires motivation stemming from the potential for self-evaluation (additive model), then there should be a goal setting effect when the criterion is valid, but not when it is invalid, because in the latter case, the contribution of self-evaluation has been eliminated. Consistent with the "experimenter evaluation only" interpretation, Harkins et al. (2000) found goal setting effects whether the goal was based on the performance of similar or dissimilar others.

Harkins et al. (2000) pitted the experimenter evaluation only interpretation against the additive model in a second way. Participants in the experimenter evaluation/do your best condition outperform participants in the no experimenter evaluation/do your best condition because of the potential for experimenter evaluation. There is no opportunity for self-evaluation, because the participants have no criterion against which to compare their performance. The additive model suggests that the improvement from this do-your-best level of performance to the level required for a goal setting effect reflects the influence of motivation stemming from the potential for self-evaluation provided by the goal. No striving instruction should be required. Whether or not the experimenter asks the participants to strive, the goal provides a criterion for self-evaluation. In contrast, the experimenter evaluation only interpretation suggests that it is simply the experimenter's instruction to strive to reach the stringent goal that produces the additional performance. Without this striving instruction, there should be no goal setting effect, only performance at the do-your-best level. Once again, consistent with the experimenter evaluation only interpretation, when participants were provided a stringent criterion only as a piece of information (no striving instructions), Harkins et al. found performance at the do-your-best level, whether the criterion was based on the performance of similar or dissimilar others.

Taken together, these findings show that setting stringent goals leads to better performance than do your best instructions, but only when there is the potential for external evaluation. And, once again, consistent with our previous research (Harkins & Szymanski, 1988; Szymanski & Harkins, 1993), we find strong support for the argument that concern over the potential for experimenter evaluation supplants interest in self-evaluation. However, in this research we have used simple tasks about which the participants knew nothing except that the experimenter had asked them to perform them. When subject to the experimenter's evaluation, the participants followed his/her instructions, "doing their best" when asked to do so, and striving to reach the goal when given that criterion. However, when not subject to external evaluation, participants were motivated enough by the potential for self-evaluation to "do their best," but no more. We would argue that this level of effort gives them a sense of how well they can perform the task, and because no one else will know how well they have done, this suffices. If this is the case, if we were to increase the importance of their performance to them, the motivation stemming from interest in the potential for self-evaluation may be sufficient to produce a goal setting effect. Perhaps under these circumstances, concern over the potential for external evaluation would not overwhelm interest in self-evaluation.

Ego-Involvement

Utman and Harkins (1996, Experiment 2) increased participants' ego-involvement in a task by leading them to believe that the task was a test of intellectual ability and then set goals for performance. We found that if the participants were ego-involved, the potential for self-evaluation led to a goal setting effect, just like the potential for external evaluation. These findings suggest that the potential for self-evaluation can be as potent as the potential for experimenter evaluation when participants have a stake in their performance. However, this experiment does not tell us what happens to interest in the potential for self-evaluation when it is combined with concern about the potential for experimenter evaluation under these conditions. That is, when participants are assigned a goal for performance on a simple task, we know that concern over the potential for experimenter evaluation supersedes interest in the potential for self-evaluation (e.g., Harkins, et al., 2000), but what about when participants have a stake in their performance?

This question can be answered by looking at the effects of increased ego-involvement in Harkins, White, and Utman's (2000) experimental paradigm. In the previous description of this experiment, we divided the findings in terms of striving instructions. For our present purposes, we present the findings in the conditions in which experimenter evaluation was possible followed by the findings in the no experimenter evaluation conditions.

In the experimenter evaluation conditions, participants responded to the striving instructions, but not to the manipulation of criterion validity. Whether the criterion was based on the performance of similar (valid criterion) or dissimilar (invalid criterion) others, when given striving instructions, participants produced a goal setting effect, but when the criterion was presented only as a piece of information (no striving), they performed at the do-your-best level. On the other hand, in the no experimenter evaluation conditions, participants were not responsive to the striving instructions. Instead they responded to the similarity instructions. Whether or not the experimenter asked them to strive, when the criterion was based on the performance of similar others (valid criterion), participants performed at the do-your-best level, but when the criterion was based on the performance of dissimilar others (invalid criterion), they loafed.

This experiment (Harkins, White, & Utman, 2000) shows that participants who are not subject to experimenter evaluation are responsive to the manipulation of criterion validity, but not to the manipulation of striving instructions. Utman and Harkins's (1996) Experiment 2 shows that participants who are not subject to experimenter evaluation are also responsive to a manipulation of ego-involvement. In fact, increased ego-involvement motivated these no experimenter evaluation participants to perform not just at the do-your-best level, but to produce a goal setting effect. Of course, Utman and Harkins's Experiment 2 did not incorporate a manipulation of striving, but if it had, we would not expect these no experimenter evaluation participants to respond to it, just as participants who were not subject to experimenter evaluation failed to respond to this manipulation in Harkins et al.'s research.

This analysis suggests that we can determine whether concern over the potential for experimenter evaluation supersedes interest in self-evaluation when ego-involvement is high by looking at the effect of high ego-involvement on participants who are subject to the evaluation of the experimenter but are given no striving instructions. We know that the potential for self-evaluation is sufficient to produce a goal setting effect when ego-involvement is high. We have no reason to believe that this effect depends on striving instructions. In fact, we can test this hypothesis simply by comparing the performance of no experimenter evaluation/high ego-involvement/striving participants to that of their no striving counterparts. We should find goal setting effects in each case. Given this outcome, if experimenter evaluation/high ego-involvement participants who are given no striving instructions produce a goal setting effect, it would suggest that the effect could be due to the potential for self-evaluation. If there is no goal setting effect, it would suggest that the potential for experimenter evaluation supersedes interest in self-evaluation even when ego-involvement is high.

In this experiment (Utman & Harkins, 1996, Experiment 3), participants were randomly assigned to one of twelve conditions in a 2 (experimenter evaluation versus no experimenter evaluation) x 3 (criterion presented as a goal toward which the participants are urged to strive (striving) versus criterion presented as a piece of information in which the participants might be interested (no striving) versus do your best instructions) x 2 (low ego-involvement instructions versus high ego-involvement instructions) design, and were asked to generate uses for a common object. In those conditions in which participants were provided a criterion, they were told that it was based on the performance of similar others.

As shown in Table 1, the results of Experiment 3 replicated the findings of our previous research. As found by Harkins, White, and Utman (2000), in the low ego-involvement conditions, participants subject to experimenter evaluation were responsive to the striving instructions. When asked to strive, they produced a goal setting effect, but when the criterion was presented as a piece of information in which they might be interested, participants performed only at the do-your-best level. Participants who were not subject to evaluation by the experimenter performed only at the do-your-best level, regardless of the striving instructions.

Under high ego-involvement, participants in the no experimenter evaluation/striving condition produced a goal setting effect, replicating the effect found by Utman and Harkins (1996) in Experiment 2. And, as in Harkins et al. (2000), we found that no experimenter evaluation participants were not responsive to the striving manipulation. But in Harkins et al.'s (2000) research no experimenter evaluation participants performed only at the do-your-best level whether or not the experimenter asked them to strive. In Utman and Harkins's Experiment 3, under high ego-involvement instructions, no experimenter evaluation participants produced goal setting effects whether or not they were asked to strive.

This pattern of findings indicates that we produced the conditions necessary to determine whether or not concern over the potential for experimenter evaluation supersedes interest in the potential for self-evaluation when ego-involvement is high. In the absence of experimenter evaluation, when ego-involvement was high, the potential for self-evaluation produced goal setting effects whether the participants were asked to strive or not. If it is the potential for self-evaluation that is driving performance in the high ego-involvement/experimenter evaluation/no striving condition, we should also see a goal setting effect in this condition. But we do not. Participants performed at the do-your-best level despite the fact that their no experimenter evaluation counterparts produced a goal setting effect. This finding suggests that concern over the potential for experimenter evaluation supersedes interest in self-evaluation even when ego-involvement is high.

Table 1. Mean uses for a "knife": Exp. 3, Utman & Harkins (1996)

	Low Ego-involvement			High Ego-involvement		
	Do Your Best	No Striving	Striving	Do Your Best	No Striving	Striving
Experimenter Evaluation	30.6	31.5*	39.4‡	30.6	30.7*	40.1‡
No Experimenter Evaluation	21.2	27.7*	32.7*	30.1	40.1‡	41.8‡

* = do-your-best effect ‡ = goal setting effect

Experimenter-set versus Self-Set Goals

One could also argue that the ascendancy of social evaluation depends on the fact that the goals have been set by the experimenter, and would not hold if participants were allowed to set their own goals. After all, the goal setting literature is unequivocal in its suggestion that when participants are asked to set their own goals, goal setting effects are produced. As Locke and Latham (1990b) write: "A surprising finding of research on goal commitment is that assigning goals to individuals generally leads to the same level of commitment and performance as letting individuals participate in the setting of their goals or letting them set their own goals (Latham & Lee, 1986; Locke & Latham, 1990a). Participation is not less effective than most social scientists (including ourselves) assumed it would be; rather assigned goals are more effective than predicted" (p. 241). That is, the surprise is not that participatively-set and self-set goals produce goal setting effects; rather, the surprise is that assigned goals lead to performance as good as participatively-set and self-set goals. In fact, Locke and Latham (1990a) believe that the literature is so compelling on this point that they write: "Further research on the motivational effects of different goal setting methods would appear to have limited value" (p. 171).

However, White, Kjelgaard, and Harkins (1995) found that when participants were asked to set their own goals, they set them far too low to produce goal setting effects. When the experimenter suggested appropriately stringent goals (White et al., 1995; Harkins & Lowe, 2000), participants set their goals only at the do-your-best level, far short of the level necessary to produce goal setting effects. Participants who were subject to experimenter evaluation did produce goal setting effects, but they did so by working past the goals that they set.

In an attempt to resolve this apparent discrepancy, we (Harkins & Lowe, 2000) examined two reviews (Wright's (1990) meta-analysis, and Locke & Latham's (1990a) narrative review), and found no support for the notion that self-set goals produce goal setting effects. Of course, these reviews were not intended to demonstrate the existence of self-set goal effects, and so, we undertook our own meta-analysis of this literature. Our meta-analysis showed that self-set goals do produce goal setting effects but only when two conditions are met: (1) Prior to setting their goals, participants must have had sufficient experience on the task to provide a basis for setting the goal; and (2) The experimenter must have access to the goals and to the performances of the participants.

The experiments included in the meta-analysis did not provide enough information about the goals for meaningful analysis, and so, our interpretation of the process was based on the performance outcomes. However, if the goals themselves drive the self-set goal effect, we argued that it was the participants' experience with the task that provided the basis for setting these stringent goals. Without this experience, the participants are unwilling or unable to do so. The stringent goals then drive the participants' performances.

This logic was tested in an experiment in which participants were asked to solve single-digit arithmetic problems across multiple trials of equal length. For the first trial, participants were asked to solve as many problems as they could in 3 minutes after having been led to believe that the experimenter would or would not be able to evaluate their output. The first trial was meant to provide the requisite experience. Before each of the next three 3-minute trials, participants were asked to do the best they could (do your best), or to set and then try to achieve the goals that they set for themselves (self-set). In the experimenter evaluation/self-set goal condition, the participants knew that the experimenter would have access to both their goals and their performances; in the no experimenter evaluation condition, the participants knew that the experimenter would have access to neither.

Consistent with the outcome of the meta-analysis, participants who were subject to experimenter evaluation and had experience on the task (Trial 1) set stringent goals and attained them, producing self-set goal effects on Trials 2-4. Without the potential for experimenter evaluation, no self-set goal effects were obtained. Thus, it is not the fact that participants have been asked to strive to reach experimenter-set rather than self-set goals that accounts for the ascendancy of social evaluation.

Self-Set Goals and Ego-Involvement

One could argue that the potential for self-evaluation was not sufficient to produce goal setting effects even when goals were self-set because the task was not ego-involving. Of course, Utman and Harkins (1996) tested this notion, and found that concern over the potential for external evaluation superseded interest in self-evaluation even when ego-involvement was high, but this finding characterized performance when goals were set by the experimenter.

Lowe (1997) tested the possibility that the potential for self-evaluation would be sufficient to produce goal setting effects when goals were self-set. If it were, the next question would be whether this effect would be superseded by concern over the potential for external evaluation. In addition, in this research we tested an implication of the "requisite experience" explanation for self-set goal effects. Although the results of the multi-trial experiment (Harkins & Lowe, 2000, Experiment 2) were consistent with the results of the meta-analysis, this experiment left an aspect of the "requisite experience" account unexamined. In the four-trial experiment, self-set participants were not asked to set a goal until Trial 2. We claimed that there would have been no self-set goal effect on Trial 1 even if these participants had been asked to set a goal, because they had no basis for doing so (i.e., no requisite experience). However, this claim was just that, because these participants were not asked to set a goal on Trial 1. In our next experiment (Lowe, 1997), this notion was tested by asking participants to self-set goals on the first trial.

The low ego-involvement condition of this experiment allowed us to test the prediction that there would be no self-set goal effect on Trial 1. Consistent with the "requisite experience" analysis, when participants were subject to experimenter evaluation and were asked to self-set goals on Trial 1, there was no goal setting effect. However, on Trial 2, after their experience on Trial 1, experimenter evaluation/self-set participants did produce a reliable goal setting effect. As predicted, without the potential for experimenter evaluation, there was no goal setting effect on either Trial 1 or Trial 2.

Utman and Harkins (1996, Experiment 2) found that, with *experimenter-set goals*, the high ego-involvement manipulation motivated no experimenter evaluation participants to produce a goal setting effect. Lowe (1997) replicated this effect. However, when goals were self-set, Lowe (1997) found that the high ego-involvement manipulation was not sufficient to motivate no experimenter evaluation participants to produce this effect. In fact, under high ego-involvement, the self-set goal effect produced by experimenter evaluation participants on Trial 2 under low ego-involvement was eliminated.

Apparently when ego-involvement is high, the fact that the experimenter has set the goal gives it a potency that cannot be ignored even when only the participant will know how well s/he has done. On the other hand, when the participant sets his/her own goal, s/he can take advantage of this opportunity to avoid the possible discovery by the experimenter or self that s/he is not capable of achieving a stringent criterion on an important task. The fact that increasing the importance of the task did not motivate participants in the no experimenter evaluation condition to produce self-set goal effects suggests that it was not lack of interest that accounted for the absence of a self-set goal effect in the low ego-involvement condition. These findings suggest that the ascendancy of social evaluation holds for both experimenter-set and self-set goals.

Summary

Taken together, these findings provide strong support for the claim of the primacy of the potential for external evaluation in both the do-your-best and the goal setting paradigms. There are some situations in which the potential for self-evaluation motivates performance to the same extent as the potential for external evaluation (e.g., when the experimenter only asks participants to "do their best"). In fact, the potential for self-evaluation can lead to better performance than the potential for external evaluation. For example, as shown in Table 1, Utman and Harkins (1996) found that under high ego-involvement with no striving instructions, no experimenter evaluation participants produced a goal setting effect whereas experimenter evaluation participants produced only a do-your-best effect. But in this research, we used the bell jar provided by the laboratory to examine separately the effects of experimenter and self-evaluation. It is under these special conditions that we can find some few instances in which the potential for self-evaluation is as potent as, or even more potent than, the potential for social evaluation.

Even under the conditions produced in the bell jar, the potential for external evaluation is more powerful than the potential for self-evaluation in most instances. For example, when goals are experimenter-set and the experimenter can evaluate performance, goal setting effects are produced whether or not the participants have had previous experience with the task (Harkins & Lowe, 2000), whether or not the participants are ego-involved (Utman and Harkins, 1996), and whether or not the goals are based on the performance of similar others (Harkins, White, & Utman, 2000). In fact, the experimenter can produce goal setting effects by only suggesting goal levels (White, Kjelgaard, & Harkins, 1995; Harkins & Lowe, 2000).

When goals are self-set, if the participant has taken part in an initial session equal in length to the test session, under low ego-involvement, the potential for experimenter evaluation produces self-set goal effects but the potential for self-evaluation does not. Increasing ego-involvement in the self-set goal paradigm does not enhance the potency of self-evaluation. In fact, under these conditions, even the potential for evaluation by the experimenter does not produce a self-set goal effect.

In any event, in the "real world" and in the traditions encompassed by the three-variable model, the potential for social and self-evaluation most often co-exist. Under these circumstances, we have found that concern over the potential for evaluation by the experimenter supersedes interest in the potential for self-evaluation, even under high ego-involvement (Utman & Harkins, 1996). What is more, this effect does not depend on the power of the experimenter (Szymanski, Garczynski, and Harkins, 2000). The potential for evaluation by a coactor, a less powerful source, has the same effect on self-evaluation as the potential for evaluation by the experimenter. These findings argue for the primacy of the potential for external evaluation under a wide range of conditions that, at the very least, encompass those incorporated in the various traditions represented in the three-variable model.

Task Complexity

Once again, we wish to make the claim that the three variables incorporated in the model are all that is required to produce the basic performance effects of each tradition. However, up to this point, our analysis has focused on the simple half of the three-variable model. We now consider performance on complex tasks.

Social Loafing/Social Facilitation

Of course, the unified model of social loafing/social facilitation described in Chapter 5 easily accommodates performance on complex tasks. According to this model, loafing and facilitation are complementary phenomena. In social facilitation research, when participants coact their outputs can be compared, and this potential for evaluation leads to enhanced performance on simple tasks and debilitated performance on complex tasks. In social loafing research, when participants work together their outputs cannot be evaluated and the absence of the potential for evaluation leads to poorer performance on simple tasks and better performance on complex ones. For example, Jackson and Williams (1985) found that participants in a coaction/evaluation condition performed better on simple mazes, but worse on complex mazes, than participants in a coaction/no evaluation condition. Likewise, Sanna (1992) found that participants who were subject to experimenter evaluation solved more simple RAT (Remote Associates Test) items than those who were not, but when participants were asked to solve difficult items, the outcome reversed. Participants subject to experimenter evaluation solved fewer RAT items than those who were not subject to this evaluation. Of course, we replicated this finding in the experiment using RAT items described in Chapter 5.

Goal Setting

The extension of this analysis to the goal setting literature is also quite straightforward. The bulk of the research on goal setting has used tasks that are very simple, like reaction time, use-generation, simple arithmetic, perceptual speed, sewing machine work, typing, and production work (Wood, Mento, & Locke, 1987). These tasks are exactly like the ones used in research on social loafing and social facilitation. And, on tasks like these, when the experimenter has access to the participants' performances, participants assigned a stringent goal outperform participants who are only asked to do their best. The stringent goal requires a higher level of performance than "do your best" instructions, and when the experimenter can evaluate their performances, the participants strive to reach it. Given that the task is simple, this additional effort leads to better performance.

But what about complex tasks? As Tubbs notes (Chapter 2, p. 34-35), of the tasks in the studies reviewed by Wood et al. (1987), "a sizeable minority (34 out of the 125 they reviewed) were reasonably complex, and included: college coursework, employee supervision, middle management, technician work, and science/engineering work (Locke & Latham, 1990)." Tubbs notes that these "all represented rather complex real-life tasks quite different from the typical 'widget-making' tasks found in many laboratory studies" (Chapter

2, p. 35). In their meta-analysis, Wood et al. (1987) found reliable goal setting effects for these "reasonably complex" tasks even though the effect size was smaller than that found on simpler tasks.

However, Tubbs also notes that many of the studies in which "complex" tasks were used were conducted in the field, and the participants had had extensive experience with the tasks. In these cases, participants have had ample opportunity to learn how to perform the task, a situation that stands in marked contrast to the experience awaiting participants in loafing and facilitation research as they face the complex task most likely for the first time. In fact, in the few goal setting studies that have used novel, complex tasks (e.g., Earley, Connolly, & Ekegren, 1989; Kanfer & Ackerman, 1989), participants in the goal conditions have performed more poorly than participants in the "do your best" conditions. This finding is consistent with the notion that the goal represents a greater source of pressure than "do your best" instructions which, in combination with the pressure arising from concern about the potential for evaluation by the experimenter, undermines performance on complex tasks.

Thus, we would argue that the three-variable model is well-supported in the social loafing, social facilitation, and goal setting literatures, although more research is required on the effects of goal setting on complex task performance. If there is to be a problem with the simple/complex task dichotomy, it lies in its extension to the intrinsic motivation/creativity and achievement goal literatures.

Intrinsic Motivation/Creativity Research

Researchers in the intrinsic motivation/creativity tradition (e.g., Amabile, 1996; Hennessey, Chapters 3 and 8) focus on the interest the participants have in the task. They argue that participants must perform the task for the sheer enjoyment and pleasure of the activity itself rather than for some external goal. In addition, these researchers argue that to be creative a response must represent a novel and appropriate solution to a task that requires a heuristic, rather than an algorithmic, solution. On algorithmic tasks, the path to the solution is clear and straightforward, whereas heuristic tasks are open-ended, and require search for the appropriate solution path.

This distinction between algorithmic and heuristic tasks comes from a review by McGraw (1978), which was aimed at determining the conditions under which reward produces detrimental effects on performance. As McGraw writes: "What emerges from this review and analysis is the claim that incentives will have a detrimental effect on performance when two conditions are met: first, when the task is interesting enough for subjects that the offer of incentives is a superfluous source of motivation; second when the solution to the task is open-ended enough that the steps leading to a solution are not immediately obvious" (p. 34). Of course, the conditions under which reward produces detrimental effects are exactly those conditions that Hennessey identifies as necessary for creative performance.

Given the importance of McGraw's (1978) review to Hennessey's analysis of creative performance, it is worth a closer look. In his article, McGraw (1978) first reviews research on discrimination learning, concept attainment, insight and creativity, and incidental learning and finds evidence of the detrimental effects of reward in each of these domains. To reconcile these findings with the more familiar finding of reward facilitation, McGraw (1978) suggests that tasks that show facilitation and those that show disruption differ in their attractiveness for the participants. According to McGraw, tasks that show the detrimental effects of reward are attractive to the participants, whereas those that show facilitation are not (e.g., marble dropping, lever pressing, letter canceling, and vigilance). Thus, tasks that show the detrimental effect of reward "appear to be tests of intelligence; and subjects, at least those in the student population, are generally motivated to do well regardless of whether they are rewarded. In contrast, the perceptual-motor tasks that predominate in the literature on facilitating effects of reward involve little intelligence" (p. 41).

On unattractive tasks, participants are not motivated unless they are rewarded. As McGraw (1978) writes: "Reward subjects will presumably engage wholeheartedly in any task, no matter how odious, if the reward is perceived as equitable" (p. 41). This is not the case for nonreward participants. They must be motivated by the task. Thus, the first condition necessary to produce the detrimental effect of reward is a task sufficiently attractive to elicit the best efforts of participants who are not rewarded.

However, this aversive-attractive dimension is not sufficient to predict when reward will have a facilitating effect and when a detrimental one, because there are many attractive tasks on which reward does not have a detrimental effect (e.g., research on mental multiplication, serial learning, paired-associate learning and perceptual recognition). According to McGraw: "By determining in what way the tasks differed when the effects of reward differed, a second crucial dimension for predicting reward's effect can be isolated" (p. 47). His analysis revealed that the attractive tasks for which reward had a facilitating effect were algorithmic. That is, "the paths to solutions were well mapped and straightforward, just as they are on other tasks where reward has been found to facilitate, like lever pressing and signal detection" (p. 47). In contrast, there were tasks on which the algorithm must be developed as the task unfolds. It is these tasks that McGraw termed heuristic. McGraw (1978) argued that "by adding the algorithmic-heuristic distinction to the attractive-aversive distinction, much better predictions of reward's effect on performance can be made, with the most favorable case for detrimental effect of reward being in the case where attractive tasks requiring heuristic solutions are used" (p. 47).

Taken together, the variables produce a 2 (reward vs. no reward) x 2 (attractive vs. unattractive) x 2 (algorithmic vs. heuristic) design, and, based on his review of the literature, McGraw predicted that only when the participants were faced with an attractive, heuristic task would reward have a detrimental effect on performance. In all other cases, he predicted that it would have a facilitating effect. In his review, McGraw provides examples of facilitation effects for both attractive and unattractive algorithmic tasks. There are no examples of experiments with unattractive, heuristic tasks that produce facilitation effects, but McGraw suggests that such cases are easily imagined: "It would hold when an otherwise interesting and heuristically solvable task is not presently interesting for reasons of momentary subject factors such as fatigue" (p. 47).

This approach is not theory-driven, nor does McGraw suggest an explanation for the effects that emerge from his prediction model. He simply surveys the literature and, based on this review, notes the conditions under which it appears that reward has detrimental effects on performance. However, the evidence that he provides for the importance of task attractiveness in this analysis is not compelling. First, task attractiveness does not appear to matter on algorithmic tasks. McGraw cites research that shows that reward has a facilitating effect on performance on algorithmic tasks whether the task is attractive or not. On heuristic tasks, he argues that reward has a detrimental effect on performance on attractive tasks, but not on those that are unattractive. Of course, there are many examples of the detrimental effect of reward on the performance of attractive, heuristic tasks, but we are left to rely on our imaginations to supply examples of cases in which reward has a facilitating effect on heuristic, unattractive tasks. However, not only are there no examples of such findings, such a prediction appears to be inconsistent with his own analysis.

McGraw (1978) points out that his distinction between algorithmic and heuristic tasks is very similar to one proposed before. As he writes: "Spence's (1956) use of the position of the correct response in the habit family hierarchy as a determinant of the effect of incentive on performance covers much of what we mean by making the nature of the solution (algorithmic or heuristic) a determinant of reward's effect" (p. 56). On algorithmic tasks, the correct response lies at or close to the top of the habit hierarchy, whereas on heuristic tasks, the correct response falls toward the bottom of the hierarchy. The multiplicative relationship between incentive (K, reward in this case) and habit strength results in the increased likelihood of a correct response when this response is high in the habit hierarchy, but a decreased likelihood of the correct response when the correct response is low in the habit hierarchy.

It is inconsistent with this analysis to predict that reward will have a facilitating effect on unattractive, heuristic tasks. Using McGraw's example, even if one were fatigued, thereby rendering a heuristic task uninteresting, the correct response would still fall toward the bottom of the habit hierarchy, and the incentive produced by the reward would still be expected to debilitate performance relative to a condition in which no reward was supplied. Thus, whether the task is attractive or not, reward would be expected to have a detrimental effect on performance.

Consequently, on algorithmic tasks, because the correct answer lies at the top of the habit hierarchy, reward should facilitate performance whether the task is attractive or not. And on heuristic tasks, because the correct answer falls toward the bottom of the habit hierarchy, reward should have a detrimental effect on performance, whether the task is attractive or not. Zajonc (1965) also used the notion of habit hierarchy in his drive account of social facilitation/debilitation effects. In his analysis, the presence of others served as the source of motivation, which increased the likelihood of the emission of the dominant response (most likely response in the habit hierarchy). If the dominant response was correct (as when the task is simple or well-learned), performance should be facilitated, but if the dominant response is incorrect (as when the task is complex or not well-learned), performance was debilitated. Thus, McGraw's (1978) distinction between algorithmic and heuristic tasks is essentially nothing more than the simple-complex distinction in the social facilitation literature.

In Chapter 3, Hennessey described Amabile's (1996) maze metaphor for the creative enterprise: "There is one starting point, one entrance into this maze but there are a variety of exit points and many different paths of those exits" (p. 66). When one is subject to evaluation, the most straightforward route is chosen. According to Hennessey, to generate a creative idea, one must be willing to test alternative pathways. Using McGraw's terminology, Hennessey describes this as a heuristic task, but, once again, this is nothing more than a complex task. Just as the "creative" response is the less likely one, the "correct" response on a complex task is the less likely one, and the potential for evaluation makes this response even less likely. Thus, this aspect of McGraw's (and Hennessey's) analysis maps directly on to the simple/complex dimension of our model.

Bartis, Szymanski, and Harkins (1988) have reported findings consistent with this analysis. They asked one-half of their participants to generate as many uses for an object as possible without regard to creativity, whereas the other half of the participants were asked to generate uses that were as creative as possible without regard to number. Replicating previous findings (e.g., Harkins & Jackson, 1985), when given number instructions, participants who were subject to experimenter evaluation generated more uses than participants who were not, but there were no differences in the creativity represented by these responses. However, when given creativity instructions, participants who were subject to experimenter evaluation generated uses that were less creative than participants who were not, and there was no difference in the number of uses generated. Thus, manipulating the potential for experimenter evaluation alone produced a pattern of results identical to that found in the social facilitation/social loafing literature. That is, on the simple task (number instructions), the potential for evaluation led to better performance, whereas on the complex task (creativity instructions), it led to debilitated performance. Of course, under creativity instructions (complex task), the pattern of results replicates the findings of creativity researchers in the intrinsic motivation literature (e.g., Amabile, 1979; Hennessey, Chapters 3 and 8).

Achievement Goal Theory

Elliott and Dweck (1988) argue "that there are two major goals that are pursued by individuals in achievement situations: (a) performance goals, in which individuals seek to maintain positive judgments of their ability and avoid negative judgments by seeking to provide, validate, or document their ability and not discredit it; and (b) learning goals, in which individuals seek to increase their ability or master new tasks (Nicholls & Dweck, 1979)" (p. 5). In his meta-analysis of this research, Utman (1997) found that, as hypothesized, mastery (learning) goals led to better performance than performance goals, but noted that "the learning goal advantage may be limited to relatively complex tasks" (p. 170). As was noted in Chapter 5, when participants with performance goals "seek to maintain positive judgments of their ability . . .," it is not clear whether the participants seek to maintain the judgments made by external sources, by the self, or both. In any case, the potential for experimenter evaluation is present in the "performance goal" conditions of all of the experiments that Utman (1997) reviewed, and it is under these conditions that our research has shown that concern over the potential for external evaluation supersedes interest in self-evaluation. As a result, we would argue that the potential for experimenter evaluation is a salient aspect of the "performance goal" manipulation. Thus, it could well be concern about the evaluation of performance on complex tasks by this source that leads to poorer performance in the "performance goal" condition than that found in the "learning goal" condition in which the potential for experimenter evaluation is either not present, or is less salient.

Thus, we argue that, on complex tasks, all that is required to produce performance better than that found in the experimenter evaluation (performance goal) condition is the absence of the potential for evaluation. Of course, this is exactly what is found in the social loafing/social facilitation literatures (e.g., Jackson & Williams, 1985; Sanna, 1992). On the other hand, achievement goal theorists argue that participants in learning goal conditions outperform participants with performance goals because the former are motivated to increase their abilities and to master new tasks. As Elliott and Dweck (1988) write: "individuals who pursue learning goals are concerned with developing their ability over time and can be seen as posing the question, How can I best acquire this skill or master this task?" (p. 5).

However, social comparison theory (Festinger, 1954) would suggest that, under these circumstances, there is little, if any, opportunity for participants to feel that they have "mastered" the task. Festinger proposed that in the absence of objective, nonsocial means of evaluation, people turn to social comparison. That is, they judge the validity of their attitudes and the adequacy of their abilities by comparing themselves to similar others. Of course, there is no such opportunity in the learning goal conditions in which participants are neither provided a goal prior to their performance, nor promised a criterion afterwards (e.g., average performance of previous participants). Instead achievement goal theorists (e.g., Elliott & Dweck, 1988) argue that participants given learning goal instructions are motivated by the opportunity to compare their performance at one point to their performance at an earlier point. However, the instability of such self-judgments is one of the key pieces of evidence that led Festinger to develop social comparison theory in the first place. Knowing that one is doing better this time than the time before does not allow an accurate appraisal of one's ability. Thus, given the information available in this setting, it is difficult to see how one could conclude that the task has been mastered.

If research demonstrated that a learning goal advantage were produced when participants had the opportunity to track their performance across time, but not when there was no such opportunity, this finding would provide strong support for the achievement goal account. However, there appear to be no such findings. Instead, in his meta-analysis of this literature, Utman (1997) cites a number of studies that show that the "learning goal" advantage is produced in single-trial experiments, which provide no such opportunity (e.g., Graham & Golan, 1991; Grolnick & Ryan, 1987). In these experiments, the most that a participant can know about his/her performance is that he or she can perform the rudiments of the task. That is, the person knows that she or he can solve an anagram, keep a pinball in play, etc., but she or he will know no more. These single-trial experiments suggest that the ability to track one's performance is not needed to produce this performance advantage.

Summary

It should come as no surprise to learn that the three-model model can accommodate findings for performance on both simple and complex tasks from the social loafing, social facilitation and goal setting traditions. After all, it was research from these traditions that led to the proposal of the three-variable model in the first place. If there were a compelling case to be made against the model, it would come from the intrinsic motivation/creativity and/or achievement goal traditions. But our review of these literatures suggests that instead of generating evidence that is inconsistent with the model, the findings generated within these traditions are quite consistent with it.

The intrinsic motivation/creativity tradition argues that to be creative, participants must perform a task that requires a heuristic solution for the sheer enjoyment and pleasure of the activity itself rather than for some external goal. This approach draws heavily on McGraw's (1978) analysis of the conditions under which reward produces detrimental effects on task performance. However, our review of McGraw's analysis suggests that the case for the importance of task attractiveness has yet to be made, and that what McGraw means by the term "heuristic" is the same as what is meant by the term "complex" in the social loafing/social facilitation literatures. In addition, the proponents of this view would agree that the anticipation of external evaluation represents one way of undermining creativity (see Hennessey, Chapter 3). Thus, research from the intrinsic motivation/creativity tradition fits quite well into the complex half of the three-variable model. The potential for experimenter evaluation leads to poorer performance on complex ("creative") tasks than its absence.

The potential for external evaluation is also a salient aspect of the performance goal manipulation in the achievement goal tradition. Achievement goal theorists argue that learning goal instructions lead to better performance than performance goal instructions because the former instructions lead participants to focus on increasing their abilities and mastering new tasks. However, this tradition provides no evidence that the opportunity to track one's trajectory of improvement is necessary to produce learning goal effects. Indeed, in his meta-analysis, Utman (1997) reports "learning goal effects" in single-trial experiments in which there is no opportunity for the participants to judge their improvement. Thus, consistent with the three-variable model, the simple absence of the opportunity for external evaluation is sufficient to produce "learning goal effects" on complex tasks.

Occam or Procrustes?

We have evaluated the contention that placing the key findings from each of the five traditions in the three-variable model is essentially a Procrustean enterprise by considering three arguments that could be made by proponents of these traditions. First, it could be argued that the three-variable model disregards the "group" nature of the social loafing effect. Second, the three-variable model argues that concern over the potential for external evaluation supersedes interest in the potential for self-evaluation. Proponents of the other traditions could argue that the primacy accorded social evaluation is not warranted. Third, the three-variable model claims that tasks that produce creative performance and "learning goal" effects are essentially just complex tasks. Proponents of these traditions could claim that this view leaves out essential characteristics of these tasks. In each case, we argue that our review of the relevant literature supports the three-variable model. Of course, we have considered only three such arguments. Perhaps there are other arguments to be made that will not sustain this analysis, but for now, we would argue that the three-variable model represents the most parsimonious means of representing these findings. Thus, we are seeing the action of Occam's razor rather than Procrustes's bed.

PROCESS MODELS

Our analysis argues that the manipulation of the variables incorporated in our model is all that is required to produce findings consistent with those found in each of these traditions. But the model has nothing to say about how these variables have their effect on task performance. It just suggests a set of independent variables, which, when manipulated, will produce the outcomes predicted by the traditions. Any comprehensive account of these performance effects must fill in the black box that lies between the independent variables and the performance effects. Because each of these traditions includes a process model that could provide guidance in this regard, we will briefly review them. Given our argument that the tasks used in each of the traditions map directly on to the simple/complex task dichotomy, we will pay particular attention to how the traditions account for performance on simple and/or complex tasks.

Social Loafing

Shepperd (Chapter 1) has proposed an expectancy-value theory of social loafing that consists of three components: expectancy, instrumentality, and value. Expectancy refers to the perception that performance is contingent on effort. Instrumentality refers to the perception that one's performance will determine one's outcome. Value refers to the importance the person attaches to the outcome less any costs associated with it. Shepperd argues that in group settings where efforts are pooled, it is often the case that individual efforts are "redundant or relatively inconsequential, resulting in low expectancy" (Chapter 1, p. 5). Instrumentality "may be low because of the often tenuous relationship between individual performance and attaining the group outcome" (p. 5), and "the group outcome may not be equally valuable to all members of the group" (p 5). The multiplicative nature of the model ensures that if any of the components contribute little, the resultant effort motivation will be low.

In a typical social loafing experiment (e.g., Williams, Harkins, and Latané, 1981), participants shouted alone on some trials and were told that they were shouting along with others on other trials. The basic finding was that participants put out less effort when they were told that they were shouting with others than when they shouted individually. Shepperd argues that this is a reflection of the value component of his model. He notes that: "When people pool their efforts and individual contributions cannot be identified, the social rewards for contributing or social sanctions for failing to contribute cannot be administered" (Shepperd, Chapter 1, p. 13). "By contrast, when people perform alone or when their inputs are identifiable, they can be associated more easily with their efforts: they can be evaluated negatively should they perform poorly or fail, and positively should they perform well or succeed" (Shepperd, Chapter 1, p. 14).

In his chapter, Shepperd goes on to argue that this model can accommodate a variety of moderators of the loafing effect. However, all of this research utilizes simple tasks. Certainly performance on a complex task could have an effect on the expectancy component of Shepperd's model. That is, as participants begin working on complex tasks, they may come to believe that greater effort will not result in better performance. Instead, they may conclude that good performance is beyond their ability, or that the amount of effort devoted to performance and performance quality are unrelated. In these cases, the model would predict less effort motivation. But this reduction in effort motivation would apply equally to those participants who are subject to evaluation and those that are not, and could not account for the findings in social loafing research that when performing complex tasks participants who are subject to evaluation perform more poorly than those who are not (e.g., Jackson & Williams, 1985; Sanna, 1992).

However, performance on a complex task would also have an effect on the value component. Shepperd defines value as "the difference between the reward for achieving the outcome and the cost (psychological, physical, and material) of achieving the outcome" (Shepperd, Chapter 1, p. 3). According to Shepperd, value "ranges from -1 (the outcome is not rewarding and very costly) to +1 (the outcome is highly rewarding or important and the costs are negligible)" (Shepperd, Chapter 1, p. 3). On simple tasks, the participants have reason to believe that they will do well, and as a result, when they are subject to the experimenter's evaluation, they may anticipate a positive evaluation. In this case, the potential for evaluation would lead to greater effort and better performance than its absence. However, when working on a complex task, participants may come to believe that good performance is beyond their ability, and as a result, when they are subject to the experimenter's evaluation, they would anticipate a negative evaluation. Under these circumstances, Shepperd's model would predict less effort on the part of participants subject to experimenter evaluation than on the part of those who are not. Thus, this model would suggest that performance on complex tasks of participants subject to evaluation by the experimenter is worse than that of those who are not because the former are withdrawing effort under these circumstances.

Social Facilitation

In the 1960s and 1970s, Geen (1989) notes that the drive theory of social facilitation (Zajonc, 1965) was dominant. Drive theory suggested that the presence of others produced arousal, which functioned as a drive. The likelihood of a given response was a "multiplicative function of the habit strength for that response and drive level, as given in the Hull-Spence equation E = DxH" (Geen, 1989, p. 17). On simple tasks, the dominant response was correct, and so, the presence of others improved performance, but on complex tasks, the dominant response was incorrect, and the presence of others debilitated performance.

By the '80s, however, Geen (1989) argued that drive theory, although not totally rejected, was no longer the dominant approach in the area, and reviewed a number of other approaches, each of which could "explain certain features of the phenomenon without fully accounting for all of the aspects of the problem" (p. 43). Geen (1989) organized these theoretical approaches into three broad classes. One class of theories incorporated those approaches that continue to rely on the notion that the presence of others increases drive. Baron's (1986) distraction/conflict theory suggested that the simple presence of others may be distracting enough to trigger attentional conflict and increased drive. Cottrell's (1972) suggested that the presence of others can come to be associated with evaluation and/or competition, and the resulting evaluation apprehension leads to increased drive. Guerin and Innes's (1982) social monitoring interpretation suggested that the presence of others leads to uncertainty and increased drive when the behavior of these others cannot be monitored. For Zajonc (1980), the mere presence of others leads to a feeling of uncertainty that produces increased drive.

Geen's second class of theories included those approaches that suggest that "the presence of others creates either explicit or implicit demands on the person to behave in some specific way" (Geen, 1989, p. 31). Bond's (1982) self-presentation approach suggested that the prospect of evaluation leads to concerns about self-presentation. People try to present themselves in the best light possible. Given this motivation, the presence of coactors will lead them to work hard, and to be particularly concerned about the possibility of failure. On easy tasks, it is unlikely that they will fail, and so, the increased motivation is likely to lead to improved performance, but complex tasks are often failed. As Geen (1989) writes: "Embarrassment elicited by such failure may cause stress and cognitive interference of sufficient intensity to disrupt performance" (p. 33). Carver and Scheier (1981) suggested that the potential for evaluation makes one self-aware which leads to greater attention to how performance matches some standard. If there is a discrepancy between the standard and the current level of performance, action is initiated to bring them into alignment. On easy tasks, this action is likely to be successful. However, "if subjects estimate their chance of actually bringing behavior into line with the standard to be poor, their response will be to stop trying and to withdraw from the situation" (Geen, 1989, p. 32).

The third class of theories consists of Baron's (1986) information processing view of distraction/conflict, which proposed that the presence of others affects focus of attention and information processing. He suggests that the simple presence of others and/or their potential for evaluation may be distracting enough to create an attentional overload affecting focus of attention. That is, "the effect of audiences and coactors is mediated by a temporary condition of *stimulus overload* to which the person responds with a defensive narrowing of attention" (Geen, 1989, p. 40). Because simple tasks require attention to a relatively small number of central cues, performance on these tasks is enhanced. On the other hand, to perform well on complex tasks, one must attend to a wide range of cues, and a restricted range of attention leads to poor performance.

This list of explanations is not meant to be exhaustive. It is meant to show the range of explanations that have been offered to account for the same set of findings. In my view, what is most noteworthy about these accounts is the fact that there is not even any agreement on whether participants subject to evaluation are working hard on complex tasks, but failing nonetheless (or as a consequence), or are withdrawing effort and failing as a result.

That is, the drive approaches would suggest that participants are putting out more effort when they work with coactors, and this increased effort enhances performance on simple tasks (correct answer high in the habit hierarchy), but debilitates performance on complex tasks (correct answer low in the habit hierarchy). Bond's self-presentation approach suggests that participants are working hard in the presence of coactors but concern over the embarrassment of potential failure causes cognitive interference. Baron's focus of attention interpretation would suggest that it is not a motivational effect, but a cognitive one. They are working as hard as participants facing easy tasks. The presence of others leads to a narrowing of attention, which debilitates performance on complex tasks because these tasks require attention to a wide range of cues.

In contrast to these approaches, Carver and Scheier (1981) suggest that debilitated performance on complex tasks results from the withdrawal of effort. That is, the presence of others makes participants self-aware, which leads them to be "more cognizant of both the level of performance being manifested at the moment and the salient standard" (Geen, 1989, p. 32). When they find that they have little chance of bringing their performance into alignment with the standard, they stop trying. Thus, within the social facilitation tradition, there is not even agreement about something as basic as whether people working with coactors perform poorly on complex tasks because they are working hard, hardly working, or if the effect is cognitive rather than motivational.

We have argued that social facilitation and social loafing are complementary phenomena, representing opposite sides of the same coin. However, adding Shepperd's analysis of social loafing to the accounts offered for social facilitation effects simply adds another account that suggests that the poorer performance on complex tasks of those subject to evaluation is the result of the withdrawal of effort. Of course, there is no compelling evidence that this is what is actually happening.

Sanna (1992) has proposed a unified model of social loafing and social facilitation that draws on Bandura's (1986) self-efficacy theory. Sanna argues that "self-efficacy expectancies develop spontaneously while participants work on easy or difficult tasks" (p. 780). Sanna suggests that a positive expectancy develops during the course of performance on a simple task, whereas a negative expectancy is produced by performance on a complex one. Of course, the expectancy that one can perform a task well does not mean that one could expect favorable outcomes from this performance. Sanna notes that one must also take into account outcome expectancy. As Sanna (1992) writes: "What type of social recognition can a participants expect from the experimenter when he or she cannot be individually identified and evaluated? Likely, not much" (p. 776). Thus, Sanna (1992) predicts that participants who work on a simple task develop high-efficacy expectations, and if they have high outcome expectancy (experimenter evaluation), they will expect positive evaluation from the experimenter, resulting in improved performance compared to participants with low outcome expectancies (no experimenter evaluation). On the other hand, participants who perform a difficult task develop low-efficacy expectancies, and if they have high outcome expectancies (experimenter evaluation), they will anticipate negative evaluation from the experimenter, resulting in impaired performance compared to participants with low outcome expectancies (no experimenter evaluation).

What is not clear from this account is how the expectation of negative evaluation from the experimenter produces the impaired performance. That is, one could imagine that when a person comes to believe that she or he is performing poorly and must soon face the evaluation of the experimenter, if anything, the person would work harder. On the other hand, one could simply withdraw effort and give up. And so, we see once again that this account does not clarify what happens during the performance of complex tasks.

Recently, Blascovich has applied his biopsychosocial model of challenge and threat to the phenomenon of social facilitation (Blascovich, Mendes, Salomon, & Hunter, 1999). "The biopsychosocial model (Blascovich & Mendes, 2000; Blascovich & Tomaka, 1996) describes challenge and threat motivational states, marked by distinctive cardiovascular response patterns, as resulting from the interplay of learned and unlearned affective and cognitive mechanisms" (p. 75). "Challenge occurs when the individual experiences sufficient resources to meet situational demands in a goal-relevant performance situation. Threat occurs when the individual experiences insufficient resources to meet such situational demands" (p. 75).

In applying this model to the social facilitation literature, Blascovich argues that the presence of others increases the goal relevance of performance situations, which, in turn, increases the likelihood of challenge and threat responses. When performing well-learned tasks, participants "should experience greater challenge and exhibit the characteristic cardiovascular response pattern that accompanies challenge because of the resources (i.e., task mastery) they bring to the performance situation" (p. 70). When performing tasks that are not well-learned, participants should experience threat with its characteristic cardiovascular response pattern, because they lack the resources necessary for the task. Consistent with these predictions, Blascovich et al. (1999) found the pattern of cardiovascular reactivity associated with challenge when participants performed well-learned tasks in the presence of others, whereas the presence of others was associated with the pattern of cardiovascular reactivity associated with threat when participants worked on tasks that were not well-learned. On the other hand, "participants performing the task alone, regardless of whether it was learned or unlearned, demonstrated no appreciable reactivity from baseline" (p. 74).

This work advances our understanding of social facilitation by identifying precise physiological patterns of cardiovascular reactivity that are associated with the facilitation and debilitation of performance. However, Blascovich and his colleagues "do not yet claim that the cardiovascular patterns associated with socially facilitated enhancement and impairment effects identified in the present research necessarily mediate social facilitation effects" (p. 75). So, this work does not tell us whether the physiological reactions are causes, concomitants, or the results of the performance effects. In addition, because the timing period for the cardiac measures was limited to the first minute of the testing period, we know only that the participants performing the unlearned task in front of the audience were displaying the cardiac pattern associated with threat at that time. We do not know whether these participants continued to exhibit this patterning as the timing period continued, nor do we know whether these participants continue their striving in an effort to perform the task successfully or if they withdrew their effort. Thus, we are left with exactly the same question that is left unresolved in the other accounts of social facilitation effects.

Goal Setting

According to Tubbs (Chapter 2), the models of motivation employed in the goal setting literature "reflect the influence of theoretical perspectives from the psychological literature on behavioral intentions, expectancy-valence judgments, and cybernetic control systems" (p. 38). So, for example, the expectancy-valence framework focuses on influences on the expectancy (i.e., likelihood) of attaining the goal and the valence (i.e., value or importance) of successful of goal attainment. Thus, "from an expectancy-valence theory perspective, the most immediate influence of an assigned goal should be on one's judgments of the valence and expectancy attached to the task itself and to the performance of levels above and below the assigned goal" (Tubbs, Chapter 2, p. 39). This analysis is, of course, compatible with the one provided by Shepperd (Chapter 1).

At a more molecular level, Tubbs notes that Locke and Latham (1990a) specify four mechanisms through which they hypothesize that goals affect performance. "The first three, directing attention, mobilizing effort, and encouraging persistence, are motivational in nature and can be seen as related to the three facets of behavior: direction, intensity, and duration" (Tubbs, Chapter 2, p. 39). The fourth, more cognitive mechanism, "comes into play in the case of complex tasks where available knowledge may not suffice to allow successful performance. Locke and Latham (1990) believe that goals encourage the development of more appropriate task performance strategies in that context" (Tubbs, Chapter 2, p. 39).

Tubb's (Chapter 2) review makes it quite clear that when simple tasks are used, goal setting is a very powerful motivational tool. However, as noted previously, the findings are less clear for complex tasks. In fact, Tubbs (Chapter 2) writes that: "Arguably the most important trend in the current literature has been the investigation of possible explanations for the relatively weak (and sometimes detrimental) effects of assigned goals on complex tasks" (p. 40). He cites DeShon, Brown, and Greenis (1996) as having suggested three explanations for the complex task findings: (1) The pressure to meet goals leads to dysfunctional strategy choices; (2) The presence of a specific performance goal results in poor performance because attentional resources are expended on self-regulation activities like performance monitoring instead of on skill acquisition; and (3) Goals on complex tasks may be improperly framed. He then goes on to suggest that the findings do not clearly support any one of these explanations, and calls for more research. Thus, at present, it does not appear that the goal setting literature provides a compelling explanation for the effect of goal setting on complex tasks.

Intrinsic Motivation/Creativity

Hennessey, (Chapter 3) suggests several possible mechanisms to account for the deleterious effect that anticipated evaluation has on creativity. For example, she notes that Simon (1967) argues "that the more intense the motivation to achieve a goal, the less attention will be paid to environmental aspects that are seemingly irrelevant to achieving that goal" (Hennessey, Chapter 3, p. 66). Thus, when one anticipates evaluation, the resulting motivation will make it less likely that one will test alternative pathways, and direct attention toward more seemingly incidental aspects of the task and the environment. But this is exactly what needs to be done to be creative. This explanation seems to suggest that the potential for external evaluation increases task motivation, and this motivation restricts the focus of attention, which undermines creativity.

A second explanation offered by Hennessey comes from the early work on intrinsic motivation. In this work, researchers (e.g., Lepper, Greene, & Nisbett, 1973) proposed that "when a behavior is overjustified (when there exists both a possible internal and an external cause for one's own or another's behavior), each of us will tend to overlook the internal cause (the presence of intrinsic task motivation) in favor of the external cause (an evaluation was at stake)" (Hennessey, Chapter 3, p. 65). As a result, participants may "feel less positively toward the task and less inclined to devote their energy and attention to it" (p. 67). However, Hennessey goes on to note that this explanation cannot account for the effect that anticipated evaluation has on children who have consistently been shown "to lack the cognitive capabilities necessary for weighing multiple sufficient causes and employing discounting" (Hennessey, Chapter 3, p. 67). She notes that: "One viable alternative to the discounting explanation is that the reduction of intrinsic interest in young children (and perhaps all of us) is driven primarily by the learned expectation that evaluations are usually paired with activities that need to be done -- activities that are often not fun and sometimes even aversive" (p. 67). According to Hennessey, the resulting negative affect may lead to decrements in intrinsic interest.

Whether it is an overjustification effect or the effect of negative affect, these explanations seem to suggest that the potential for evaluation leads participants to withdraw effort, and it is this reduction of effort that undermines creativity. On the other hand, the first explanation suggests that the potential for evaluation leads to increased motivation, which narrows the focus of attention, thereby undermining creative performance. We have argued that the tasks used in creativity research correspond to what we term complex tasks. Performance on these tasks could be damaged either because participants who can be evaluated are more motivated or less motivated than participants who are not subject to evaluation. But it cannot be both.

In her review, Hennessey also describes findings for what she terms algorithmic tasks, tasks in which the path to the solution is clear and straightforward. So, for example, in these types of tasks the dependent variables are the number of responses made or the number of different categories of responses. These tasks would seem to correspond to what we have termed simple tasks, and, consistent with research using simple tasks, the potential for evaluation improved performance. The focus of attention explanation could account for this finding because the narrowed focus of attention that results from the potential for evaluation could aid in the performance of a task that requires attention only to central cues. However, it is difficult to see how explanations that suggest that the potential for evaluation leads participants to withdraw effort could account for the performance findings on algorithmic tasks.

Achievement Goal Theory

According to Harackiewicz, Barron, and Elliot (1998), "an emerging consensus suggests a fundamental distinction between two types of achievement goals (Ames & Archer, 1988; Pintrich & Schunk, 1996). *Performance goals* highlight normatively based standards and promote the demonstration of ability relative to others, whereas *mastery goals* are self-referential, focusing on the development of skill and competence relative to the task and one's own past performance" (p. 2). A focus on mastery goals should lead participants to seek "to develop and improve their competence." "As a result, these individuals should seek out challenge and persist at tasks even in the face of difficulty" (Harackiewicz et al., 1998, p. 2). "In contrast, when pursuing performance goals, individuals focus on how their performance compares to others and are concerned with demonstrating their ability" (Harackiewicz et al., 1998, p. 2). Given this orientation, even if participants view themselves as competent at performing a given task, they are likely to "to sacrifice learning opportunities to look good in front of others (Elliott & Dweck, 1988). Furthermore, when pursuing performance goals, individuals who encounter performance difficulties are likely to interpret negative outcomes as a reflection of their level of ability, and rather than risk continued failure, they are likely to withdraw effort or give up" (Harackiewicz, et al., 1998, p. 2).

In his meta-analysis of performance effects in the achievement goal literature, Utman (1997) found a performance advantage for mastery goals when the tasks were complex. On complex tasks, participants with performance goals are likely to encounter performance difficulties, which would lead them to withdraw effort. According to this view, participants with mastery goals would persist at these tasks even in the face of difficulty. Thus, this approach would suggest that the performance advantage enjoyed by participants given mastery goals stems from the fact that they persist in the face of difficulty encountered on complex tasks whereas participants given performance goals withdraw effort.

However, Harackiewicz and her colleagues argue that strong conclusions about the negative effects of performance goals may be premature. In Chapter 4 of the current volume, Tauer and Harackiewicz examine the effects of competition on intrinsic motivation, testing predictions following from a version of Harackiewicz and Sansone's (1991) process model of intrinsic motivation adapted to characterize the processes involved in competition. This model argues that it is important to take into account people's goals as they approach activities and identifies evaluative contingencies (e.g., competition) and personality variables (e.g., achievement orientation) that may affect these goals. "In addition, the model predicts that individual differences (e.g., achievement motivation) may moderate the effects of the evaluative situation" (Tauer & Harackiewicz, Chapter 4, p. 80). That is, people differing in achievement motivation may adopt different goals in the same situation. So, for example, because participants who are high in achievement motivation (HAMs) seek challenge, desire to attain competence, and wish to outperform others, they should respond positively to competition. On the other hand, participants low in achievement motivation (LAMs) find situations that involve evaluation aversive and avoid them.

The model also identifies three motivational processes that can be engaged during task performance: competence valuation, an individual's emotional commitment to attaining competence on the task; task involvement, an individual's absorption in the task; and perceived competence, an individual's sense of competence during task performance. "Intrinsic motivation can be enhanced to the extent that individuals care about doing well, become involved in a task, and develop a sense of competence while performing an activity" (Tauer & Harackiewicz, Chapter 4, p. 81). Finally, the model incorporates the feedback that participants eventually receive in the evaluative situation.

In their chapter, Tauer and Harackiewicz report support for this process model in their examination of the effects of competition on intrinsic motivation. They note that: "HAMs and LAMs approached competition differently, and this affected their perceptions of challenge and values going into the task, as well as their affect at task conclusion" (Chapter 4, p. 87). Thus, there was no overall effect of competition. Instead, HAMs enjoyed the activity more than LAMs when participants were instructed to compete, whereas LAMs enjoyed the task more than HAMs when there was no competition. And this relationship was not dependent on the availability or the valence of feedback.

Tauer and Harackiewicz (Chapter 4) go on to review a series of studies in which Harackiewicz and her colleagues have examined the effects of mastery and performance goals on intrinsic motivation. In these experiments, participants given performance goals are told that their performances will be compared to those of others, whereas participants in the mastery goal conditions are simply asked to improve their skills. These studies show that achievement motivation mediates the effect of goal type "such that HAMs enjoyed an activity more than LAMs when assigned a performance goal, whereas LAMs enjoyed the activity more than HAMs when assigned a mastery goal" (Tauer & Harackiewicz, Chapter 4, p. 92). Based on these studies, Tauer and Harackiewicz argue that, contrary to conventional wisdom that would claim that evaluation, competition, and performance goals undermine intrinsic motivation, "evaluative contingencies need not undermine intrinsic interest in an activity for everyone" (Tauer & Harackiewicz, Chapter 4, p. 94).

But this analysis focuses on the effects of performance goals on *task interest*. What about their effects on *task performance*? Although processes involved in task performance are included in Harackiewicz and Sansone's (1991) model (e.g., competence valuation, perceived challenge), in most of their research, task performance is treated only as a way station on the road to their destination, an examination of factors that influence intrinsic motivation. Given this goal, it makes sense to control or manipulate various aspects of the participants' experience during task performance. Unfortunately, these manipulations mask the effects of the independent variables on the dependent variable of interest for our present purposes, task performance.

For example, in some of Harackiewicz and her colleagues' research, participants' pinball performance is controlled to ensure that all participants perform at similar levels (e.g., Elliot & Harackiewicz, 1994; Harackiewicz & Elliot, 1993; Harackiewicz & Elliot, 1998). Other means of controlling the participants' performance have also been used. In Tauer and Harackiewicz's (1999) Experiment 1, an effort was made to convince participants that their performances were improving or deteriorating by giving them either a difficult problem followed by a simple one (improving) or a simple problem followed by a difficult one (deteriorating), respectively. It is quite likely that the participants' performance on the second puzzle was affected by their experience on the first one, which was the point of the manipulation. Because the investigators report only total puzzle performance, we cannot even see the effects of the independent variables on task performance in the first trial. Efforts to control and/or manipulate the participants' experience of task performance have been made in other experiments in this line of research (e.g., Epstein & Harackiewicz, 1992; Tauer & Harackiewicz, 1999, Experiment 2). As a result, we do not know what effects these independent variables would have on task performance.

However, Tauer and Harackiewicz (Chapter 4) do cite recent research by Barron and Harackiewicz (2001) in which participants performed a multiplication task without any intervention. Barron and Harackiewicz (2001) note that in previous experimental research in the achievement goal literature, participants have been assigned either mastery or performance goals, but not both. In this research, they tested the hypothesis that motivation for everyone might be optimized in a multiple goal condition in which both performance and mastery goals were assigned.

When Barron and Harackiewicz manipulated whether participants were assigned mastery goals, performance goals, or both (Experiment 2), they replicated the usual pattern of findings for mastery goals and performance goals. Thus, LAMs exhibited more *task interest* when assigned mastery goals than when assigned performance goals, whereas HAMs showed the opposite pattern. In their test of the multiple-goal hypothesis, Barron and Harackiewicz found that HAMs and LAMs both exhibited an intermediate amount of task interest when provided with both goals. However, Barron and Harackiewicz (2001) found no differences in *task performance* as a function of goal type or achievement motivation. The failure to find a performance difference between participants given only a performance goal and participants given only a mastery goal does not replicate the typical finding of a mastery goal advantage reported in the achievement goal literature (e.g., Utman, 1997). Perhaps Barron and Harackiewicz's manipulation of achievement goals was not potent enough to produce this effect, or perhaps the "difficult" math problems were not as difficult as the tasks typically used in the achievement goal literature.

Whatever the explanation may be, to test the multiple goal hypothesis for *task performance*, one first must replicate the typical mastery goal advantage when single achievement goals are assigned. Given an effective manipulation of single achievement goals, we would predict that if participants were given both types of goals, concern over evaluation would overwhelm interest in "mastery" goals, and performance would drop to the level found in the condition in which participants were assigned performance goals alone. This test must await additional research, but it is not clear that Harackiewicz and her colleagues would expect their findings for task interest to translate directly into performance differences anyhow. In Chapter 4, Tauer and Harackiewicz do not suggest that there is a direct relationship between task performance and intrinsic motivation. They suggest that intrinsic motivation "should help people develop long-lasting interest in an activity. In turn, developing intrinsic motivation may promote increased performance over an extended period of time" (Tauer & Harackiewicz, Chapter 4, p. 78). Consistent with this position, Harackiewicz, Barron, and Elliot (1998) write: "Moreover, given that interest and performance both develop throughout the course of an educational process, it is possible that they can affect one another. Particularly intriguing is the possibility that intrinsic interest can influence learning and performance" (p. 4).

In any event, in the research in the achievement goal literature that has focused on *task performance* as opposed to *task interest*, participants given performance goals (for whom evaluation is salient) perform more poorly than participants given mastery goals (for whom we would argue evaluation is not salient). And, according to Harackiewicz, Barron, and Elliot (1998), the achievement goal literature would suggest that the poor performance results from the withdrawal of effort of participants focused on performance goals.

Summary

Taken together, the explanations provided by these traditions suggest that, after more than 100 years of research on the effects of evaluation on performance, there is no agreement about what process(es) mediate(s) these effects. Perhaps the most striking example of this state of affairs is the fact that there is not even agreement about whether the potential for evaluation on complex tasks results in poor performance because these participants are putting out *more* or *less* effort than participants for whom evaluation is less salient. Shepperd's expectancy-value model of social loafing (Chapter 1) and the achievement goal literature (Tauer & Harackiewicz, Chapter 4) would suggest that performance on complex tasks is worse when evaluation is salient because effort is withdrawn. In the social facilitation literature, it has been suggested that the potential for evaluation leads to greater effort (e.g., the drive explanations) and to less effort (e.g., Carver & Scheier), resulting in debilitated performance on complex tasks. It has also been suggested that it is a cognitive effect, stemming from the fact that the potential for evaluation creates an attentional overload (e.g., Baron, 1986). Sanna (1992) argues that social facilitation and social loafing effects can be explained by taking into account feelings of self-efficacy and outcome expectancies, but, in fact, this approach does not make clear whether it is that participants subject to experimenter evaluation are working hard or hardly working on complex tasks. Hennessey's (Chapter 3) explanations for the effects of evaluation on creativity are subject to the same criticism. That is, one of her explanations (focus of attention) suggests that the potential for evaluation undermines creative performance because it increases motivation, whereas the other two explanations (overjustification effect or the effect of negative affect) suggest the potential for evaluation leads participants to withdraw effort. Finally, Tubbs (Chapter 2) suggests that no definitive explanation has been offered for the effects of goal setting on complex tasks.

THE BLACK BOX

I would argue that state of affairs exists, at least in part, because we have focused our efforts at the molar rather than the molecular level of analysis.

That is, we are much more likely to be interested in and rewarded for theory construction than for the molecular analysis that is required to learn exactly how performance unfolds on a given task. Of course, one might think that such an analysis would be an integral part of theory development, but such has not been the case. I believe that a lack of attention to this level of analysis characterizes all of the traditions included in this volume, which this prevented us from making as much progress as we should have. For the purpose of demonstrating this shortcoming, I will use my own work using the Remote Associates Test.

Performance on the RAT

In the experiment in my first chapter (Chapter 5), we replicated the typical findings of the various traditions using the Remote Associates Test. So, for example, we replicated the typical findings of social loafing and social facilitation research: Participants given do-your-best instructions who were subject to external evaluation solved more simple items, but fewer complex ones, than participants who were not subject to external evaluation. Based on 20 years of social loafing research, we would certainly expect that participants subject to evaluation solved more simple RAT items than those who were not because the former worked harder than the latter. However, there is ambiguity about this effort explanation even on these simple items. For example, even if it is an effort effect, the locus of the effect could be at the level of the booklet or at the level of the item.

That is, participants who were not subject to the evaluation of the experimenter could have performed more poorly on the simple items simply because they looked at fewer of the 20 triads than the more highly motivated participants subject to experimenter evaluation. Certainly if they never looked at the triads, they could not solve them. On the other hand, it is also possible that the explanation for the performance difference lies at the level of the item. This interpretation would suggest that participants who were and were not subject to evaluation by the experimenter spent the same amount of time working on the task, and looked at each of the items. However, participants subject to experimenter evaluation put more effort into solving each triad than participants who were not.

Thus, even when it comes to the simple triads, we are unsure as to the source of the performance effects. This provides just one example of why a more molecular analysis of task performance is required to have any chance of understanding what is going on inside the black box. As a first step in this effort, we conducted a pilot study using the RAT task reported in Chapter 5. Participants were given the same 20 triads, pre-tested to be relatively simple or difficult. All participants were given do-your-best instructions and were led to believe either that their performances would be subject to evaluation by the experimenter or would not. However, this version of the experiment was presented on a computer so that the participants could move among the pages of the "booklet" by clicking on "next item" or "previous item." The participants responded to each triad by typing their answer in a box on the screen on that triad's page. In this version of the task, they were given an additional two minutes (for a total of 12 minutes). They were told that they could spend their 12 minutes in whatever way they wanted, moving back and forth among the triad pages, changing their answers if they wished. They were also told that the task would be stopped after time expired, or that they could stop earlier if they wished by clicking on "end experiment" on the computer screen. Unbeknownst to the participants, the computer kept track not only of all of their responses, but also all of their movements among the triads along with the times of these movements. This record allowed us to evaluate the "booklet" versus "item" account for the findings on the simple task in our RAT experiment. However, we would argue that this analysis also provides some insight into the source(s) of performance differences on complex tasks, thereby demonstrating the potential value of a molecular analysis of task performance.

Pilot Experiment

We have run 36 participants in the 2 (experimenter evaluation vs. no experimenter evaluation) x 2 (simple vs. complex) design with the measure described above. At the molar level of analysis, we replicated the pattern of findings for participants given do-your-best instructions that was reported in Chapter 5. Participants subject to evaluation by the experimenter solved more simple triads (M = 15.33) than participants who were not (M = 11.33), F (1, 32) = 9.51, $p < .01$. But when faced with complex triads, participants who were not subject to experimenter evaluation solved more items (M = 5.56) than participants who anticipated evaluation by the experimenter (M = 2.33), F (1, 32) = 6.17, $p < .02$.

The Booklet versus Item Explanation

As a first step in our molecular analysis, we evaluated the "booklet" versus "item" explanations for the simple RAT items. An analysis of the total time spent on the task revealed no reliable difference between those participants who were subject to evaluation and those who were not, $p > .40$ (Overall M = 680.7 of the total possible 720 seconds). Of course, the participants could spend the same amount of total time looking at items, but the "booklet" hypothesis would suggest that participants who are not subject to experimenter evaluation could be spending this time looking at fewer items. In fact, however, each of the participants who were not subject to evaluation by the experimenter looked at each of the 20 triads, as did each of the participants who were subject to this evaluation.

We then compared the amount of time participants who were and were not subject to evaluation spent looking at the triads within each fourth of the task. Each participant saw the twenty triads in the same order, and so we divided the twenty items into four sets of five, and averaged the amount of time participants spent looking at the items within each of these fourths. These data were analyzed in a 2 (experimenter evaluation vs. no experimenter evaluation) x 2 (simple triads vs. complex triads) x 4 (average time spent looking at the five items in each of the four sets) ANOVA. This analysis revealed that experimenter evaluation and no experimenter evaluation participants did not differ in the amount of time they spent on the triads in each fourth of the task, $p > .50$. These findings suggest that the performance difference on these simple items cannot be explained by the fact that no experimenter evaluation participants failed to look at some subset of the items. Instead, the explanation seems to lie at the level of the individual triad, and so, we moved to an examination of performance at this level.

Findings for the Simple Items

As noted above, participants subject to evaluation by the experimenter solved more of the simple items ($M = 15.33$) than participants who were not ($M = 11.33$), $p < .01$. However, these participants did not differ in the amount of time that they took to provide answers for the triads that they did successfully solve. Participants who were not subject to experimenter evaluation, on average, took 17.0 seconds/triad whereas participants who were subject to this evaluation took 20.2 seconds/triad, $p > .60$. So, when no experimenter evaluation participants solved a triad, they did so as quickly as participants subject to experimenter evaluation.

Next, we looked at the two types of errors participants could make on this task. Participants could simply leave an item blank, or they could provide an answer, but one that was incorrect. The potential for experimenter evaluation made no difference in the first type of error. Participants who were subject to the potential for experimenter evaluation left as many items blank ($M = 2.33$) as those who were not ($M = 2.33$). In addition, participants who were not subject to experimenter evaluation spent as much total time looking at triads for which they did not provide an answer ($M = 96.5$ seconds/triad) as participants who were subject to evaluation by the experimenter ($M = 89.5$ seconds/triad), $p > .60$.

However, the participants did differ in the number of answers that they produced that were incorrect. Participants who were subject to experimenter evaluation produced fewer incorrect answers (*M* = 2.33) than participants who were not subject to this evaluation (*M* = 6.33), F (1, 32) = 4.34, $p < .05$. Not only did participants subject to experimenter evaluation produce fewer incorrect answers, but they also waited substantially longer before producing them (*M* = 60.0 seconds/incorrect answer) than participants who were not subject to the experimenter's evaluation (*M* = 36.1 seconds/incorrect answer), F (1, 30) = 9.95, $p < .01$.

Of course, one could argue that from the participants' points-of-view, these responses were not errors at all. The "incorrect" answers were responses that tended to be related to one or two of the three clue words, but not to all three. For example, in response to the triad "Family Apple House," a participant responded "Green." In this case, "Green" could be associated with "Apple" and "House," but not with "Family." Nonetheless, the participant may have assumed that this answer was correct, even though she or he did not know the nature of the relationship between "Green" and "Family." Likewise, the response "Rich" goes with two members of a triad, "Chocolate" and "Fortune," but not with "Tin."

We tested the hypothesis that participants viewed these "incorrect" answers as correct by examining their estimates for the number of RAT items they solved correctly. If they considered these "incorrect" answers to be correct, they should have included them in their estimates of the number of RAT items that they correctly solved. However, they did not. There was no reliable difference between the number of triads correctly solved and the participants' estimates of the number of items they solved, $p > .50$. In addition, the absolute difference between the number of items that participants actually solved correctly and their estimate of the number of items that they correctly solved was reliably smaller (*M* = 2.61) than the absolute difference between the number of items correctly solved plus the "incorrect" answers and their estimates of items correctly solved (*M* = 5.28), F (1, 32) = 6.23, $p < .02$. Thus, participants did not include these "incorrect" answers in the number of triads that they estimated that they correctly solved. This finding is also consistent with the fact that participants subject to experimenter evaluation took longer to supply these incorrect answers. They knew that the answer was incorrect, but they simply could not think of the correct answer.

These findings suggest that participants who were not subject to experimenter evaluation performed more poorly than those who were because they simply did not make the requisite effort on a subset of the simple items. Instead of trying to come up with an answer that related to all three of the clue words, they were satisfied to enter an answer that was related to one or two of the words in the triad. When they did put in the requisite effort, they solved the triads as quickly as participants subject to experimenter evaluation. Of course, this behavior could be enacted in a number of ways. For example, participants who were not subject to experimenter evaluation could start out working as hard as participants subject to this evaluation, and then begin loafing. However, Figure 1, which plots the number of triads solved in two-minute bins across the twelve-minutes of the task shows that this was not the case. All of the action was at the beginning of the task. Participants who were not subject to evaluation by the experimenter began loafing within the first two minutes of the task. Participants subject to experimenter evaluation solved 5.56 triads in the first two minutes, whereas those who were not subject to this evaluation solved only 3.67, F (1, 160) = 7.76, $p < .05$. In the second two minutes, experimenter evaluation participants solved 4.11 triads, whereas those who were not solved only 2.67, F (1, 160) = 4.51, $p < .05$. There were no reliable differences in the number of triads solved after the first four minutes, *ps* > .20. The linear trends suggested by the shapes of these functions were highly reliable for both experimenter evaluation, linear F (1, 160) = 38.56, $p < .0001$ and no experimenter evaluation participants, linear F (1, 160) = 27.17, $p < .0001$. And in each case, the deviations from linearity were not reliable, *ps* > .50.

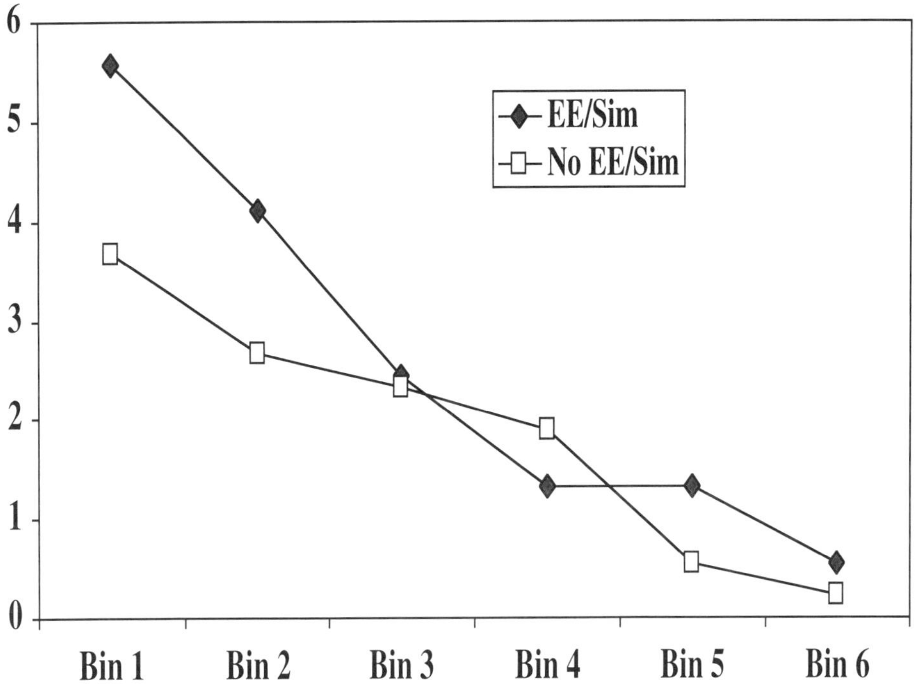

Figure 1. Simple RAT Items Solved Correctly in Two-Minute Bins Across the Twelve-Minute Task

Findings for the Complex Items

The findings for simple items are consistent with our previous research on social loafing (e.g., Latané, Williams, & Harkins, 1979) in suggesting that participants who are not subject to experimenter evaluation put out less effort than those who are. Our findings also suggest that this same low level of effort characterized the performance of no experimenter evaluation participants faced with complex triads. Of course, the difficulty of the complex triads led to poorer performance by no experimenter evaluation participants faced with these items than by no experimenter evaluation participants working on simple items (57% versus 28%), but in every other way the performances of these participants were similar. For example, no experimenter evaluation participants reached solutions for the complex items that they did solve as quickly (M = 20.99 seconds) as their simple triad counterparts (M = 17.01 seconds), $p > .50$. They supplied no more incorrect answers for complex triads (M = 8.11) than their simple triad counterparts (M = 6.33), $p > .35$, and they took the same amount of time to provide these responses (M = 34.8 seconds) as their simple triad counterparts (M = 36.1 seconds), $p > .80$. In Figure 2, the mean number of complex triads correctly solved by the no experimenter evaluation (and experimenter evaluation participants) in each two minutes of the twelve-minute task has been added to the plot for simple triads. As can be seen in Figure 2, the performance of no

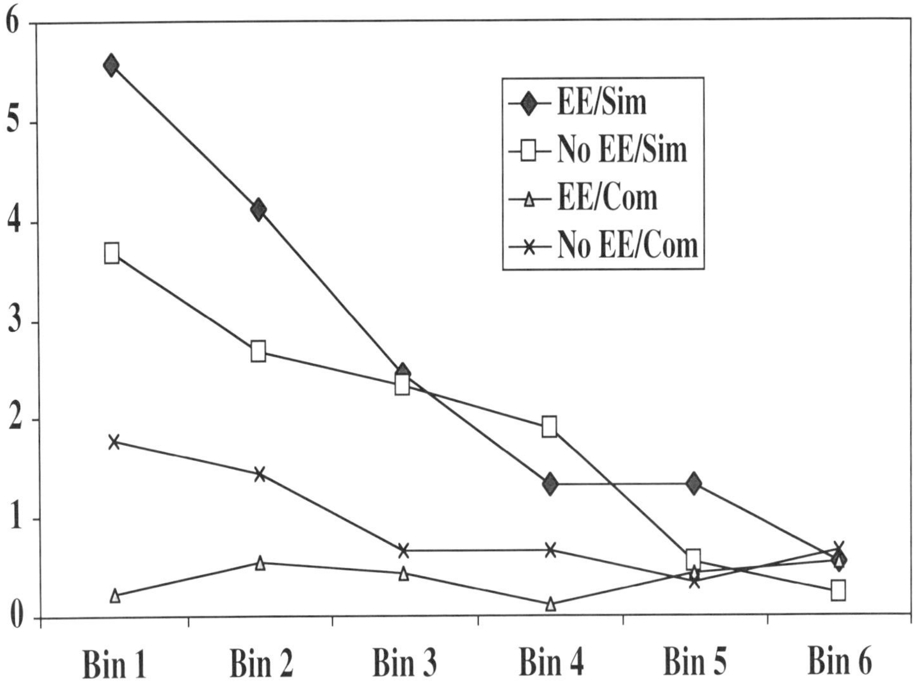

Figure 2. Simple and Complex RAT Items Solved Correctly in Two-Minute Bins Across the Twelve-Minute Task

experimenter evaluation participants faced with complex triads has the same general form as the performance of no experimenter evaluation participants who worked on simple items, but is simply shifted downwards reflecting the greater difficulty of the triads. And, as was the case for simple triads, the function is well fit by a linear function, linear F (1, 160) = 9.43, $p < .01$, and the deviations from linearity are not reliable, $p > .50$.

In contrast, when faced with complex triads, the performance of experimenter evaluation participants fell completely apart. Although participants subject to evaluation by the experimenter solved 77% of the simple triads, experimenter evaluation participants who worked on complex triads solved only 12%. Experimenter evaluation participants facing complex triads took longer to reach solutions on the items that they did solve (M = 38.00 seconds/triad solved) than their simple triad counterparts (M = 20.2 seconds/triad solved), F (1, 32) = 7.36, $p < .05$. In addition, on complex triads, experimenter evaluation participants produced more incorrect responses (M = 8.33) than their simple triad counterparts (M = 2.33), F (1, 32) = 9.76, $p < .05$, and produced these incorrect answers more quickly (M = 36.59 seconds) than their counterparts faced with simple triads (M = 60.0 seconds/incorrect response), F (1, 30) = 9.56, $p < .05$.

Figure 2 shows the profound effect that the potential for evaluation by the experimenter had on the performance of these participants. When experimenter evaluation participants were faced with simple triads, they achieved their best performance in the first two minutes of the task, but when faced with complex triads the performance of experimenter evaluation participants was no better in the first two minutes than in any other two-minute block of time, $ps > .50$. As a result, the linear trend for RAT items solved by experimenter evaluation participants faced with complex triads is not reliable, $p > .60$, nor are any of the other trend components, $ps > .50$.

This reaction to the potential for experimenter evaluation led to better performance by participants who were not subject to experimenter evaluation (M = 5.66) than by participants who were subject to this evaluation (M = 2.33), F (1, 32) = 6.17, $p < .02$. As was the case for simple triads, the action is seen at the beginning of the timing period. Thus, the performance of no experimenter evaluation participants was at its best in the first two minutes of the task and fell off from there through the rest of the twelve-minute task. In fact, it was only in the first two minutes that participants who could not be evaluated by the experimenter solved more of the complex triads (M = 1.78) than experimenter evaluation participants (M = .22), F (1, 160) = 5.28, $p < .05$. Thereafter, the performance of experimenter evaluation and no experimenter evaluation participants did not differ, $ps > .20$.

More Effort or Less Effort on Complex Items?

It is important to note that the procedures leading up to the performance of the simple and complex versions of the RAT task were identical. In each case, participants were presented with the same two sample items on the computer to show them how the procedure worked, after which they began the task. Thus, we have every reason to believe that experimenter evaluation participants working on complex triads began the task putting out the same high level of effort that characterized the behavior of experimenter evaluation participants working on simple triads. They then immediately ran into trouble. As noted previously, the performance of participants subject to experimenter evaluation was worse than that of no experimenter evaluation participants by the end of the first two minutes of the task. In fact, however, this dramatic effect can be seen within the first four moves that the participants made. No experimenter evaluation participants solved more triads within their first four moves (M = 1.00) than participants subject to experimenter evaluation (M = .11), F (1, 16) = 5.75, $p < .05$. And this effect was produced despite the fact that participants subject to experimenter evaluation took more total time to make these first four moves (M = 108.11 seconds) than no experimenter evaluation participants (M = 63.44 seconds), F (1, 16) = 6.33, $p < .03$. In addition, within their first four moves participants subject to experimenter evaluation had already produced more incorrect answers (M = 1.67) than no experimenter evaluation participants (M = .78), F (1, 16) = 4.61, $p < .05$.

In general, accounts that argue that participants withdraw effort suggest that participants work on the task long enough to decide that they are not doing well, and then withdraw their effort. It is this withdrawal of effort that accounts for their debilitated performance. This pattern of behavior does not describe what we find on the RAT task. On simple triads, each of the participants subject to experimenter evaluation solved a problem in their first two moves. Taken together, these participants solved 24 items correctly in their first 36 moves (4 moves for each of nine participants), while producing only four incorrect answers. In contrast, when faced with complex triads, participants subject to experimenter evaluation produced only one correct response in their first 36 moves, while providing 15 incorrect answers. After four moves, the participants had seen at most one-fifth of the triads. As a result, they had no reason to give up yet. Thus, it was not that participants started out working hard and then ended up hardly working. Rather it appears that it was the motivational state in which participants subject to experimenter evaluation began the complex task that was the culprit, and this state characterized their behavior throughout the twelve-minute task.

CONCLUSIONS

This volume represents a first effort to integrate (or at least, juxtapose) five research traditions in which it has been shown that the potential for evaluation affects task performance. As my contribution to this effort, I presented a model consisting of only three variables that I argued could encompass the basic findings from these traditions (see Chapter 5). In fact, I intended to use this three-variable model only as a starting point, assuming that the model would not prove equal to the task. However, after having considered these research traditions more thoroughly, I have come to the conclusion that this simple, three-variable model remains viable.

Certainly this model leaves only bare bones, cutting away much of the theoretical meat of the various traditions. However, I would argue that nothing essential is lost as a result of this surgery. For example, the model assumes that the basic social loafing effect (e.g., Latané, Williams, & Harkins, 1979; Harkins, Williams, & Latané; Williams, Harkins, & Latané, 1981) is nothing more than an evaluation effect. This claim is supported by Karau and Williams's (1993) meta-analysis and by the results of manipulation checks that we have incorporated in our work (e.g., Harkins & Szymanski, 1989; Szymanski & Harkins, 1987). The model also suggests that the potential for external evaluation is sufficient to produce the basic effects of each tradition. The research that we have conducted so far supports this claim, and there are no findings from these traditions that are inconsistent with this view.

The model suggests that the tasks used in the intrinsic motivation/creativity and achievement goals literatures can be subsumed by the simple/complex distinction used in the social facilitation literature. Researchers in the intrinsic motivation/creativity literature could argue that this simple/complex classification does not capture the difference between algorithmic and heuristic tasks, and, thus, misses an essential feature of creative performance. However, McGraw (1978), who is cited by intrinsic motivation/creativity researchers as the source for this algorithmic/heuristic distinction, acknowledged that his conception is very similar to Spence's (1956) notion of a habit family hierarchy. As he points out, on algorithmic tasks, the correct response lies at or close to the top of the habit hierarchy, whereas on heuristic tasks, the correct response lies at the bottom. The multiplicative relationship between incentive (e.g., reward, external evaluation) and habit strength results in a greater likelihood of a correct response when the response is high in the habit hierarchy than when it is low. Of course, Zajonc (1965) also used Spence's notion of a habit hierarchy in his drive theory of social facilitation. This theory suggests that the presence of others increases drive, which facilitates the performance of simple or well-learned tasks (correct answer near the top of the habit hierarchy), and debilitates performance on complex or not well-learned tasks (correct answer near the bottom of the habit hierarchy). Thus, the simple/complex and algorithmic/heuristic classifications share a common ancestry, and we would argue that there is nothing special about the open-ended tasks used in the intrinsic motivation/creativity tradition that is missed by the simple/complex classification. Certainly there are no data that would substantiate a claim of special status for open-ended tasks. In fact, as noted previously, Bartis, Szymanski, and Harkins (1988) have replicated the complex task finding (i.e., poorer performance by participants subject to evaluation than by those who were not) in the social loafing paradigm, using a task that required participants to produce creative responses.

Clearly many other issues may be raised concerning the three-variable model that could require its revision. For example, the model accords specific, quantitative goals a status that may not be warranted. Research from our laboratory suggests that participants may need only believe that an external source expects a "high" level of performance from them, and that the source has some means of gauging whether they have achieved this level of performance. For example, Utman and Harkins (1994) urged participants to strive to generate the number of uses produced by a participant whose performance fell at the 90th percentile of a use-generation task, but they were also told that they would not be provided with the number of uses that corresponded to this level of performance until after they finished the task. As a result, while they were working, the participants had no idea how many uses they needed to generate to meet this criterion. They only knew that the experimenter wanted them to try to reach and/or exceed this "high" number, and that he would know exactly how well they did. Utman and Harkins (1994) found that under these circumstances, participants generated reliably more uses than participants in the experimenter evaluation/do your best condition, a "goal setting effect." Participants given these striving instructions who were not subject to experimenter evaluation performed only at the level of participants in the experimenter evaluation/do your best condition.

On the other hand, Harkins, White, and Utman (2000, Experiment 1) promised to provide participants with the score at the 90th percentile after they performed, but it was described only as a piece of information in which they might be interested. Without striving instructions, participants subject to experimenter evaluation performed no better than participants in the experimenter evaluation/do your best control group. In this case, the experimenter had had not asked the participants for "high" performance by urging them to strive to reach the criterion. So, performance greater than that found in the experimenter evaluation/do your best control group was produced: (1) when participants were subject to evaluation by the experimenter; (2) the experimenter made clear that he wanted "high" performance; and (3) he could gauge whether or not the participants achieved this level of performance. A specific, quantitative goal was not necessary.

Additional research in our lab is also consistent with this speculation. Harkins and Lowe (2000) suggested that to produce self-set goal setting effects, two conditions must be met: (1) Prior to setting their goals, participants must have had sufficient experience with the task to provide them with a basis for setting the goal; and (2) The experimenter must have access to the goals and the performances of the participants. However, in research that followed up these findings, we found that participants can produce self-set goal effects with no prior experience (e.g., Lowe, 1997). Participants were asked to take a brief ability assessment test that they were told would be highly predictive of their performance on a subsequent arithmetic test. The experimenter scored this test but provided no feedback to the participants who were then either asked to do their best or to self-set goals for the arithmetic task. The ability assessment manipulation made no difference to participants given do-your-best instructions. They performed no better than participants given do-your-best instructions with no ability assessment test. Of course, these participants were only asked to "do their best." They had not been asked for a "high" level of performance.

In contrast, the self-set goal instructions let participants know that the experimenter did want a "high" level of performance. And when the experimenter could evaluate their performances, they knew that the ability assessment test provided him/her with the means of determining whether or not they had achieved this "high" level. Under these circumstances, the participants produced a "goal setting effect" on the first trial, even though they had no previous experience on the arithmetic task. If experimenter evaluation, ability assessment, or self-set goal instructions were missing, no self-set goal effect was produced. Apparently it is not that participants need experience to be able to self-set goals that they then strive to achieve, but rather that the participants believe that the *experimenter* needs this information in order to determine whether or not they have met his/her requirement for "high" performance. In the absence of this means of judging them, the participants feel no need to exceed their do-your-best level of effort.

Thus, this research calls into question the special status that the three-variable model accords goals. Additional research will be required to determine whether a revision of the model that places the role of goals in a broader context is warranted. There are other issues that could be raised as well. For example, the three-variable model does not take task attractiveness into account. We make the argument that whether tasks are attractive or not, task performance will depend on whether the required responses are well-learned or are not, and it is this difference in task complexity that drives performance. Certainly task attractiveness could account for why someone would approach a task in the first place, but the model is based on research in which participants did not select the task that they are asked to perform. Task attractiveness could also affect the extent to which a person persists in task performance, but in the research on which the model is based, participants are often facing a task for the first time, and are asked to perform, at most, a few trials. In any event, it could be argued that persistence would influence task performance by changing the extent to which the necessary responses are well-learned, and the model could account for these effects.

The model also does not take into account individual difference variables like the need for achievement. It could well be that the performance differences that we have documented would be accentuated or minimized if we were to take this personality variable into account. While acknowledging this point, we would note that the effects produced in our research are found quite reliably without taking this variable into account. In addition, McClelland (1987) has argued that differences between participants high and low in need for achievement emerge most strongly on tasks that are of moderate difficulty. In fact, he cites research that shows that the performance of participants who differ in need for achievement does not differ on tasks that are simple and difficult, but does differ on tasks of moderate difficulty. For example, McClelland (1987) writes: "Karabenick and Yousseff (1968) showed that subjects high in n Achievement performed better than subjects low in n Achievement only when learning moderately difficult paired associates as compared with very easy or very difficult ones" (p. 240). Of course, the three-variable model is based on research in which simple and complex tasks have been used. These tasks are easier and more difficult, respectively, than the tasks on which performance differences between participants high and low in need for achievement emerge, suggesting that the need for achievement would not affect performance on these tasks.

Of course, these are only examples of the variables that may need to be taken into account in a revision of the three-variable model. But whether the model requires revision or not, it serves only to organize the findings of the different traditions. It tells us nothing about the process(es) through which the independent variables produce these effects, nor do the process models provided by the various traditions offer any help in this regard. Perhaps most striking is the fact that there is not even any agreement about whether participants subject to evaluation perform more poorly on complex tasks than participants who are not subject to this evaluation because the former participants put out *more* effort or *less* effort than the latter ones.

We argue that this state of affairs exists because researchers have focused on the molar level of analysis when a molecular approach may be required. That is, we claim that to understand the process(es) through which these variables have their effects on performance, we must look at exactly how task performance unfolds, rather than being satisfied with accounts that essentially only suggest what might have happened. We made an initial attempt at such a molecular analysis by conducting an item by item analysis of performance on the Remote Associates Task (RAT). This analysis suggests that the impaired performance of participants working on complex RAT items is not a result of the fact that these participants withdraw effort after they conclude that things are not going well. Instead these data suggest that participants subject to experimenter evaluation are putting out more effort than participants who are not subject to this evaluation.

Of course, this is just the smallest of first steps. For example, if it is not withdrawal of effort that accounts for the poor performance, then what is it? Geen (1991) reviewed the social loafing/social facilitation literature, and proposed that concern about evaluation produces social anxiety, and it is this anxiety that produces the performance effects. As Geen (1991) writes: "Theory and research on both social facilitation and social loafing suggest that evaluation apprehension is an important motive for human behavior in social settings. Each phenomenon may therefore be thought of as a manifestation, in some ways, of a more general influence of social anxiety" (p. 390).

Geen argues that this social anxiety can have both cognitive and motivational effects. The motivational effect manifests itself in "the person's desire to protect the self image by engaging in behaviors that make the person look good, or perhaps even more important, allow him or her to avoid looking bad" (Geen, 1989, p. 44). In the case of the tasks used in the research encompassed by the present analysis, the participants would be motivated to look good by performing as well as possible.

The cognitive effect is a state of attentional overload, which results in the "selective narrowing of attention to a relatively small number of central stimuli" (Geen, 1989, p. 40). This reduction in the range of stimuli to which the person attends has the same effects on the performance of simple and complex tasks as the effects attributed to drive. Simple tasks are hypothesized to require attention to a small number of central cues, whereas complex tasks require attention to a wider range of cues. To the extent that attentional overload reduces attention to the same range of cues whether the task is complex or simple, performance on simple tasks may be improved because attention to peripheral irrelevant cues is reduced, whereas performance on complex tasks may be debilitated because the same restricted focus eliminates task-related cues.

This is a plausible explanation for participants' performance on the RAT. That is, one could imagine that simple RAT triads are easily solved because the correct answer is highly related to each of the triad members, whereas complex triads are difficult because the relationships between the correct answer and the triad members are more remote. If one's attention is narrowed as a result of the potential for evaluation, the highly associated answers would emerge more quickly, and the remotely associated answers would be less likely to emerge at all. Although this account is plausible, this is not enough. Requiring plausibility alone left us not knowing whether the potential for evaluation on complex tasks debilitates performance because these participants are putting out more or less effort than participants who are not subject to this evaluation. We must provide compelling evidence that the specified process mediates performance at the level of the individual triad.

For example, we do not even know what makes RAT triads differ in difficulty. We chose the items on the basis of pre-testing in which participants were presented with a large number of triads. We then selected a set of items that most respondents solved, and labeled those "simple." Another set of items that some participants, but not all, missed, were labeled "complex." Of course, this process generates triads differing in difficulty, but it tells us nothing about what it is that makes the triads simple and complex.

In my chapters in this volume, I have argued that the bulk of the conceptualizations of the various traditions can be cut away, revealing the action of only three variables. The parsimony of this model in organizing the findings of the five traditions may be appealing, but, in the absence of a compelling demonstration of the mediating process(es), any account that we offer (e.g., social anxiety) will simply remain a member of the long list of plausible (and contradictory) "explanations" that have accumulated over the years. If the proponents of the traditions encompassed by the three-variable model believe that the model does violence to the corpus of their respective domains, they may reclaim their lost parts by filling in the same black box. Regardless of the fate of attempts to integrate these parallel traditions in general, and of the three-variable model in particular, it is only through such efforts that any progress will be made in our attempts to understand the effects of evaluation on performance. And, in my view, the key to such efforts lies not in psychophysiology nor in causal modeling with correlated measures (although both may help), but in a molecular analysis of task performance.

REFERENCES

Amabile, T. (1979). Effects of external evaluation on artistic creativity. *Journal of Personality and Social Psychology, 37*, 221-233.

Amabile, T. M. (1996). *Creativity in context.* Boulder, CO: Westview.

Ames, C., & Archer, J. (1988). Achievement goals in the classroom: Students' learning strategies and motivation processes. *Journal of Educational Psychology, 80*, 260-267.

Bandura, A. (1986). *Social foundations of thought and action: A social cognitive theory.* Englewood Cliffs, NJ: Prentice-Hall.

Baron, R. (1986). Distraction-conflict theory: Progress and problems. In L. Berkowitz (Ed.), *Advances in experimental social psychology* (Vol. 19, pp. 1-40). New York: Academic Press.

Barron, K. E., & Harackiewicz, J. M. (2001). Achievement goals and optimal motivation: Testing multiple goal models. *Journal of Personality and Social Psychology, 80*, 706-722.

Bartis, S., Szymanski, K., & Harkins, S. (1988). Evaluation of performance: A two-edged knife. *Personality and Social Psychology Bulletin, 14*, 242-251.

Blascovich, J., Mendes, W., Salomon, K., & Hunter, S. (1999). Social "facilitation" as challenge and threat. *Journal of Personality and Social Psychology, 77*, 68-77.

Blascovich, J., & Mendes, W. (2000). Challenge and threat appraisals: The role of affective cues. In J. Forgas (Ed.), *Feeling and thinking: The role of affect in social cognition* (pp. 59-82). London: Cambridge University Press.

Blascovich, J., & Tomaka, J. (1996). The biopsychosocial model of arousal regulation. *Advances in Experimental Social Psychology, 28*, 1-51.

Bond, C. (1982). Social facilitation: A self-presentational view. *Journal of Personality and Social Psychology, 42*, 1042-1050.

Brickner, M. A., Harkins, S. G., & Ostrom, T. M. (1986). Effects of personal involvement: Thought-provoking implications for social loafing. *Journal of Personality and Social Psychology, 51*, 763-769.

Carver, C., & Scheier, M. (1981). The self-attention-induced feedback loop and social facilitation. *Journal of Experimental Social Psychology, 17*, 545-568.

Cottrell, N. (1972). Social facilitation. In C. McClintock (Ed.), *Experimental social psychology* (pp.185-236). New York: Holt, Rinehart & Winston.

Davis, J. (1969). *Group performance.* Reading, MA: Addison-Wesley, 1969.

DeShon, R. P., Brown, K. G., and Greenis, J. L. (1996). Does self-regulation require cognitive resources? Evaluation of resource allocation models of goal setting. *Journal of Applied Psychology, 81*, 595-608.

Earley, P. C., Connolly, T., and Ekegren, G. (1989). Goals, strategy development, and task performance: Some limits on the efficacy of goal setting. *Journal of Applied Psychology, 74*, 24-33.

Elliott, E., & Dweck, C. (1988). Goals: An approach to motivation and achievement. *Journal of Personality and Social Psychology, 54*, 5-12.

Elliot, A. J., & Harackiewicz, J. M. (1994). Goal setting, achievement orientation, and intrinsic motivation: A mediational analysis. *Journal of Personality and Social Psychology, 66*, 968-980.

Epstein, J., & Harackiewicz, J. (1992). Winning is not enough: The effects of competition and achievement orientation on intrinsic interest. *Personality and Social Psychology Bulletin, 18*, 128-138.

Festinger, L. (1954). A theory of social comparison processes. *Human Relations, 7*, 117-140.

Geen, R. (1989). Alternative conceptions of social facilitation. In P. Paulus (Ed.), *Psychology of group influence* (pp. 15-51). Hillsdale, NJ: Erlbaum.

Geen, R. (1991). Social motivation. *Annual Review of Psychology, 42*, 377-399.

Graham, S., & Golan, S. (1991). Motivational influences on cognition: Task involvement, ego involvement, and depth of information processing. *Journal of Educational Psychology, 83*, 187-194.

Grolnick, W., & Ryan, R. (1987). Autonomy in children's learning: An experimental and individual difference investigation. *Journal of Personality and Social Psychology, 52*, 890-898.

Guerin, B., & Innes, J. (1982). Social facilitation and social monitoring: A new look at Zajonc's mere presence hypothesis. *British Journal of Social Psychology, 7*, 81-90.

Harackiewicz, J., Barron, K., & Elliot, A. (1998). Rethinking achievement goals: When are they adaptive for college students and why? *Educational Psychologist, 33*, 1-21.

Harackiewicz, J., & Elliot, A. (1993). Achievement goals and intrinsic motivation. *Journal of Personality and Social Psychology, 65*, 904-915.

Harackiewicz, J., & Elliot, A. (1998). The joint effects of target and purpose goals on intrinsic motivation: A mediational analysis. *Personality and Social Psychology Bulletin, 24*, 675-689.

Harackiewicz, J., & Sansone, C. (1991). Goals and intrinsic motivation: You can get there from here. In M. L. Maehr, & P. R. Pintrinch (Eds.), *Advances in motivation and achievement* (Vol. 7, pp. 21-49). Greenwich, CT: JAL.

Harkins, S., & Jackson, J. (1985). The role of evaluation in eliminating social loafing. *Personality and Social Psychology Bulletin, 11*, 457-465.

Harkins, S., Latané, B., & Williams, K. (1980). Social loafing: Allocating effort or taking it easy? *Journal of Experimental Social Psychology, 16*, 456-465.

Harkins, S. & Lowe, M. (2000). The effects of self-set goals on task performance. *Journal of Applied Social Psychology, 30*, 1-40.

Harkins, S., & Szymanski, K. (1988). Social loafing and self-evaluation with an objective standard. *Journal of Experimental Social Psychology, 24*, 354-365.

Harkins, S., & Szymanski, K. (1989). Social loafing and group evaluation. *Journal of Personality and Social Psychology, 56*, 934-941.

Harkins, S., White, P., & Utman, C. (2000). The role of internal and external sources of evaluation in motivating task performance. *Personality and Social Psychology Bulletin, 26*, 100-117.

Jackson, J., & Williams, K. (1985). Social loafing on difficulty tasks: Working collectively can improve performance. *Journal of Personality and Social Psychology, 49*, 937-942.

Kanfer, R., & Ackerman, P. L. (1989). Motivational and cognitive abilities: An integrative/aptitude-treatment interaction approach to skill acquisition. *Journal of Applied Psychology, 74*, 657-690.

Karabenick, S. A., & Yousseff, Z. I. (1968). Performance as a function of achievement level and perceived difficulty. *Journal of Personality and Social Psychology, 10*, 414-419.

Karau, S., & Williams, K. (1993). Social loafing: A meta-analytic review and theoretical integration. *Journal of Personality and Social Psychology, 65*, 681-706.

Latané, B., Williams, K., & Harkins, S. (1979). Many hands make light the work: The causes and consequences of social loafing. *Journal of Personality and Social Psychology, 37*, 823-832.

Latham, G., & Lee, T. (1986). Goal setting. In E. Locke (Ed.), *Generalizing from laboratory to field settings*. Lexington, MA: Lexington Books.

Lepper, M., Greene, D., & Nisbett, R. (1973). Undermining children's intrinsic interest with extrinsic rewards: A test of the "overjustification" hypothesis. *Journal of Personality and Social Psychology, 28*, 129-137.

Locke, E., & Latham, G. (1990a). *A theory of goal setting and task performance*. Englewood Cliffs, N.J.: Prentice Hall.

Locke, E. & Latham, G. (1990b). Work motivation and satisfaction: Light at the end of the tunnel. *Psychological Science, 1*, 240-246.

Lowe, M. (1997). *An examination of the effects of self-set goals on task performance.* Unpublished doctoral dissertation, Northeastern University.

McClelland, D. C. (1987). *Human Motivation.* Cambridge: Cambridge University Press.

McGraw, K. (1978). The detrimental effects of reward on performance: A literature review and a prediction model. In M. Lepper & D. Greene (Eds.), *The hidden costs of reward.* Hillsdale, NJ: Lawrence Erlbaum Associates.

Nicholls, J. G., & Dweck, C. S. (1979). *A definition of achievement motivation.* Unpublished manuscript. University of Illinois at Champaign-Urbana.

Pintrinch, P., & Schunk, D. (1996). *Motivation in education: Theory, research and applications.* Englewood Cliffs, NJ: Prentice Hall.

Sanna, L. (1992). Self-efficacy theory: Implications for social facilitation and social loafing. *Journal of Personality and Social Psychology, 62,* 774-786.

Simon, H. (1967). Motivational and emotional controls of cognition. *Psychological Review, 74,* 29-39

Spence, K. (1956). *Behavior theory and conditioning.* New Haven: Yale University Press.

Szymanski, K., Garczynski, J., & Harkins, S. (2000). The contribution of the potential for evaluation to coaction effects. *Group Processes & Intergroup Relations, 3,* 269-283.

Szymanski, K., & Harkins, S. (1987). Social loafing and self-evaluation with a social standard. *Journal of Personality and Social Psychology, 53,* 891-897.

Szymanski, K., & Harkins, S. (1993). The effect of experimenter evaluation on self-evaluation within the social loafing paradigm. *Journal of Experimental Social Psychology, 29, 268-286.*

Tauer, J. M., & Harackiewicz, J.M. (1999). Winning isn't everything: Competition, achievement orientation, and intrinsic motivation. *Journal of Experimental Social Psychology, 35,* 209-238.

Utman, C. (1997). Performance effects of motivational state: A meta-analysis. *Personality and Social Psychology Review, 1,* 170-182.

Utman, C., & Harkins, S. (1994). *Acceptance of performance standards: The effects of perceptions of criterion stringency.* Paper presented at Midwestern Psychological Association, Chicago, IL.

Utman, C. & Harkins, S. (1996). *The effect of ego-involvement on the use of goals in self-evaluation.* Midwestern Psychological Association, Chicago, IL.

White, P., Kjelgaard, M., & Harkins, S. (1995). Testing the contribution of self-evaluation to goal setting effects using the social loafing paradigm. *Journal of Personality and Social Psychology, 69,* 69-79.

White, S., Mitchell, T., & Bell, C. (1977). Goal setting, evaluation apprehension, and social cues as determinants of job performance and job satisfaction in a simulated organization. *Journal of Applied Psychology, 62,* 665-673.

Williams, K., Harkins, S., & Latané, B. (1981). Identifiability as a deterrent to social loafing: Two cheering experiments. *Journal of Personality and Social Psychology, 40,* 303-311.

Wood, R. E., Mento, A. J., & Locke, E. A. (1987). Task complexity as a moderator of goal effects: A meta-analysis. *Journal of Applied Psychology, 72,* 416-425.

Wright, P. M. (1990). Operationalization of goal difficulty as a moderator of the goal difficulty-performance relationship. *Journal of Applied Psychology, 75,* 227-234.

Zajonc, R. (1965). Social facilitation. *Science, 149,* 269-274.

Zajonc, R. (1980). Compresence. In P. Paulus (Ed.), *Psychology of group influence* (pp. 35-60). Hillsdale, NJ: Lawrence Erlbaum Associates.

AUTHOR INDEX

Abrahams, 68, 83, 197, 199
Abrams, 78
Ach, 30
Ackerman, 31, 38-41, 123, 182, 223
Ajzen, 38, 157
Alexander, 41
Amabile, 48, 50, 53-54, 56-59, 62-66, 68-71, 121-122, 126, 140, 143, 158, 163, 166, 174, 177-179, 181-182, 185-186, 193, 199-200, 223, 226-227
Ames, 91, 238
Andia, 37, 41
Archer, 91, 238
Argyris, 27
Asch, 118
Atkins, 40
Baca, 2
Bailey, 123
Bandura, 25, 38, 123, 158, 234
Baron, R. A., 26, 28, 42
Baron, R. S., 118-120, 232-233, 242
Barret, 126
Barrick, 40, 161
Barron, 79, 91, 93-94, 203, 238, 240-242
Bartis, 122, 127, 143, 226, 252
Bedeian, 26, 29, 42, 181
Bell, 109, 135, 212
Bem, 65, 70, 176
Benedict, 19
Benjamin, 28
Benware, 126
Berglas, 63, 200
Berlyne, 49
Berscheid, 20
Betley, 78
Bingham, 27
Blascovich, 235
Blum, 27
Boehne, 40, 161
Boggiano, 48, 126
Bond, 118, 232-233

Brackfield, 58-59, 62, 66, 199
Brickner, 15, 102-103, 210
Bright, 40
Brown, K. G., 40, 123, 167, 236
Brown, K., 37
Brown, R., 68
Brown, S. P., 40
Bruun, 2, 7-8, 14, 100, 194
Butkowsky, 67, 176
Button, 40, 161
Cacioppo, 15
Campbell, J. P., 166
Campbell, W. K., 202
Campion, 31, 38-39, 158
Cardy, 166
Carter, 93, 203
Carver, 38, 118, 158, 233, 242
Cascio, 62
Cattell, 27
Cheek, 68, 178
Cheung, 91
Chidester, 30, 32
Cohen, H. A., 52
Cohen, J., 32
Cole, 79
Collins, 68, 178-179
Connolly, 40, 123, 167, 223
Conti, 68-69, 126, 178, 182, 200
Coon, 69, 179, 182
Cooper, 31, 39, 161
Cortina, 40
Cottrell, 118, 232
Cron, 40
Csikszentmihalyi, 84, 197
DaFoe, 67
Dahl, 40, 161
Davis, 209
Dawes, 18, 20
De Leo, 11
deCharms, 49, 65, 121, 176, 195
Deci, 48-49, 62, 70-71, 78, 82, 84, 121, 126, 176, 179, 185-186, 192-193
Denny, 30
Deppe, 200
DeShon, 40-41, 123, 167, 236

Dickson, 27
Doyle, 16
Drucker, 30
Dugdale, 41, 182
Dugosh, 145
Dunnette, 26
Dunning, 136, 141
Dweck, 91, 121, 126, 227-228, 238
Dzindolet, 145
Earley, 37, 40, 123, 167, 223
Edney, 18
Ekeberg, 31, 38-39
Ekegren, 40, 123, 167, 223
Elliot, 80, 91-93, 195, 200, 202-203, 238, 240-242
Elliott, 91, 121, 126, 227-228, 238
Emery, 48
Epstein, 82-83, 87, 90, 197, 202, 240
Etzioni, 26, 29, 181
Evans, 5
Faler, 202
Feren, 30
Festinger, 112, 228
Fishbein, 38, 157
Fisher, 202
Flink, 126
French, 166
Frey, 2
Friedman, 48
Gange, 118
Garbarino, 48
Garczynski, 211, 221
Garfield, 52
Gargano, 2
Geen, 118, 232-234, 255
Gist, 161
Goetz, 52
Golan, 228
Goldfarb, 58-59, 62, 66, 199
Graham, 228
Graves, 1
Greenberg, 26, 28, 42, 160
Greene, 48, 67, 78, 237
Greenis, 40, 123, 167, 236
Greenwald, 80, 177, 194

Greenwood, 30
Grigsby, 30, 32
Grolnick, 126, 228
Gryskiewicz, N., 69
Gryskiewicz, S., 69, 179, 181
Guerin, 118, 232
Gully, 40
Guzzo, 30, 32, 162
Hackman, 160
Haladyna, 91
Hanson, 37
Harackiewicz, 62-63, 68, 79-96, 134, 146, 149, 162-163, 173, 175-179, 181, 185, 190-191, 193-203, 238-242
Harkins, 2, 6, 8, 14-15, 17, 19, 25, 100-107, 109-116, 118-119, 122, 124, 126-127, 135-138, 143, 150-151, 155, 164, 173, 182-186, 190-191, 193-196, 198-199, 203, 208-221, 226, 231, 247, 251-253
Hart, 147, 149-150
Harter, 49, 84
Hebb, 49
Hennessey, 50, 56, 60-61, 67, 71, 134, 140, 143, 158, 162-163, 167, 176, 190-191, 193, 199-200, 208, 223-224, 226-227, 229, 237-238, 242
Hidi, 95
Higgins, 195
Hill, 69, 71, 179, 182
Hollenbeck, 31, 37-38, 40, 161
Hough, 26
Hughes, 47
Hunter, J. E., 30, 32
Hunter, S., 235
Ilgen, 11, 31, 39, 157, 161
Ingham, 1
Innes, 118, 232
Ivancevich, 42, 161
Jackson, D. N., 82
Jackson, G. B., 32
Jackson, J. M., 2, 14, 19, 101, 119, 122, 126, 151, 222, 226-227, 231
Jette, 30, 32
Jones, 200
Judd, 87
Jussim, 68
Kahle, 78
Kahn, 26
Kakuyama, 161
Kanfer, 31, 38-41, 123, 182, 223

Karabenick, 254
Karau, 2, 5, 7-8, 17, 20, 101, 147, 209, 251
Karniol, 62
Karren, 30, 32
Kasmer, 15
Kasof, 140
Katz, 26
Katzell, 30, 32
Kay, 166
Kelley, 65, 176
Kenny, 87
Kernoodle-Loveland, 48
Kerr, 2, 7-8, 14, 18, 20, 100, 147, 194
Kimble, 66
Kjelgaard, 107, 135, 212-213, 218, 221
Klein, 31, 37-40, 161-162
Klimoski, 27
Klinger, 119-120
Kohlhepp, 68
Kohn, 95
Kravitz, 133
Kristoff-Brown, 37
Kruglanski, 48
Krusell, 62
Kuhl, 38
Landers, 119
Landis, 40
Landy, 26-27
Larey, 145
Latané, 2, 13-14, 100, 102-103, 107, 115, 118, 126, 208-209, 231, 247, 251
Latham, 25, 29-33, 35-39, 100, 107-108, 123-125, 137, 157-158, 161, 165, 208, 212, 218, 222, 236
Lauer, 91
Lawler, 2, 4, 162
Lawrence, 26, 160
Lazenby, 69
Lee, C., 37, 40, 161
Lee, T. W., 40
Lee, T., 218
Leggett, 91
Lehto, 203
Lepper, 48-49, 54, 67, 78, 237
Lett, 52
Levinger, 1

Lewin, 30, 95, 178
Ley, 68
Likert, 27-28
Locke, 13, 25, 29-41, 100, 107-108, 123-125, 137, 157-158, 161, 164-165, 180, 208, 212, 218, 222, 236
Lorch, 26
Lord, 31, 38-39, 158
Lowe, 218-221, 253
Luchins, 64
Lynn, 18
Mace, 30
Manderlink, 83, 193, 199, 201
Markus, 119
Martens, 119
Martin, 133
Mathieu, 40, 161
Matsui, 161
McAuley, 79
McCaleb, 30
McClelland, 80, 177, 194, 254
McCloy, 166
McCullers, 48
McCullough, 47
McGraw, 48, 53-54, 57, 223-226, 229, 251
McGregor, D., 27-28
McGregor, H. A., 202
McTavish, 20
Mendes, 235
Mento, 30, 32-34, 36, 164, 180, 222
Messick, 18
Meyer, 166
Miner, 31
Mitchell, T. R., 2, 4, 11, 13, 29, 109, 135, 161, 212
Moore, 119-120
Morgan, 67
Motowidlo, 162
Mount, 40, 161
Muchinsky, 26, 28, 156
Mulvey, 40, 162
Munsterberg, 27
Murray, 80
Murtha, 41, 182
Napoli, 28
Naylor, 27, 29, 31, 39, 157, 161

Nebeker, 11, 31, 39, 161
Nelson, 41, 182
Nicholls, 91, 121, 227
Nida, 2
Nisbett, 48, 78, 237
Nolen, 91
Ochse, 140, 145
Okada, 161
Oldenquist, 18
Oldham, 160
O'Leary, 40
O'Leary-Kelly, 40
Olley, 48
Olson, 79
Oppler, 166
Orbell, 18
O'Reilly, 27
Orne, 33
Ostrom, 15, 102, 210
Owen, 52
Parks, 156
Patashnick, 91
Paulus, 119-120, 140, 145
Pearce, 67, 176
Peckham, 1
Peters, 11
Petty, 2, 6, 8, 15, 101, 136, 194-195
Phan, 40
Phillips, E. D., 179
Phillips, J. M., 40
Picariello, 68, 178
Pinder, 31
Pintrich, 238
Pittman, 48
Pollak, 68-69, 126, 179, 182
Poole, 52
Porac, 78
Porter, 2, 4
Pritchard, 11, 161
Pulakos, 166
Ragan, 79
Raina, 52
Ransen, 67
Reeve, 78-79, 84

Reid, 79
Reidel, 31, 39, 161
Reiss, 182
Rodgers, 30
Roethlisberger, 27
Roland, 145
Ross, 62
Roth, 52
Rousseau, 156, 160
Ryan, R. M., 70-71, 78, 82, 84, 121, 126, 176, 179, 185-186, 192-193, 228
Ryan, T. A., 30
Saari, 30
Sachau, 202
Sager, 166
Sagotsky, 67
Sales, 161
Salomon, 235
Samuelson, 18
Sanders, 119-120
Sanna, 120, 122-123, 126, 151, 222, 227, 231, 234, 242
Sansone, 79-84, 87-88, 90-93, 95-96, 175-177, 190, 193-194, 199, 201-202, 239-240
Scheier, 38, 118, 158, 233, 242
Schkade, 119-120
Schmidt, 32
Schmit, 162
Schmitt, 27
Schunk, 238
Scott, 27
Sedikides, 202
Seta, 119-120
Shaklee, 20
Shanfield, 67, 176
Shapira, 48
Shaw, K. N., 30
Shaw, N. R., 30
Shea, 162
Shepperd, 2-3, 9, 11, 16, 137, 161, 173, 179-180, 190-191, 193-196, 210, 230-231, 234, 236, 242
Shultz, 67, 176
Simon, 66, 237
Simonton, 140, 145
Slocum, 40
Smith, 67, 176

Soffin, 68
Spence, 66, 225, 251
Spreitzer, 160
Stahl, 68, 178
Stasson, 147
Steel, 30, 32
Sternberg, 140, 145
Strauss, 40, 161
Stroebe, 2
Sushinsky, 182
Szilagyi, 42
Szymanski, 2, 15, 17, 102-107, 109-110, 112-114, 122, 127, 143, 183-184, 198, 210-214, 221, 226, 251-252
Tammen, 79
Tauer, 84-86, 89-90, 93, 134, 146, 149, 162-163, 173, 175-179, 181, 185, 190-191, 196, 198, 201-203, 239-242
Taylor, F., 27-28, 30
Taylor, K., 9, 11, 137
Taylor, M. S., 161
Taylor, M., 19
Tighe, 71
Tomaka, 235
Torrance, 52
Triplett, 117-118
Trumbo, 26
Tubbs, 30-40, 139, 161, 173, 180-182, 184, 190-191, 193, 196, 203, 222-223, 236, 242
Turner, 160
Utman, 109, 111-112, 115, 121, 124, 127, 135, 185, 196, 213, 215-217, 219-221, 227-229, 238, 241, 252
Vallerand, 79
VandeWalle, 40
Vroom, 2, 4-5, 13, 38, 161
Wageman, 68, 83, 162, 197, 199
Wallace, 42
Wallach, 53
Walster, E., 20
Walster, G. W., 20
Weber, 28
Weinberg, 79
Weir, 202
Weldon, 2
White, K., 52
White, P., 107-116, 124, 135, 196, 212-213, 215-216, 218, 221, 252

White, R. W., 49, 84
White, S., 109, 135, 212
Whitney, 69, 179, 182
Williams, A. J., 52
Williams, C. R., 161
Williams, K., 2, 5, 7-8, 13-14, 17, 20, 100-102, 107, 115, 118-119, 122, 126, 151, 208-209, 222, 227, 231, 247, 251
Wood, J., 112
Wood, R. E., 30, 32, 34-35, 40-41, 164, 180, 222-223
Wood, R., 123
Wright, P. M., 40, 218
Wright, R. A., 16
Wundt, 27
Yamagishi, 18-19
Yang, 145
Yousseff, 254
Yukl, 30
Zaccaro, 2, 16
Zajac, 40, 161
Zajonc, 118, 226, 232, 251
Zammuto, 26, 29, 42, 181
Zeevi, 48

SUBJECT INDEX

Achievement goal theory, 91, 99, 121-127, 155, 162, 165, 167, 183, 185-186, 196, 202, 207-208, 223, 227-229, 238, 241-242
Achievement motivation, 80, 82-83, 86-88, 90-95, 133-134, 146-147, 152, 161, 177-178, 181, 193, 239, 241, 254
Achievement motivation, high in (HAM), 80, 82-90, 92-94, 146-150, 152, 177-178, 196-197, 200, 202, 239-241
Achievement motivation, low in (LAM), 80, 82-90, 92-94, 146-150, 177-178, 196-197, 202, 239, 240-241
Achievement orientation, 85, 87, 90, 194, 196-197, 200, 202, 239
Actual evaluation, 62-63, 66-67, 71, 157-158, 163, 165
Affect, 67, 82, 84-88, 126, 149, 161-162, 175-178, 181, 185, 191, 193, 235, 237, 239, 242
Algorithmic task, 50, 53-54, 56-57, 59, 72, 162, 180, 201, 223-226, 238, 251
Anticipated evaluation (see also Expected evaluation), 157, 163, 165, 237
Anxiety, 142, 146, 161, 166, 255-256
Assigned goals, 25, 30-31, 36-40, 158, 160, 182, 189, 196, 202, 212, 217-221, 236
Attention, 66, 144, 233, 237-238, 242, 255
Better-than-average effect, 136, 141
Biopsychosocial model of challenge and treat, 235
Brainstorming, 49, 145
Challenge, 235
Challenge, perceived, 84-90, 95-96, 146, 149, 177, 183, 191-196, 202-204, 238-240
Close-ended tasks, 190, 199, 201
Coaction, 118-120, 126, 151, 212, 221-222, 232-233
Cognitive evaluation theory, 78-79, 173, 176
Collective performance, 7, 10-11, 15-17, 21, 133
Competence valuation, 80, 83. 85, 87-90, 93, 95-96, 191, 194-195, 200-204, 239, 240
Competence, 62-63, 77, 80-81, 83, 86-87, 91
Competence, perceived, 78, 81-82, 85-88, 95-96, 177, 191-194, 196, 198, 202, 239
Competition, 47, 52, 64-65, 68, 72, 77-80, 82-92, 94-96, 118, 145-146, 150, 159, 162-163, 166, 175-178, 189, 192-193, 201-202, 239-240
Compresence, 118
Conditioned association explanation, 144
Conjunctive task, 7, 194-195
Conscientiousness, 40, 161, 181

Consensual Assessment Technique (CAT), 50-52, 56, 60, 63-64
Control theory, 31, 38, 41, 158, 236
Control, sense of, 49
Creativity, 47-69, 71-72, 102, 121-122, 127, 133-134, 140-145, 152, 155-156, 162-167, 173-177, 179-186, 198-200, 204, 208, 223-224, 226-229, 237, 242, 251-252
Criterion validity, 213-215
Deadlines, 48
Discounting principle, 65, 67, 176, 237
Disjunctive task, 7
Dispensability, 6-8, 136, 145, 148
Distraction, 144, 182
Distraction/conflict, 118, 232-233
Dominant responses, 118, 226, 232
Drive theory, 118, 226, 232-233, 242, 251, 255
Effort expectancy, 2, 5-6, 136, 138-140, 142, 150, 152
Effort motivation, 3-5, 180, 192, 194-195, 202
Ego-involvement, 38, 121, 200, 215-217, 219-221
Empowerment, 160
Evaluation apprehension, 118, 232
Evaluative contingency, 79-84, 90-92, 94-96, 175-178, 189-193, 197-198, 200-202, 204, 239-240
Evaluative criterion, 100, 102, 104, 107, 209
Expectancy-value theory, 1-3, 31, 38-40, 133-135, 137-140, 144-145, 148, 151-152, 161, 179, 194, 230, 236, 242
Expected evaluation, (see also Anticipated evaluation), 47, 50, 52, 54, 58-60, 62, 66, 68-69, 71-72, 158, 162-163, 174-179, 182-184, 186, 197, 201
Expected reward, 47-48, 179
Experimenter evaluation, 100, 102-111, 113-117, 120, 122-125, 135, 140, 165, 183-184, 189, 197, 207-208, 211-221, 223, 226-227, 231-234, 242-250, 252-253
External evaluation, 52, 100, 103, 121-122, 124, 126, 140, 150, 155-159, 161, 165, 184, 207-208, 210, 212, 214-215, 219-220, 229, 236-238, 242, 251
Extrinsic incentives, 78, 146, 160, 166, 174, 177, 179
Extrinsic motivation, 48, 53, 62, 65-68, 70-71, 121, 126, 133-134, 144, 160, 163, 166, 174-177, 179, 183, 185-186, 195
Extrinsics in Service of Intrinsics Cycle, 70
Feedback, 79-80, 82-90, 92, 94-95, 107, 202, 239
Feedback, negative, 83, 90, 94, 200-201
Feedback, positive, 83, 87-88, 90, 92, 94, 201-202
Free-riding, 6-7, 18-20, 136
Goal acceptance, 36-38
Goal commitment, 36-38, 40, 161, 218
Goal difficulty hypothesis, 31-34, 134-135, 139

Goal setting effect, 32, 100, 107-109, 111, 114, 116-117, 124-125, 161, 164-166, 212-221, 223, 253
Goal setting paradigm, 173
Goal setting, 25, 29, 31, 79, 99, 109, 123, 125, 133-139, 141, 152, 155-158, 160-162, 164-167, 180-181, 183-184, 186, 195, 202, 207-208, 217-218, 222-223, 236, 242, 253
Goal specificity hypothesis, 31-34, 41, 134-135, 139
Group cohesiveness, 17
Habit family hierarchy, 225-226, 232-233, 251-252
Hawthorne effect, 27
Heuristic task, 50-51, 53-54, 56-59, 162, 186, 223-226, 229, 251
Hydraulic model, 67-68, 174
Industrial/organizational psychology, 25-29, 38, 155- 157, 165-167, 173, 180-181
Instrumentality (Performance Expectancy), 2-3, 5, 10-12, 137, 139-141, 148, 150, 152, 230-231
Intrinsic motivation principle of creativity, 48, 52, 62, 69-71, 174
Intrinsic motivation, 15-16, 47-49, 52-54, 57-58, 62-63, 65-67, 69-72, 77-84, 87-88, 90-91, 94-96, 99, 121-126, 133-134, 140, 142-144, 146-147, 150, 152, 159-160, 162-163, 166-167, 174-181, 183-186, 189-204, 207, 223, 227-229, 236-237, 239-241, 251
Job characteristics model, 160
Job enrichment, 160
Laboratory vs. field settings, 33, 165, 181
Learning goals (See also Mastery goals), 40, 91-94, 121-122, 126-128, 161-162, 181, 196, 203, 208, 227-230, 238-242
Management by objectives, 30
Mastery goals (See also Learning goals), 40, 91-94, 121-122, 126-128, 161-162, 181, 196, 203, 208, 227-230, 238-242
Mere presence, 118-119, 151, 232
Motivational synergy, 70, 174
Multiple goals, 241
Need for cognition, 15
Normative evaluation, 196-197, 202-203
Objective criterion, 104
Open-ended task, 51, 53-54, 66, 68, 180, 183-186, 190, 198- 201, 204, 223, 252
Outcome Value, 2-3, 5, 12, 16-17, 136-141, 143, 148, 150-152, 161, 230-231
Overjustification hypothesis, 65, 67, 143, 176, 237, 242
Overjustification paradigm, 54, 176
Participatively-set goals, 31, 36, 212, 218
Performance appraisal, 166
Performance evaluation, 166, 168, 189

Performance feedback (knowledge of results), 31, 33-35, 37, 157-158, 163, 165-166, 177, 192-193, 203
Performance goals, 40, 91-95, 121, 126-127, 161-162, 181, 196, 203, 227, 229, 238-242
Performance monitoring, 41, 182
Performance-contingent reward, 62
Process model of intrinsic motivation, 79-80, 87-88, 90-92, 95-96, 176-177, 190, 239
Quality, 134, 140-143, 145, 152, 159, 180
Quantity, 134, 140-141, 143, 152, 159, 180
Remote associates test (RAT), 120, 122-125, 127, 185-186, 222, 242-250, 254-256
Reward, 1-3, 5, 9-14, 19, 21, 28-29, 38, 41-42, 47-48, 62, 64, 70, 78, 133-134, 137, 142, 144-146, 152, 160, 166, 179, 223-226, 229, 231, 251
Scientific management, 27-28, 42
Self-awareness, 118, 233
Self-efficacy, 38, 49, 158, 163, 233, 242
Self-evaluation, 15, 100, 102-103, 105-109, 111-115, 117, 120, 124-125, 127-128, 137-138, 177, 183-184, 186, 195, 208-217, 219-221, 227, 229
Self-handicapping, 200
Self-presentation, 118, 232-233
Self-set goals, 158, 160, 212, 217-221, 253
Shyness, 68, 163, 178
Social comparison, 102, 109, 112, 228
Social evaluation, 211-212, 217, 221, 229
Social facilitation, 99, 117-120, 122-123, 125-126, 150-151, 164, 173, 207-208, 222-223, 226-227, 229, 232-233, 235, 242, 251, 254
Social loafing effect, 208, 229, 251
Social loafing paradigm, 103, 105, 107, 209-210, 213, 252
Social loafing, 1-2, 11, 13-14, 17, 21, 99-103, 106-107, 111, 113, 115, 118-119, 122, 124-126, 133-134, 136, 140, 143, 146, 150-151, 155, 159, 161-162, 173, 179-180, 183-184, 194-195, 207, 222-223, 227, 229-231, 233, 235, 242, 247, 254
Social monitoring, 118, 232
Status, 211
Sucker effect, 18-21
Surveillance, 47-48
Task attractiveness, 224-226, 229, 253
Task complexity, 33-37, 40-41, 54, 99-100, 159, 164, 166-167, 180, 182-185, 221
Task difficulty, 89, 93-94, 136, 190, 199
Task engagement, 49, 177, 182, 189-190, 192-193, 195, 198, 200-204
Task enjoyment, 86-90, 93, 134, 149, 159, 174, 178, 190, 193, 223
Task interest, 185-186, 240-241

Task involvement, 81, 93, 95-96, 174, 183, 191, 197, 199-200, 203, 239
Task novelty, 36, 40, 159, 162, 165-166, 182
Task output, 100, 102, 104, 107, 209
Task-contingent reward, 62
Tasks, complex, 118-128, 159, 165-167, 182, 185-186, 199, 204, 207, 221-223, 226-239, 242-245, 247-252, 254-256
Tasks, simple, 119-120, 122-125, 127, 159, 185, 190, 207, 211, 214-215, 221-222, 226-228, 230-236, 242-252, 254-256
Threat, 235
Torrance Tests of Creativity, 52
Type A behavior, 161
Uniqueness of contribution, 6, 194
Use-generation task, 100, 104-105, 110, 119, 135, 147, 149, 198, 209, 211, 222, 226-227
Vigilance task, 104-105, 119, 198, 209, 211